Beyond Gridlock

Beyond Gridlock

Thomas Hale and David Held

with

Garrett Wallace Brown, Michael Clarke,
Camila Villard Duran, Ann Florini, Lucas Kello,
Andreas Klasen, Kyle McNally, James Orbinski,
Tom Pegram, Taylor St John, Kevin Young

Polity

First published in 2017 by Polity Press

Polity Press
65 Bridge Street
Cambridge CB2 1UR, UK

Polity Press
101 Station Landing, Suite 300
Melford, MA 02155, USA

ISBN-13: 978-1-5095-1571-4
ISBN-13: 978-1-5095-1572-1(pb)

A catalogue record for this book is available from the British Library.

Library of Congress Cataloging-in-Publication Data

Names: Hale, Thomas (Thomas Nathan), editor. | Held, David, editor.
Title: Beyond gridlock / [edited by] Thomas Hale, David Held.
Description: Cambridge, UK ; Malden, MA : Polity Press, 2017. | Includes bibliographical references and index.
Identifiers: LCCN 2017004155 (print) | LCCN 2017022001 (ebook) | ISBN 9781509515745 (Mobi) | ISBN 9781509515752 (Epub) | ISBN 9781509515714 (hardback) | ISBN 9781509515721 (pbk.)
Subjects: LCSH: International cooperation. | Economic policy–International cooperation. | Environmental policy–International cooperation. | Globalization–Political aspects. | World politics.
Classification: LCC JZ1318 (ebook) | LCC JZ1318 .B483 2017 (print) | DDC 337–dc23
LC record available at https://lccn.loc.gov/2017004155

Typeset in 10.5 on 13 pt Swift
by Toppan Best-set Premedia Limited
Printed and bound in Great Britain by CPI Group (UK) Ltd, Croydon

For further information on Polity, visit our website:
politybooks.com

Contents

Figures and Tables

Figures

Tables

Abbreviations

AMR	antimicrobial resistance
APT	advanced persistent threat
ARPANET	Advanced Research Projects Agency Network
ASEAN	Association of Southeast Asian Nations
BCBS	Basel Committee on Banking Supervision
BIS	Bank for International Settlements
BIT	bilateral investment treaty
BRICS	Brazil, Russia, India, China and South Africa
BWC	Biological Weapons Convention
C6	US Federal Reserve, European Central Bank, Bank of Japan, Bank of England, Swiss National Bank, Bank of Canada
CAT	Convention against Torture
CEM	Clean Energy Ministerial
CFE	Contingency Fund for Emergencies (WHO)
CGFS	Committee on the Global Financial System
CMIM	Chiang Mai Initiative Multilateralization
COP	Conference of the Parties
COP21	21st Conference of the Parties to the UNFCCC, Paris, 2015
CPSS	Committee on Payments and Settlement Systems
CRA	Contingent Reserve Arrangement
CRD	Capital Requirements Directive
CTBT	Comprehensive Nuclear-Test-Ban Treaty
CWC	Chemical Weapons Convention
DAH	development assistance for health

DSM	dispute settlement mechanism
EU	European Union
FATF	Financial Action Task Force
FDI	foreign direct investment
Fed	United States Federal Reserve
FSB	Financial Stability Board
FTA	free trade agreement
G7	Group of Seven (Canada, France, Germany, Italy, Japan, UK, US)
G8	Group of Eight (G7 plus Russia)
G20	Group of Twenty (major economies)
G30	Group of Thirty (consultative group of academics and financiers)
G77	Group of Seventy-Seven (developing countries)
GATS	General Agreement on Trade in Services (WTO)
GATT	General Agreement on Tariffs and Trade
GDP	gross domestic product
GEG	global energy governance
GFATM	Global Fund to Fight AIDS, Tuberculosis and Malaria
GFF	Global Financial Facility
GHSA	Global Health Security Agenda
GICNT	Global Initiative to Combat Nuclear Terrorism
GSM	Global Stabilization Mechanism
HRC	Human Rights Council
HSS	health system strengthening
IAASB	International Auditing and Assurance Standards Board
IADI	International Association of Deposit Insurers
IAEA	International Atomic Energy Agency
IAIS	International Association of Insurance Supervisors
IASB	International Accounting Standards Board
ICANN	Internet Corporation for Assigned Names and Numbers
ICC	International Criminal Court
ICRC	International Committee of the Red Cross
ICSID	International Centre for Settlement of Investment Disputes
IDA	International Development Association
IDP	internally displaced person
IEA	International Energy Agency
IEF	International Energy Forum
IGO	intergovernmental organization
IHR	International Health Regulations
IIF	Institute for International Finance

IMF	International Monetary Fund
IOPS	International Organisation of Pension Supervisors
IOSCO	International Organization of Securities Commissions
IPCC	Intergovernmental Panel on Climate Change
IRENA	International Renewable Energy Agency
ISDS	investor–state dispute settlement
IWG	International Working Group on Export Credits
LDCs	least developed countries
LNG	liquefied natural gas
MAI	Multilateral Agreement on Investment (OECD)
MDB	Multilateral Development Bank
MDG	Millennium Development Goal
Mtoe	million tons of oil equivalent
NAFTA	North American Free Trade Agreement
NATO	North Atlantic Treaty Organization
NGO	non-governmental organization
NHRI	national human rights institution
NPT	Treaty on the Non-Proliferation of Nuclear Weapons
OCHA	UN Office for the Coordination of Humanitarian Affairs
ODRF	Over-the-Counter Derivatives Regulators' Forum
OECD	Organisation for Economic Co-operation and Development
OHCHR	UN Office of the High Commissioner for Human Rights
OPCAT	Optional Protocol to the Convention against Torture
OPCW	Organisation for the Prohibition of Chemical Weapons
OPEC	Organization of the Petroleum Exporting Countries
OSCE	Organization for Security and Co-operation in Europe
OTC	over-the-counter derivatives
P5	Permanent Five (members of the United Nations Security Council)
PEF	Pandemic Emergency Financing Facility (World Bank)
PEPFAR	President's Emergency Plan for AIDS Relief
PSI	Proliferation Security Initiative
R&D	research and development
R2P	Responsibility to Protect
SALT	Strategic Arms Limitation Treaty
SARS	severe acute respiratory syndrome
SDG	Sustainable Development Goal
SDR	Special Drawing Right
SE4ALL	Sustainable Energy for All
SML	Local Currency Payment System
START	Strategic Arms Reduction Treaty

TCP/IP	Transmission Control Protocol/Internet Protocol
TPP	Trans-Pacific Partnership
TRIMs	Agreement on Trade-Related Investment Measures
TTIP	Transatlantic Trade and Investment Partnership
TW	terawatt
UHC	universal health coverage
UK	United Kingdom
UN	United Nations
UNAIDS	Joint United Nations Programme on HIV/AIDS
UNCITRAL	United Nations Commission on International Trade Law
UNCTAD	United Nations Conference on Trade and Development
UNEP	United Nations Environment Programme
UNFCCC	United Nations Framework Convention on Climate Change
UNGGE	United Nations Group of Governmental Experts
UNHCR	United Nations High Commissioner for Refugees (UN Refugee Agency)
US	United States
USAID	US Agency for International Development
WHO	World Health Organization
WMD	weapons of mass destruction
WTO	World Trade Organization
XDR-TB	extensively drug-resistant tuberculosis

Notes on the Authors

Garrett Wallace Brown is Professor of Political Theory and Global Health Policy in the School of Politics and International Studies, University of Leeds. His research includes work on cosmopolitanism, globalization theory, global justice, international law and global health governance. He has published widely on issues in global health and has recently published *Global Health Policy* (2014) and *The Global Politics of Health Reform in Africa* (2015). His current Medical Research Council research is investigating whether performance-based financing is an effective policy mechanism for African health system strengthening.

Michael Clarke was Professor of Defence Studies at King's College London from 1995 and was the Director General of the Royal United Services Institute from 2007 to 2015. He remains Visiting Professor at King's and also at the University of Exeter and is a Specialist Advisor both to the House of Commons Defence Committee and to the Joint Committee on the National Security Strategy. In 2016 he began chairing an Inquiry into drone warfare on behalf of the All Party Parliamentary Group on Drones.

Camila Villard Duran is an Assistant Professor of Law at the University of São Paulo. She was an Associate Fellow of the Oxford-Princeton Global Leaders Fellowship Program run by the Global Economic Governance Programme at the University of Oxford and the Woodrow Wilson School of Public and International Affairs at Princeton University (2014–2016). Camila Villard Duran was awarded her joint-PhD degree in Law by the University of São Paulo and the University of Paris 1

Panthéon-Sorbonne (2009–2012). She works on issues related to regulation of money and finance, international economic law, the sociology of economic law, and central bank swaps.

Ann Florini is Professor of Public Policy, School of Social Sciences, Singapore Management University, and Academic Director of SMU's Master of Tri-Sector Collaboration. She is also Non-resident Senior Fellow in the Foreign Policy Studies Program at the Brookings Institution in Washington, DC. She is an authority on new approaches to global governance. Her work currently focuses on the roles of tri-sector collaborations involving government, civil society and the private sector in addressing global issues. Her books include *China Experiments: From Local Innovation to National Reform* (with Hairong Lai and Yeling Tan, 2012); *The Right to Know: Transparency for an Open World* (2007); *The Coming Democracy: New Rules for Running a New World* (2003); and *The Third Force: The Rise of Transnational Civil Society* (2000).

Thomas Hale is Associate Professor of Public Policy (Global Public Policy) at the Blavatnik School of Government, University of Oxford. His research explores how we can manage transnational problems effectively and fairly. He seeks to explain how political institutions evolve – or not – to face the challenges raised by globalization and interdependence, with a particular emphasis on environmental and economic issues. His books include *Between Interests and Law: The Politics of Transnational Commercial Disputes* (2015), *Transnational Climate Change Governance* (with Harriet Bulkeley et al., 2014) and *Gridlock: Why Global Cooperation Is Failing When We Need It Most* (with David Held and Kevin Young, 2013).

David Held is Master of University College, Durham and Professor of Politics and International Relations at Durham University. Among his publications are *Gridlock: Why Global Cooperation Is Failing When We Need It Most* (with Thomas Hale and Kevin Young, 2013), *Cosmopolitanism: Ideals and Realities* (2010), *Globalization/Anti-Globalization* (with Anthony McGrew, 2007), *Models of Democracy* (2006), *Global Covenant* (2004), *Global Transformations: Politics, Economics and Culture* (with Anthony McGrew, David Goldblatt and Jonathan Perraton, 1999), and *Democracy and the Global Order: From the Modern State to Cosmopolitan Governance* (1995). His main research interests include the study of globalization, changing forms of democracy and the prospects of regional and global governance. He is a Director of Polity Press, which he co-founded in 1984, and General Editor of *Global Policy*.

Lucas Kello is Senior Lecturer in International Relations at Oxford University. He serves as Director of the Cyber Studies Programme, a major research and teaching initiative on all aspects of the modern information society. He is also Co-Director of the university's interdisciplinary Centre for Doctoral Training in Cyber Security.

Andreas Klasen is Professor of International Business at Offenburg University, Senior Honorary Fellow at Durham University and Visiting Fellow at Newcastle Business School. Previously, he was a Partner with PricewaterhouseCoopers and Managing Director of the official German Export Credit and Investment Insurance Agency. Until 2014, he also served as Berne Union Vice President. His research focuses on trade, innovation and economic development.

Kyle McNally is a Post-Doctoral Research Fellow in the Global Policy Institute at Durham University. His current research is focused on humanitarianism, global health governance and forced migration policy. His publications include an upcoming book entitled *Internal Displacement* (2017) and *Lessons from Intervention in the 21st Century* (co-editor and contributing author, 2014). Kyle McNally was awarded his PhD from Durham University and his MSc in Development Studies from the London School of Economics and Political Science.

James Orbinski has over 30 years of international experience in humanitarian medicine, having worked in situations of war, genocide, famine and epidemic disease. He was international president of Médecins Sans Frontières/Doctors Without Borders from 1998 to 2001. He is Professor and CIGI Research Chair in Global Health at the Balsillie School of International Affairs, Laurier University. He is also a full Professor at the University of Toronto Dalla Lana School of Public Health. His research touches on humanitarian medicine, emerging and re-emerging infectious diseases, global health governance, and the global health impacts of climate change.

Tom Pegram is Senior Lecturer in Global Governance at University College London and the Deputy Director of the UCL Global Governance Institute. He completed his DPhil in Politics from Nuffield College, University of Oxford. His research interests lie at the boundaries of global governance, international organizations, and the transnational politics of human rights implementation. He is co-editor of *Human Rights, State Compliance, and Social Change: Assessing National Human Rights Institutions* (with Ryan Goodman, 2012) and his scholarly articles have appeared in *International Organization, European Journal of International Relations, Human Rights Quarterly* and *Governance*, among others.

Taylor St John is a Postdoctoral Research Fellow at PluriCourts, University of Oslo, and a Senior Research Associate at the Global Economic Governance Programme, University of Oxford. Her research concerns the international architecture for investment dispute resolution and the politics of foreign investment more generally. Her book *The Rise of Investor–State Arbitration: Law, Politics, and Unintended Consequences* will be published in 2017.

Kevin Young is an Associate Professor at the University of Massachusetts Amherst, and works on the political economy of financial market regulation, elite networks and transnational governance. He is co-author of *Gridlock: Why Global Cooperation Is Failing When We Need it Most* (2013) and has published widely, in journals such as *Regulation and Governance, Journal of Banking Regulation, Review of International Political Economy, Business and Politics, Socio-Economic Review* and *Public Administration*.

Preface

There are increasing signs that the liberal international order created after 1945 now verges on collapse. While populism and nationalism are on the rise across the world, asserting the claims of particular peoples and places, we are more linked than ever before. These links require global cooperation and careful management. And yet we are not rising to this challenge. A series of global collective action problems, from the spread of weapons of mass destruction to climate change, threaten to render our societies weaker, poorer, and more violent. There is a substantial risk that humankind may not end the twenty-first century as well as we began it.

How these existential challenges are governed, and why their governance has been so inadequate, has preoccupied us for many years. In *Gridlock: Why Multilateralism Is Failing When We Need It Most*, published with Kevin Young in 2013, we sought to understand and explain the achievements and the limits of the postwar order. We concluded that deep structural trends, rooted in the extraordinary success of international cooperation and the transformations it allowed, now undermined its continued effectiveness and responsiveness. We set out a bleak picture of how gridlock paralyses multilateral governance, with dangerous implications.

This grim picture has stayed with us, and in some cases darkened further. However, it does not capture significant anomalies to the argument. Across world politics, some resilient pathways endure, and new pathways of change unfold. Over the last three years we have explored and examined these exceptions, and tried to understand the balance between the pressures of gridlock, on the one side, and pressures for change, on the other. Without understanding these trends, we cannot begin to break the cycle of gridlock.

Beyond Gridlock is distinctive in two ways. First, it offers a unique and comprehensive insight into political stasis and change at the global level – what works, and why, and where. Second, it has been written in an innovative way, drawing on the expertise of outstanding academics and policy experts working in a diverse range of problem areas. We brought this group together twice, once in Durham in 2015 and once in Oxford in 2016. These were far-ranging and intense discussions in which expertise on specific topics came into dialogue with arguments concerning cross-cutting global trends. This process laid the foundations for the work on this book, which began as an edited volume of essays but ended as a highly integrated, multi-authored text that deploys jointly developed theoretical and analytic tools. The result is an original and comparative analysis of the fundamental challenges of global governance in the twenty-first century.

We would like to thank all those who contributed in these discussions. These include all the contributors to this book, as well as Oliver Stuenkel, Vanda Felbab-Brown, Seyom Brown, Eva Maria Nag, Robert Wade, and Saba Mahmood. We also thank the Global Challenges Foundation for their support of the two workshops. Finally, Polity Press has been hugely supportive; we thank everyone there for their professionalism.

Thomas Hale and David Held
Oxford and Durham, 2017

1

Introduction

Pathways beyond Gridlock

Thomas Hale and David Held

Conventional wisdom now sees the greatest challenges facing humanity in the twenty-first century as inherently transnational. From climate change, to economic stability, to deadly pathogens, to migration, to criminal networks, to terrorism, the issues governments must address often ignore the borders that divide political authority between sovereign states. It is no exaggeration to maintain that human welfare depends more than ever before on effective transborder governance at all scales.

Conventional wisdom also holds that we lack the effective international cooperation we need to meet transnational challenges. Contemporary global governance has been called "unfit for purpose" (Goldin 2013), in a state of "permanent deficit" (Lamy 2014), and, in our own formulation, increasingly "gridlocked" (Hale, Held and Young 2013). Even while our need for cooperation grows, our ability to achieve it seems to be flagging.

The dangers of persistent gridlock in global governance are difficult to overstate. As our response to collective action problems fractures, states devise strategies in isolation and according to short-term self-interest. These challenges have grown even starker in recent years as nationalism has risen in nearly every corner of the world. This anti-global backlash can be seen as part of a negative cycle that compounds gridlock. In part driven by a failure to manage globalization and interdependence effectively, nationalism further erodes our ability to cooperate through international institutions. It is, at one and the same time, a consequence of gridlock and a reinforcing factor.

While the conventional wisdom carries considerable weight, it is time for a reassessment. Any evaluation of our capacity to resolve twenty-first century challenges needs to be mindful of the complexities and nuances that characterize individual problems. Not all areas of world politics exhibit the same degree of gridlock. Moreover, beneath the surface of deadlock and drift, movements can be detected which, in a number of cases, reveal instances of policy reform and fresh pathways through crises. Such developments emerge from varying circumstances. For example, in the climate realm shifting institutional models at the 2015 Paris climate summit helped recalibrate the regime after the two decades of lacklustre multilateral negotiations. Questions about the future ability of the International Monetary Fund to manage global crises come alongside new arrangements for monetary cooperation in the global South. And in trade, the death of multilateral negotiations in the Doha Round and "mega-regional" trade agreements across the Atlantic and Pacific has coincided with other proposals, such as China's Regional Comprehensive Economic Partnership or the "One Belt, One Road" programme of investment to link the economies of Central and Southeast Asia. In sum, gridlock is a central condition of contemporary global governance, but is it the whole story?

This book takes the dominant trends that cause gridlock and stagnation in international cooperation as a starting point, but, at the same time, asks if there are systematic pathways through or beyond gridlock that we can detect and build on. The pages that follow do not simply attempt to list exceptions or qualifications. Rather, any good theory must use anomalies to consider if such evidence reinforces, alters, or even overturns previous understandings. Our goal, then, is not just to assess gridlock, but to learn something more general about the patterns through which, and conditions under which, multilateral blockages are created, adapted to, and potentially overcome in contemporary world politics.

To achieve this, the book compares different issue areas. It explores gridlock, and systematic exceptions to it, in global governance and uses the results of that analysis to evaluate prospects for more effective global governance going forward. We focus on a significant range of policy sectors in order to explore whether and how change is possible. By identifying pathways through and beyond gridlock in these sectors, the book shows which pathway (or pathways) explain change in which policy sectors, and why. It allows a comparison of what works where, and thereby helps illuminate which pathways are most likely to yield significant policy shifts in the direction of a more effective governance, and under what circumstances. While this book is, at core, a social scientific effort to compare current and past trends in global governance, it is prospective and normative as well.

This introduction begins by recalling the thesis set out in the book *Gridlock: Why Global Cooperation Is Failing When We Need It Most* (Hale, Held and Young 2013). The sections that follow highlight the debate about this book and criticisms levelled at it; identify exceptions and anomalies that compromise, qualify, or enrich the argument; and explore the steps needed to examine how gridlock can be overcome. It remains our judgement that the dynamics discussed in the following chapters do not overturn the relevance of the core gridlock argument (see below); rather, they explore and highlight how global governance can adapt, modulate, and even succeed despite – and even, in some cases, because of – gridlock. In this way, the book seeks to create an evidence base for more effective management of global challenges in the twenty-first century.

The Gridlock *Argument*

The impetus for *Gridlock* came from the observation, particularly commonplace around the start of the decade, that multilateral institutions had stalled across issue domains ranging from the Copenhagen climate summit, to the Doha trade round, to the inability to agree effective financial regulation in the wake of the 2008–9 crisis. The book attempted to offer a general explanation for this phenomenon that made sense of various trends in world politics.

Gridlock is defined as the inability of countries to cooperate via international institutions to address policy problems that span borders. It refers both to deadlock or dysfunctionality in existing organizations and the inability of countries to come to new agreements as issues arise. If we look only at the creation of new international institutions, just one useful indicator for gridlock, we find some disturbing trends. The bars in figure 1.1 show the number of international organizations, plus their offshoots, in the world from the middle of the twentieth century to the present. The line shows the rate of growth of these organizations from year to year. Two striking trends are clear. First, there has been an explosion of formal global governance in the years since World War II, with several thousand international organizations now operating in every domain of human activity. Second, the creation of new international organizations has now essentially stopped,

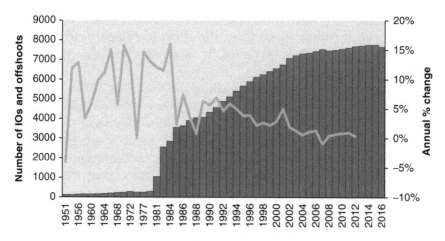

Figure 1.1   International organizations and their offshoots, absolute number (bars) and annual rate of growth (line)

Source: Union of International Associations 2016.

even as interdependence reaches new levels. While there is of course more to gridlock than just the creation of new international institutions, the trend exemplifies the larger problem.[1]

The primary goal in *Gridlock: Why Global Cooperation Is Failing When We Need It Most* was to explain the growing stagnation and deadlock in multilateral governance. We were not alone in recognizing the difficulties of multilateralism at the time (Narlikar 2010a; Victor 2011b; Goldin 2013). At least one book has made the counter-argument that global governance is, if not ideal, at least a marked improvement over previous historical episodes and close to what can be realistically expected of it (Drezner 2014). Our own contribution to this literature argued that the past successes of multilateral cooperation were indeed very significant and generated a deeper level of interdependence; but we went on from here to argue that this higher level of interdependence now makes current and future cooperation more difficult.

Global cooperation, we contended, is gridlocked across a range of issue areas. The reasons for this are not the result of any single underlying causal structure, but rather of several underlying dynamics that work together. In order to understand why gridlock has come about it is important to understand how it was that the post–World War II era facilitated, in many respects, a successful form of "governed globalization" that contributed to relative peace and prosperity in large parts of the world over several decades. This period was marked by peace between the great powers, although there were many proxy wars fought out in the global South. This relative stability created the conditions for what now can be regarded as an unprecedented period of prosperity that characterized the 1950s onwards. Although it is by no means the sole cause, the United Nations (UN) is central to this story, helping to create conditions under which decolonization and successive waves of democratization could take root, profoundly altering world politics. The Bretton Woods institutions created in the wake of World War II were the economic counterparts to the UN – providing a forum for economic cooperation heretofore unseen and mechanisms for economic development. The leading role of the United States in the creation and maintenance of these institutions, and the associated geopolitical and distributional implications, are of course a central piece of this story (Ikenberry 2001), though postwar global governance became much more than an epiphenomenon of US power (Keohane 1984).

The record of postwar multilateral organizations is, of course, mixed. Nonetheless, while the economic performance of the postwar years varies by country, many experienced significant economic growth and living standards rose rapidly across significant parts of the world. By the late 1980s a variety of East Asian countries were beginning to grow at an unprecedented speed, and by the late 1990s countries such as China, India and South Africa had gained significant economic momentum, a process that continues to this day, though some countries, notably China, are beginning to shift to a slower, less export-oriented growth model.

Meanwhile, the institutionalization of international cooperation proceeded at an equally impressive pace (figure 1.1). There was substantial growth in the number of international treaties in force, as well as the number of international regimes, formal and informal. At the same time, new kinds of institutional arrangements have emerged alongside formal intergovernmental bodies, including a variety of types of transnational governance arrangements such as networks of government officials, public–private partnerships, as well as exclusively private governance bodies (see Hale and Held 2011).

All these postwar institutions helped create socio-economic conditions, according to the gridlock thesis, under which a multitude of actors could benefit from forming multinational companies, investing abroad, developing global production chains, forming transnational advocacy networks, and engaging with a plethora of other social and economic processes associated with globalization. These conditions, along with technological innovation and the expansionary logic of capitalism, changed the nature of the world economy, radically increasing dependence on people and countries from every corner of the world. This interdependence, in turn, created demand for further coordination, which states and non-state actors, seeking the benefits of cooperation, provided by creating new and stronger institutions, beginning the cycle anew.

This is not to say that international institutions were the only cause of the dynamic form of globalization experienced over the last few decades. Changes in the nature of the world economy, including breakthroughs in transportation and information technology, are obviously critical drivers of interdependence. However, all of these changes were allowed to thrive and develop because they took place in a relatively open, peaceful, liberal, institutionalized world order. By preventing World War III and another Great Depression, the multilateral order arguably did just as much for interdependence as microprocessors or email (see Mueller 1990; O'Neal and Russett 1997).

This "self-reinforcing interdependence," as we defined it in *Gridlock*, has now progressed to the point where it has altered our ability to engage in further global cooperation. That is, economic and political shifts in large part attributable to the *successes* of the postwar multilateral order are now among the factors grinding that system into gridlock. Because of the remarkable achievements of global cooperation in the postwar order, human interconnectedness weighs much more heavily on politics than it did in 1945. The need for international cooperation has never been higher. Yet the "supply" side of the equation, institutionalized multilateral cooperation, has stalled in many critical areas. In areas such as nuclear proliferation, the explosion of small arms sales, terrorism, failed states, global economic imbalances, financial market instability, global poverty and inequality, biodiversity losses, water deficits, and climate change, multilateral and transnational cooperation is now increasingly in question. Gridlock is not unique to one issue domain, but appears to be becoming a general feature of global governance: it represents a basket of trends that is today making international cooperation more difficult, even as deepening globalization and interdependence mean that we need global cooperation now more than ever. Put simply, cooperation seems to be increasingly difficult and deficient at precisely the time when it is needed most.

Gridlock identified four specific trends that now make global governance more difficult: increasing multipolarity, more complex problems, institutional inertia, and growing fragmentation. Because these trends partially emerge from previous successes of the institutionalized world order, we characterize them as "second order" cooperation problems. Each can be thought of as a growing trend that embodies a specific mix of causal mechanisms (see table 1.1). We explain each trend below.

Table 1.1 Gridlock trends and their mechanisms

Trends	Mechanisms
1. Growing multipolarity	• Increased transaction costs • Exacerbated legitimacy dilemma • Divergence of interests between critical states
2. Harder problems	• Extensity: scope of problems has increased • Intensity: problems penetrate more deeply into societies
3. Institutional inertia	• Formal lock-in of decision-making authority • Entrenchment of dysfunctional cognitive and organizational focal points
4. Fragmentation	• Increased transaction costs • Inefficient division of labour, redundancy • Excessive flexibility

Growing multipolarity   The absolute number of states has increased by 300 per cent in the last 70 years, meaning that the most basic transaction costs of global governance have grown. More importantly, the number of states that "matter" on a given issue – that is, the states without whose cooperation a global problem cannot be adequately addressed – has expanded by similar proportions. At Bretton Woods in 1945, the rules of the world economy could essentially be written by the United States with some consultation with the United Kingdom and other European allies. In the aftermath of the 2008–9 crisis, the Group of Twenty major economies (G20) has become the principal forum for global economic management, not because the established powers desired to be more inclusive, but because they could not solve the problem on their own. However, a consequence of this progress is now that many more countries, representing a diverse range of interests, must agree in order for global cooperation to occur. Against this background, it is seen as both less effective and less legitimate for a few large states to dictate policies that affect others. Broadening global decision-making beyond the traditional powers represents a positive evolution in the postwar order, but it can make agreement harder to reach.

Harder problems   As interdependence has deepened, the types and scope of problems around which countries must cooperate has expanded. Problems are now both more extensive, implicating a broader range of countries and individuals within countries, and more intensive, penetrating deep into domestic policy space and even the daily lives of individuals. Consider the example of trade. For much of the postwar era, trade negotiations focused on reducing tariff levels on manufactured products traded between industrialized countries. Now, however, negotiating a trade agreement requires also discussing a host of social, environmental, and cultural subjects – genetically modified organisms, intellectual property, health and environmental standards, biodiversity, labour standards – about which countries often disagree sharply. In the area of environmental change a similar set of considerations applies. To clean up industrial smog or address ozone depletion required fairly discrete actions from a small number of top polluters. By contrast, the threat of climate change and the efforts to mitigate it involve nearly all countries of the globe. Yet, the divergence of voices and interests within both the developed and developing worlds, along with the sheer complexity of the incentives needed to achieve a low carbon economy, have made a global deal extremely difficult to achieve (Falkner, Stephan and Vogler 2010; Victor 2011b).

Institutional inertia The postwar order succeeded, in part, because it incentivized great power involvement in key institutions. From the United Nations Security Council, to the Bretton Woods institutions, to the Treaty on the Non-Proliferation of Nuclear Weapons, key pillars of the global order explicitly grant special privileges to the countries that were wealthy and powerful at the time of their creation. This hierarchy was necessary to secure the participation of the most important countries in global governance. Today, the gain from this trade-off has shrunk while the costs have grown. As power shifts from West to East, North to South, a broader range of participation is needed on nearly all global issues if they are to be dealt with effectively. At the same time, following decolonization, the end of the Cold War, and economic development, the idea that some countries should hold more rights and privileges than others is increasingly (and rightly) regarded as morally bankrupt. And yet, the architects of the postwar order did not, in most cases, design institutions that would organically adjust to fluctuations in national power. Instead, what we see is the existing constellation of interests entrenched within traditional organizational and cognitive structures.

Fragmentation The institution-builders of the 1940s began with, essentially, a blank slate. But efforts to cooperate internationally today occur in a dense institutional ecosystem shaped by path dependency. The exponential rise in both multilateral and transnational organizations has created a more complex multi-level and multi-actor system of global governance. Within this dense web of institutions, mandates can conflict, policy interventions are frequently uncoordinated, and scarce resources are subject to increased competition. In this context, the proliferation of institutions can lead to dysfunctional fragmentation, reducing the ability of multilateral institutions to provide public goods. When funding and political will are scarce, countries need focal points to guide policy (Keohane and Martin 1995), which can help define the nature and form of cooperation. Yet, when international regimes overlap, these positive effects are weakened. Fragmented institutions, in turn, disaggregate resources and political will, while potentially increasing transaction costs like arranging meetings and coordinating policies and standards. At the same time, the proliferation of institutions allows actors to "forum shop" across them, increasing flexibility and weakening the ability of any single cooperative framework to compel convergence on a single policy goal.

In stressing four trends to gridlock we emphasized the manner in which contemporary global governance problems compound each other, although different pathways carry more significance in some domains than in others. The challenges now faced by the multilateral order are substantially different from those faced by the 1945 victors in the postwar settlement. They are second-order cooperation problems arising from previous phases of success in global coordination. While "first order" cooperation problems familiar to students of international relations of course continue to apply, the gridlock trends place additional barriers before problem solving and reform at the global level.

Gridlock *Revisited*

Gridlock attracted a healthy mix of praise and criticism in print, in seminars, and in conversations with readers. Some thought we overemphasized the role of multilateralism in the postwar period. As many observers noted, global governance was hardly smooth sailing between the end of World War II and the fall of the Berlin Wall. Others questioned our diagnosis that current global governance was failing by asking what the appropriate counterfactual should be. Contemporary multilateralism is certainly not meeting all our needs, but does that mean it is failing, or simply that political reality always falls short of our normative goals? What is the appropriate benchmark of success?

In addition, some critics of postwar global governance, particularly in the global South, pointed out that gridlock has been beneficial for preventing certain strategies by leading states, and the United States in particular, for steering world affairs to their benefit. In this context, gridlock opens new possibilities for southern-led interventions in world politics, such as the New Development Bank led by Brazil, Russia, India, China, and South Africa, the so-called BRICS. These discussions highlighted the importance of the distributional implications of global governance. Who wins and who loses from different kinds of international cooperation? What one country may see as gridlock, another may see as liberation.

Another set of criticisms questioned the causal mechanisms of the argument. In a number of domains observers noted the importance of traditional geopolitical rivalries in impeding cooperation, "first order" cooperation problems that we under-emphasized. Some also questioned the relative emphasis we placed on the different causal mechanisms within our argument, with some seeing multipolarity as more important than the others. We were also criticized for paying insufficient attention to the nature of contemporary global capitalism as a core explanation for global governance outcomes, the argument being that weak outcomes in global governance are in fact the expression of elite interests.

In our view these criticisms usefully identify scope conditions that help qualify our argument, but do not challenge the core analytic insight that deepening interdependence, growing from cooperation in the postwar period, set in motion key trends that now create obstacles to further cooperation even as the functional need for global governance grows. Instead, in our own reflections on the argument, what gave us most pause was how gridlock seemed to manifest more acutely in some issue areas than in others. While we saw gridlock as the dominant tendency, it struck us that some issue areas and institutional settings seemed more beset by it than others, as the chapters that follow explicate. We attempted to address this issue in the final chapter of *Gridlock* in the context of assessing various ways in which states and other actors might overcome the trends we identified in the book, but this was the most speculative section of the book.

Looking beyond Gridlock: *Anomalies and Exceptions*

Since *Gridlock* was published, we have been increasingly interested in exploring the anomalies and exceptions to our somewhat grim diagnosis of contemporary multilateralism. Are the anomalies sufficiently significant to undo the gridlock logic? Is global governance more adaptive and resilient than we previously believed? How does rising nationalism in various countries affect these issues? Answering these questions is critical not only to enhance our understanding of world politics, but also, crucially, to help think through practical solutions to the very real dilemmas of managing interdependence in the twenty-first century.

In thinking about responses to these issues, we invited a number of subject experts[2] to explore the applicability – or not – of the gridlock thesis to various domains in a three-day workshop held at University College, Durham University, in June 2015 and a follow-up workshop at the Blavatnik School of Government, University of Oxford, in March 2016. From the outset, we sought to include in the discussions a wide number of policy areas in world politics, from economics to security to the environment, in order to ensure a comprehensive test of the gridlock argument. Both workshops examined how, in each field, past and current governance may be understood as effective or successful; how, and in what ways, it has failed or succeeded; and what challenges are likely to characterize future governance. They also involved a critical discussion concerning if, and how, the trends of gridlock (see table 1.1) manifest in each area; and if they are absent, what else could explain (in)effectiveness in that sector. Finally, participants were invited to think about the implications of their analysis for institutions, states, and social groups.

Several conclusions emerged from these discussions. In most policy domains, it was widely recognized that global governance is manifestly inadequate for the needs of human societies in the globalized, interdependent, multipolar twenty-first century. The four "second order" gridlock trends – multipolarity, harder problems, institutional inertia, and fragmentation – were, as previously noted, identified as significant impediments to more effective governance. While there is no single appropriate benchmark for "successful" global governance (see below), there was little disagreement that building more effective global governance in almost every area of world politics is an urgent task in these sectors with enormous implications for human welfare.

At the same time, participants identified significant variation in the effectiveness of global governance across sectors, as well as across institutions or regimes within sectors. Certain institutions, like the Berne Union, the system of transnational commercial arbitration, the Chemical Weapons Convention, or the World Trade Organization (WTO) dispute settlement mechanism (DSM) were recognized as effective in some crucial respects. In short, while global governance as a whole is lacking, there are some positive exceptions to this rule that reform efforts might emulate and build upon.

Most importantly, the detailed discussion of concrete issue areas allowed participants to identify a range of instances in which gridlock has not prevented effective global governance from emerging. The authors distilled these into seven general "pathways" out of gridlock; that is, a set of causal mechanisms and processes that under certain conditions lead to improvements in global governance arrangements. These pathways form the analytic core of this book.

Before describing the individual pathways, it is important to be more specific about what we mean by moving "through" and "beyond" gridlock. These terms refer to positions along a continuum of change in the outcomes of interest. "Through" connotes incremental yet significant improvements. "Beyond," in turn, refers to a more fundamental transformation. While we expect moves through gridlock to be, on average, shorter in term than moves beyond gridlock, we do not assume a single temporal relation between the two. Various incremental steps may cascade into more profound transformations; alternatively, critical junctures or "punctuated equilibria" may provoke large realignments with great speed.

We are ultimately interested in how global governance can become more robust and effective vis-à-vis the transborder policy challenges it seeks to address. Analytically, it is useful to separate this object of analysis into two sets of outcomes.

First, we are concerned with the institutions and processes of global governance. Do we see more cooperation and compliance, new, or newly effective, institutions, or simply stagnation? Here we are particularly interested in explaining the creation, use, and effectiveness of transborder institutions and the patterns of state and non-state behaviour that play out around them. Are rules created that stand a reasonable chance of shaping behaviour? Do institutions emerge that provide collective benefits? Are existing institutions reformed to become more efficacious? An example of moving "through" gridlock in this sense might be, say, effective coordination in the UN Security Council on humanitarian crises. Moving "beyond" gridlock in this setting, in turn, could refer to a deeper shift such as a fundamental reform of the Security Council's voting rules to reduce the power of veto-holders.

Second, we are concerned with the impact of global governance on human welfare. Does more cooperation lead to better outcomes? If new or stronger intergovernmental or transnational institutions emerge, do they have a significant and positive impact on the prob-lems they seek to address? Or is their impact negligible? Continuing with the above example, a pathway "through" gridlock in this realm would be Security Council authorization of effective peacekeeping missions capable of maintaining a fragile order, while "beyond" would require a model of authorized intervention which was reliable and effective enough to, for example, drastically reduce the number of people killed in civil wars each year.

Regarding this second set of impact-oriented outcomes, it is of course essential to ask *for whom* the impact of global governance is positive or negative. In the abstract, we may wish to define effective-ness in general terms of public good provision. Do global governance arrangements in a given issue area meet the functional needs created by interdependence or not? For many issues, of course, the impact of global governance creates both winners and losers. Shifts in global governance may both help to resolve the functional dilemmas of inter-dependence while also disadvantaging or privileging specific actors or groups. Teasing out these differentiated impacts is crucial to the analysis presented here.

In the chapters that follow, then, we understand pathways through and/or beyond gridlock as causal processes that (a) improve the insti-tutions and processes of global governance and/or (b) improve the impact of global governance on human welfare broadly, with particu-lar attention to the range of potential positive and negative impacts that may apply to different groups.

To address these issues satisfactorily requires of course a meaning-ful counterfactual. Does the process or impact of global governance improve *compared to what*? Because there is no single appropriate coun-terfactual, the chapters that follow evaluate the outcomes of interest against several different benchmarks, triangulating among them as appropriate. First, they consider the process and impact of global governance in an issue area compared to previous time periods. For example, is the global trade regime more or less effective after the creation of the WTO? Second, they consider actual outcomes against alternative proposals that have been made or attempted by various actors in a given issue domain. In investment, for example, some countries have proposed replacing the current bilateral system with a multilateral treaty, such as the Multilateral Agreement on Investment that was actively negotiated in the 1990s. Third, the chapters compare outcomes against the null scenario – what if nothing had been done? While reasonable readers may disagree with the specification of some of the counterfactuals employed in the chapters below, we seek to make our evaluations and arguments as transparent as possible by being explicit about our assumptions and points of comparison. It seems to us that such an approach is unavoidable. Implicitly or explicitly, all evaluations of current effectiveness or prospects for future effectiveness entail some counterfactual analysis; the point is to be clear about it.

Pathways through and beyond Gridlock

Each chapter in this book will explore how one or more of the seven core pathways through which gridlock may be overcome relates to a distinct issue area in global governance. We use these pathways both retrospectively, to explain a certain positive outcome, and prospectively, to evaluate the likelihood of reaching a particular outcome. Before setting out the substance of the chapters that follow, it is important to be clear about the analytical core of each of the pathways, their relationship to each other, as well as what we mean by "pathways" in the first place. The pathways are described below and summarized in table 1.2.

Each pathway describes a constellation of conditions and causal mechanisms that apply across various domains. The pathways emphasize general factors like the preferences of states and other actors, the material and ideational processes that generate these preferences, the strategies actors employ, the institutional arrangements in which they operate, and power relations between them. Because we are interested in exploring tangible ways to advance effective global governance, the pathways emphasize relatively proximate and immediate dynamics, as opposed to more remote, structural, and long-term trends (see below).

1   Shifts in major powers' core interests

It is a core tenet of international relations theory that when one or more great powers have a strong national interest in policies that create a global public good, they will be willing and often able to provide that public good. Hard versions of Realist theory see this condition as the only setting in which global public goods are likely to be provided, and it has been advanced as a prominent explanation for the postwar global order (Gilpin 1981). A central argument of *Gridlock* is that this mechanism has been decreasingly common

Table 1.2 Pathways through and beyond gridlock and their mechanisms

Pathways	Mechanisms
1. Shifts in major powers' core interests	• Gridlock can provoke or exacerbate systemic or regional crises creating incentives for major powers to provide global public goods
2. Autonomous and adaptive international institutions	• The accrual of authority in some international institutions has made them increasingly autonomous from the interests of their members • Some international organizations possess generative rule-making capacity to adapt to new circumstances
3. Technical groups with effective and legitimate processes	• Issue area in which states delegate to experts are relatively insulated from gridlock trends • Transparent and rational procedures add legitimacy to technocratic decision-making
4. Multiple, diverse organizations and institutions coalesce around common goals/norms.	• Possible for "additive" or "expansionary" contexts, not "absolute" issue areas • Diffusion and entrenchment of common principles, norms, and goals across a policy domain
5. Mobilization of domestic constituencies for cooperation and compliance	• Socializing communities of actors in particular practices and norms • Institutional channels give leverage to domestic and regional actors
6. Civil society coalitions with reformist states	• Coalitions across state–civil society boundaries generate new political possibilities • Do not challenge the core interests of key states
7. Innovative leadership as a reaction to gridlock	• Gridlock provokes innovative and entrepreneurial strategies (e.g. norm entrepreneurship).

in more recent decades, as growing multipolarity (1) increases the number of great powers that are required to act to provide a global public good in many issue domains; (2) increases the heterogeneity of interests among the great powers because states with very different political and economic systems weigh more heavily on world politics. Both of these effects make it less likely for a sufficient coalition of major powers to come together to provide a public good. For example, preventing global financial contagion requires a much larger coalition of countries to act than in, say, the 1970s and those countries' preferences are shaped by very different domestic political economies.

But while gridlock has reduced the conditions under which major powers will be able to provide global public goods as a positive externality of their national interests, it still remains possible, of course. Moreover, it may be the case that gridlock, by reducing the efficacy of multilateralism, generates exactly the kinds of crises that are most likely to bring together great powers in specific instances, despite long-term trends to the contrary. Such dynamics can be seen in the (fragile) P5+1 coalition (Permanent Five members of the UN Security Council plus Germany) that negotiated a nuclear settlement with Iran; in transgovernmental networks like the Financial Action Task Force (focused on money laundering, especially when connected to terrorist networks); in efforts to counter piracy around the Horn of Africa; in the launching of a concerted effort to tackle Ebola in West Africa; and in other security-oriented fields. Though growing multipolarity has made it less possible for a great power (or coalition of powers) to provide global public goods unilaterally, it remains possible. For issues where (a) a great power (or sufficient coalition of powers) has a strong interest in solving a problem and (b) no other great powers are willing and able to oppose, we can expect action to overcome gridlock. Such occasions typically arise only in the face of incontrovertible security threats when the relevant powers can gain much more from cooperation than from conflict.

2   *Autonomous and adaptive international institutions*

Gridlock argued that the past 70 years of international institution-building has had a profound effect on world politics, with many positive outcomes, but also a number of second-order cooperation problems (e.g. institutional inertia and fragmentation) that result from a denser institutional landscape. While it is of course well recognized that under some conditions international institutions have become formidable autonomous actors in world politics (Barnett and Finnemore 2005), on average, we might expect gridlock to reduce the ability of international institutions to act proactively in world politics, as they become stymied by diverging member state interests, challenged by alternative fora under growing fragmentation, or find that new and more complex problems exceed their mandates and functional resources.

But there may also be systematic ways in which international organizations remain more autonomous and adaptive than these trends suggest, or even gain authority as multilateralism gridlocks. First, some international institutions have not seen their mandates or capabilities reduced under gridlock. The International Energy Agency (IEA), for example, possesses significant autonomy to decide when fuel reserves should be released, and its restrictive membership (only countries in the Organisation for Economic Co-operation and Development (OECD)) has ensured that it has not been hamstrung by multipolarity. More generally, while an organization's autonomy is not independent of the underlying problem structure or interests of states (which had to decide to set it up that way in the first place), there are various reasons to expect institutions created under conditions of relatively less gridlock to retain at least some of their autonomy even under conditions of increasing gridlock.

Additionally, some international institutions have been given unique capacities to adapt to emerging issues and shifting constellations of power and interests. This ability may be particularly strong for legal institutions, which possess a "generative" function, the ability to decide new rules for situations not originally envisioned by states. For example, the WTO Dispute Settlement Mechanism has been increasingly called upon to adjudicate cases for which WTO members have established no clear sets of rules. Many of these controversial cases have even involved members states, such as China, that joined the WTO significantly after the treaty-making process had occurred, and which we might therefore expect to challenge existing rules. Despite these difficult circumstances, the WTO adjudicators have developed a careful, politically informed jurisprudence that has been able to resolve disputes over a number of issues beyond what the WTO's creators originally envisioned, and has ensured a relatively high rate of compliance with these decisions. Ironically, gridlock in trade negotiations between countries may have strengthened the DSM's autonomy by forcing it to fill some of the rule-making gaps countries have left unfilled.

3   *Technical groups with effective and legitimate processes*

A related, but conceptually distinct pathway emphasizes the ability of technical groups to work effectively in a "low politics" context. It has long been recognized that cooperation is easier for more technical issues that avoid excessive interest conflicts or matters of "high politics." Even when distributional problems exist, the low salience and complexity of such issues buffer them from conflictive politics. For these reasons, we would expect gridlock to apply significantly less in these areas. Like the autonomous and adaptive institutions discussed under pathway 2, these entities are somewhat insulated from conflicts between member states. But unlike the other category, this insulation stems from the expertise-based nature of the issue, not necessarily an explicit delegation of authority by states or other power resource possessed by the institutions. To be sure, some institutions, like central banks, combine both autonomy and expertise.

But even purely technocratic institutions are vulnerable to the charge that they are unrepresentative, or privilege certain actors or others. The World Intellectual Property Organization, for example, has been subject to such challenges from developing countries. We therefore expect technocratic institutions to be especially insulated from the dangers of gridlock when they embody fair and transparent procedures that are likely to be seen as legitimate by a wide range of actors. The Internet Corporation for Assigned Names and Numbers (ICANN), for example, has managed to govern a potentially very contentious area of world politics, assigning domain names and protocols to govern the internet, an issue in which political and commercial actors have significant stakes. Yet these conflicts have not managed to upset the basic functioning of the institution, which has been able to provide an essential global public good.

4   Multiple, diverse organizations and institutions coalesce around common goals/norms

Gridlock focused on the negative effects of fragmentation in global governance, such as the increase in transaction costs that may result, or the way in which forum shopping can undermine incentives for cooperation. However, there may also be ways in which fragmentation can represent an adaptive and effective response to the challenges of cooperation under conditions of gridlock. This may be particularly true when public goods provision is being held back by just a small group of spoilers and the good in question is not "absolute" but "additive" in nature. For example, this is one interpretation of the way that gridlock in the WTO has led to a proliferation of bilateral and, more recently, plurilateral trade agreements. To the extent that this "spaghetti bowl" of agreements creates competing rules, it may increase transaction costs, but to the extent that it fosters economic growth and development, and avoids blockages in the WTO, it may generate benefits. Note that such an arrangement would arguably be less compelling in issue areas where just a small number of non-participants can significantly undermine the value of the public good that is created, such as in nuclear non-proliferation.

A proliferation of diverse organizations and institutions may be particularly efficacious when common rules or principles give coherence to an otherwise fragmented institutional landscape. As Slaughter (2017) identifies, well-designed "webs" can provide effective governance in many different areas. For example, transnational commercial arbitration represents a common set of practices and procedures for resolving disputes between commercial actors across borders. While it depends in part on international treaty law, the work of actually adjudicating disputes is carried out by hundreds of private legal organizations around the world specializing in commercial dispute resolution. The decisions of these bodies are then given force through domestic courts under both international and domestic law. Because common practices and rules guide this enormously diverse, pluralistic landscape, the regime functions in a strikingly consistent way across diverse countries and institutions. It has also proven highly resilient, enduring across geopolitical shifts, including gridlock, that have undermined more formalized institutions.

5   *Mobilization of domestic constituencies for cooperation and compliance*

Because growing multipolarity can increase the divergence of preferences within the minimal set of states required to achieve cooperation, *Gridlock* expects cooperation to stall. Other scholars have instead emphasized the way in which global governance may shift states' interests in ways that promote cooperation over time, for example by "socializing" states in cooperative patterns or creating and reinforcing domestic interest groups that push for greater cooperation (Ikenberry 2001). This raises the possibility that states or other actors may make strategic interventions to mobilize certain constituencies in other states that may increase the willingness of those states to cooperate or otherwise promote effective transborder governance. For example, various human rights institutions were created precisely to strengthen the role of pro-law, pro-rights bodies within domestic politics by elevating their voice to the international level. Likewise, international human rights norms can be used to mobilize significant political action by domestic actors (Keck and Sikkink 1998). Alternatively, the large investments that rich, green jurisdictions have made in renewable energy have lowered the costs of those technologies, making climate policies more attractive to less rich, less green countries by reducing opposition from economic groups concerned about the price of energy (Hale and Urpelainen 2015). The 2015 Paris Agreement on climate change is animated by a similar logic, deploying various instruments – the review process, technical support for countries implementing climate policies, orchestration of climate action by transnational networks of sub- and non-state actors – that aim to strengthen support for pro-climate policies in countries over time.

6   *Civil society coalitions with reformist states*

Some of the greatest successes in global governance in the 1990s came about from concerted civil society efforts. When activist groups have been able to partner with progressive countries, significant shifts have been possible, such as the Mine Ban Treaty, the creation of the International Criminal Court (ICC), the Responsibility to Protect (R2P) doctrine, the Guiding Principles for Internal Displacement, or the Framework Convention on Tobacco Control. Transnational business interests have also proved adept at organizing support for certain global governance initiatives in partnership with their governmental allies.

Gridlock has likely increased the barriers to success for such coalitions by making it easier for recalcitrant states to block would-be reformers. Still, mobilization of such coalitions likely provides a meaningful way to achieve results in global governance. Civil society groups and social movements tend to be more successful in agenda-setting and policy impact if (a) they work with states and (b) seek change that, while reformist, can be accommodated within existing structures and organizational principles, at least in the short to medium term. More structural transformations in who gets what, when, and how tend to be the outcome of longer-term struggles and exchange between civil society/social movements and structures of power.

7   *Innovative leadership as a reaction to gridlock*

Gridlock and related arguments about the ineffectiveness of global governance typically rely on structural explanations, with shifts like increasing multipolarity and complexity playing a key role. Such theories, though perhaps insightful on average, de-emphasize the agency of individual actors and specific leaders. Emphasizing general patterns over idiosyncratic behaviours makes social scientific theories usefully parsimonious. But this exercise of course assumes that general patterns exist and explain a large amount of the phenomenon or outcomes of interest compared to more anecdotal accounts.

But is it possible that the very fact of gridlock can itself increase the likelihood that individual actors will develop new forms of agency to overcome it? Faced with both an increasingly stymied international system, and with deepening interdependence and challenges that affect their interests, individuals, states, and other actors may innovate and develop more sophisticated and effective strategies to meet the new challenges they face. In other words, it is possible that more difficult global challenges help generate innovative behaviours to overcome them. Even if such leadership remains the exception that proves the rule, it may be a significant dynamic in discrete areas of world politics, and offer hope and guidance to policymakers seeking proactive change in a gridlocked world.

One particularly salient example of leadership is often referred to in the literature as "norm entrepreneurship." By this we mean strategic efforts by states or other actors to create sets of beliefs that become sufficiently widespread and deeply held to change the preferences and behaviours of other actors in world politics. This strategy constitutes leadership because it seeks to decisively reshape the "rules of the game" by altering many actors' basic beliefs. The campaigns around the Responsibility to Protect and the International Criminal Court both have this quality, though of course both the norm of state responsibility for protection of civilians and universal accountability for crimes against humanity remain incomplete and contested.

Theorizing Pathways through and beyond Gridlock

The pathways through, and beyond, gridlock outlined above are an attempt to identify general mechanisms through which effective global governance can be achieved even in the presence of second-order cooperation problems. The remainder of this book interrogates them and explores how they apply in a wide range of global issue areas. Before summarizing those contributions, it is useful to stress several overarching ideas regarding how to think about the role of these pathways vis-à-vis gridlock in world politics. We return to these ideas at the end of the book.

First, as with the four gridlock trends, we do not expect each pathway through or beyond gridlock to apply in each sector. Rather, different pathways may manifest in different combinations in different areas. In some areas, only a single pathway may be identified, while in others none may apply. In the final chapter, we identify some patterns in these combinations and their distribution across issues.

Second, it is important to note that pathways through or beyond gridlock may only be partial, or may be more effective in certain settings than in others. None of the pathways elaborated here or explored in the following pages can be recognized as silver bullets or panaceas. Our focus is instead on relative improvements in outcomes compared to plausible counterfactual outcomes, as discussed above.

Third, we are curious about the extent to which different pathways interact or combine to produce outcomes. Some of them may work in concert with each other in such a way that the net effect is greater than the sum of the parts. Or, it may also be the case that pathways counterbalance each other – with some leading a sector out of gridlock, and others exacerbating gridlock. Forced migration is a good example of this. The roles of civil society groups (Brookings Institution, the Quakers, etc.) plus state partners help us understand developments in the formation of policy for internal displacement; for example, the creation of the *Guiding Principles on Internal Displacement* and the Kampala Convention for the protection and assistance of internally displaced persons in Africa. These initiatives exemplify elements of pathway 6. However, the fact that forced migration is seen as a threat to states (pathway 1) is in fact one of the drivers of internal displacement in the first place. Given security concerns, states (with a few notable exceptions) are increasingly resistant to accepting refugees, leading to the introduction of containment policies. This, in turn, has led to a situation wherein the number of internally displaced persons now far exceeds the number of refugees. The push and pull of these different forces can lead to contradictory outcomes.

Alternatively, sometimes pathways can work in concert. The Organisation for the Prohibition of Chemical Weapons (the implementing secretariat of the Chemical Weapons Convention), or perhaps the IEA, are examples of organizations based on highly technical expertise (pathway 3), while also enjoying the benefits of relative autonomy (pathway 2).

Fourth, as noted above, this book intentionally highlights pathways through and beyond gridlock that (a) have a proximate causal force on the outcomes of interest, (b) operate in relatively short time frames, and (c) emphasize the strategies and actions that actors in world politics can choose to take. This emphasis reflects the book's aim of highlighting concrete and tangible pathways towards more effective global governance. To succeed in this goal, however, our analysis must of course also consider factors further back along the causal chain, forces that play out over long historical time frames, and conditions that emerge from structural factors in world politics. Shifts in such background conditions and environments can decisively alter the nature of world politics and thus the effectiveness of global governance. Consider, for example, how postwar trade liberalization fundamentally altered the economic structure of the OECD countries over several decades, creating multinational firms and supply chains linked through intra-industry and intra-firm trade, with decisive consequences for states' preferences over global economic governance (Milner 1988). Or note, as the energy and cyber security chapters do, how changes in technology fundamentally altered the governance challenges that states faced. Perhaps most consequentially, it is important to emphasize how fundamental ideational shifts have altered world politics over significant time scales. Shifting ideas around slavery, colonialism, human rights, democracy, environmentalism, and sovereignty have all had significant effects on global governance. While the rise of multipolarity can bring with it ideational heterogeneity, marked by clashes of interpretation about core ideas and priorities, in the long term these contestations have the potential to result in paradigm shifts in the global order. Examples of such shifts in the postwar period include widespread agreement on basic human rights, the prohibition of genocide, the humanitarian standing of refugees and a recognition of climate change risks. Indeed, in the long term, changes in these larger trends may be the only thing that decisively moves the world "beyond" gridlock.

Finally, while gridlock and pathways through it are theories of international politics, we are acutely aware that these dynamics are inextricably linked to and conditioned by domestic political forces, particularly those in the major powers. In *Gridlock* we noted how political challenges in several major powers made gridlock increasingly entrenched. Regrettably, we do not see much evidence that the situation has improved in the intervening years. Indeed, the opposite has occurred. In the conclusion to this book we develop the idea of "self-reinforcing gridlock," in which the failure to manage global problems contributes to an anti-globalist backlash in various countries. The resulting nationalist turn in domestic politics makes it even more difficult for countries to cooperate effectively, deepening the problem of gridlock.

Evidence of this dynamic can be found across the world. For many years in the United States, increasing partisanship driven by the rise of the radical right within the Republican Party (McCarty, Poole and Rosenthal 2006) limited the country's ability to legislate on major issues. It has also rendered all but impossible the ability of the US Senate to ratify international treaties, prompting the executive branch during the Obama presidency to take unprecedented measures to commit credibly to international cooperation. Subsequently, the election of Donald Trump, who vigorously campaigned against trade, immigration, and the global role of the United States, suggests a sharp reduction in US efforts to either facilitate or strengthen global cooperation in the years to come. In Europe, the ongoing tension between economic and political integration remains unresolved, while global challenges like migration from the Middle East threaten to roll back hard-won integration. With the future of the European Union itself in the balance, European countries struggle to come together to play a proactive role on the world stage. China has emerged as a stronger voice for effective global governance, but there are mixed signs as to whether the present leadership will embrace this role. Moreover, the challenge of reforming the economy from a highly polluting investment- and export-led model to one that emphasizes domestic consumption and human welfare, even as the economy slows and the population begins to age and contract, threatens to substantially distract the government from global affairs. Across these diverse jurisdictions, cross-cutting trends like growing (intra-country) inequality raise fundamental challenges that we believe are likely to exacerbate gridlock. While these domestic-level dynamics fall outside the focus of this book, they can reinforce gridlock and therefore affect our consideration of pathways beyond it.

Normative Considerations of Moving beyond Gridlock

While the arguments in this book are analytic and empirical, we are interested in gridlock and pathways through and beyond it because we see these dynamics as fundamental drivers of human welfare in a globalized world. The ability of political institutions to manage interdependence is crucial for a world in which our peace and security, prosperity, health, and natural environment are shaped by transnational forces.

That said, as noted above, it is important to avoid the overly facile framing that all gridlock is necessarily "bad" and all pathways through it unambiguously "good." A pathway out of gridlock that results in changes in policy, decision-making procedures, or institutional design does not automatically imply "good governance"; the outcomes of breaking gridlock may lead to unequal outcomes for different groups, enhance overall inequality, and further entrench privilege or power in the global order. For example, one of the positive regulatory steps taken in the wake of the 2008–9 global financial crisis was to require globally significant banks to keep more of their money on-hand instead of over-extending ("leveraging") their balance sheets. But these regulations have also made it more difficult, in some cases, for developing countries to access international credit markets. Almost all shifts in global governance are likely to produce losers as well as winners, both domestically and globally.

More generally, the discussion of gridlock and pathways through it that follows should be understood in the context of realistic counterfactuals. We very much doubt that any of the pathways explored in this book, singly or in combination, will imminently usher in a radically more effective set of global governance arrangements. Our concern, instead, is in identifying systematic mechanisms that can reasonably ameliorate or undo the more pernicious consequences of multilateral gridlock. Our hope is that the analytic arguments advanced here will increase our understanding of which political strategies can best advance human welfare in a globalized, gridlocked world.

Structure of the Book

Each chapter that follows is structured by an initial assessment of gridlock, and then goes on to evaluate the particular pathways through and beyond gridlock in the given field. The main contours of the institutional architecture and its relevant history are traced. Following an assessment of the presence or absence of gridlock, the chapters consider those pathways through or beyond it that can be observed in existing arrangements or current processes of change. The chapters also consider, prospectively, what pathways may come to play a role – or not – in the future. The last chapter of the book draws together these observations about past, present, and prospective governance arrangements in the issue area, and the causal logics that govern them. Table 1.3 lists the chapters and summarizes which pathways pertain to each, providing an overview of the scope of the

Table 1.3 Pathways through and beyond gridlock across areas of world politics examined in this book

	Shifts in major powers' core interests	Autonomous and adaptive institutions	Technical groups with effective and legitimate processes	Multiple, diverse organizations and institutions around common goals/norms	Mobilization of domestic constituencies	Civil society coalitions with reformist states	Innovative leadership as a reaction to gridlock
Finance	P	P	P	XP		XP	
Monetary Policy		P	P				
Trade	FP	P	P	FP			
Investment	P	P	P	P		P	
Energy	P		P	P			P
Humanitarianism				P		P	P
Human Rights	P	P		P	P		
Health	P		P	P			P
Climate	P		P	P	FP		P
Cyber Security	FP		FP			FP	FP
Weapons of Mass Destruction	P	P	P	XP		XP	FP

P = Pathway through or beyond gridlock.
FP = Pathway may apply in future.
XP = Pathway unlikely to apply.

book. Overall, the book offers a comprehensive assessment of the relevance of the gridlock argument and pathways through or beyond it, in critical areas of world politics.

In the conclusion, we summarize our findings and develop their implications. In particular we assess the pressures generating gridlock and the opportunities for moving beyond it. We note that gridlock metastasizes by feeding into anti-global backlashes in national politics, reactions that further reduce our ability to cooperate internationally. But we also argue, drawing on the comparative analysis in the chapters, that numerous paths forward can be detected. Many of these offer incremental steps, and some promise more fundamental transformations. The preponderance of incrementalism is hardly surprising given the complex and densely intermeshed world order we live in. But incremental should not be confused with unimportant. Even small steps through gridlock can point to avenues beyond it. And larger transformations, noted by some authors, offer the promise of new paradigms for problem solving. In short, the pathways through and beyond gridlock mapped in this book guide us towards an understanding of how to change the world.

2

Finance

Risk and Progress

Kevin Young

Many scholars have confronted the question of why more has not changed in global financial governance since the crisis. Why has there not been more substantial reform of this system since the greatest economic catastrophe in 80 years? Despite some changes to regulatory governance institutions, and to policy ideas about regulation, a common position accepted by the majority of scholars working in this area is that the extent of these changes is modest in comparison to the severity of the financial crisis itself (Helleiner 2012; Moschella and Tsingou 2013; Baker 2013; Young and Park 2013; Mügge 2013). For many, the system of global financial governance in 2017 looks too much like the way it looked in 2006, and the "new Bretton Woods moment" that some were expecting never came (see Helleiner and Pagliari 2010). This is a big, important puzzle that begs explanation. How might we understand the conditions for stasis or transformation from the level of global governance institutions?

The theory behind *Gridlock* suggests that challenges associated with generating a more robust system of global governance emerge historically, inherited from past international cooperation. Challenges of global cooperation are thus situational, specific to historical context, and not something that can simply be derived from predictions about the likelihood of different parties coming to agreement or trusting one another in the international system. "Second order" cooperation problems emerge because the development of prior multilateral cooperation has been successful enough to foster a new set of challenges and situations which are not easily dealt with under earlier models of multilateralism that were so successful in the past. Global cooperation is always difficult; but prior cooperation can, paradoxically, make present cooperation more difficult, as institution-building is locked into a cycle of self-reinforcing interdependence (Hale, Held and Young 2013; 2016).

Is there gridlock in global financial governance? If that state of affairs is meant to mean no change at all, then no. If the status of grid-lock is meant to indicate that effective global governance is chroni-cally undersupplied relative to demand, then yes. The fact that global financial governance is not as robust as is needed is widely accepted, as noted above. Yet there has been movement. Without question, a series of policies, institutional arrangements, and ways of thinking about financial risk have changed since the crisis. But this change is more akin to a gradual drift than a reformulation, and it is certainly not the revolution in regulatory thinking and practice that many expected. In what follows I first outline the state of governance arrangements in global finance and describe the state of gridlock in this area. I argue that problems of institutional inertia continue to prevent more ambitious transformation of existing governance arrangements, and that for all its policy output in the form of global financial standards, the institutional ecology of global financial governance has lacked a centralizing authority to coordinate and adapt to new challenges. I point to evidence at the heart of North Atlantic powers: fissures of cooperation between the United States and European Union (EU) on a variety of issues related to financial regulation.

Turning to potential pathways out of gridlock in this area, I focus on four particular pathways identified in the introduction to this volume: multiple institutions and actors coalesced around common norms/goals, non-state actor coalitions with reformist states, autonomous and adaptive international institutions, and technical groups with effec-tive and legitimate processes. I argue that recent experience should cause us to question the potential for civil society coalitions to push for movement beyond gridlock, or for coherence to emerge from the existing regime complex for financial regulation. Instead I argue that a more likely route beyond gridlock is one which combines the potential for transformation by autonomous international organizations with technical groups characterized by effective and legitimate processes.

The Global Financial System: A Complex Organizational Ecology

The "Bretton Woods" governance institutions such as the World Bank and the International Monetary Fund (IMF) pervade any discussion of how global financial governance works. As *Gridlock* emphasized, these are very important institutions, they have evolved in important ways since the 1970s, and they often have set the stage for the promotion of neoliberal reform since then. Yet as important as the IMF and the World Bank are, there is a lot more to the system of global financial regulation than the functions these organizations carry out. The so-called "transnational standard setting" bodies such as the Basel Committee on Banking Supervision (BCBS), the International Organization for Securities Commissions (IOSCO), the International Association of Insurance Supervisors(IAIS) and many others also plan important roles in setting standards for states and for financial institutions and practices. They are transnational or "transgovernmental" in character (see Keohane and Nye 1974; Hale and Held 2011; Thiemann 2014; Baker 2010), which makes them organizationally distinct from traditional multilateral organizations. This refers to the fact they are rule-making institutions which are organized above the level of the state but which are not strictly composed of state representatives, and do not possess coercive authority. They are also distinct from multilateral governance institutions like the IMF and the World Bank in that they have very small administrative bureaucracies but coalesce as an organized elite network.

Transnational regulatory policymaking has traditionally occurred in a very special kind of social setting – largely an informal one. Those engaging in the design of some international financial standard are, for all intents and purposes, highly specialized technocratic officials. Meetings held within bodies such as the BCBS or the IOSCO for example are seen as highly opaque and not generally well known even to the attentive educated public. This feature of their operations, as I will highlight below, has changed in some ways since the crisis. The extent to which transnational regulatory policymaking is "technocratically insulated" from politics has been explored both as a subject of empirical enquiry and also as a normative concern (see Helleiner and Porter 2010). There has traditionally been a striking lack of formal accountability mechanisms for these bodies. The BCBS for example has been characterized "by virtual separation from any accountable political process" (Underhill and Zhang 2008: 29). The decisions made by these transnational standard-setting bodies – despite their crucial importance to the operation of the global economy and thus to human welfare – have not traditionally been subject to the formal approval of any external body (this too, as I shall argue below, has changed).

These institutions don't simply generate standards on their own, autonomously; they exist in co-dependency relationships with other institutions. The Financial Action Task Force, for example, produces recommendations for the regulation of illicit financial activities that are meant to guide the behaviour of both state policymakers and financial institutions themselves (see Tsingou 2010). The International Accounting Standards Board (IASB) produces international accounting standards for listed companies; the BCBS produces international standards for banking; the International Association of Deposit Insurers (IADI) generates international standards for the conduct of financial deposit insurance schemes, and so on. However the standards that these institutions create are themselves utilized as yardsticks of country performance by the IMF. Standards generated are evaluated by the Financial Stability Board (FSB). International financial market activity also provides an evaluation role. Sometimes international standards are put together explicitly by a collection of different transnational regulatory institutions. The prime example of this is a transnational body called the Joint Forum, which is an organization composed of participants from the IOSCO, the BCBS and the IAIS. Other examples of inter-institutional cooperation also exist, such as that between the Group of Eight (G8), the World Bank, the IMF and the Joint Forum following the 11 September 2001 attacks on the United States (see Tsingou 2010; Biersteker and Eckert 2007).

Private governance organizations also play numerous roles in either trying to shape existing standards or create their own. For example the global standards for the accounting profession are produced by the IASB, which is essentially a global private international club of professionals which operates in such as a way as to generate international standards for the accounting industry (see Botzem 2012). The IASB generates the International Financial Reporting Standards that are used around the world, and have become an essential part of corporate governance. In the EU these standards have been used as formal requirements for all listed companies (see Nölke 2010). Many other organizations that contribute to international standards formation are essentially global business associations, such as the International Swaps and Derivatives Association and the Institute of International Finance (IIF), two organizations that both try to influence existing transnational standards and try from time to time to create their own (see Young 2012). Global financial governance also features hybrid organizations that serve as intellectual hubs for the development and maintenance of operational paradigms about how global finance should be governed. Among the most important is the Group of Thirty (G30), which is a forum of elite professionals from within finance, financial policy and academia (and often reflecting individuals who "revolve" through each of these spaces) (see Tsingou 2015). The line between elite policy think tank and advocacy organization often becomes blurred. Relatedly many members of the G30 have also held prominent positions within the IIF, for example.

This complex system of global financial governance was not designed. It evolved into what it is today as a result of discrete attempts to address particular areas of concern within global governance in the absence of an overarching organizational framework for doing so. Thus the particular historical development of these various institutions has given rise to a highly decentred structure of governance, which resembles a network much more than a hierarchy (Slaughter 2004; Young 2014b). This makes global financial governance much less like the system of global trade governance (which is largely centred around one large multilateral institution, the WTO) and much more like the global environmental regime (which features a panoply of institutions from the United Nations Environment Programme (UNEP) to the Intergovernmental Panel on Climate Change, in that it is constituted by significant "regime proliferation" or akin to what Keohane and Victor (2011) refer to as a "regime complex." Perhaps the best characterization of this system is that it is complex organizational ecology. Formally, organizational ecology is a framework that emphasizes how factors such as organizational density and resource availability change the composition and behaviour of organizations within a given system. Using this framework, Abbott, Green and Keohane (2016) have recently demonstrated how the proliferation of private transnational regulatory organizations has crowded out space for public intergovernmental organizations. According to their argument, the continued growth of public intergovernmental organizations is constrained by this crowding in the organizational environment. Private transnational regulatory organizations have thrived. While Abbott, Green and Keohane apply their analysis to the empirical case of environmental governance, the analysis could easily be extended to global financial governance.[1] The characterization of the system of global financial governance as an ecological system is appropriate because it is a "grown" order, not a "made" one. It is the product of human action but not of human design (Held and Young 2013). Some of its strengths and many of its weaknesses are a product of this structure.

It might be contended that, as problematic and messy as the organizational ecology of global financial governance is, it is not "gridlocked." Other contributions in this volume suggest reasons to believe that governance innovation can take place and be resilient in the face of change. A number of scholars who have emphasized the network-like character of global financial governance have argued that existing arrangements helped to foster enhanced cooperation during and after the crisis (see Kahler 2013; Kahler and Lake 2013; Drezner 2012). As Helleiner summarizes, "International economic institutions are seen to have been significant in providing focal points for coordination, rules that constrained behavior and reduced uncertainty, and expertise that helped to promote shared understandings" (2014: 19). There is much to agree with in this statement. Existing arrangements did help to prevent a true downward spiral in the global economy. Yet this does not mean – this time to quote Drezner (2012) – that "the system worked." The system helped recover from the brink, but the system also failed. As emphasized in *Gridlock*, existing arrangements of global economic governance helped to turn a disaster into a *mitigated* disaster.

Continued Gridlock or Forward Momentum Out?

How has the system of global financial governance evolved since the crisis, in terms of adaptation to new challenges and addressing long-standing ones? One way to assess this is to measure the policy output of this system. Viewed from this perspective alone, there has not been "gridlock" but rather a proliferation of output. Since the crisis, the organizations within this ecology have done much more of what they have always done: generate more and more financial regulatory standards. Figure 2.1 counts the number of global financial regulatory standards from 1983 to 2015.[2]

This figure illustrates the fact that there has been a significant increase in the number of standards agreed on since the crisis. Yet a key weakness within global financial governance has not been that there have been too few standards. It has been the weakness of central-izing governing authority and the productive coherence among these standards. I note in this context that a key part of the argument in *Gridlock* is not *just* that effective global governance is in short supply but that the process of self-reinforcing interdependence is producing, and will continue to produce, new problems that give rise to new global public policy demands. Put bluntly, new problems arise that the existing system cannot deal with well. Global finance is no less competitive and cutthroat than it was before the crisis. But there have been signs of global cooperation weakening, especially between the North Atlantic powers.

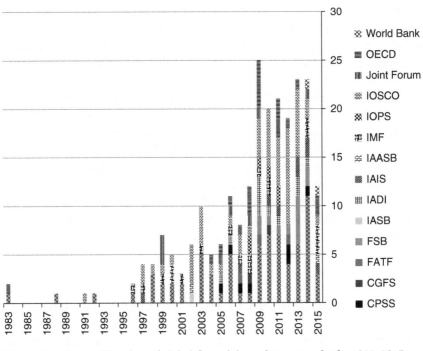

Figure 2.1   The proliferation of global financial regulatory standards, 1983–2015

Source: Financial Stability Board, data compiled by Stefano Pagliari.

In this context it is worth reflecting on which of the originally hypothesized *Gridlock* trends and mechanisms have been at work since the financial crisis. *Growing multipolarity* seems to have been a much less important threat to continued global financial governance cooperation than was envisaged before the crisis. The expansion of the existing transnational financial standards bodies has come with its challenges but it is not clear that adding additional countries to include the entire G20 has inhibited progress. *Institutional inertia* has persisted in some ways but has been weakened in others. While there is considerable institutional inertia within the IMF, the institution has also proven that it is capable of evolving, albeit in constrained ways, since the crisis (see Ban and Gallagher 2015). Transnational financial standard-setting bodies have continued their logic of informal consensus decision-making but since the crisis have also sought external authorization through the G20, which represents a significant change since the crisis. Importantly, not all of the work done by international institutions has been seeking to protect the status quo. There has been considerable rethinking of what the ends of financial governance should be, especially in light of environmental sustainability goals, by the UN Environment Programme (see UNEP Inquiry 2015; 2016a).

In contrast, *harder problems* and *institutional fragmentation* have persisted and taken new forms, and I focus on these two gridlock mechanisms in particular in what follows below. These are manifest in three different forms which show evidence of continued gridlock in global financial governance: the rise of financial protectionism, the slow and uneven advance in the coordination of derivatives regulatory reform, and the lack of material compliance within new global banking standards. Together these examples constitute evidence of a fissure between the US and the EU. I do not want to argue that these practices are leading to some dangerous cataclysm. The reason why they are instructive in a discussion of *Gridlock* is because their emergence, and the lack of them being addressed systematically, speak to weaknesses in global financial governance within the North Atlantic core of the system.

The rise of financial protectionism

The fear of protectionism (it is only a *fear* among *some* – since some see protectionist policies as generating comparative advantage) usually comes in the form of trade protectionism. Yet when countries executed the multifarious bailout packages for their financial systems, they engaged in a wide array of policy manoeuvres to support their own financial industry at the expense of foreign rivals. It is hard to blame them for succumbing to this anti-globalist pressure, given the enormous transfers involved from the public purse into the most profitable industry in the world that had just nearly tanked the economy.

Yet other financial protectionist practices started to emerge once the dust settled. Protectionism evolved (see Young 2014a). A set of practices known as "ring fencing" began to emerge. Ring fencing refers to a practice whereby national financial regulators impose a requirement on a foreign bank subsidiary operating in their jurisdiction that treats that subsidiary as if it were a distinct entity for regulatory purposes – that is, effectively ignoring the fact that it is connected to an *international* banking group. Ring fencing has generated serious concerns among policymakers and industry, given that it could generate a pattern of international retaliation or at least catch on as a regulatory trend. This is exactly the kind of emerging governance challenge – a coordination problem, in this case – that the system of global financial regulation should have responded to. Context makes this emergent problem

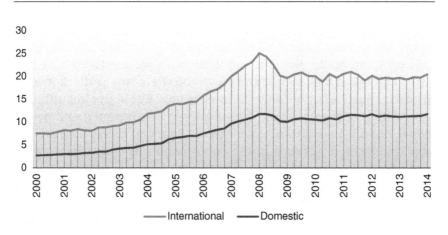

Figure 2.2   Bank lending in international and domestic components, 2000–2014 (US$ trillions)

Note: International time series measures international bank claims on a consolidated and immediate borrower basis. Domestic time series measures local currency claims on local residents on an immediate borrower basis.

Source: Bank for International Settlements database.

more worrying from the perspective of governance capacity. The European Central Bank estimated that between mid-2011 and 2012, international overnight money markets fell by about a third. Indeed, in the years immediately following the crisis there was a marked downturn in international bank lending, followed by a plateau that suggested a slowdown in financial globalization. Figure 2.2 shows domestic and international bank lending from 2000 to 2014.[3]

Many large international banks have essentially been seeking to make their subsidiaries self-funded, which means matching their liabilities and assets on a country-by-country basis. National regulators encouraged banks, sometimes formally, sometimes informally, to restrict the fungibility of the banking groups' capital across borders, for example by instituting greater scrutiny of inter-group transfers within the operations of a given banking group (IMF 2013: 20). As banks have been pursuing more of a subsidiary form, they are forced to rely increasingly on their own funding, whereas in the past, thanks to financial globalization, they could rely on funding from their parent ("home country") bank when needed. What this has meant is that banks began to make disproportionately large cuts to their international exposures (IMF 2012: 55; 2013: 20).

In the US, regulators made a significant move that had a consequence of exacerbating global trends. At the end of 2012, the Fed released proposals to require operations of foreign banks to establish a holding company structure over all bank and non-bank subsidiaries operating in the United States. What this meant was that these foreign subsidiaries will be subject to the same capital and liquidity requirements as domestic US banks, without acknowledging the fact that foreign bank subsidiaries operating in the United States are part components of international banking groups (see IMF 2013: 20). This represented a monumental reversal of US banking regulatory policy. The EU Commissioner for the Internal Market, Michael Barnier, warned in April 2013 that the Fed's move posed a threat to global regulation and risked "a protectionist reaction" (see Menon, George-Cosh and Douglas 2013; Plender 2013). Jonathan Faull, the head of the European Commission department handling financial regulation, made similar warnings.

Global financial regulatory bodies have, to be sure, identified these kinds of practices as a rising problem. The Financial Stability Board for example identified ring fencing as an affront to its global ethos (see Verma 2012), and its head, Mark Carney, argued against the US move (see Foley 2013). The IMF also identified it as an important risk factor several times in its *Global Financial Stability Report* (IMF 2012: 8, 55; IMF 2013: 20). Yet they have not been able to do anything about it, with the exception of soft "moral suasion." Large and important private sector associations like the IIF and the Global Financial Markets Association denounced these kinds of practices as well, but since it divides the industry into winners and losers on the basis of national jurisdiction, there are limits to their mobilization. One can only speculate whether the resurgence of new right populist tendencies in the North Atlantic may exacerbate these tendencies. The incoming Trump regime in the United States has rattled the trade protectionist sabre; it is an open question whether financial protectionism will be on the agenda as well. If it is, then the prospects for continued gridlock in global financial governance are strong indeed.

OTC derivatives reform

Another example of the kinds of weaknesses that have emerged in global financial regulatory governance concerns the regulation of over-the-counter (OTC) derivatives. International cooperation on the regulation of OTC derivatives is an excellent litmus test for the robustness of global financial governance in light of pressing challenges because the regulation of OTC derivatives has been flagged as a pressing policy issue and one where there was virtually no regulatory infrastructure before the crisis.

In 2009, two significant developments occurred in this area. First, the G20 made ambitious commitments to generate a system of global OTC derivatives reform by 2012. Second, in true informal technocratic fashion, the crisis produced a new organization in 2009, called the Over the Counter Derivatives Regulators' Forum (ODRF), as a communication, monitoring and deliberation body among central banks, banking regulators and other government authorities with authority over OTC derivatives market infrastructure. With respect to the G20's ambitious commitments for global OTC derivatives reform, this was later extended from 2012 to 2015, yet as Knaack remarks "the gap between the 2009 G20 commitments and the reality of their global implementation … remains considerable" (2015: 1239). With respect to the ODRF, rather than this specialist organization advancing and attaining greater prominence over time, it scaled down its operations. Seeing the existing global standard-setting bodies and domestic authorities as taking care of the regulatory infrastructure that was needed, in 2014 it officially reduced its operating mission and has since decided to focus on the use of an important but ultimately very limited area: data quality of trade repository issues.

Given this attrition, a key issue for the diagnosis of regulatory cooperation in this area is whether and how the two key jurisdictions covering (at present) most of the world's OTC infrastructure, the US and the EU, have been cooperating. Knaack (2015) notes a striking lack of cross-border regulatory cooperation between them on this very issue. Documenting the challenges faced in recent years, Knaack argues that intergovernmental networks are weak and incomplete due to a fragmented domestic regulatory system in both the EU and the US. Compounding these problems has been the fact that legislators in both jurisdictions have hindered cross-border harmonization at several stages. The latter shows that the salience of financial regulation does not lead to stronger global cooperation but can sometimes weaken it.

There were significant divisions between the US and EU in terms of including financial services in the projected Transatlantic Trade and Investment Partnership (TTIP). Given the significant G20 commitments and all the prior cooperation between the US and the EU in this area, it is remarkable that financial services got left off the agenda. Jones and Macartney (2016) argue that the attempts by the US to move more quickly in financial regulatory reform have given rise to "venue shopping" on the part of the largest financial firms.

The divide in global financial standards implementation

The US–EU divide has also grown with respect to how the new global financial standards generated in the wake of the financial crisis have been implemented years later. As Helleiner (2014: 18) notes, at the beginning of the crisis European policymakers were very enthusiastic in calling for more radical change in global financial governance. Yet these ambitions were overcome by local considerations: the eurozone crisis meant a diversion from issues related to governance reform and cast a shadow on the eurozone's capacity to manage problems even in its own backyard. European policymaking also proved a more porous forum for financial industry lobbying than in the US (see Jones and Macartney 2016). This has occurred at the same time as EU regulatory centralization and capacity has been built up (see Pagliari 2012a; 2012b).

With respect to global financial standards implementation, the EU has traditionally been a loyal implementer of global standards; the US, in contrast, has traditionally been more reticent, but this has been in areas related to accounting and the bifurcation of its banking system. With respect to global banking regulatory reform the US has been a relatively loyal steward of BCBS standards, accepting the required minimum levels and calibrating national regulatory policies in line with it, and in many cases going beyond global standards. In contrast, the EU has selectively reshaped the content of Basel III – the highly technical and systematic revamp of the pre-crisis Basel Accord – in a variety of ways. The two keystone policy packages for banking regulatory reform in the EU, the Capital Requirements Directive (CRD) IV and the Capital Requirements Regulation, specified a wide range of exceptions – from a more flexible implementation of leverage ratio requirements to less stringent credit risk and liquidity requirements.

Reviews conducted by a peer evaluation subcommittee of the BCBS concluded that the EU was "materially non-compliant" with the new Basel III rules (BCBS 2014: 4). The CRD IV allowed EU banks to engage in more practices of grandfathering of securities (grandfathering allows banks to continue to engage in practices that were in place before the new regulations), and has offered more flexibility in the inclusion of financial instruments counted as high quality "Tier 1" capital. EU banks are even permitted under certain circumstances to apply a zero risk weight to EU sovereign exposures and to give preferential treatment to a host of EU member state authorities, such as central banks, regional governments, and local authorities. Equity exposures related to government programmes designed to promote specific sectors of the economy are also allowed to be given special treatment. Regardless of the appropriateness of these policy moves, such adaptations of the global standards represent defiance from what was agreed globally. The BCBS of course monitors progress of the implementation of its rules in different jurisdictions. Already in June 2012 it signalled warnings that EU implementation plans were looking more lax than the global rules (see Brunsden 2012). Such moves were reported to the G20 in 2012 but neither the global standard-setting bodies nor the G20 have the authority to undo EU regulation, only to "identify, name and shame" (BCBS 2012: 6). After studying these revisions, a BCBS subcommittee even concluded that these adaptations generated a material overstatement of banks' Tier 1 capital (BCBS 2014: 20).

There has, of course, always been variation in the actual concrete implementation of global banking standards (see Oatley 2001; Chey 2006; Walter 2008). The point I wish to make about the recent divergence between the US and the EU is that significant variation in compliance among the North Atlantic powers is not a good sign of the robustness of global financial governance, since these jurisdictions have been at the heart of the system. The fact that it has not led to a tangible disaster is beside the point; the two biggest centres of economic activity have quite significantly parted ways when it comes to their adherence to global regulatory standards that they all had an active hand in shaping in the first place.

Prospects for the Future

If there are signs of continued gridlock within the system of global financial governance since the crisis, what about the prospects for the future? In the remainder of this chapter, I reflect on particular pathways identified in the introduction as leading beyond gridlock. This reflection is intended to be forward looking but with evidence from recent experience.

Beginning from the most remote pathways to the more likely, it is very difficult to imagine *shifts in major powers' core interests* in this area. The governance of finance remains a key driver for national accumulation strategies and is not likely to shift in its importance or orientation. With respect to the mechanism of *mobilization of domestic constituencies for cooperation and compliance*, this volume posits the possibility that states' interests might shift in a way that promotes greater cooperation over time, either through socialization through international interactions or through shifts in domestic constituencies' interests.

The pathways in this book also encourage us to consider a variety of actor constellations which often fall outside the gambit of usual international relations scholarship. They point to pathways such as *multiple, diverse organizations and institutions coalescing around common goals/norms*, and no*n-state actor coalitions with reformist states*. There are of course a very wide variety of potential constellations of actors that might be involved in such activity when it comes to global financial governance. When it comes to non-state actors such as private business associations and individual firms, the potential is certainly great that global cooperation may be encouraged in different ways. Large transnational financial firms usually do not like regulatory fragmentation across borders and prefer standardized rules that allow them to operate in multiple jurisdictions with greater ease and flexibility. Yet as a constituent group they do not necessarily want to push for more robust governance standards. Nor do they, after many years of tooling themselves up in line with existing financial standards regimes, seek to push for more stringent financial regulatory rules. Though there are exceptions to this (in particular when large firms seek to edge out competitors), the financial sector itself is unlikely to be a force for change as a constituency working with reformist states or as a force trying to organize other actors around a new set of norms, etc. The "non-financial" business community is another non-state actor that might be considered to be a potential catalyst for change in this area, given that non-financial business interests are sometimes at odds with those of the financial community. This too seems unlikely, on the basis of recent evidence. In particular non-financial business groups tend to coalesce as a supportive force for the status quo when it comes to financial sector regulation (see Young and Pagliari 2017).

One non-state actor group which many hold out as an important potential catalyst for change in global financial governance are non-business civil society organizations, such as non-governmental organizations (NGOs), consumer protection groups, and research institutes/think tanks. The introduction to this volume highlights how these groups can potentially work alongside reformist states, and/or be part of a diversity of organizations and institutions organizing around common goals. Indeed civil society is often held out as an important and significant progressive force for reform. I first examine the prospects for this, before turning to a more likely prospect, *the assertion of autonomous agency within and among technocratic organizations*.

Civil Society's Potential Contribution out of Gridlock

There are two reasons why civil society actors are unlikely to act as pivotal catalysts for pathways out of gridlock in global financial governance in the future. The first is that many civil society organizations are inherently suspicious of global governance arrangements in the area of finance. The properties of the gridlock trend of "institutional inertia" is relevant here, in that many see existing governance arrangements as shot through with elite interests or neoliberal policy programmes, rather than as changeable, complex institutions with problems but also potential. Key organizations like the IMF, BCBS, Bank for International Settlements and now the FSB have been seen as instruments for powerful states at best, or at worst as completely "captured" institutions that simply do the bidding of private financial institutions. Regardless of the empirical accuracy of such claims, this has socialized many civil society actors, as well as the social movements they often depend on, with an anti-global governance orientation. Years of campaigning by civil society organizations have generated an entrenched discourse that *global governance = rules for the powerful*. Governance capacity – the social and bureaucratic infrastructure within and among international organizations and their surrounding organizational ecology – is not something that civil society mobilizations tend to focus on or promote. Thus delegation of (or agglomeration of) public authority to global financial governance institutions is treated with suspicion. Change is always possible, and it is possible that civil society can reorient itself in the future. Yet its recent orientation is strikingly different from other areas of policy and of global governance. For example, the movements for human security and the movement for environmental sustainability recognize, on the whole, that international organizational arrangements are genuine arenas of social struggle; while their targets for reform are often multi-level in character, they are not strongly anti-globalist.

Second, there has been a general dearth of organizational responsiveness of civil society organizations directed at global financial governance institutions outside of the IMF and World Bank, and it is just that kind of responsiveness that is needed to urge a pathway beyond the current state of gridlock. An exception to this would be the struggle over global taxation reform, where there has been significant mobilization (see Seabrooke and Wigan 2015), as well as organizations such as New Rules for Global Finance and FinanceWatch, which is particularly active within the EU (see Lindo and Fares 2016). Mobilizing for reform beyond gridlock is not just about orientation and about the organizational capacity of any one group. An entire network of civil society groups needs to be directed towards a problem, as this allows global civil society organizations to frame agendas and bolster resource mobilization (see Carpenter 2007). Yet the available research on general trends within civil society mobilization suggests that the kind of dense network of civil society organizations that exists in other domains is unlikely to be focused around global financial governance unless some radical break with the past takes place. Yagci (2016) shows that the Occupy protests – which emerged impressively in 88 different countries – were systematically related to low growth and to the presence of inequality. This would suggest that civil society's radical edge may have a bright future indeed; however Occupy was squarely focused on national concerns, and not international governance institutions. Data on responsiveness to regulatory policy proposals in finance have allowed scholars to study the conditions under which interest groups generate the conditions for pluralist politics, and at different levels of governance. Pagliari and Young develop a measure of "mobilized dissent" generated among interest groups as they respond to different regulatory policymaking proposals in different individual countries, at the EU level, and within global standard-setting bodies like the IOSCO, FSB and BCBS. They find a significant negative association between the technical complexity of regulatory proposals and the degree of mobilized dissent – especially among trade union organizations and NGOs (Pagliari and Young 2016: 18). What is more, despite the fact that mobilized dissent has increased since the crisis, it tends to come from different groups at different times. What this means is that while there is some interest group pluralism in financial governance, it is highly disjointed.

I do not want to discount the role of civil society altogether. This diverse group has, under favourable conditions, made important contributions to financial governance reform within particular countries and regions (see Kastner 2014). In this sense they may act as part of future coalitions, potentially within states that seek to reform global governance through some catalytic or leadership role. However, in the larger scheme of pathways through and beyond gridlock, their role is likely to be muted relative to other forces. The same cannot be said, I would argue, for the assertion of autonomous agency within and among technocratic organizations, which I now focus on.

Assertion of Autonomous Agency within and among Technocratic Organizations

I have noted above a lack of centralized authority within the system of global financial governance. This was emphasized in *Gridlock* (Hale, Held and Young 2013) but as I have demonstrated there are some continued signs that this continues to be a problem, for example when it comes to coordinating policy implementation of global standards. In this section I argue that the most promising prospect for pathways beyond gridlock is in the assertion of autonomous agency within and among international organizations with significant technocratic capacity. This approach combines two of the pathways emphasized in this book.

Since the crisis there have been several initiatives in place to induce greater centralizing authority within the system of global financial governance – to truly "govern" the complex organizational ecology that has built up over the last few decades. The crisis meant that existing institutions "took the helm" – trying to exercise leadership, competence authority and ultimately trying to steer the agenda of reform within the existing system. In looking forward it is possible to see prospects for further activity on these fronts as new challenges arise amidst the conditions of self-reinforcing interdependence.

The IMF has been one example of this trend. Prior to the crisis the IMF had been suffering in terms of both funding and legitimacy. Middle-income countries had ceased to take out loans from the IMF, preferring other sources that required less macroeconomic re-engineering. During the crisis the IMF asserted its competence authority as the institution responsible for the stability of the global financial system. Indeed, the IMF has reinvented itself. In the years before the crisis, lending from the IMF fell to its lowest levels since the early 1970s, and lending to middle-income countries and large emerging economies came to an end. As Reinhart and Trebesch (2016) summarize, "A view emerged that perhaps an institution whose primary roles were economic surveillance and crisis management had outlived its usefulness." There have been some important changes in IMF policy, in particular in the way it treats states' attempts to manage capital flows. When it comes to capital inflows, the IMF has become significantly more permissive than when it used to treat this kind of behaviour with hostility. The clientele for IMF programmes also shifted, and the IMF made its largest loans not to developing countries but to wealthy economies in the EU (in particular to Greece).

The G20 has also taken on a more central role in acting as an international steward for crisis reform than previously. The G20 – an ad hoc construction in the first place – was created in the aftermath of the East Asian financial crisis of 1997–8, and was not considered particularly noteworthy within the International Political Economy finance literature (see Germain 2001). Yet since the crisis the rise of this body in setting the global financial regulatory agenda has been of great interest to recent scholarship in the field (e.g. see Vestergaard and Wade 2013; Helleiner 2012). The rise of the G20 as a global governing body was unexpected but impressive given the need for centralizing authority. As Helleiner put it, "Immediately after its creation, the G20 leaders' forum was seen as a major institutional innovation in global financial governance that would help manage the financial crisis" (2014: 5). Among the most historically significant moves the G20 made early in the crisis was a broad call to reform the formal memberships of existing financial governance bodies. This occurred rapidly within the space of a few months (see Helleiner and Pagliari 2011). It is possible, and even likely, that the reason why multipolarity has not been a serious problem for global financial governance is because of this greater formal inclusiveness. Countries such as China, for example, have played a very reserved and "mainstream" role in global banking negotiations (see Nölke 2015).

The leadership of the G20 was important for agenda-setting during the crisis but short-lived in its importance. It was the formal institutionalization of the Financial Stability Board that was the true innovation and more significant change. The FSB represents a transformation from the previous Financial Stability *Forum*, which was simply a discussion forum. The FSB, in contrast, was to serve as the keystone organization within the ecology of global financial governance, by coordinating and monitoring activities within other organizations. While the G20 was a forum of executive-level political leaders, the FSB was a mix of central bank governors, finance ministers, and also representatives of other international organizations such as the BCBS and the IMF. The creation of the FSB was correctly seen as significant but relatively uncertain early on (see Helleiner 2010). From the beginning it had very few administrative resources, despite the fact that it was heralded as being the "fourth pillar" of global economic governance. Having a keystone organization is an excellent idea, and shows that G20 leaders at least recognized the fragmentation problem in global financial governance. The FSB Charter has been criticized as weak and significantly limits its abilities to compel its members to abide by its decisions. While the FSB is designed in part to undertake reviews and coordinate the development of global standards and codes, its Charter ensures that these organizations fully maintain their independence. As Knaack argues, the institutional design of the FSB has been criticized as lacking a strong legal foundation and has "no teeth" (2015: 1221; see also Davies 2014).

Each of the aforementioned changes are significant because of the sheer lack of coordination and centralization authority within global financial governance prior to the crisis. They suggest a possibility for a path through gridlock. The introduction notes that highly technocratic institutions may offer a way out of gridlock because its key mechanisms may not operate within or on such institutions. Moreover, technocratic organizations may also derive legitimacy and therefore authority as a product of their rational and transparent procedures. This latter characteristic may be less applicable to the present case, since most financial governance institutions have a long way to go in terms of their input or output legitimacy.

The FSB is an inherently technocratic organization, but one with a degree of legitimacy given its creation under the auspices of the G20 in recognition of a lack of centralizing authority. My confidence in this pathway beyond gridlock in global financial governance is strengthened by relatively low-profile but significant events demarcating the changing relationship among technocratic transnational organizations in finance. Specifically in 2012 the G20 urged the FSB to strengthen its autonomy. Subsequently it formalized its legal status (as a Swiss charity) and has taken moves that suggest a level of technocratic autonomy. The FSB's staff and secretariat is still very small, but it has a larger Steering Committee, standing committees and a variety of working groups. It has also set up six different "regional consultative groups": in the Americas, Asia, Commonwealth of Independent States, Europe, the Middle East and North Africa, Sub-Saharan Africa. It sits as the "spider" (Davies 2014) in the web of global financial governance, coordinating and monitoring the policy output and coordination of other institutions in the complex organizational ecology of global finance.

Institutions like the FSB may move beyond gridlock by instituting what is sometimes referred to as "transformative incremental change." Chwieroth (2014) argues persuasively that international organizations tend to respond to situations of change by a process of "layering" whereby new policies are put atop old ones, rather than a course correction. This incremental bias within international organizations is in-built because of internal path-dependent cultural features within their bureaucracies. This practice of layering thus makes change slow moving. Yet it also allows international organizations to build coalitions amidst a diverse world. Chwieroth argues that rather than simply reproducing existing practices (see Weaver 2008: 29), changes that appear gradual "can culminate over time into significant institutional and organizational discontinuities" (Chwieroth 2014: 446; see also Baker 2013). The question is not whether or not there is evidence of such "transformative" incremental change to date but whether it will develop over time. Among other alternative pathways laid out in this volume, this one seems the most likely future prospect.

Conclusion

Tendencies towards gridlock in global financial governance have persisted despite massive calamity and politicization in that sector. In this chapter I argued that problems of institutional inertia continue to prevent a more ambitious transformation of existing governance arrangements, and that for all its policy output in the form of global financial standards, the organizational ecology of global financial governance has lacked a centralizing authority to coordinate and adapt to new challenges. Despite a persistent concern with rising multipolarity, in financial governance there have been a surprising number of fissures in regulatory cooperation among the North Atlantic powers, specifically between the US and the EU.

In terms of pathways beyond gridlock I reviewed the potential of multiple, diverse organizations and institutions organizing around common goals/norms, and non-state actor coalitions with reformist states. Both have potential that is highly conditional on the politics of the future and therefore invite speculation as well as modesty about what political futures are to come. As such, I focused attention on an actor category that many might expect to be prominent in both of these pathways: the role of non-business civil society groups. I argued that recent experience should cause us to question the potential for civil society coalitions to push for movement beyond gridlock. Instead I argue that a more likely pathway beyond gridlock is one that combines the potential for transformation by autonomous international organizations with technical groups with effective and legitimate processes.

3

Monetary Policy

Making Fragmentation Work

Camila Villard Duran

Why has global monetary cooperation been failing when it is most needed? After the 2008 crisis and ten summits of the G20,[1] little has changed in the global monetary architecture. The International Monetary Fund, created by the Bretton Woods agreements in the 1940s, was supposed to be the central forum for international monetary cooperation. The economic crisis that began in East Asia in 1997 and then spread internationally was a global event in which the Fund played a key role as a forum for monetary cooperation. For the first time in its history, the IMF dealt with a capital account crisis due to sudden reversals of capital flows in a very complex international environment. However, since the 1990s crisis, this international organization has been suffering from political stigma created by its lending programmes (IMF 2014; IEO IMF 2014; Duran 2015b).

Once the 2008 crisis hit, the global economic landscape was different from previous decades. A shift of global economic power was already in motion. Emerging countries in Asia and Latin America were important drivers of global growth. Nevertheless, Bretton Woods institutions, notably the Fund, did not reflect this shift in their governance structure. Developed and emerging countries resorted to the G20 to promote changes in the Fund's governance and make it more legitimate and effective. However, due to institutional inertia, only modest changes have resulted.

Monetary cooperation at the multilateral level has been challenged by growing multipolarity and institutional fragmentation. Newly relevant state actors, such as emerging countries in Asia and Latin

America, are reshaping the international monetary system. In the aftermath of 2008, these countries formalized, or reinforced, regional and bilateral monetary arrangements. They are investing in institutions parallel to the IMF to respond to future liquidity crises. In addition, they are challenging the key role played by the US dollar as the main monetary and investment vehicle of the Bretton Woods system. The formalization of new arrangements could be described as "contested multilateralism," a concept that emphasizes that "contemporary multilateralism is characterized by competing coalitions and shifting institutional arrangements, informal as well as formal" (Morse and Keohane 2014: 386).

A central argument of this chapter, based on the theoretical framework proposed in *Gridlock*, is that growing multipolarity (emerging countries with economic and political power at the global level) combined with institutional inertia (related to the IMF) and harder problems (recurrent liquidity crises in capital accounts) are leading to a more fragmented and diversified global order.

To go through gridlock in monetary governance, short-term responses to the US dollar system have been formulated. Based on foreign exchange reserve accumulation, emerging economies formalized regional arrangements and created, or reinforced, parallel institutions to the IMF. At the same time, through bilateral initiatives, some emerging countries have invested in the emergence of new currencies to escape from the dependence of international money supplied by advanced economies.

Both bilateral and regional initiatives clearly have a multilateral intent, that is, they are promoting cooperation among countries and aligning different interests in approaching global monetary challenges. On the one hand, these strategies are aggregating economies around shared goals and adding more sources of liquidity to be accessed in case of balance of payment imbalances. On the other hand, these strategies are reinforcing fragmentation in monetary governance. It seems that institutional fragmentation is both a response to, and a driver of, gridlock.

To go beyond gridlock in monetary governance, two pathways are emerging: (1) technical groups with good processes, and (2) autonomous and adaptive international institutions. For the former, the complexity of monetary governance and shared ideas on money among a specific epistemic community, such as central banks, are the main drivers of changes in the international monetary system. The emergence of currency swaps[2] in regional and bilateral arrangements is contributing to a shift in the locus of decisions on monetary affairs from international organizations towards central banks.

For the latter pathway, the IMF is trying to overcome institutional inertia by linking its programmes to new regional arrangements, as well as reinforcing the emergence of new global currencies. For instance, since 2016, the Fund has been running tests to connect the Asian Chiang Mai Initiative Multilateralization (CMIM), a regional arrangement, to its lending programmes. In addition, in 2015, the IMF decided to include the Chinese currency in the Special Drawing Rights (SDR)[3] basket, which tends to reinforce Chinese policies sustaining the internationalization of the renminbi.

Currently, the most challenging task for the international organization is how to connect the multilateral level with bilateral initiatives promoted by central banks. The Fund's staff proposed creating a multilateral hub for swaps between central banks, but the idea was not approved by the Fund's directors (IMF 2010a). Meanwhile, the growing power of national central banks is reshaping monetary cooperation at the global level (Duran 2015b). This fragmentation will likely be reinforced in coming years, with more bilateral monetary agreements based on central banks' networks and financial operations, in traditional global currencies or new "monies." The Bretton Woods agreements are silent on this issue. There are no clear international obligations related to central bank operations at the global level, or regarding the convertibility of currencies in capital accounts.

The chapter is divided as follows. In the next section, I present a brief analysis of the evolution of the Bretton Woods framework and how the US dollar became its key currency. The section also explores the gridlock argument in global monetary governance due to the growing multipolarity of the system. In the following section, I present evidence on the institutional fragmentation caused by the creation, or the reinforcement, of regional and bilateral monetary arrangements formulated by G20 emerging powers in Asia and Latin America, in the aftermath of 2008. I evaluate the practical consequences of these arrangements, notably their impact on the global monetary architecture. Emerging countries are using this pathway to go through gridlock, as a short-term response to global challenges. Then I explore pathways beyond gridlock: the role of central banks (technical groups) and the main attempts of the IMF to overcome its institutional inertia (autonomous and adaptive international institutions). Critical barriers to moving beyond gridlock are stressed.

Growing Multipolarity, Harder Problems and Institutional Inertia: The Gridlock in Monetary Cooperation

Since the end of World War II and the establishment of the Bretton Woods institutions, the International Monetary Fund has been in charge of assuring global monetary cooperation, through financial support to member countries in case of balance of payments imbalances (i.e. as an international lender of last resort) as well as serving as a forum for monetary dialogue (Boughton 2001; Fischer 1999; James 1996). After 1969, the Fund was also responsible for managing a newly created international reserve asset, the SDR.

The idea of the Bretton Woods founders was to ensure states had macroeconomic autonomy, a major intellectual change by comparison with the international gold standard prevailing up to 1914. In the 1940s, the international monetary system was originally conceived as a global order in which different currencies were supposed to be used in international transactions without hierarchy between them. Each country was to fix a par value for its domestic currency by using gold or another currency tied to gold. The long-run par value would be adjusted after an agreement with the IMF and, in the short run, each state was to manage its currency and keep it within 1 per cent of the par value. Therefore, the agreement's original intention was to use national currencies symmetrically for foreign transactions.

However, the rules and the real practice of the Bretton Woods system differed greatly (McKinnon 1993). The US dollar quickly became the key currency of the international monetary system. In practical terms, the system evolved to a "fixed-rate dollar standard" in the 1960s (McKinnon 1993: 15), which became the most stable financial system ever experienced by countries, empirically less subject to liquidity crises.

After the end of the par value system in the 1970s, the US dollar and its issuer, the Federal Reserve (Fed), became even more central to the Bretton Woods system. Since this currency was no longer linked to gold by an international agreement, the Fed's monetary policy determined the value of this hegemonic currency at the global level and has decisively influenced its demand by other countries. Currently, the US dollar is the main reserve currency for national central banks, representing more than 60 per cent of total international reserves, even achieving more than 70 per cent at the end of the 1990s.[4] In this order centred on the US dollar, countries rely on the supply of international money by the American central bank, the Fed, and access to it in times of crisis through the IMF's credit operations.

Over its history, the Fund consolidated its role as a financial actor in a complex international environment, as well as an institution responsible by the "transmission of ideas" for money management (James 1996: 133) and an "arbiter of economic policies" (Mohan and Kapur 2015: 12). With the recurrence of international crises after the 1970s, the IMF gained more power as global lender, expanding the number of its credit operations. For instance, the total outstanding Fund's credit grew from US$20 billion in 1981 to US$60 billion in 1995, reaching US$100 billion in 2001 and more than US$140 billion in 2012 (Mohan and Kapur 2015).

The IMF's responsibility as international lender of last resort was heavily reinforced during the 1990s crises in Asia and Latin America. With Michel Camdessus as managing director, the Fund was the central organization in global monetary cooperation, formulating responses to developing countries facing liquidity crises. However, this was also a historical period in which the organization was highly criticized by its approach to political conditionalities.

After the 1990s, developing countries were suffering crises in their capital accounts for the first time in their history – instead of the crises in current accounts common in the past (Lastra 2015: 540). Capital account crises are characterized by abrupt reversals of capital flows, causing falls in exchange rates and economic activity. Growing global capital mobility made crisis in capital accounts the rule rather than the exception. It was – and is – a source of harder problems to be solved by the Fund.

Despite the importance of the IMF in dealing with the crisis in the 1990s, the organization has been suffering from criticism since then. The institution is encountering difficulties in overcoming inertia. In the last three decades, a major shift in global economic power has occurred. The share in global gross domestic product (GDP) of advanced economies changed from more than 58 per cent in 1992 to approximately 43 per cent in 2014.[5] In the same period, the share of emerging and developing countries increased from 41 per cent to 57 per cent and it is expected to be over 60 per cent in 2020.[6] Yet governance structures in the monetary field did not adjust accordingly. The share of emerging and developing economies in the IMF quotas changed merely (and after long periods of negotiations) from 36 per cent in 1992 to 42.4 per cent in 2016.

To explain the failure of global cooperation and deadlock in multilateral institutions (the *Gridlock* argument), Hale, Held and Young (2013) identify trends making international governance more difficult in different issue areas. These pathways are growing multipolarity, harder problems, institutional inertia and fragmentation. In monetary affairs, it seems that the growing multipolarity (emerging powers with economic power), harder problems (recurrent liquidity crises in capital accounts) and institutional inertia (related to the IMF governance structure) are the main drivers of a more fragmented and diversified global order. Fragmentation, then, is both a response to, and a driver of, gridlock in monetary affairs.

In the post-2008 crisis, the G20 called for changes in the balance of voting power at the Fund, arguing that they would make the IMF's decisions more legitimate and efficient in responding to the emerging needs of monetary cooperation.[7] There is a demand for more representation for emerging countries in multilateral institutions to better reflect the global shift of economic power.

Nevertheless, the IMF's 2010 General Quota Review, agreed among the G20 countries, only took effect on 26 January 2016, due to a delay in US Congress approval. Furthermore, merely 5.7 per cent of the Fund's voting power was shifted towards emerging countries, notably to the benefit of China, Brazil, India, Mexico and South Korea. China was probably the only country which had a relatively successful outcome: it saw its voting share almost doubled (from 3.6 per cent to 6 per cent) and it is today the third-largest member country of the Fund, after the US and Japan. The US, however, still maintains a veto power over key decisions at the Fund, retaining 16.5 per cent in voting share. A majority of 85 per cent is required, for instance, for adjustment in quotas, any amendment to the Fund's Articles of Agreement and the allocation of new SDRs. The governance structure of the IMF reveals a particular trend: an "institutional inertia" characterized particularly by "formal lock-in in decision-making authority" (Hale, Held and Young 2013).

In addition, new lending instruments created by the IMF for emerging economies, based on ex ante conditions and with precautionary effects, such as the Flexible Credit Line and the Precautionary Credit Line, had low demand after 2008 (IMF 2014). Only Mexico, Colombia and Poland had access to the first and Morocco to the second. Mexico and Colombia are still attached to this instrument and they are suffering from "exit stigma" (IMF 2014). From 2008 to 2011, the Fund was only an international lender of last resort for small developing countries in Latin America and a few emerging economies in Europe (IEO 2014). Other countries in Asia and Africa, without systemically important financial centres (such as Angola, Mongolia, Sri Lanka and Pakistan), were also counterparties of these agreements with the Fund. However, the biggest emerging economies avoided using the IMF as the main lender of last resort, even though cooperation was needed.

Which Pathways Lead through and beyond Gridlock in Global Monetary Cooperation?

In the 2000s, benefiting from high price levels for commodity goods, emerging countries in Latin America and Asia could accumulate foreign exchange reserves to counter capital flows and assure some degree of independence in designing their monetary responses in times of crisis. This type of unilateral action had precautionary purposes.[8] Figure 3.1 shows the progression of reserve accumulation by G20 emerging economies in Latin America and Asia from 1990 to 2015. This practice was reinforced after the 2008 crisis.

The motivation behind the accumulation of reserves was attributed to political stigma attached to the Fund, created by the conditions imposed particularly in the 1990s lending programmes (Duran 2015b; IMF 2014; IEO 2014). The conditions associated with these lending programmes and the ideas supporting them were perceived as not applicable to or even suitable for emerging economies. This is an issue related to political legitimacy and the economic efficiency of the Fund's programmes.

However, the accumulation of reserves was not (and is not) free from costs. Since they are held in national currencies issued by advanced

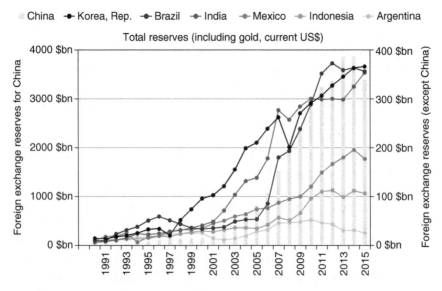

Figure 3.1   Foreign exchange reserve accumulation in G20 emerging countries in Asia and Latin America, 1990–2015

Source: World Bank.

countries, this unilateral strategy implies a transfer of resources from developing countries towards developed economies (Stiglitz et al. 2010: 110), whose central banks are issuers of international money. Thus, this system has inherent characteristics of inequality and dependence on the supply of international money by developed economies' central banks, notably the Fed.

Once the 2008 crisis hit, monetary cooperation was needed and the accumulation of reserves was used as a political tool: this unilateral action assured political leverage to emerging powers (Duran 2015b). They were able to choose their lender of last resort – some of them had direct access to temporary currency swaps with the Fed instead of going to the IMF.[9] But most importantly: they could design regional and bilateral arrangements as alternatives to the multilateral organization.

Fragmentation revisited: a pathway through gridlock in monetary governance

Growing multipolarity is producing more fragmentation in the international monetary system. In the aftermath of 2008, the G20 emerging countries in Asia and Latin America were able to formulate new arrangements for monetary cooperation to respond to balance of payment imbalances. The unilateral model of monetary action, that is, foreign exchange reserve accumulation, created the economic conditions which assured political leverage to design monetary strategies for cooperation. The monetary plans had a multilateral aim: to gather emerging countries around common goals on how to cope with the next liquidity crises.

The arrangements involved two main political actions: (1) designing parallel institutions to the IMF to serve as lenders of last resort in times of crisis, through regional arrangements based on the pooling of reserves in US dollars; and (2) to promote cross-border transactions in other national currencies to challenge the international uses of the US dollar, the main currency of the Bretton Woods system.

For the first political strategy (1), one can mention the reinforcement of the Chiang Mai Initiative,[10] originally established in 2000 after the Asian crisis (Hameiri and Wilson 2015; Grimes 2011). It was multilateralized in 2009, that is, became a multilateral currency swap arrangement governed by a single contractual agreement, the CMIM. A surveillance pillar was also introduced with the creation of a macroeconomic research office in Singapore, in 2011.[11] The institution of

Table 3.1 Institutional fragmentation in the international monetary system: regional arrangements in US dollars created or reinforced by the G20 emerging countries after the 2008 crisis

Regional monetary initiatives International lenders of last resort in US dollars	Among G20 emerging powers
Multilateralization of the Chiang Mai Initiative Total of US$240bn	China, South Korea and Indonesia
Creation of the BRICS Contingent Reserve Arrangement Total of US$100bn	China, India and Brazil
No new regional arrangement in US dollars	Mexico and Argentina

Source: ASEAN+3 website; Treaty for the Establishment of a BRICS Contingent Reserve Arrangement (http://brics.itamaraty.gov.br/media2/press-releases/220-treat y-for-the-establishment-of-a-brics-contingent-reserve-arrangement-fortaleza-july-15). Elaborated by the author.

the Contingent Reserve Arrangement (CRA) by the BRICS[12] countries in 2014 was inspired by the legal design of the CMIM (table 3.1). The CRA is "a framework for the provision of support through liquidity and precautionary instruments in response to actual or potential short-term balance of payments pressures" (Article 1 of the Treaty of the Establishment of the BRICS CRA). Interestingly, both regional agreements have a particular legal design: they are not created as international organizations, but rather as a network of currency swaps between central banks.

For the second political strategy (2), the incentive for cross-border transactions in national currencies, the main legal instruments were bilateral currency swaps formalized between central banks to ensure access to currencies for short-term liquidity operations as well as trade settlement (table 3.2).

Both tables reveal a more fragmented and diversified monetary architecture in the post-2008 period. It seems that China is the main country driving this change: through the formalization of regional arrangements (i.e. the CMIM and the BRICS CRA) based on the pooling of reserves in US dollars, as well as through the promotion of its own currency, the renminbi, as global money. India, South Korea and Indonesia are also participating in this latter strategy. Bilateral swaps among emerging countries' central banks are usually three-year term contracts and capped to a certain amount. The total value of these arrangements is not negligible.

Table 3.2 Institutional fragmentation in the international monetary system: arrangements in national currencies created by the G20 emerging countries after the 2008 crisis

G20 emerging powers	Bilateral monetary arrangements in national currencies
China	Bilateral currency swaps in renminbi – 32 agreements (Hong Kong SAR, South Korea, Singapore, Australia, Malaysia, Indonesia, Thailand, New Zealand, Mongolia, Pakistan, Sri Lanka, Kazakhstan, Uzbekistan, European Central Bank, United Kingdom, Canada, Brazil, Russia, Switzerland, Argentina, United Arab Emirates, Qatar, South Africa, Chile, Ukraine, Turkey, Hungary, Belarus, Iceland, Albania, Suriname and Armenia) Equivalent of US$465.67bn
South Korea	Bilateral currency swaps in Korean won – 4 agreements (China, Australia, Indonesia and Malaysia) Total: equivalent of US$74.5bn
Indonesia	Bilateral currency swaps in rupia – 3 agreements (China, Korea and Japan) Total: equivalent of US$13.8bn
India	Bilateral currency swaps in rupee (Japan and South Asian Association for Regional Cooperation nations – Afghanistan, Bangladesh, Bhutan, Maldives, Nepal, Pakistan and Sri Lanka). Total: equivalent of US$52bn
Brazil	Bilateral currency swaps in reais (1 agreement – China) Total: equivalent of US$18.3bn Creation of the SML – Local Currency Payment System (Argentina and Uruguay) Total: equivalent of US$160m
Mexico	*No strategy*
Argentina	Bilateral currency swaps in peso (1 agreement – China) Total: equivalent of US$2.5bn Creation of the Local Currency Payment System (SML) (Brazil and Uruguay) Total: equivalent of US$160m

Source: Central Bank websites; *Financial Times*; IMF 2015: 56; Brazilian Law no. 11.803/2008. Elaborated by the author.

Mexico is the only G20 emerging economy not investing in alternatives to the Bretton Woods system – possibly, because of its political proximity to the United States and the IMF.[13] Brazil and Argentina are investing in a traditional Latin American mode of monetary cooperation: the organization of clearing houses and the establishment of official credit lines among central banks for mainly trade purposes.[14] The total value, however, is insignificant compared to initiatives based on currency swaps among other emerging economies.

Central bank swaps in national currencies, other than the US dollar, point to the potential emergence of new "monies" that can serve as cross-border means of payment in the future. This global monetary network tends to become more complex, since more emerging countries could consider expanding international transactions in their own currency. This institutional change points to currency competition in the future (Eichengreen 2011), despite the current centrality of the US dollar (Cohen and Benney 2014).

China can be considered a crucial country for the functioning of the Bretton Woods system, if one takes into account the financial power granted by its huge reserves in US dollars (almost US$4 trillion) – the system's key currency. Foreign reserves are also allowing other emerging countries to pool their reserves into regional arrangements.

However, up to the present, regional monetary responses seem to be short-term adaptations to a US dollar-centred global system. These agreements are still relying on the issuance of international money by the Fed, the key currency of the Bretton Woods system. In addition, they depend on a *continuum* process of reserve accumulation, with its inherent economic costs. In contrast, bilateral initiatives based on swaps in national currencies could eventually serve as a pathway to go beyond gridlock. However, a more certain structure could be required to further develop this monetary initiative.

Beyond Gridlock? Technical Groups with Effective Processes and Autonomous and Innovative International Organizations

Technical groups with effective processes: the role of central banks

Central bank swaps are not a new phenomenon. To sustain the dollar–gold parity in the 1960s, currency swaps among central banks in developed economies and the Bank for International Settlements (BIS) supported the stability of the Bretton Woods regime and the parity between the US dollar and gold (Moessner and Allen 2010: 25–7; Kindleberger and Aliber 2011: 249–50; Coombs 1976). Nevertheless, this practice of central bank cooperation was discontinued. The argument made by the Fed, in 1998, was that arrangements for international monetary cooperation were in place and central bank swaps were no longer needed.[15]

From December 2007, however, the Fed re-established swaps with central banks in advanced economies to cope with the financial crisis (Bank of England, European Central Bank, Bank of Japan, Swiss National Bank, Reserve Bank of Australia, Bank of Canada, Danmarks Nationalbank, Reserve Bank of New Zealand, Norges Bank and Sveriges Riksbank). Later this practice was extended to a few emerging countries (e.g. Brazil, South Korea, Singapore and Mexico).[16]

These temporary swaps were aimed at dealing with the 2008 crisis. In reactivating these arrangements, the economic literature identified the Fed as the lender of last resort for the world (Aizenman and Pasricha 2010; Allen and Moessner 2010; Moessner and Allen 2010; McDowell 2012; Chey 2012; Broz 2015). Going further in this practice, in 2013 the Fed set up a permanent and unlimited network of swaps with the European Central Bank, the Bank of Japan, the Bank of England, the Swiss National Bank and the Bank of Canada: the so-called "C6" (Mehrling 2015: 8).

In the aftermath of 2008, the novelty of central bank swaps was their rapid proliferation, their formalization in US dollars as well as other national currencies, and the participation of emerging countries in this global network (McDowell 2012). Currency swaps, underpinning regional or bilateral initiatives, account for the development of a network of the equivalent of almost US$1 trillion (tables 3.1 and 3.2), excluding the unlimited size of swaps among the C6. As a comparison, the IMF has US$668 billion in quotas in lendable resources and a further US$668 billion in additional pledged and committed resources. This international network can potentially perform a more significant economic role than the Fund.

Central banks are technical institutions reshaping political choices at the global level and they are using their own instruments: currency swaps. These agencies could be considered an epistemic community, with shared values and ideas, as well as modes of policy actions (Haas 1992; Marcussen 2009).

As I argued elsewhere (Duran 2015b: 13), central banks have been engaging in "bureaucratic competition" to occupy a policy space in monetary affairs by ensuring that new policies fall within their "territory." "Territory" (Downs 1967: 212–13) is the policy portion where the monetary authority substantially controls the expertise and the resources required for implementation. This applies to the management of foreign exchange reserves and the issuance of national money. The use of swaps, in bilateral and regional arrangements, is an example.

The growing complexity of monetary policy and the well-established network of central bankers made central banks the winners in the dispute for policy options in the period after the 2008 crisis. The "Great Moderation" and the accumulation of foreign exchange reserves empowered central banks and their agents, whether in advanced economies or in emerging countries (Duran 2015b). The interests and preferences of these central banks are then central to understanding the outcomes of monetary cooperation at the international level.

Particularly where emerging economies' central banks are concerned, it seems that they are not willing to delegate their financial role to an international organization. They are pushing the IMF to be a financial actor for smaller developing countries. In relation to regional arrangements, they are designing them as a network of swaps. Therefore, emerging economies are aspiring to a model of monetary cooperation based on central bank relationships and communication, which has already been implemented by developed countries' central banks.

Nonetheless, these structures can carry more uncertainty in times of crisis. Swaps rely on national authorities' discretion for the transfer of resources and these agencies have national mandates and interests as their priorities. Currency swaps involve "pre-committed" resources, which are not permanently attributed to a global institution with a specific mission. For instance, members of the CRA can opt out of providing financial support, or can request early repayment, if a balance of payment need arises (Article 15*c* and 15*d*, Treaty for the Establishment of a BRICS CRA). Since there is no international organization with a specific mandate, once a crisis hits it is difficult to assess the solvency of their counterparties and uncertainty tends to be greater in this case.

Furthermore, central banks are not only regulatory agencies, but also banks. They tend to be more exposed to market interests, including at the global level. The growing complexity of the international monetary order poses threats to the effectiveness of their accountability frameworks. Central banks have a fiscal background and are supposed to be accountable to taxpayers in their own countries. In addition, their specific national mandates could conflict with the global interest in financial stability during crises.

Autonomous and adaptive international organizations: the role of the IMF

To date, the Fed's formalized and unlimited bilateral swaps are only with developed economies' central banks. Emerging countries have limited (and relatively uncertain) access to liquidity through regional and bilateral structures. Yet institutional fragmentation could lead to a pathway beyond gridlock in the medium and long term. It depends on the capacity of multilateral organizations to adapt themselves to the emerging needs of cooperation involving central banks.

Since the central banks of emerging and less developed countries were not allowed to be part of the Fed network, they needed a multilateral institution to ensure access to international money in times of crisis, including, in the near future, to other currencies adopted as a means of payment for trade and investment purposes. The managers of swap networks, that is, the central banks, are good agencies for planning and responding to crisis in the short and medium term, but given their limited mandates and toolkit, they cannot play a full role as lenders of last resort at the global level.

In this sense, if multilateral institutions are going to play a less important financial role (that is replaced by central banks), their specific contribution to avoid systemic risks posed by a fragmented monetary system is to support countries in need of international money in times of crisis and connect different levels of monetary governance (multilateral, regional and bilateral).

Throughout its history, the process of change in the global monetary order has already revealed the capacity of the IMF to adapt itself to new conjunctures (Boughton 2001; James 1996). Since the 2008 crisis, the Fund has been mainly working on three fronts related to central banks: (1) in 2010, the Fund's staff proposed the creation of Multicountry Swap Lines renamed the Global Stabilization Mechanism (GSM) (IMF 2010a), which was supported by South Korea at the 2010 G20 Summit; (2) in 2015, the Chinese currency, the renminbi, was included in the Fund's SDR basket of currencies (the decision took effect in October 2016; IMF News 2016), which reinforced the policies of China's currency internationalization; and (3) since May 2016, the IMF has been running tests jointly with the CMIM to strengthen the connections between regional and multilateral levels of monetary governance.[17]

In relation to (1), the proposal on a multilateral swap arrangement was later abandoned by the Fund due to a lack of support from its directors. The idea was to provide resources of the Fund to sustain bilateral initiatives. However, according to the meeting's minutes,

> Many Directors saw merit in exploring the GSM as a key tool to enhance the Fund's ability to carry out its mandate to promote global economic stability, including by coordinating global responses to systemic events with central banks, regional institutions, and systemic-risk bodies, as appropriate. *Many others did not see a need for a formalized framework, noting the adequacy of the revamped lending toolkit, the existence of the emergency financing mechanism, and the risks of moral hazard.* (emphasis added; see IMF 2010b)

However, since 2010, the IMF has been monitoring the development of swap networks and is producing regular reports on this issue (IMF 2016). In 2015, the former Indian Reserve Bank governor, Raghuram Rajan, called again for the institution to guarantee a multilateral swap arrangement among central banks (Mallet and Crabtree 2015). He insisted on the idea that the Fund could financially support countries in need of international currency in collaboration with central banks. This proposal still implies, however, that the Fund could actually overcome its institutional inertia. Mr Rajan recognized that emerging markets would like to implement this type of arrangement, but he admitted there was no interest among advanced economies.

In my previous work (Duran 2015a), I proposed, as a second-best option, that the G20 could lead a "coalition of the willing" to establish a multilateral framework to exchange global currencies. Bilateral and regional arrangements based on swaps have a multilateral goal. They are structured to promote the exchange of global currencies between countries in times of crisis. The network, although currently less formal, can be further reinforced. If the IMF is not able to implement this type of arrangement, the BIS could manage the monetary agreement. Since this institution previously sustained the Bretton Woods par value system in the 1960s, this proposition would thus revive the monetary role of the BIS. In this case, it would require autonomous and adaptive actions on the part of the BIS as well.

The other front of action (2) led by the IMF was the inclusion of the Chinese currency in the SDR basket. This strategy was particularly successful. Despite the US veto power inside the institution for the negotiation of relevant issues, the Chinese currency was included in the basket – a type of decision requiring 70 per cent of voting power. As an international reserve asset, the SDR has minor practical relevance for the global monetary system, representing less than 3.4 per cent of global reserves.[18] The share in the total global reserve has never exceeded 6 per cent in its entire history (Obstfeld 2011). However, the SDR can produce symbolic effects. The inclusion of the renminbi in its basket maybe reveals a path to the emergence of new global currencies.

The Fund supported the consolidation of the renminbi's internationalization process, declaring it a "freely usable currency," that is, a currency widely used to make payments for international transactions and widely traded in the principal exchange markets (Article XXX(*f*) of the Fund's Articles of Agreement). In practice, the IMF recognized that the concept of "freely usable currency" does not mean full convertibility, which allowed China to continue its policy of "managed" convertibility.[19] This decision concerning the SDR basket was a case where the Fund was able to overcome its inertia. It can potentially contribute to a perception of the organization as more legitimate at the global level.

In relation to the third front (3), the IMF has been exploring forms of connections with a regional arrangement based on swaps. There is a de jure link between the Fund and the CMIM. If a country wishes to access more than 30 per cent of its "share" in the regional agreement, it needs to provide evidence of existing financing arrangements with the multilateral organization. The main aim is to "outsource" conditionalities.

Therefore, since 2016, the Fund has been running tests on crisis resolution facilities with the CMIM, to connect multilateral and regional levels. The intention is to provide an institutional link between the Fund's lending facilities and the IMF-linked portion of the CMIM. In this sense, fragmentation could produce good effects: providing additional liquidity coverage for emerging and developing countries in times of crisis, as well as more certainty in access to resources, when linked to the multilateral level.

All these three fronts reveal that the multilateral institution is trying to change its governance structure and adapt itself to a new environment, even though it still suffers from institutional inertia.

Conclusion

In monetary governance, growing multipolarity, institutional inertia and harder problems are the main drivers of a more fragmented and diversified global order, characterized by increased transaction costs. The 2010 quota reform of the IMF hardly changed its governance structure – only 5.7 per cent of its voting power was shifted to emerging economies. In addition, the United States retains its institutional veto power over the Fund's key decisions.

In this context, G20 emerging countries are trying to reshape the global monetary landscape. They are creating, or reinforcing, regional and bilateral arrangements. This process is causing fragmentation of the global order. Institutional fragmentation, therefore, is a reaction to, and a driver of, gridlock.

Yet regional arrangements rely on the supply of international money by advanced economies and are based on unilateral, costly monetary actions, that is, foreign exchange reserve accumulation. Up to the present, these agreements have not produced a significant transformation of the international monetary architecture, but merely incremental changes. Regional structures are contributing to the fragmentation of the international monetary system without guaranteeing certain and timely access to liquidity in the event of a crisis. They represent short-term responses to the US-dollar centred order – an immediate reaction through gridlock in monetary affairs.

To go beyond gridlock, two pathways emerge: technical groups with effective processes (central banks) and an autonomous and adaptive institution (the IMF). The growing power of central banks at the global level and the emergence of new international currencies are shifting the centre of monetary cooperation away from the Bretton Woods institutions. However, bureaucracies such as central banks are agencies with national mandates and interests, which could conflict with international responsibilities in times of crisis.

In this sense, the capacity of the IMF to adapt itself to the global shift of economic power is crucial for monetary cooperation and the role this international organization will play in the next liquidity crisis. For instance, the inclusion of the renminbi in the SDR basket had symbolic effects, which tends to reinforce the legitimacy of the multilateral organization. However, the main challenge is how to connect and support the multifaceted network created by central banks. For the next crisis, global risks may arise from the connections among the three levels of monetary governance: multilateral, regional and bilateral. It seems that only a multilateral organization can provide shared governance on this issue.

4

Trade

Gridlock and Resilience

Andreas Klasen

The benefits and harms of economic interaction across borders have been the subject of political contestation for thousands of years. Ancient philosophers such as Democritus (c. 460–370 BCE) and Xenophon (c. 430–354 BCE) describe basic economic concepts such as comparative advantages in their works. Hesiod (c. 750–650 BCE) and Plato (c. 427–347 BCE) mention the benefits of foreign trade and the importance of international exchange of merchandise goods (Michaelidis, Kardasi and Milios 2011; Amemiya 2007; Skultety 2006). Today, global trade and foreign investments are key drivers for economic growth. A global economy producing, trading, and consuming goods and services across borders is a reality for billions of people and countless firms.

Our extraordinarily global economy would not exist but for a complex series of institutions and rules, which governments, international organizations, and private bodies have created over the previous decades of globalization. But despite numerous gains from free trade between countries, multilateral efforts to enhance the global governance of trade seem to have come to a standstill, most notably with the collapse of the Doha Round of negotiations under the World Trade Organizations (Destradi and Jakobeit 2015; Lee 2012; Narlikar 2010b). Broader trends are also putting the global trading system into question. In some industries, digitalized processes and procedures and new forms of production involving automation or three-dimensional printing are eroding the economic rationale for cross-border production. And the rise of nationalist and populist politicians in many key economies has put in question the political consensus around the "embedded liberalism" (Ruggie 1982) that sustained economic openness for much of the postwar period. While global trade remains at historically high levels, its rate of growth has slowed.

The multilateral trading system faces a new set of challenges with harder problems and a fragmented policymaking landscape leading to a breakdown of international cooperation in many areas (Hale, Held and Young 2013). At the same time, there has been a vast proliferation of trade agreements at bilateral and regional levels, including a series of proposed "mega-regional" agreements such as the Regional Comprehensive Economic Partnership in Asia. Crucial questions for global governance in trade today include: Are the WTO's missed objectives and deadlines the new reality, or are multilateral trade agreements still possible? Are bilateral and regional trade and investment partnerships a solution to gridlock, or part of the problem? Away from the gridlock of global trade negotiations, do less formal or more technocratic processes and organizations offer a way forward? Finally, have the politics of economic openness now shifted against globalization, putting the future of the existing regime into question?

This chapter discusses gridlock and pathways through and beyond it in global trade governance. It outlines the history, architecture, and successes of trade and multilateral governance. The presence and absence of gridlock in the current trade universe is then analysed, which highlights the role of institutional inertia, harder problems, and a growing number of bilateral initiatives leading to fragmentation in an increasingly multipolar world.

Turning to pathways through and beyond gridlock, the chapter then analyses several existing trends. First, it notes the autonomy and adaptability of the WTO's legalized dispute settlement processes, which are able to partially adjust to new problems as they arise through the generative power of adjudication. Second, the chapter investigates the functioning of technical groups such as the Berne Union, the International Chamber of Commerce, and the Organisation for Economic Co-operation and Development, which play a critical, though often underappreciated, role in sustaining global trade. Finally, the chapter considers a challenging and partly unsuccessful pathway beyond gridlock: a plurality of actors and institutions around common goals and voluntary global standards in the context of export finance.

The Multilateral Trade Environment: History, Architecture, and Successes

Successful free trade in a truly global setting is a comparatively recent phenomenon. Trade liberalization among European states in the latter part of the nineteenth century contributed to a first wave of globalization, although it coexisted with colonial trading relationships between Europe and territories around the world. Political support for liberalization in key countries, notably the United States, receded after World War I before succumbing totally to the nationalist turn in the 1930s. After World War II, countries sought to rebuild a managed form of trade integration. The creation of the General Agreement on Tariffs and Trade (GATT) signed in 1947 was one of the key achievements after World War II. The rules of GATT enhanced trade relationships in a variety of ways. In particular, concessions between any two members were passed to other participants according to the principle of the "most-favoured nation." Since the 1950s, many multilateral organizations have adopted a rule-based approach that have given states increasing confidence to liberalize their economies and reduce tariffs, quotas, and other barriers to trade. Some 20 years ago, a strengthening of GATT led to the development of the most important organization for world trade governance, the World Trade Organization.

Growing out of the GATT in 1995 and now the only truly global multilateral organization dealing with the rules of trade between countries, the WTO aims to help manufacturers, service providers and thus exporters and importers to conduct their business (Matsushita, Schoenbaum and Mavroidis 2015; Hoekman and Mavroidis 2007). In providing legal rules for international commerce, the overall purpose is to help trade flow between countries and regions by removing obstacles and ensuring transparent and predictable rules of international trade. These rules give individuals, companies and governments confidence that there will be no sudden changes of policy, and that conflicting interests can be resolved in a fair manner.

Since 1995, the international trade regime has, for the first time ever, a strong legal basis, a sustainable organizational structure, and an effective dispute settlement process (Capling and Higgott 2009). During the first decade of its existence, the WTO had several positive effects on free trade policy and dispute enforcement. Countries have tended to comply with WTO rules, and, when they have not, the dispute settlement mechanism has been largely effective at compelling compliance. The principle of transparency in negotiations and disputes found its way into the trade regime through the introduction of the WTO's decision-making procedures and the dispute settlement system (Delimatsis 2014).

As a result, the expansion of international business activities through a multilateral trading system provided a major pillar for growth enjoyed by industrialized countries in the last century.

Although developing economies were latecomers to international trade and foreign direct investment, many of them have significantly benefited from open markets and the prevention of protectionist measures (Klasen and Bannert 2015), especially through concessional trade access granted under the Generalized System of Preferences. The WTO was able to prevent numerous unilateral tariff increases or quantity restrictions, and even extremely difficult trade disputes such as the multibillion-dollar Airbus–Boeing dispute between the European Union and the United States are now transparently resolved in an international forum.

While the WTO sits at the centre of the global trade regime, it is hardly alone. Over the past decades there has been a proliferation of bilateral investment treaties and preferential and free trade agreements (FTAs) on a bilateral or regional basis (Garcia et al. 2015), which now number over 300, making the landscape of global trade liberalization into a "spaghetti bowl." There have also been a number of "plurilateral" trade deals on specific issues – for example, on trade in services – under which a subgroup of WTO members liberalize trade on a certain set of issues. While most of these agreements have no formal links to the WTO, many rely on the WTO's dispute settlement procedures to guarantee their credibility.

Critically, the broader trade regime is not limited only to agreements to liberalize tariffs or remove trade barriers. A wide range of institutions exist to set standards on technical, environmental, or health issues, to provide specific kinds of financing to underwrite cross-border transactions, or to otherwise ease the flow of goods and services across borders. For example, transnational commercial arbitration providers facilitate crucial dispute resolution functions for firms operating internationally (Hale 2014; 2015). While many of these institutions are more technocratic in nature, they are a crucial and sometimes underappreciated element of the global trade regime.

Absence and Presence of Gridlock in Trade

The expansion of the multilateral trading system shaped by the WTO was and still is effective in many cases. It gives developed and developing economies greater leverage than they would have outside the system. However, the Doha Round, also known as the Doha Development Agenda, the latest round of multilateral trade negotiations, has shown the immense difficulties of the WTO. Launched in 2001, the key objective was to make the international trading system fairer for developing economies. The main issues at stake were to improve developing countries' access to global markets and to revise rules with regard to agricultural subsidies. For the agricultural sector, the aim was to eliminate export subsidies and reduce distorting domestic support, but also deal with non-trade concerns such as rural development and food security.

Two major problems made it difficult to bring talks to a successful conclusion: although highly industrialized countries committed to promote development in poorer economies without asking them to reduce import barriers to the same extent, disagreement grew with regard to protection of industries and market access. This applied, in particular, for the agricultural sector. US farmers vigorously lobbied for easier access to foreign markets through reduced tariffs and increased quotas, offering in return to cut trade-distorting subsidies at home. But such bargains remained out of reach, with stalemate prevailing in the agricultural negotiations. Second, economic conditions in countries such as China and India substantially changed during the decade of talks over which negotiations took place. Some emerging economies started producing export surpluses but insisted on sticking with the original principles exempting them from opening their markets, refusing requests from European members and the US to lower import barriers and cut agricultural subsidies.

Faith in the WTO was partially restored after the Bali Ministerial Conference in 2013. Governments formally agreed on the WTO's first truly multilateral pact in nearly 20 years, accepting a new agreement on trade facilitation. The core of the agreement was to cut down the cost of doing business by easing customs procedures. But more importantly, avoiding failure was crucial to rebuilding the WTO's credibility. It was an important achievement in its own right that members reached a consensus. Bali was enthusiastically welcomed, and there were further substantial successes at the 2015 Ministerial Conference in Nairobi, for example by outlawing agricultural export subsidies. However, major challenges remain to revive multilateral negotiations after the de facto failure of the Doha Round. Bali and Nairobi were significant in showing that the WTO is still a living animal, but the agreed results are only small steps forward. The agreements on trade facilitation that emerged have been described as asymmetric deals: although developing economies benefit from Bali, gains from trade facilitation will be primarily realized by developed countries (Wilkinson, Hannah and Scott 2014). The least developed country (LDC) package was criticized because of too many non-legally binding agreements. For several areas, LDCs only secured a set of "best endeavour" provisions — a weaker form of obligation — such as with regard to preferential rules of origin that benefit exports from the poorest countries. The package also included a reiteration that members accepted to provide duty-free/quota-free market access, but failed to establish additional measures such as preference schemes. Challenges of legitimacy deficits and institutional weakness (Narlikar 2010b), as well as a need for a reform of negotiation procedures, have been continuously discussed as well (Albin 2008). And in a world which is increasingly dominated by regional as well as bilateral trade and investment agreements, WTO members are confronted with core issues such as domestic agriculture subsidies that have divided them for years.

Gridlock identified four key barriers to cooperation: growing multipolarity, fragmentation, harder problems, and institutional inertia. Each can be observed in the realm of trade.

First, the global trade environment is increasingly multipolar. For decades, governance of the multilateral trading system has been configured around political and economic interests of highly industrialized states. But from a perspective of relative economic size, the world today is more multipolar than it has ever been since the 1960s. The impasse of the failure of the Doha Round is partly the consequence of two major trends, and it is expected that greater diffusion is set to continue into the future. The first trend is the significant role of the BRICS (Brazil, Russia, India, China and South Africa) in the export of goods and services, showing substantial growth and increasing their share in world exports from 8 per cent in 2000 to 19 per cent in 2014 (WTO 2015a). These structural changes over the past years parallel the BRICS countries' behaviour in WTO negotiations. Economies such as China and India are increasingly assuming an importance in the growth picture relative to the advanced economies, such as the eurozone and Japan. And while they may not yet have reached an advanced level of development, the trend towards regional integration is progressing rapidly. The BRICS are, and this applies in particular for China, at the forefront of the entire multipolarity phenomenon. Their greater involvement in the future direction of the global economy means that decoupling between the advanced and emerging world may finally come to pass.

In addition, South–South trade is becoming increasingly important, further reducing the relevance of traditional industrialized countries in the northern hemisphere. Total South–South exports have doubled over the last two decades. The substantial growth resulting in a share of 42 per cent of developing countries' total merchandise trade in 2015 is visible in South American and Asian developing economies, coinciding with the economic dynamism in these regions. And although Asia, Europe and North America have accounted for 88 per cent of total merchandise trade of WTO members over the past ten years, South–South trade from least developed countries in Africa also significantly climbed. As a result of this development, countries engaged in South–South trade are now influential players building coalitions in multilateral trade negotiations to increase their power and interests (Rolland 2007). They are also much more willing and able to challenge industrialized WTO member countries because of their divergent interest, in particular regarding agricultural policies. Activism of developing economies during the Doha Round negotiations has made gridlock the standard rather than the exceptional circumstance (Lee 2012).

Fragmentation, which is related to increased transaction costs but also excessive flexibility, complements growing multipolarity as a second major trend. As noted above, in part due to a persistent deadlock in multilateral talks, regional initiatives to advance trade liberalization or to protect economies have grown outside the WTO framework. The new regional and bilateral trade agreement landscape is an immense challenge. Trade initiatives are not only sprouting on a regional level, a major trend in trade policy is also bilateral solutions. Policymakers increasingly remove existing multilateral trade strategies, focusing much more on FTAs. Nationalism and regionalism are thus likely to occupy a growing role in trade governance (Reyes, Wooster and Shirrell 2014). Drivers of these trends include different policy preferences affected by interest configuration, defensive motives with economies experiencing limitations to economic growth, and the growth of lobbying by companies towards their national government to bolster their competitive position via free trade agreements (Manger 2005).

India, in particular, has been aggressively pushing bilateral foreign trade agreements, with mixed results. While the country's exports stagnated, imports from bilateral partner countries into India increased. Bilateral agreements have been immensely popular throughout Asia (Aggarwal and Lee 2011; Park 2009). China signed FTAs with, for example, Australia, India and Korea in order to expand its markets and secure long-term supply of natural resources. The increasing number of bilateral deals in Asia is described as a "noodle bowl," often with more harm than good. Bilateral FTAs mostly include complicated rules, and too many and overlapping "noodles" create complex regulatory environments leading to higher costs for exporters.

A third reason for gridlock is the emergence of harder transborder problems. Because of previous successful efforts to reduce tariffs and quotas, firms operate in a more politically, economically and legally challenging global environment. The issues trade must address now increasingly occur "behind the border," involving, for example, environmental or health standards. Furthermore, the growing reliance on outsourcing, production networks and complex supply chains has created a higher significance of behind-the-border rules such as investment clauses, diffluent competition norms and non-tariff barriers. This creates harder transborder problems in the WTO negotiation process due to the fact that the right level of integration, regulatory cooperation and coherence has to be found (Elsig 2016). Such coherence is difficult because countries often disagree on these substantive standards, resulting in gridlock.

Finally, institutional inertia is a major area of concern. Power structures of international organizations with great importance for international trade such as the IMF, the World Bank and the WTO are regarded as dominated by the United States and larger European countries (San Juan 2011; Wade 2011; Harrigan, Wang and El-Said 2006). There is severe criticism that there is systematic bias towards rich economies and multinational corporations. Institutional inertia is also a pressing topic because important areas such as social and environmental issues seem to be continuously ignored. In particular, traditional multilateral organizations have been criticized for being an "economic cartel" dominated by the United States, and for pursuing free trade and open markets at the expense of the poorest and least developed countries. Emerging economies feel discriminated against regarding power and influence within multilateral institutions, although there is an obvious transformation in the global economic structure, for example towards the East.

The WTO as an institution has to face continuous criticism on two further topics: capacity-building and internal democracy, as well as transparency and external accountability. First, skills and knowledge about trade policy, tariffs, subsidies or trade finance instruments are often limited in developing and least developed countries. Such countries often lack institutional capacity, and the WTO seems not to be able to react accordingly. Second, institutional inertia comes from an alleged or actual lack of transparency and accountability. With limited access to information leading to distrust regarding democratic accountability, there is a growing public perception of institutional inertia. For the WTO, an appropriate balance between an open flow of information and protected space for negotiations presents a difficult trade-off between legitimacy and effectiveness.

Pathways through and beyond Gridlock

While the global trading system in some ways represents a textbook case of gridlock, there are critical exceptions that force a more nuanced evaluation. I focus on several pathways identified in the introduction to this book: autonomous and adaptive international institutions, technical groups with effective and legitimate processes, innovative leadership, as well as multiple and diverse organizations and institutions coalescing around common goals as a reaction to gridlock.

An adaptive and autonomous international institution: WTO revisited

The successes, challenges and deficiencies of the World Trade Organization have been analysed above, and there have been numerous discussions about a reform of the WTO. While gridlock on average reduces the ability of international organizations to act proactively, one of the pathways through gridlock is via autonomous international organizations that are able to adapt to shifting interests. One of the most important examples of this mechanism is the highly legalized WTO dispute settlement mechanism.

The DSM is undoubtedly one of the major success stories of the WTO. In more than 20 years, more than 500 disputes have been brought to the WTO, many more than the 300 disputes GATT received in nearly 50 years. Compared to the more "power-oriented" dispute settlement in the GATT, which avoided the term "dispute" and focused on diplomatic consultations, the WTO DSM saw the introduction of greater "legalism" and a more "rules-oriented" system. It provided legitimacy while also creating a more effective mechanism for imposing liberal trade rules (Chorev 2005). In addition, formality and transparency make it difficult to bypass the legal process without other states taking notice. When the WTO dispute settlement system was built on the pre-existing GATT regime, it was not envisaged that more and more developing economies would use the system to pursue their trading rights. However, Dispute Settlement Bodies and Appellate Bodies have proven themselves as a system in which asymmetry in political power and influence is not significant for the legal result. One of the most prominent examples was the Brazil–United States cotton dispute where the WTO issued the decision that US support for the cotton industry was inconsistent with obligations under the Agreement on Subsidies and Countervailing Measures. Further evidence for the autonomy of the system is that WTO members comply with the rulings of the dispute settlement system in about 90 per cent of cases (WTO 2015b).

In addition, the dispute settlement mechanism is a vivid example of how the WTO is adaptive and able to keep up with the rapid changes in the global environment. Dispute Settlement Bodies and Appellate Bodies have been successful through a kind of judicial lawmaking in classic commercial disagreements. However, present areas of global concern such as environmental protection are now highly relevant for the DSM as well (Cosbey and Mavroidis 2014; Lewis 2014). Several disputes related to the sustainable exploitation of natural resources and green energy programmes. Appellate Body reports addressed, for example, controversial domestic content requirements for solar and wind power technologies. India recently complained about support given to the renewable energy sector in the US, alleging illegal subsidies. But twenty-first-century disputes also include animal welfare issues such as the treatment of seals and the protection of dolphins. And a panel dealing with the global concern over healthcare, involving package regulations on tobacco products, attracted more WTO members as complainants than any other case. In grappling with these difficult issues, the DSM has shown how it can adapt to shifting circumstances and make rules beyond those negotiated between member states, but still consonant with their interests. This generative quality makes the DSM more adaptive and robust than less autonomous bodies would be.

However, the autonomy and adaptivity of the system is also a threat because member countries are becoming more and more reluctant to commit to future deals because of the important consequences of the DSM's enforcement mechanism and the severe criticism of domestic pressure groups about an alleged non-transparency of dispute panels (Matsushita, Schoenbaum and Mavroidis 2015). In addition, the characterization of the WTO as an autonomous organization is limited to the legal effect under the dispute settlement mechanism. Looking at the negotiation function of the World Trade Organization, it is clearly a member-driven institution which makes it increasingly non-autonomous in combination with its two other pillars of consensus decision-making and single undertaking, which means that new WTO members have to accept all agreements, preventing them from "cherry-picking." And although the DSM's ability to adapt by solving twenty-first century problems is valuable in itself, there are major concerns about how to balance, for example, nations' abilities to transition to low carbon economies and basic principles of the global trade regime.

Technical groups: effective processes with strong leadership

A related pathway identified in the introduction is technical groups with effective and legitimate processes. While most observers of the trade regime focus on the WTO and related institutions through which countries mutually agree to remove barriers to trade, the global exchange of goods and services depends on a much broader array of institutions for standard setting (Büthe and Mattli 2011), export financing and trade credits (Meyer and Klasen 2013), standardized contracts and commercial guidelines, commercial dispute settlement (Hale 2015), and other critical functions. A full consideration of the trade regime should keep in mind these more technical groups as well. Indeed, many of them are able to avoid or even overcome some of the barriers associated with gridlock in the WTO, in large part because technical groups are often able to escape geopolitics as well as governmental influence and concentrate on business-related topics. Two vivid examples are the International Chamber of Commerce and the Berne Union.

The International Chamber of Commerce is a global organization providing a forum for businesses to understand and improve conditions for global trade (Pair and Frankenstein 2011). Its commissions discuss and prepare policy products, for example for trade and investment, as well as for arbitration and anti-corruption. The International Chamber of Commerce also develops legal tools that businesses can apply directly to cross-border commerce, including voluntary rules, guidelines, and codes supporting cross-border transactions. For example, its standards on financing and security do not have the status of laws but are rather part of self-regulation by companies. International rules for the interpretation of trade terms, so-called Incoterms, are worldwide standards for facilitating international trade. The body is also a leading provider of private arbitration services, a form of dispute resolution for cross-border contracts that plays a major role in the global economy. While the International Chamber of Commerce is in many ways the focal private institution for global commerce, hundreds of trade associations and other similar groupings provide similar functions in many areas of the world economy. Major commodities (such as agricultural products or other raw materials) typically benefit from highly organized industry groups that set standards, develop standardized contracts, arbitrate disputes, and otherwise allow for global commerce. Because many of these bodies are private or quasi-private in nature, and focused on technical details, they avoid many of the gridlock dynamics observed at the WTO.

Another technical group providing effective processes for global governance in trade is the Berne Union. As the leading global organization for the export credit and investment insurance industry, Berne Union members collectively financed or insured US$1.9 trillion of exports and foreign direct investment in 2015, which is more than 10 per cent of international trade. The Berne Union facilitates cross-border trade by supporting international acceptance of sound principles in export credits and investment insurance. It also provides a forum for professional exchange about technical questions such as underwriting or trade finance claims among 82 members, including government institutions and private organizations from a wide range of countries such as Armenia, Brazil, China, Germany, Oman and the United States. Government export credit agencies and private credit insurers share views as well as detailed information on their business, data and statistics within the Berne Union (Klasen 2011).

Because the International Chamber of Commerce and the Berne Union are not traditional multilateral legal bodies but groups of senior trade executives, they show how cooperation among officials, market players, and civil society actors can work by focusing more on technical and less on political issues (Scholte 2010). Berne Union members follow a value statement of guiding principles which cover aspects such as ethical values, sound business practices, environmental issues and money laundering (Levit 2008; Moravcsik 1989). Members as a whole share the opinion that there is a need and a role for a variety of institutions to keep trade and project finance at healthy levels, agreeing on sound and sustainable business practices. For example, mutually agreed standards of documentation and evidence of market liquidity are commonly seen as criteria of critical importance for the success of any particular asset class in capital markets. Developing distinct norms for assets financed by export credit agencies carries the promise of a much deeper liquidity pool for medium- to long-term export financing, benefiting in particular small and medium-sized exporters. In addition, Berne Union members agree that harmonizing documentation and continued dialogue have the potential to pave the path towards the creation of the capital markets needed in both international and local currencies to support trade in emerging markets and developed economies.

The OECD is a further model of effective processes, at least in part. The organization has both political and technical elements; here I concentrate on processes in the technical work. In committees and groups such as the Export Credit Group, there is a forum for exchanging information on members' export promotion systems and activities. Members discuss and coordinate national policies relating to good governance issues (Erkkilä and Piironen 2014). Experts also work out common guiding principles and consider possibilities for improving cooperation between members with prior consultation, or prior notification. The OECD acts by soft law and peer pressure, mostly with non-binding instruments producing standards and models (Tyler 2011; Ruffing 2010). Examples are guidelines for sustainable lending, or guidelines on corporate governance and environmental practices. In foreign trade, OECD member countries have cooperated regarding officially supported export credits since the 1970s with the so-called OECD consensus in order to create a "level playing field" for trade and export finance.

Three main aspects make these voluntary standards for trade and export finance successful (Drysdale 2015): comprehensive rules, real-time transparency, and an ongoing evolution of rules to meet the needs of both governments and markets. First, the rules provide a level playing field among participants because they are comprehensive. The OECD consensus covers not only minimum premium rates and interest rates for export financing. It also determines other relevant factors for credit agreements such as maturity and repayment structure. For example, a competitive advantage for aircraft manufacturers based on generous state financing support is not possible because OECD rules require governments to prescribe minimum upfront payments, minimum premium rates and maximum repayment terms. As a result, comprehensive rules equalize the competitive dimension of financing. Second, the system provides for real-time transparency, including access to transaction-based data. It gives a forum in which confidential information can be exchanged, including a process for resolving disagreements before the financial commitment in a transaction. Peer pressure is generated because there are no secret financing terms and thus no competitive advantages to be gained from deviating from the rules. Third, the voluntary rules are constantly evolving, adapting to changing needs of users and the market. Over the last decade, governments have negotiated regular updates and upgrades, including revised sector understandings for large energy projects. The Large Aircraft Sector Understanding is a further success-ful example for the creation of a level playing field.

The OECD pioneered the cooperation approach with its evidence-based analysis, tools and a transparent forum for sharing experience. But most importantly, peer pressure among members may be one of the most distinctive features that describes the functioning of the OECD. These practices of voluntary agreements are success stories and exemplification for effective trade governance. They are, however, not a success story of truly global trade governance. The main weakness is that the OECD was unable to fully include emerging economies, and China and India still are not and might never be members. A pathway beyond gridlock would be to rewrite the success story of voluntary agreements and peer pressure by including countries such as these.

Limited success: diverse organizations and processes around common goals

I have observed that growing multipolarity, often in combination with fragmentation, is a major reason for gridlock in international trade. The proliferation of bilateral, regional, and plurilateral trade agreements underscores this dynamic. However, as the introduction to the book notes, fragmentation can also appear as an adaptive and effective response if multiple and diverse organizations and institutions act around common goals or norms. I will discuss how this approach has led to mixed results using the examples of cooperation between multilateral development banks (MDBs) and a recent initiative for global standards in export credit, the International Working Group on Export Credits (IWG).

Alongside their more traditional lending functions, MDBs provide financial investments and business services to numerous developing countries, and supporting trade by providing trade finance is one of their important objectives. This role is key in order to keep supply chains open for developing and least developed economies. As regulatory pressures mount on major commercial banks, companies need increased MDB support for the continuation of their trade finance activities. Trade finance stands at the interface between trade policy and financial market regulation. As development institutions, MDBs seek to address market failures in trade finance that commercial financial institutions are unable or unwilling to address, and help provide more holistic trade finance solutions, keeping in mind development goals.

There is an opportunity for MDBs to coordinate their activities in order to create a pathway beyond gridlock in trade. Regionally oriented MDBs offer apolitical support for member countries around a common goal, and they are increasingly cooperating on a multilateral level. For example, technical assistance from the European Investment Bank for the African Trade Insurance Agency is a new multilateral initiative in trade finance to mobilize resources for climate finance. That said, MDBs still mostly concentrate on their regional mandates, with few pushing broad initiatives for global governance in trade finance. There is a lack of collective approaches, or successful partnerships or cooperation around common goals, to fill the trade finance gap.

Such efforts have been attempted, notably the International Working Group on Export Credits initiated by former US President Obama and China's President Xi Jinping. As an initiative to build new global standards outside the institutional framework of the OECD, representatives from the European Union and the United States as well as other OECD countries, but also important developing economies such as Brazil, China and Russia participate in the IWG. The goal is to agree jointly upon improved standards for financial terms and conditions for export credits provided by national governments. The IWG holds regular meetings and has focused on ships and medical equipment as two specific sectors in its first phase, with the aim of proceeding to a more general perspective in a second phase.

Many exporters would celebrate the IWG if governments could agree on joint rules for mandatory practices for financing global trade, and pressure on governments to establish such a framework has intensified. For exporters, the development and application of truly international norms ensuring global trade governance is crucial. Many exporters in the OECD believe they are at a disadvantage vis-à-vis non-OECD exporters because countries outside the OECD are not bound by similarly stringent export finance rules. Exporters now therefore lobby their home governments to create global rules for trade finance governance.

However, these efforts need refinement. The organization of the IWG has been rudimentary, and there is limited progress locking domestic decision-makers into a global framework. Selective participation and engagement in the IWG stems from collective action problems, and disagreement on enhanced financing conditions of trade promotion prevents positive integration. More than five years after they began, negotiations for global standards have met little success. There is a continuing divergence of interests and still institutional inertia. In sum, the establishment of novel global standards outside the established international organizations by accepting and using the plurality of national trade institutions, as well as complementing existing multilateral agreements, is possible, but challenging to implement.

Conclusion: Reinvigorating the Multilateral Trading System

In sum, the global trade landscape suffers from extensive gridlock, a condition that has brought its core postwar function, negotiating progressively lower barriers to trade, to a halt. But at the same time, elements of the trade regime have proven remarkably resilient and adaptive, including the WTO DSM and technical organizations like the International Chamber of Commerce, the Berne Union, and the OECD. Though the trade regime remains gridlocked, it still functions thanks to these different institutions working at different levels.

At the same time, the pluralization of trade agreements has not necessarily brought coherence. As the IWG example demonstrates, gridlock trends like rising multipolarity can be so strong as to prevent the minimum level of coherence required to make plurality work.

But can the trading regime endure? With political leaders threatening to turn away from free trade across major economies, the question arises of whether "business as usual" will be sufficient, or if deeper transformations are required to move global trade arrangements through or even beyond gridlock. Or, indeed, to prevent them from deteriorating.

In this context, innovative and adaptive leadership from the WTO itself may be able to at least partially reinvigorate the regime as a whole. Since 1995, the WTO has been a main pillar of multilateral economic governance in trade. Despite its weaknesses, solutions through and beyond gridlock without a strong involvement of the WTO are hardly imaginable. To reinvigorate the WTO, however, policymakers in developed and developing countries would have to admit and accept that amendments in policymaking and organizational settings are necessary.

Beyond gridlock in trade means enhancement; the WTO needs a stronger voice in areas of major concern, and a stronger involvement of developing countries is a key success factor. Institutional reforms must start with the WTO Secretariat. Furthermore, the increasing number of bilateral and regional agreements is not only a challenge but also an institutional opportunity. Governments can use the WTO for creating effective rules to supervise regional and bilateral agreements, and regional conflicts can be regulated by the independent multilateral dispute settlement mechanism. The majority of members would benefit from an agile WTO Secretariat, and an adaptive organization is necessary due to the high number of global challenges with an effect on trade. Following a demand-driven approach, the Secretariat must move away from a "pull" strategy – following the demands of member states – to a "push" strategy of providing political leadership for crucial topics.

Several steps are critical. First, institutional reforms will help the WTO to strengthen its capability and credibility. A more independent Secretariat driven by its thought leadership and considerable economic and political expertise will boost the organization's credibility. Enhancing the openness and transparency of the WTO's governance is a key issue; the Secretariat has to create a credible reform process that increases its overall legitimacy. Institutional reforms require increased capacity-building for members in order to develop the analytical skills and knowledge of developing and least developed country governments. Making more use of the Secretariat's expertise together with member representatives as well as external consultants will strengthen the Secretariat's role and impact. Furthermore, more systematic information and data management will enhance the WTO's relevance and creditability. Although the Secretariat already produces a substantial amount of information, including statistics and staff working papers, there is a demand for more surveillance of new policy developments and information about regulatory matters (Elsig 2016; Toohey 2014; Steger 2009). Similar to other institutions such as the OECD, the WTO Secretariat can grow into a role as a leading provider of information for the member countries.

Institutional reform also includes bringing regional and bilateral trade agreements closer to the WTO. Elsig (2016) proposes the creation of a committee to develop proposals and rules for preferential and free trade agreements, which would allow WTO members to benefit from plurilateral agreements more effectively. These preferential and free trade agreements could extend benefits to members on an unconditional or conditional basis, and this committee's work would be beneficial both for countries in terms of results and for the WTO in terms of institutional strengthening.

Second, being an adaptive institution requires a stronger involvement of developing economies (Delimatsis 2014; Albin 2008). Developing countries now comprise two-thirds of the membership of the WTO, and their inclusion into global trade governance should be seen not as a challenge but as an opportunity. Developing countries mostly accept that trade liberalization is beneficial, but are often concerned about adjustment costs. Governments need and ask for more flexible approaches to negotiations which are in line with needs of their individual economies. The WTO must accept these individual needs and move beyond the approach of purely multilateral and all-or-nothing negotiations. The provision of technical assistance, the role of the separate committee on trade and development, and the inclusion of special provisions on developing countries in trade agreements have to be strengthened. The WTO as an institution must lead this process of gradual integration to better involve developing economies.

Third, the World Trade Organization has to increase its participation in areas of crucial concern, for example on climate change (Millimet and Roy 2015; Braun 2014; Neumayer 2004). During the 2007–8 financial crisis, the WTO created a task force and was involved in numerous discussion with governments and other international financial institutions. The WTO was able to give evidence of its importance during and after the financial crisis as a driver and neutral moderator. Although governments provided substantial financial aids into economically necessary or politically deserving industries, the WTO successfully assumed its role by, for example, averting prohibited export subsidies. However, the lack of participation in other global challenges relevant for trade such as financial regulation, food security or climate change has to be converted into an active role of the WTO.

Finally, the contrast between increasing globalization and the removal of trade and investment barriers, on the one hand, and the decline in support for open markets in large sections of the population, on the other hand, has to be tackled (He 2014; Capling and Higgott 2009). The World Trade Organization has to deal with growing concerns about job losses in industrialized countries, fear of stagnant salaries and wages, as well as growing income inequality, reflecting key issues in the political debate in many countries. Policy responses must not only cover appropriate arrangements such as including non-governmental organizations in global-level policymaking. The WTO also has to stand up for trade by better explaining and successfully addressing questions around global inequality as well as social justice. There is a continuous need for re-examining and remaking the case that global trade is as much part of the solution as part of the problem. This includes marshalling both empirical evidence and effective arguments to show that economies turning inwards and erecting new barriers will hurt the poorest the most.

5

Investment

Contestation and Transformation

Taylor St John

A t first glance, the governance of foreign direct investment (FDI) is a graveyard for multilateral cooperation. Describing or analysing a "global investment regime" has long seemed more fantasy than reality. Keohane and Ooms observed in 1975 that: "Writing about alternative international regimes to deal with direct foreign investment may seem to be somewhat like discussing a perpetual motion machine: most people would like one for their own purposes; no one has ever built one; and discussions about their construction often take on a certain air of unreality." Today, 40 years later, there is still no international organization mandated with the governance of direct investment. The repeated negotiating failures and absence of formal organization-building in the postwar period gives the governance of direct investment a different trajectory than most issue areas discussed in the original *Gridlock* volume. Direct investment is not a new phenomenon – flows of FDI have been high throughout the postwar period. Yet formal multilateral cooperation did not succeed in creating a dedicated organization or core convention to govern those flows in the immediate postwar era, unlike the pattern observed in other issue areas and described in *Gridlock*.

The development of postwar investment governance does fit the pattern discussed in *Gridlock* in other ways, however. The postwar stability and prosperity of most OECD countries enabled firms to expand across borders and send record amounts of investment. Deepening interdependence and decades of high FDI flows led to more complex, second-order cooperation problems. This has led investment governance to exhibit many characteristics of gridlock. The second section of this chapter briefly describes the contemporary investment regime and the extent to which it is characterized by gridlock – arguing that it is characterized by a "harder" problem, more fragmentation, and more multipolarity. In investment governance, however, these characteristics of gridlock also contain the seeds of dynamism. These same characteristics, in particular the multipolarity and fragmentation, may provide pathways through and beyond gridlock.

The third section of this chapter identifies pathways out of gridlock in investment governance, starting with two pathways that have the potential to transform investment governance beyond gridlock. These pathways, a shift in major powers' interests and convergence around common principles, reinforce each other in investment. Due in part to their shifting interests, major powers have proposed the most profound reforms in a generation, which are currently being discussed in a series of mega-regional negotiations. The prospects for future cooperation rest heavily on the visions articulated by the European Union, the United States, and China, and the extent to which these mega-regional deals compete with each other or converge around certain principles. Even if all of these ambitious mega-regionals come into force, which requires overcoming substantial political hurdles, they will operate alongside thousands of existing treaties. Therefore, while a shift in major powers' interests and the possibility of convergence in mega-regional negotiations create the possibility for transformative change, there are reasons to doubt if these two pathways will actually propel investment governance beyond gridlock.

Three other pathways, while not offering transformative potential beyond gridlock, help to adapt the investment regime to contemporary challenges and provide pathways *through* gridlock. These pathways – autonomous and adaptive international organizations, technical groups, and civil society coalitions – can accelerate convergence, facilitate faster adaptation, and help update or terminate existing treaties that constitute the contemporary regime. All three pathways are actors, each constrained in various ways, but still capable of creating and managing incremental change. These three pathways through gridlock are also explored in the third section of this chapter. The concluding section then discusses the distributional implications of different pathways through and beyond gridlock. While the five pathways discussed in this chapter (a shift in major powers' interests; convergence around certain principles; autonomous and adaptive international organizations; technical groups; civil society coalitions) may propel investment out of gridlock, the extent to which this momentum can be translated into more inclusive and more robust multilateral cooperation in investment remains an open question.

Contemporary Investment Governance and Its Gridlock

Contemporary investment governance is decentralized. There is no single focal organization or convention at the international level around which actor expectations converge. Instead, a complex web of rules articulated at the national, transnational, and international levels governs FDI. A main reason for the decentralization and spread of investment governance across different levels is the structure of FDI, also referred to as direct investment. Direct investment – defined as long-term ownership and "a large enough ownership stake to provide the investor with some degree of corporate control" (Kerner 2014) – traditionally involves physical assets like a factory or a mine, which exist in a specific location, and are therefore subject to local laws unless the investor and government agree differently. The concerns of foreign investors vary widely, based on their relationship with the host government, the purpose of their investment, and other factors (Dunning 2000). These traits have two key repercussions for governance: first, foreign investors may not have common interests, beyond a general concern about protection from expropriation, and second, a specific domestic law or transnational contract may be the most important legal instrument for a particular investment.

Domestic law and transnational contracts are not discussed in the remainder of this chapter as part of the *international* investment regime, but these instruments are crucial in the day-to-day management of most foreign investment. Many direct investments are secured by contracts made directly between an investor and a host state. Most laws and practices relevant to specific investments are still made at the national or subnational levels, and most of the liberalizing reforms that created the conditions for high flows of FDI were implemented at the domestic level, as governments reformed their legal frameworks in order to attract more foreign investment. In a study of liberalization in 116 developing countries from 1992 to 2001, Kobrin (2005) found that 95 per cent of the changes in FDI policy (1,029 of 1,086 changes) were liberalizing rather than restrictive during these years. These reforms followed a decline in expropriation that begin in the late 1970s and continued through the 1990s and 2000s (Kobrin 1984; Minor 1994). These reforms were part of the shift away from import-substitution policies towards initiatives that actively sought to attract foreign investment (in particular to replace lost debt financing after the 1980s debt crisis). National governments and states, provinces, or even municipalities often provide a package of incentives – including tax holidays or reductions – to attract particular investors (Thomas 2007; James 2009) as well as reforming licensing practices or other regulations to become business-friendly jurisdictions and improve their place in rankings (Kelley and Simmons 2016).

Bilateral treaties and diplomatic activities at the bilateral level constitute the bulk of contemporary global governance in investment. Home governments – that is, the government of the investor – have long played an important role in investment rule-making, despite not being part of the central FDI relationship between investor and host state. These home governments were instrumental in crafting and negotiating the first bilateral investment treaties (BITs) – many with their former colonies or other newly independent developing states. In the 1990s, governments around the world began to embrace BITs, leading to a proliferation of treaties, with over 3,000 BITs in force today. These BITs have fundamentally reshaped the investment regime, in many cases providing broad protections to investors and backing those protections up with binding dispute resolution, in the form of investor–state arbitration (also called "investor–state dispute settlement" or ISDS). Home governments do much more to shape the investment regime than negotiate treaties, however. They provide a substantial proportion of political risk insurance and tend to take a more active role in facilitating investment than is commonly assumed, through agencies like the US Foreign and Commercial Service, economic attachés at embassies, or early government involvement in mediating disputes.

At the multilateral level, investment governance has been characterized by high-profile negotiating failures throughout the postwar era. Out of five attempts to draft multilateral conventions on investment between 1948 and 1998, four failed. The first attempt included investment protection within the broader Havana Charter for an International Trade Organization, which was signed in 1948, but never came into force. The second attempt was a dedicated Convention on the Protection of Foreign Property, discussed within the OECD from 1961 until 1967. The third attempt occurred at the UN Centre on Transnational Corporations in the 1970s–1980s, this time with greater participation from developing countries and an aim to create a balanced agreement with obligations for both investors and host states. During the fourth attempt, investment issues were brought on the agenda of the Uruguay Round of trade negotiations. The Uruguay Round ended with two successful agreements that relate to investment, one that relates directly but has a very narrow scope – the Agreement on Trade-Related Investment Measures (TRIMs) – and a second that has a broader scope but relates to investment indirectly – the General Agreement on Trade in Services (GATS). Shortly after the Uruguay Round concluded, negotiations were launched at the OECD towards the Multilateral Agreement on Investment (MAI).

The MAI was the most recent attempt at a formal, multilateral convention in investment. Initially, the MAI contained strong liberalization provisions in addition to high standards of treatment and direct access to investor–state arbitration, the result of an agenda-setting process with heavy participation from firms (Walter 2001). A transnational coalition of NGOs mobilized to oppose the MAI, arguing that it would grant unprecedented rights to corporations without addressing their responsibilities to the environment, workers, and communities. The MAI developed a toxic public reputation, and officials came to perceive the MAI as a "vote loser" (Henderson 1999: 23). To salvage the effort, key provisions were reworded, leading the text to lose the support of the business groups that had been integral in its initiation (Walter 2001). The MAI's failure prompted serious reflection within the OECD Secretariat and outside it about how to facilitate multilateral cooperation in investment.

In the shadow of these high-profile failures, several less ambitious multilateral initiatives were successful. Two multilateral conventions that provide the cornerstones of contemporary investor–state arbitration, the 1958 New York Convention and the 1966 International Centre for Settlement of Investment Disputes (ICSID) Convention, were agreed. The New York Convention provides enforcement for commercial or investor-state arbitration decisions, while the ICSID Convention outlines arbitration procedures for the resolution of investor–state disputes and provides enforcement for investor–state arbitration decisions. There are also several soft-law initiatives, like the OECD Guidelines on Multinational Enterprises or the UN Global Compact, which provide focal points for cooperation on investment governance. The OECD Guidelines and the Global Compact suggest obligations for investors, unlike BITs. If international investment governance is divided into regulatory versus market enabling (Levy and Prakash 2003), then one observes that regulatory initiatives, like the OECD Guidelines or the Global Compact, tend to be crafted as soft law, while market-enabling initiatives, like BITs or liberalizing reforms in domestic law, are likely to be binding.

In summary, contemporary investment governance is decentralized and occurs across multiple levels. While a series of attempts to craft a multilateral treaty failed, bilateral treaties proliferated, creating a network of thousands of BITs in force today. Bilateral treaties have become the central instrument of international cooperation in investment governance. Is this bilateral network gridlocked? In the remainder of this section, I argue that contemporary investment governance does display three characteristics of gridlock: a "harder" problem, fragmentation, and growing multipolarity.

"Harder" problem

The governance of direct investment has become a harder problem as the focus has shifted from outright expropriation to regulatory expropriation. In the immediate postwar era, the primary cooperation problem in investment that OECD governments confronted was to protect foreign property owned by their citizens from seizure. It is relatively straightforward to identify outright expropriation and to determine an appropriate remedy.[1] The number of outright expropriations peaked in the 1960s and 1970s, and then declined sharply (Kobrin 1984). Today outright expropriation has largely disappeared, with a few exceptions that tend to be concentrated in sectors with high sunk costs, such as utilities and natural resource extraction.

The defining problem of investment governance today is indirect or regulatory expropriation (Lowe 2002; Dolzer 2002; OECD 2004; Newcombe 2005). Indirect expropriation is difficult to define precisely, but can include any state measures with the effect of substantially reducing the value of an investment. Relevant state measures include, for instance, the revocation of a licence or increases in tax rates or new packaging requirements, if these actions are deemed to erode the investor's rights. There is a tension between what constitutes indirect expropriation and legitimate governmental regulation: "a clear conflict arises between the regulatory interests of states and the interest in the protection of investments" (Kriebaum 2007: 717). This type of expropriation is a more intensive problem – that is, one which penetrates much deeper into domestic policy space and daily life – as these expropriations concern domestic regulation, occasionally in sensitive areas like health or environmental standards. Indirect expropriation came to widespread public attention in North America after the *Ethyl* and *Methanex* arbitrations, in which the two firms claimed that restrictions on fuel additives meant they suffered losses so significant that the regulations in question were tantamount to expropriation. Drawing a boundary between regulation and expropriation is a much harder problem than defining direct expropriation, and makes forging international agreement on expropriation more difficult today.

Fragmentation

Contemporary investment governance is undeniably fragmented. The investment regime displays all three of the characteristics of fragmentation: increased transaction costs, inefficient division of labour, and excessive flexibility.

Creating and complying with the complex web of legal agreements described above creates substantial transaction costs for governments. Since there is no focal international organization tasked with monitoring or harmonizing this web of agreements, the opportunities for information-sharing or capacity-building that occur in the hub of a multilateral regime, say in Geneva for the trade regime, have no analogue in the investment regime. This disproportionately affects small and low-income countries, whose ministries are more likely to lack resources and technical expertise (Busch, Reinhardt and Shaffer 2009). Technical assistance and advisory centres like the Geneva-based Advisory Centre on WTO Law, which operates in the context of trade disputes, are less likely without a central hub. Investment negotiators tend to be based in national capitals, meeting only for negotiations or short conferences, curtailing opportunities for informal coordination or experience sharing. In addition, capacity-constrained ministries may have a difficult time assessing which of the various international initiatives most deserve their time. Many international organizations have initiatives on direct investment, but none of these organizations have a mandate to govern it or be the undisputed hub for investment policymaking. This leads to a wide array of initiatives and Roundtables, which, combined with the complex web of legal agreements, create a regime with high transaction costs.

There is considerable redundancy at the international level and no division of labour. Countries may negotiate investment provisions in a bilateral free trade agreement, and then negotiate similar investment provisions in a plurilateral agreement. For instance, the Australia–US Free Trade Agreement and the North American Free Trade Agreement (NAFTA) both contain investment provisions that will coexist with the provisions on investment in the Trans-Pacific Partnership (TPP).

Countries may negotiate BITs that overlap with (or contradict) investment provisions in other agreements, like the TRIMs Agreement or the GATS.

The fragmented nature of the investment regime also creates excessive flexibility and inconsistency. Investors can structure their firms or change their corporate nationality in order to be eligible for treaty protection or use more favourable treaty provisions. This treaty shopping is relatively common in the investment regime, with the bilateral treaties of some countries, such as the Netherlands, acknowledged as investor favourites because of their expansive provisions (van Os and Knottnerus 2011; Schrijver and Prislan 2013: 554). The structure of arbitration and particularly its roots in commercial arbitration create the conditions for inconsistent decisions. In commercial arbitration, the aim is to settle a specific dispute efficiently and confidentially, and not to create precedent or even *jurisprudence constante* (in which previous decisions are persuasive but not binding precedents). Investor–state arbitration tribunals can, and have, come to opposite conclusions on virtually identical facts (Waibel 2007). The system provides no means of reconciling this inconsistency, which increases perceptions of the regime as too flexible and too fragmented.

Growing multipolarity

Investment governance is affected by growing multipolarity, but this multipolarity is both a contributor to gridlock and a potential engine of cooperation. Under conditions of gridlock, growing multipolarity is expected to increase transaction costs, exacerbate legitimacy dilemmas, and lead to greater divergence of interests. In investment, multipolarity has enabled more open challenges to existing governance arrangements (exacerbating legitimacy dilemmas) and sparked competing proposals. Yet it also spurs dynamism and facilitates a convergence of interests among major powers.

Rising multipolarity has not increased transaction costs in investment governance, because transaction costs were high even in the immediate postwar era. While the presence of a stable hegemon has long been associated with public goods provision in economic and security cooperation (Kindleberger 1973; Krasner 1976), unquestioned US hegemony did not lead to the public good of multilateral rules on direct investment. If anything, US hegemony resulted in US intransigence in investment rule-making. The US government was in such a commanding position that it had the ability to set very high standards for investment protection, with little need to compromise. Until the 1990s, the US government perceived investment treaties solely as instruments to protect American property abroad; investment law was not reciprocal in practice. In recent years, treaties have become more reciprocal: in 2013, when President Obama opened formal negotiations with the European Union on investment, or in 2014, when his administration received an open letter from the leaders of large firms supporting an investment agreement with China, there was no question but that the investment provisions would be fully reciprocal. These governments are not just securing protections for their investors, they are also writing rules that will apply to their own actions. This combination of multipolarity and reciprocity creates a fundamental shift in major powers' interests. The shift opens up a pathway beyond gridlock, as the next section elaborates.

Rising multipolarity has also facilitated open challenges and new proposals from governments that are historically investment "ruletakers." South Africa decided to exit the majority of its investment treaties and focus on a new domestic legal framework for foreign investors. Brazil developed a new type of investment treaty, called an Agreement on Cooperation and Facilitation of Investment, that focuses more on practical problems facing foreign investors, such as licences or visas, and eschews some of the legal standards in traditional investment treaties. A group of 12 South American states proposed a new investment arbitration centre with innovative legal features that respond to criticisms of existing international institutions. These proposals demonstrate the dynamism and experimentation that is possible in a decentralized system. While they respond to legitimacy dilemmas, they also strengthen the perception that larger, systemic reform is needed, because these proposals provide piecemeal reforms and many have not yet been fully realized.

The perception that investment governance needs reform is shared by a growing number of governments. In investment, it is not just the "rule-takers" who view the rules as outdated and inappropriate – increasingly, powerful countries that wrote the rules (sometimes not expecting them to apply to their own actions) also want them changed. Although in the short run, this manifests in competing proposals, protests, and tough negotiations, in the long run growing multipolarity and reciprocity may help drive investment governance out of gridlock.

Pathways out of Gridlock in Investment Governance

Investment governance is undoubtedly gridlocked. Yet what seem like sources of dysfunction can also be sources of dynamism. For instance, while fragmentation is a defining trait of gridlock, the fragmented nature of the investment regime contributes to its dynamism and adaptability (Pauwelyn 2014). This section discusses five pathways out of gridlock that apply to investment governance. The first two, a shift in major powers' interest and convergence around certain principles, appear together and may provide a path beyond gridlock. The final three, adaptive international institutions, technical groups, and civil society coalitions, are pathways through gridlock.

Shifts in major powers' interests and convergence around common norms

The ongoing mega-regional negotiations are the engine of future cooperation in investment, and these negotiations are occurring in a new world: today all major powers, including China, the EU, and the US, perceive themselves as both recipients and senders of foreign investment. This is a fundamental shift in how major powers perceive their interests. In the early postwar era, the main actors in investment were capital-exporting OECD countries, mainly France, Germany, UK, US, and to a lesser extent Belgium, the Netherlands, and other European states. When these states drafted investment treaties, their sole aim was to protect their investors abroad. Today these states look at investment treaties as both recipients and senders of FDI: as they negotiate, their governments need to consider if their treaty obligations are consistent with public health policies, environmental regulations, and procurement guidelines, to name a few of the policy areas potentially affected by investment treaties. In addition, many countries that previously perceived their interests predominately as importers of investment now seek to protect the large investments made by their citizens abroad. Governments that negotiate as exporters (in their region as well as globally) today include large states like Brazil, China, India, and South Africa, as well as smaller states like Chile, Malaysia, Mexico, Singapore, South Korea, and Turkey. In theory, more reciprocity creates a common interest that should lead to convergence, as each government seeks to negotiate standards that protect their investors abroad without unduly constraining their own domestic policy autonomy. In practice, reciprocity and shared interests are necessary but not sufficient for convergence.

The extent of convergence in contemporary investment governance is in the eye of the beholder. Many textbooks articulate "common principles" of international investment law (Dolzer and Schreuer 2012) or describe a "global regime for investment characterized by common principles, norms, rules, and decision-making processes" (Salacuse 2010). Schill (2009) conceives of a de facto multilateral regime in investment, forged through most-favoured nation clauses, arbitral *jurisprudence constante*, as well as treaties with shared content and a common origin. The common origin for investment treaties is the 1967 OECD draft, discussed above, which served as a template for the investment treaties of European governments (Schill 2009: 35–6). Then the BIT network developed as a hub-and-spoke system around the model investment treaties of OECD states. When non-OECD governments lacked a model text of their own, they sometimes anchored to the first treaty they negotiated, usually that of an OECD country (Poulsen 2014). Using text-comparison software, Alschner and Skougarevskiy (2016) find "nests" of legal consistency based around national models, and high proportions of identical text.

It is important not to overstate the degree of convergence, however. Even in instances where much of the text is identical, it is the differences that matter, as they likely indicate contentious provisions. For investors and law firms engaged in a case, the exact language of a provision can have material consequences. Removing or rewriting investment protection standards can be difficult if a highly mobilized, well-resourced constituency stands to lose from the change. Governments can face concentrated lobbying, threats to their reputation as a destination for investment, and other obstacles to changing their investment treaties or exiting their treaties (Lavopa, Barreiros and Bruno 2013).

General principles are not the same as specific text. The same principles can produce texts that differ in important ways, as the Trans-Pacific Partnership and the Transatlantic Trade and Investment Partnership illustrate. The TPP was designed to set the terms of liberalization and protection in the Pacific Rim. The TTIP was designed to harmonize European and American standards and thereby define the next generation of regulation. The US government negotiated them at the same time, yet the TPP and TTIP texts are not identical – they are distinct focal points. One clear divergence is investor–state arbitration. The TPP text finalized in November 2015 provides access to investor–state arbitration, albeit with new refinements and carve-outs, while that same month, the EU tabled a proposal for an investment court system to replace investor–state arbitration in the TTIP text.[2] Even if they never come into force, the TPP and TTIP texts may become influential models, or they may be less influential than a third focal point, contemporary Chinese proposals. On arbitration, the current Chinese negotiating position is for strong investor–state arbitration provisions, with the possibility of select carve-outs that make sense for the Chinese government. This is at odds with the current EU position (in favour of an investment court system) and with the current US position (in favour of arbitration, with regulatory carve-outs, detailed definitions, and clear constraints on scope). The question is whether these three positions will all survive as focal points, or if negotiations between these three actors will lead to harmonization.

The prospects for convergence and cooperation are also shaped by geopolitical concerns: competing mega-regional initiatives suggest a return to first-order geopolitics, to an extent. The TPP, for instance, was described by the US Trade Representative (2016) in unambiguously geopolitical terms: it is "a concrete manifestation of our strategy of rebalancing toward Asia" that "demonstrates that America remains a leading force for prosperity and security in the region." Implicit in any discussion of TPP before the US withdrew was that the agreement's strategic purpose was to exclude China. Yet the TPP bloc has always been permeable: every TPP signatory has a BIT with China except Brunei and the US. Five TPP signatories already have free trade agreements with China (Australia, Chile, New Zealand, Peru, and Singapore). In addition, the Regional Comprehensive Economic Partnership provides a regional alternative to TPP, and includes several TPP signatories plus South Korea, India, and China. These agreements vary in the breadth and strength of their commitments, and are not all equally important. Yet the high number of existing agreements suggests it is more accurate to view TPP as one (ambitious, important) agreement among many, rather than an agreement that would create an impervious bloc. While the mega-regionals may take on geopolitical overtones, high pre-existing levels of legalization mean that the borders of these blocs will be nowhere near as inviolable as economic blocs in the Cold War era. High pre-existing legalization makes convergence complicated, because even if states agree to a new standard, they will still have several agreements with different standards.

Convergence may be facilitated without treaties, through more flexible, adaptive forms of cooperation like the One Belt, One Road initiative. The Chinese-led initiative has broad aims – geopolitical, cultural, and most importantly economic – and uses different tools to facilitate investment than existing treaties. It focuses on improving trade routes and investment opportunities across the "Silk Road Economic Belt" (overland routes from China to Central Asia, the Middle East, and Europe) and the "Maritime Silk Road" (maritime routes from China to South-East Asia, the Indian subcontinent, North Africa, and Europe). The initiative could eventually include 65 countries, with 4.4 billion people. There are two characteristics that make it different from typical trade or investment treaties. First, it is backed by funding: the Chinese government is setting aside large amounts for infrastructure (estimates of the dedicated New Silk Road Fund's current assets are around US$40 billion, and the Asian Infrastructure Investment Bank's capital is US$100 billion). Second, its approach could be characterized as problem solving, in that the emphasis (at least in statements made to date) is on identifying impediments to trade or investment and fixing them. China's top planning body, the National Development and Reform Commission, issued a document on the One Belt, One Road initiative that discusses strengthening cooperation among governments, but does not mention an overarching treaty. The One Belt, One Road initiative will influence standard setting and investment governance, but likely without the transaction costs of protracted negotiations and while allowing the Chinese government to maintain control and adapt to new challenges as they arise.

In summary, these two pathways – a shift in major powers' interests and convergence around certain principles – have the potential to spark transformative change and push investment governance beyond gridlock. Today, major powers negotiate investment treaties as both recipients and senders of FDI: this perceived reciprocity is a fundamental shift in their interests. Reciprocity creates favourable conditions for convergence, because governments share the general aim of protecting their investors without unduly constraining their own autonomy. Creating favourable conditions for convergence is not the same as actual convergence, however. Currently major powers support competing proposals. While competition may itself be an engine of convergence (and these competing proposals do converge on certain points), these proposals also contain sharp divergences. Some of these divergences are superficial, but others reflect fundamental disagreements on principles, which can be exacerbated by distributional conflicts, geopolitical tensions, or sensitive domestic issues. Therefore, while these pathways have the potential to push investment governance beyond gridlock, there are serious obstacles to realizing this potential.

Autonomous and adaptive international institutions

Several international actors play important, and often under-appreciated, roles in adapting the investment regime to contemporary challenges – providing pathways *through* gridlock. Here, I identify four actors that possess a generative function and evaluate how each of these actors initiates, supports, or coordinates reforms. The actors are listed in order of best known to least understood: OECD, the United Nations Conference on Trade and Development (UNCTAD), arbitration organizations, and joint interpretation committees.

In the 1960s and the 1990s, the OECD was transformed into a negotiating forum, as member states attempted to set binding rules on investment protection. Since 1998, however, the OECD Secretariat has focused its efforts where they tend to be most successful and least controversial: facilitating intergovernmental dialogue and undertaking research. The OECD Investment Committee coordinates a Freedom of Investment Roundtable that brings together relevant officials from member states to discuss emerging developments in investment governance. These Roundtables provide opportunities for socialization and information sharing. The OECD Secretariat also produces research reports, typically providing a summary of state practices as well as a menu of possible responses to governance challenges. OECD Roundtables and reports facilitate coordination and draw attention to actions that states can take to deal with emerging issues – in a sense, paving different avenues through gridlock.

UNCTAD plays a similar role to the OECD, with a wider membership. In the absence of a focal institution, UNCTAD serves as the de facto hub of global investment policymaking. It has become the public repository for investment treaty texts and the main source of information about investment trends, policies, and arbitrations. In addition to being a clearing house of information, UNCTAD provides guidance. This guidance can take the form of investment policy reviews for individual countries, or the Investment Policy Framework for Sustainable Development, an online, global model treaty. These actions are generally intended to help officials modify their treaties to align better with national development objectives. In this way UNCTAD, like the OECD, outlines actions that governments can take to adapt the investment regime to deal with challenges, which provides an important avenue through gridlock.

The small organizations that arrange investor–state arbitrations are typically perceived as administrative organs without any generative capacity of their own. This perception is understandable but misguided; these organizations do respond to governance challenges. For instance, in response to criticisms that investor–state arbitration permits or encourages frivolous cases, the Secretariat of the International Centre for Settlement of Investment Disputes (the largest and oldest investor–state arbitration organization) invented a system of early neutral review. Under this system, an outside expert reviews the dispute before a claim is formally registered. In response to criticisms that investor–state arbitration enables inconsistent decisions, the ICSID Secretary-General wrote to an arbitration tribunal "requesting them to confirm her understanding that the Tribunal, like other ICSID tribunals, gives due consideration to published decisions" and then listed a relevant decision (Award, *Sempra Energy v Argentine Republic*, ICSID 2007: 18). This is a bold step in arbitration, where there is no formal precedent and even notions of *jurisprudence constante* are contested (Berman 2009: 664; Douglas 2006: 27). In response to the criticism that there is not enough geographical or gender diversity among arbitrators, the ICSID Secretariat created a list system, which increases the familiarity of the parties (and their law firms) with potential arbitrators who are female or from underrepresented regions. The ICSID Secretariat is taking small steps at the margins to adapt investor–state arbitration to contemporary challenges; for many observers, these steps are too little, too late (Trakman 2012).

Joint interpretive committees are created in bilateral or plurilateral treaties; their membership is composed of state treaty parties, and their purpose is to enable states to play a more active role in adapting the existing treaty to new governance needs. The NAFTA Free Trade Commission is the best known of these committees, but the texts of several investment treaties provide for joint interpretations – some create formal committees, while others merely suggest the possibility of the two governments meeting for consultations. These committees are not autonomous international organizations, but they are cooperative institutions designed to help adapt or update governance. The NAFTA Free Trade Commission has repeatedly issued Notes of Interpretation to guide tribunals and adapt investment law to deal with contemporary challenges. Joint interpretive committees can articulate a legitimate, authoritative answer to a divisive question or issue, and in this way, provide a small adaptation that prevents gridlock.

These four actors – the OECD, UNCTAD, arbitration organizations, and joint interpretation committees – are all autonomous international institutions that help adapt investment governance to contemporary challenges. While these actors generally have limited mandates, limited resources, and act largely behind the scenes, the information and recommendations they provide can lead to meaningful reforms, which can prevent gridlock or outline feasible paths through it.

Technical groups with effective and legitimate processes

Despite the increasing political salience of investment governance, there are still many low-salience issues that could be tackled by technical groups. A recent transparency reform is discussed here that illustrates the potential of technical groups, although in general this potential remains unrealized.

The Mauritius Convention on Transparency enables states to require more transparency and disclosure in investor–state arbitrations. The fragmentation of investment governance made it difficult to require transparency without individually renegotiating thousands of bilateral treaties. Therefore governments turned to a working group within the United Nations Commission on International Trade Law (UNCITRAL), created by the UN General Assembly in 1966 to promote the harmonization of trade law. UNCITRAL generally operates through draft conventions, model laws, legislative guides, and technical assistance in law reform projects. The Mauritius Convention was discussed within a UNCITRAL working group for seven years, and its drafting shows how a technical group can isolate a specific problem and slowly craft an innovative, consensus solution. Technical groups provide a place for government officials to meet outside the context of negotiations or a specific dispute, both of which can have adversarial overtones. UNCITRAL's outputs also benefit from the legitimacy that comes with good procedure and a wide membership, even if a few high-income countries drove the discussions.

The Mauritius Convention also illustrates some limits of technical groups. Since the group was operating in a fragmented context without a strong mandate, gradual steps and drafting gymnastics were required. The transparency initiative led to two instruments: Transparency Rules (which applies only to treaties that came into effect after 1 April 2014 and only to arbitrations under UNCITRAL procedural rules, around 35 per cent of all investor–state arbitrations) and the Mauritius Convention (which in principle applies to all of a ratifying government's existing treaties). Even under the Convention, however, governments can exclude certain treaties or disputes from the transparency requirement. Despite these difficulties, the UNCITRAL work on transparency is having, and will continue to have, an impact. The Convention helps "make transparency, rather than confidentiality, the default rule for investor–state disputes" (Johnson and Bernasconi-Osterwalder 2013: 26). Within investment governance, there are many issues on which technical groups with effective and legitimate processes could make substantial contributions.

Civil society coalitions with reformist states

Many civil society coalitions engage actively with investment governance. This engagement can take many forms, but by far the most influential has been advocacy against trade or investment deals, often targeting domestic political leaders. While this advocacy can exacerbate gridlock, it can also spark innovations and reforms that create pathways through gridlock.

The impact that civil society advocacy can have is illustrated vividly by a recent shift in the EU's position on investor–state arbitration. The EU's initial proposals for TTIP included investor–state arbitration, but after vocal opposition from civil society groups, the EU replaced arbitration with a proposal for an investment court system. Civil society interest in arbitration intensified after a controversial case against Germany was filed, which challenged the government's decision to phase out nuclear power without providing compensation. The circumstances of this case generated widespread anger and focused attention on the arbitration provisions in the proposed TTIP text. Demonstrations brought as many as 500,000 people onto the streets of Berlin and other European cities. These demonstrations spurred the EU Commission to open a public consultation on investor–state arbitration, which led to 145,000 submissions, the vast majority of which expressed opposition to this form of arbitration. After the consultation, the EU Trade Commissioner remarked on the "fundamental and widespread lack of trust by the public in the fairness and impartiality of the old ISDS model" (Malmström 2015). The EU Commission then made public a version of the investment chapter of TTIP that proposed an investment court system and a reader's guide enumerating how the new proposal addresses many of the concerns raised by civil society groups.

Civil society groups can also influence investment governance through working with reformist governments or through multi-stakeholder partnerships. For instance, the International Institute for Sustainable Development, a civil society group with headquarters in Canada, has long-running dialogues with many governments and drafted a model investment treaty of its own, which was subsequently adapted by a few governments. Multi-stakeholder partnerships often generate voluntary standards for investor behaviour; in so doing, they implicitly aim to "rebalance" traditional investment treaties, which create enforceable rights but not corresponding obligations for foreign investors. One prominent partnership, the Global Compact, is a set of human rights, labour, environment, and anti-corruption principles to which corporate executives commit. The Global Compact's proponents acknowledge that it falls well short of binding regulation, arguing that it operates as a "learning network" which can help to set new agendas, create new norms, and change expectations for corporate behaviour (Ruggie 2001).

Civil society groups are often associated with vocal disapproval of existing investment governance structures, but this discord is only one mode of civil society engagement, and even it can serve as an important source of dynamism. Civil society groups can generate (or demand that their governments generate) innovations and reforms that serve as pathways through gridlock.

Conclusion: Who Benefits from Investment Governance?

The consequences of investment governance are complex. While treaties and other governance instruments have long been judged by the amount of investment generated (if a treaty facilitated more investment, it was a success) this is a partial measure of the consequences of investment governance. Investment flows themselves create winners and losers. If firms decide to offshore production to a lower-cost country, this decision creates winners (share owners) and losers (production workers) in the home economy. Foreign investment also creates winners and losers in the host economy, and the overall benefits of FDI for host economies can vary greatly. While foreign investment can bring managerial expertise, create new jobs, and improve labour standards, it can also lead to irreparable environmental damage and sharp rises in the prices of essential goods, and not actually bring any new jobs, expertise, or improvements in standards. While many governments and international organizations are aware of the differential impacts of FDI, governance arrangements at the international level could do more to tackle corporate malfeasance or monitor the consequences of FDI. If proposals for a "balanced" multilateral code (that is, one which creates obligations for investors as well as creating obligations for host states), like the provisions negotiated at the UN Centre on Transnational Corporations in the 1980s, had come to fruition, arguably the international architecture would be better fit for this purpose.

Today's governance arrangements in investment are not "balanced" and not multilateral. This has many distributional consequences, but one of particular importance for overcoming gridlock is that if cooperation proceeds along the lines of mega-regional deals plus harmonization, low-income countries are likely to be largely left out. The TPP negotiations, which had the most inclusive agenda-setting process of the three mega-regional initiatives discussed above, were a discussion between 12 governments at their most inclusive. Low-income neighbours such as Cambodia, Indonesia, or Laos were not in the room and thus their concerns were not raised. Open deliberations and universal, rules-based systems bring innumerable benefits for low-income and low-capacity states. The states that stand to gain the most from multilateral rule-making are usually those with least capacity. Most discussions of the contemporary investment regime focus on how TTIP or TPP will shape it – overlooking that even if these agreements do come into force, there are 140 governments around the world that will not be directly affected by these two agreements. Governments with scarce ministerial capacity to keep current on developments in investment treaty drafting – states like Burkina Faso, Honduras, Nepal, or even states like Egypt or Libya – are the least likely to update their treaties.

Decentralization has made the international investment regime dynamic and resilient, but it also means that reforming the system requires thousands of renegotiations instead of one large renegotiation. The transaction costs of large-scale reform are overwhelming. This is a major governance challenge for investment in the future, and adaptive institutions, civil society coalitions, and especially technical groups are positioned to play a decisive role in addressing this challenge. The major, transformative push beyond gridlock in investment governance will come from shifting interests of major powers and the extent to which the new, mega-regional proposals backed by these major powers compete or converge with one another. Yet the interests of major powers and the mega-regional deals do not entirely define the future of investment. Adaptive institutions, technical groups, and civil society groups can shape the character of this governance, to make it more consistent, inclusive, and multilateral.

6

Energy

A Fundamental Transformation?

Ann Florini

The world needs a fundamental change in energy systems to meet the challenges of the twenty-first century. The task is to provide more energy to more people without fostering runaway climate change or going to war over resources. Global energy governance (GEG) as currently construed and constructed is experiencing considerable gridlock in its conventional tasks of providing reasonable stability in global fossil fuel markets. But there are promising developments in technology and the beginnings of consensus on the goals that global energy governance should seek to achieve. These developments are accompanied by shifts in the interests of great powers and an explosion of institutional innovation that may provide meaningful pathways beyond gridlock in GEG.

Energy is not just another economic sector: modern civilization depends on reliable and affordable access to energy services. The extraordinary improvements in human well-being and the extraordinary growth in human numbers of the past two centuries have occurred because humanity learned how to make widespread use of coal and oil – so the transition to a different energy system requires a thoroughgoing transformation that somehow does not disrupt the functions of modern society. Governing that transition requires rule systems that simultaneously address externalities (such as climate change), achieve global goals (such as the elimination of extreme poverty and the avoidance of conflict), and facilitate appropriate action on the part of subnational and non-state actors as well as national governments.

GEG used to be relatively simple, if difficult to do well. Through the end of the twentieth century, it focused on oil as by far the most important globally traded energy source. Since the 1990s, however, as we will see below, the geopolitics of oil have become ever more complex, with many more producers and consumers and a much greater range of relevant technologies and markets. That complexity, plus the potential growth of natural gas trade, is causing new pressure on the existing energy governance system.

At the same time, energy governance confronts major new issues. The energy and environmental aspects of global governance are inherently intertwined. Greenhouse gases from the burning of fossil fuels account for some two-thirds of the climate problem. Energy policy at the national level is now supposed to take into account national climate commitments as specified in the Nationally Determined Contributions to addressing climate change as agreed by virtually all nations at the 21st Conference of Parties (COP21) to the UN Framework Convention on Climate Change (UNFCCC) in Paris in December 2015. Meeting those commitments necessarily requires a complete transition away from fossil-based energy systems in this century.

This transition must occur while energy systems simultaneously meet growing market demand for energy services (from larger, richer populations) and make energy services available to billions of people whose access is severely limited or non-existent. The UN's Sustainable Development Goals (SDGs) include both specific commitments on sustainable energy (SDG 7), and specific goals for poverty alleviation and improvements in human well-being that will require a big increase in the availability of energy services. And the SDGs are explicit: this increase in energy access must occur while the global economy decarbonizes (SDG 13) in keeping with the Paris agreement – not an easy task given the large quantities of cheap carbon-intensive coal available to many countries and transportation systems the world over that depend almost entirely on oil.

Even to meet likely market demand for energy services without worrying about climate change would be a challenge, given expected population and economic growth. A scenario by the oil company Royal Dutch Shell points to the "zone of uncertainty" between maximum likely energy supply and minimum likely market demand by 2050 as being equal to all of energy supply today (Bentham 2014). In other words, reasonable projections about how much primary energy market forces will be able to provide and how much energy people will be willing to pay for leave us short on the supply side by a vast amount.

Success in global energy governance requires not just filling that market gap but also providing energy services to the more than 1 billion people who currently lack even the capacity to turn on a single light bulb, without exacerbating the climate change problem: the energy trilemma. That success will entail massive changes to infrastructure (including cross-border) for sustainable transport, for heating and cooling, and for sustainable electricity generation, transmission, and distribution systems. It will require spurring and disseminating rapid technological change, despite current heated disagreement over what technologies should be fostered and how.

As a result of the proliferation of energy-related goals and technologies, the challenges of global energy governance are expanding into a mishmash of unprioritized and sometimes competing goals, encompassing rapidly multiplying institutions and networks. This chapter explores the current, relatively gridlocked state of GEG in a world of increasing multipolarity, a more challenging energy agenda, and proliferating, fragmented institutions. It then considers the possible pathways beyond gridlock, via shifts in the interests of major powers, catalytic roles by technocratic institutions, pluralization around common themes, and innovative leadership that could bring about a transition to an era of sustainable, abundant energy for all under these conditions of extreme uncertainty.

The Current Energy Picture

Energy is what enables us to do work, whether the energy comes from food or gasoline or the splitting of atoms. Most of the energy we use originates from the sun, directly or via plants that turn sunlight into forms of energy we can use. Fossil fuels are simply very old forms of solar power, captured by plants and the organisms that ate them millions of years ago, then concentrated through long periods of extremely high temperature and pressure underground. The sun daily provides far more energy than humanity could conceivably use – but not in a form that we yet can easily capture on a sufficiently large scale. The challenge now is to develop both the technology and the governance systems to provide sufficient energy when and where we want it.

Understanding the scale of that challenge requires a quick vocabulary lesson. Energy is measured in various types of units. The most basic unit is the joule. One joule is roughly the energy involved in lifting a medium tomato one metre from the ground.[1] Power, the rate at which energy is used, is most often measured in watts (a watt is one joule/second), and large-scale power is measured in megawatts (1 million watts), or terawatts (TW, or trillion watts). Energy is often measured as kilowatt (thousand watts) hours or megawatt (million watts) hours – if you have a 1,000-watt hairdryer on for one hour, you use one kilowatt-hour. Large-scale energy consumption is often measured in million tons of oil equivalent (Mtoe), a common way of comparing the energy content of different primary energy sources (coal, natural gas, nuclear, renewables, etc.) using a common metric of the amount of energy released by burning 1 million metric tons of oil. One Mtoe is equal to 4.1868×10^{16} joules.

As of 2014, according to the International Energy Agency, global energy consumption was 9,425 Mtoe (IEA 2016: 28), with global power consumption of 12–13 terawatts. To have everyone in the world consume at current North American levels would require a supply on the order of 70 terawatts. Projections for likely global consumption by 2050 are in the range of 25–30TW, rising to well over 40TW by the end of this century. All of these are rough approximations, as forecasts of energy supply and demand are notoriously unreliable.[2]

Most of that energy comes from fossil fuels. Oil drives almost all transport. Coal provides the bulk of power, with natural gas on the rise. The fast and well-understood way to expand energy access is to burn much more of the world's cheapest and dirtiest primary energy source: coal. More than 40 per cent of the world's power generation is currently coal-fired (Clark 2015). And coal use is rising: contrary to expectations before the turn of the century, a number of countries, particularly in developing Asia (including China, India, and Indonesia), are proceeding to build large numbers of long-lived coal-fired power plants that could lock in decades of high CO_2 emissions and central-ized power systems (Steckel, Edenhofer and Jakob 2015).

Given the concerns about continued extensive reliance on fossil sources, attention has turned to alternatives such as solar, wind, geo-thermal, and a variety of innovative technologies. Of these, solar is by far the most promising candidate for very large-scale energy provision – the sun continuously bathes the planet with much more energy, in the order of 89,000TW. But humanity's capacity to capture that energy is not yet adequate (Tsao, Lewis and Crabtree 2006).[3]

Gridlock and Beyond in Fossil Fuel Governance

Most global energy governance is still focused around traditional large-scale energy sources: fossil fuels, and particularly oil. It is not surprising that oil has been the focus of GEG: oil remains the single largest source of global primary energy supply (accounting for roughly a third), fuels nearly all transportation in virtually all parts of the world, and is by far the most widely traded energy commodity. GEG for oil (and to an increasing degree natural gas) is about facilitating trade and providing insurance against supply shocks. The current system is suffering from considerable gridlock, with no clear pathway beyond.

Global energy governance of oil and related fossil fuels is a complex story involving several distinct organizations and rule systems (Colgan, Keohane and Van de Graaf 2012). First came the association of oil exporters. The 1961 founding statute creating the Organization of the Petroleum Exporting Countries (OPEC) explicitly states that the aim of coordinated action among members was the interests of oil producers, providing them with a steady income and a fair return on capital. OPEC once included almost all of the most significant exporters. The International Energy Agency, established in 1974 as a club for the major oil consumers under OECD auspices in response to the 1970s oil price shocks, had the explicit aims of securing oil "on reasonable and equitable terms" and creating a system to manage oil supply emergencies. That system requires all IEA members to stockpile 90 days' worth of net oil imports, to be released under IEA coordination when the agency determines that there has been a sufficient shock to global oil supply (Florini 2011).

In addition to measures taken by each of these two organizations to try to ensure the immediate interests of its member states, both intergovernmental organizations (IGOs) (and their members) have an interest in ensuring a reasonably stable oil supply system, an undertaking that requires some degree of global governance to provide the underpinnings of an effective market in this heavily traded commodity. Oil price volatility renders markets unstable. Because the nature of the oil industry requires very long-term planning and investment, this is a particularly serious market failure for both suppliers and consumers of oil. Despite this obvious common interest, structured dialogue between consumers and producers only began in the early 1990s with a series of biennial meetings of energy ministers to bridge producer and consumer nations. This was institutionalized in the form of the International Energy Forum (IEF), with the creation of a secretariat that began work in Riyadh in December 2003. The IEF's 72 member countries account for nearly 90 per cent of world oil and gas supply and demand.[4] In addition to creating structures for dialogue, the IEF supports ongoing sharing and collation of data in the notoriously opaque oil industry, in the form of the Joint Oil Data Initiative.

Despite the existence of these three institutions and the development over the past few decades of relatively robust global oil markets, global oil governance remains on shaky ground. As more countries have become major international oil suppliers and consumers, rising multipolarity has challenged existing institutions aimed at coordinating markets. OPEC has largely failed as a cartel, both because its membership now excludes a large number of significant oil producers (such as Russia) and because even its members find agreement on oil production quotas difficult to achieve. In particular, the geopolitics of the Middle East and the advent of American hydraulic fracturing ("fracking") technology have helped to drive down the price of oil and create flexibility in the form of multiple relatively small-scale production sites that can easily be taken off-line in response to market forces – not a situation with which an already enfeebled cartel can easily cope (Goldthau and Witte 2011). Similarly, the IEF dialogue has not yet led to effective mechanisms that can reliably stabilize oil prices, as became evident in the wild price swings of this century.

On the demand side, the IEA has reached out to China, India, and other non-member countries that have become major oil importers since the IEA's creation. This is crucial because the IEA is supposed to coordinate releases from its members' stockpiled oil reserves as a means of ensuring that oil supply shocks do not disrupt oil markets. Although the IEA has several times successfully played that role, the advent of huge new consumers (especially China and India) who are not IEA members and thus not included in the IEA's stockpile coordination may render obsolete one key component of global energy governance.

Although the IEA has made heroic efforts to reach out to these and other developing countries, and although the US and others have indicated they would like to see China join, China and India have no particular incentive to bring their petroleum stockpiles into the IEA system (Van de Graaf 2015; Florini 2011). At the IEA's November 2015 ministerial-level meeting, China, Indonesia, and Thailand joined the IEA as its first three Association countries, and Singapore subsequently became the fourth in October 2016. The Association initiative allows the IEA to avoid the hard question of changing its founding document to bring in new members that do not meet the original criteria, and also allows Association countries to avoid the requirement to put national oil stockpiles equal to 90 days of oil imports under the control of the IEA stockpile system.

Other transnational efforts to support energy supply security in oil (and increasingly natural gas as well) include those at the regional level. For example, energy supply security is increasingly reflected in regional agreements, notably in the ASEAN Agreement on ASEAN Energy Cooperation and the Energy Charter Treaty. However, they have limited effect in practice. The much-vaunted ASEAN energy cooperation system is currently just a set of bilateral pipeline agreements, with strictly national interests determining which are built (Carroll and Sovacool 2010).

The most significant such effort came from Europe, where the EU in particular has long promoted open trade in oil and gas (Goldthau and Sitter 2015). Reasonably efficient global markets have developed for oil (even though some 80 per cent of proven reserves are owned by states rather than private companies), and further development of such markets could provide positive-sum approaches to global energy governance. The Energy Charter Treaty, which covers energy trade, investment, efficiency, and transit (pipelines), and includes a dispute settlement procedure, began life at Dutch instigation in the early 1990s as a European effort to bring Russian pipelines into an orderly transnational arrangement – but Russia has refused to participate. More recently, this process took a major step towards reflecting the new realities of energy geopolitics, when 72 countries (notably including China), the EU, Euratom, and the Economic Community of West African States signed the International Energy Charter, a non-binding set of principles for international energy cooperation, intended as a first step towards accession to the legally binding Energy Charter Treaty. This can be interpreted as an effort to get around gridlock by substituting more flexible soft-law approaches for the intended binding constraints of the failed initial Energy Charter Treaty.

Global governance of natural gas

It is not clear how the emergence of natural gas as a more significant energy source will affect global energy governance.[5] Inexpensive gas has become more available, thanks in substantial part to fracking, particularly in the US where the substitution of gas for coal-fired power accounts for a substantial share of reduced US greenhouse gas emissions. American fracking technology continues to improve, keeping costs and prices low and supply high (Meyer 2016). Gas proponents argue that cheap and readily accessible natural gas, either locally produced or traded, would allow countries such as China and India to replace their heavy dependence on coal (the most carbon-intensive fossil fuel) with less carbon-intensive natural gas – but it is not clear why moving to gas rather than directly to non-carbon energy sources is environmentally desirable. Nor is it clear whether many other countries will enjoy a US-style fracking boom, which in the US depended on an unusual combination of geology, market structures, and governance systems.

At present, natural gas prices in the US are lower than in Europe and Asia, sparking much interest in the possibility of trade as the US begins to export liquefied natural gas (LNG). But unlike the oil industry, which over the decades has developed an elaborate infrastructure for processing and transporting oil fuels and products around the world, the investments needed to make natural gas readily tradeable have yet to be made at scale. Natural gas is different from oil because, well, it is a gas, while oil is liquid. Liquid oil is easily transported by sea, and a vast infrastructure developed over decades supports that trade. Natural gas must either travel by pipelines in gaseous form, or must be liquefied and then transported by pipelines, road tankers, or sea, then reconverted to gaseous form at its destination.

Although current predictions are that the next few years are likely to see a significant oversupply of LNG (Sheppard and Raval 2015), it is very hard to know how gas markets will progress. Such markets would require large-scale financing, LNG terminals and other infrastructure, and the development of a whole new set of rules, regulations, and market practices, especially in Asia. Singapore and China are already working to create oil-style markets and facilities, and Japan has recently announced policies aimed at creating a trading hub in Japan (Stern 2016).

The geopolitics connected to natural gas create additional uncertainties. For example, as the US is now becoming a major global player, allowing exports of LNG, its as yet unknown policy preferences could have a major effect on energy markets and related geopolitical issues: Will the US continue with the status quo, with natural gas primarily traded in long-term contracts? Or will it actively promote US LNG exports in an effort to provide Europe and Asia with an alternative to dependence on Russian gas pipelines? Or will the US lead the liberalization of gas markets to break up existing monopolies and encourage domestic production in a wider range of European and Asian countries (Medlock, Jaffe and O'Sullivan 2014)?

The New Energy World: Technological Transformation?

Technological developments have the potential to disrupt the energy sector dramatically, potentially eliminating some of the gridlock challenges that affect existing GEG, but also potentially creating new challenges. There is no shortage of technological options that could help to create a world of abundant sustainable energy. To give just a few examples:

- The costs of solar and wind-based energy are dropping so sharply that Bloomberg New Energy Finance, which has become a top source of data on renewables, contends that as of 2040, "zero-emission energy sources will make up 60% of installed capacity. Wind and solar will account for 64% of the 8.6TW of new power generating capacity added worldwide over the next 25 years, and for almost 60% of the $11.4 trillion invested" (Bloomberg New Energy Finance 2016).
- Battery technology is advancing apace, offering grounds for optimism that batteries and other energy storage approaches may help to resolve the intermittent availability of sunshine and wind power (IRENA 2015).
- Experimentation with advanced biofuels is starting to reach the commercial deployment phase, as with the new Poet-DSM cellulosic ethanol plant in Iowa (Biofuels International 2016).
- Even nuclear fusion, long known as the energy technology that is 30 years in the future and always will be, is showing promising signs via an intensive competition among well-funded start-ups as well as some large-scale government-backed projects (Grossman 2015).

Technology is fostering not only new energy sources, but also new ways of delivering energy services through much more decentralized provision such as rooftop solar. Bloomberg New Energy Finance (2016) estimates that globally small-scale photovoltaic solar will account for 10 per cent of generating capacity by 2040. Electric cars (which can run on power from any source and thus can cut oil dependence) may be poised for a massively disruptive breakout in the US and other major markets as the costs plunge and charging ports become much more widely available (Mims 2016).

There are also spillover effects of apparently unrelated technological change. New finance-sector technologies (fintech), for example, are already having significant effects in enabling the rapid diffusion of decentralized solar. In Kenya, the widespread use of mobile payments systems through M-Pesa has made it possible for the poor to pay for, and thus have access to, distributed renewable energy provided by a related business, M-Kopa. Thus access to distributed renewable energy is facilitated by fintech that in turn was made possible by policy, in the central bank's decision to allow mobile phone payments to launch a dramatic and successful assault on conventional banking. Facilitating the shift to renewable energy was clearly not the goal of central bank policy – but it is just as clearly an outcome of that policy (UNEP Inquiry 2016b: 32).

This is just one example of unexpected ways in which information and communications technologies are beginning to intersect with renewable and distributed energy technologies. Just as these technologies transformed the telecommunications industry, they could make possible a vastly different market-based decentralized approach to the provision of energy services, using a wide range of energy sources connected via everything from neighbourhood micro-grids to continent-spanning platforms.

Various technologies might also enable the world to continue to burn significant quantities of fossil fuels:

- Carbon capture and storage could permit continued use of central-ized fossil-fuel power plants and other fossil applications whose carbon emissions would be captured rather than released into the environment (IEA 2013). To date, however, there is little evidence of either substantial government funding commitment or rapid cost reduction of the kind seen recently in solar and wind energy (Clark 2015).
- Geoengineering approaches would attempt to intervene directly in planetary systems to counteract climate change, either by increas-ing the Earth's reflectivity (solar geoengineering) or by extract-ing carbon dioxide from the atmosphere (carbon geoengineering) (Oxford Geoengineering Programme 2017).

These technologies are in relatively early stages of development and have raised questions about possible unintended consequences. It seems unlikely that they will provide a silver bullet to solve the climate problem caused by the burning of fossil fuels.

No one can reliably predict how, or how quickly, any of these technologies will evolve. Technology development and deployment depends not only on inherently uncertain advances in science and engineering, but also on financing systems, trade rules, and regulatory arrangements that to date have largely served a world of fossil-based centralized power provision and oil-based transport. Thus, no one currently knows how – or whether – the energy needs of the future will be met. The outcome depends on an extraordinarily complex interplay of technology, national interests, and global governance efforts. We turn next to the role of national interests.

Potential Shifts in Great Power Interests

It is challenging, to say the least, to disentangle the complex interests involved in the energy policies of major powers, particularly the two most important: the US and China. It is possible that the core interests of the world's two largest economies are shifting in a way that will help to alleviate gridlock, but the trends are nascent and reversible.

- Both countries produce major quantities of fossil fuels, primarily for domestic consumption, and both are deeply enmeshed in energy-related trade. This suggests that they have a strong interest in protecting the global oil regime that supports the international oil market, yet China is unwilling to participate in the IEA oil stockpile system, a key ingredient in that regime.
- Both have demonstrated their willingness to engage in the use of force to safeguard fossil fuel supplies: current tensions in such volatile areas as the Middle East and the South China Sea reflect the continuing salience of the long-standing zero-sum mindset over fossil fuel access. The US has had decades of oil-related engagement in the Middle East with vast expenditures of money and blood. China's militarization of what it claims is its extensive territory in the South China Sea (despite rival claims from Vietnam, Brunei, Malaysia, Taiwan, Indonesia, and the Philippines) is clearly related to expectations that fossil fuels are plentifully available under the waters.
- Both countries are going green, with major emphasis on the development of renewables along with a determined shift away from reliance on their extensive but dirty domestic coal reserves. Both have demonstrated commitment to global climate goals – arguably it was their 2014 bilateral agreement that broke the logjam on global climate governance. Both have adopted national climate goals that will require real transformation of their domestic energy industries and energy consumption. And as we will see below, both the US and China are leading some of the most significant global

governance initiatives aimed at increasing (decarbonized) energy access for all. The future of some of these policies is now in doubt after the US presidential election of 2016, but much of the momentum in the US is happening at the state, city, and non-state actor level.

This concatenation of conflicting policies can be explained as a combination of domestic disagreements, time lags in the development and deployment of clean energy technologies, and the necessity to keep energy available and affordable in the short term on the very large scale at which both countries operate. Nonetheless, it is hard to determine to what degree national interests have actually shifted. In the case of the US, the change of administration could reverse the current commitment to the energy transition and reinforce the fossil path. China could similarly change course should it prove too difficult to bring about the energy transition while maintaining the public support that is essential to the Chinese Communist Party's grip on power. So shifts in great power interests may be providing one path to GEG for the energy transition – but not yet a reliable one.

Proliferating Institutions and Changing Technocratic Institutions: The Empirical Evidence

The energy governance agenda has moved far beyond the focus on meeting market demand for fossil fuels, to incorporate environmental and poverty concerns. As the agenda for global energy governance has exploded, so has the number and diversity of organizations and institutional arrangements addressing elements of that agenda. Various intergovernmental processes, the IEA, the United Nations, and to some degree the G20 are emerging as central nodes, with a wide variety of other initiatives and even a new IGO on the scene.

On the intergovernmental side, the most notable development is the vastly increased direct contact among energy ministers in such fora as the Clean Energy Ministerial (CEM). Starting in 2010 at the initiative of the US Department of Energy, the CEM now includes 23 countries accounting for some 90 per cent of clean energy investments (Sandalow 2016). It is an unusual inter-ministerial: as its website notes, "The CEM is based on a distributed leadership approach where any government interested in furthering a substantive idea on a clean energy technology or issue is encouraged to identify willing partners and proceed."[6] In just seven years it has had notable impact in spurring action on energy efficiency and renewable energy, bringing technical experts together with policymakers and concentrating on concrete steps rather than broad goals (Sandalow 2016).

Various national governments are promoting other intergovernmental initiatives in support of the energy transition. India, for example, is spearheading the creation of an intergovernmental International Solar Alliance, announced at the Paris climate negotiations in 2015. It is intended "to bring together countries with rich solar potential (along with solar innovators, developers, and financiers) to aggregate demand for solar across member countries, creating a global buyers' market for solar energy, and thereby reducing prices, facilitating the deployment of existing solar technologies at scale, and promoting collaborative solar R&D and capacity" (Ghosh and Chawla 2016).

Intergovernmental organizations, such as the IEA and the UN, are innovating in response to, and sometimes leading, the new agenda for global energy governance. The IEA has worked hard to expand its remit far beyond its initial focus on oil and to ensure that it has access to energy data about all countries, a necessity if it is to maintain its role as a leading global knowledge centre on energy. The Joint Ministerial Declaration under which countries become Association Members builds on two decades of outreach to and cooperation with non-member countries, and describes Association as "a non-binding and progressive relationship that will have an evolving nature and that will serve as a basis for higher levels of mutual cooperation in the future." Along with a set of "implementing agreements" on specific energy technologies open to non-members and the IEA hosting of the International Partnership for Energy Efficiency Cooperation, the intention is clearly to create a "variable geometry" that puts the IEA at the centre of global energy governance far beyond its OECD membership (Van de Graaf 2015). But the agency faces structural challenges in this endeavour, as its membership is limited in its articles of agreement to members of the OECD, and it is a tiny organization, with only some 200 staff at its Paris headquarters (Florini 2011).

The United Nations has taken on energy equity and sustainability as a key area of work. UN Energy was set up in the aftermath of the 2002 World Conference on Sustainable Development in Johannesburg as an (under-resourced) attempt to bring together the assortment of UN bodies that play some role in energy. The Sustainable Energy for All (SE4ALL) initiative, launched in 2011 by UN Secretary-General Ban Ki-moon, has three goals: to ensure universal access to modern energy services, to double the global rate of improvement in energy efficiency, and to double the share of renewable energy in the global energy mix.

The General Assembly declared 2012 the Year of Sustainable Energy for All, and then expanded the effort into a full Decade of Sustainable Energy for All (2014–24) in Resolution 67/215, formally launched by the President of the General Assembly on 5 June 2014. Somewhat confusingly, the term SE4ALL is used to refer both to the set of goals and to the organization, recently spun off as an independent organization but with ties to the UN and the World Bank. And Goal 7 of the Sustainable Development Goals essentially copies the SE4ALL goals.

Having explicit energy goals included in the SDGs is a significant step forward in global energy governance. Energy was overlooked in the SDGs' predecessor, the Millennium Development Goals. The energy goals provide focal points around which policy and implementation efforts can converge. But achieving them will be a challenge.

SE4All focuses on "four enabling Action Areas (that) characterize cross-cutting mechanisms designed to support effective sectoral action and address existing obstacles. They include: Energy Planning & Policies; Business Model & Technology Innovation; Finance & Risk Management; Capacity Building & Knowledge Sharing."[7] SE4ALL has created a tracking system to measure progress towards the three energy goals. Its first evaluation examined data from 2010 to 2012, and concluded that efforts up to that point were inadequate to achieve the goals (IEA and World Bank 2015). The significance of that finding lies mostly in the fact that a baseline for further tracking now exists, given that the political impetus sparked by agreement on the SDGs and on the Paris climate agreement only began to play out in 2015–16.

Another step in the potential GEG pathway towards the energy transition is what has become a rare event on the global stage – the creation of an entirely new intergovernmental organization with close to global membership. The International Renewable Energy Agency (IRENA) was created in 2009 outside of the UN system. Its creation was spurred by Germany's Social Democratic Party (SPD)–Green coalition government, in an initiative led by SPD member Hermann Scheer (Colgan, Keohane and Van de Graaf 2012). Interviews with people involved in the process suggest that Germany was motivated both by dissatisfaction with the renewables work of the IEA up to that point, and by German expectations that IRENA would be headquartered in Bonn – a city looking for a purpose after German reunification moved Germany's capitol to Berlin. In the event, however, Germany was outmanoeuvred by the United Arab Emirates, and IRENA is headquartered in Abu Dhabi with a technical offshoot based in Bonn. IRENA has 149 members and another 27 states in the accession process. It promotes adoption and sustainable use of renewable energy by providing:

"• renewable energy data and statistics;
• advice on best practices, policy development, etc.;
• insights on financial mechanisms and technological expertise;
• capacity-building programmes;
• a large library of publications and other resources" (IRENA 2016).

The G20 role in energy has been limited but may be growing. At the 2009 Pittsburgh Summit, leaders agreed to phase out subsidies for fossil fuels, but reality has not matched rhetoric. Unlike the Group of Seven (G7) industrialized countries, which set a target date of 2025 to phase out such subsidies, the G20 has set no timeline. The 2013 Russian presidency of the G20 saw the introduction of a new Energy Sustainability Working Group, which appears to have accomplished little. However, the 2014 G20 Summit in Brisbane, Australia saw the advent of agreement at the leaders' level on a set of principles regarding energy collaboration[8] and agreement that the G20 process would from then on include an energy ministerial, which met for the first time the following year at the Istanbul G20 summit.

In 2016, China used its chairmanship to introduce a connection between finance (the G20's historical strength) and the energy/ sustainability agenda, setting up a Green Finance Study Group in the G20's finance ministers' track to consider how financial markets can support sustainability – which largely means investment in sustainable energy. Revamping and expanding the energy infrastructure underpinning modern civilization will not be an inexpensive undertaking. It will require both public and private finance, and quite a lot of both. The rules and norms governing that finance strongly shape how energy is produced and to whom it is provided. It is thus a promising step that the 2016 Hangzhou Summit communiqué featured a paragraph on green finance, one that represents progress towards engaging the finance community in the energy and sustainability sets of issues (G20 Research Group 2016: para. 21). As of this writing, it appears that Germany, 2017 chair of the G20, will take this agenda forward.

That initiative in the G20 context arose from a process sponsored by United Nations Environment (UNEP), the Inquiry into the Design of a Sustainable Financial System. The Inquiry process began in January 2014 as a two-year investigation of what steps governments around the world were taking to align financial regulatory processes with the increasingly compelling sustainability agenda. It was at the World Bank/IMF annual meeting in October 2015 where the Inquiry's first report was released that China announced it would establish the Green Finance Study Group. The UNEP Inquiry team became the secretariat for the G20 Study Group. And UNEP continues to be a driving force in this agenda, engaging actors from the public and private sectors around the world, from the UN and the IMF to individual companies and national governments.

Beyond these large IGO and state-centric processes, an explosion of subnational, private sector, civil society, and hybrid initiatives focuses on fostering the energy transition. Many are transnational multi-sector partnerships, a rapidly growing form of global governance, especially since the 2002 World Summit on Sustainable Development in Johannesburg. That UN summit led to the creation of more than 300 formally registered partnerships, including dozens focused on energy (Szulecki, Pattberg and Biermann 2011: 714).

Some partnerships promote renewable energy and/or energy efficiency, such as REN-21 and the Renewable Energy and Energy Efficiency Partnership. Others are energy-related information disclosure programmes, usually voluntary, that aim to make markets function more efficiently, induce private actors (particularly corporations) to internalize externalities even in the absence of enforceable regulations, and/or improve democratic processes. Such initiatives as the Carbon Disclosure Project, the Extractive Industries Transparency Initiative, and the Global Reporting Initiative's G4 sector disclosures for electric utilities all aim to change behaviour by inducing actors to reveal information in various forms (Florini and Saleem 2011; Sovacool et al. 2016).

Most recently, governments and private actors have coordinated on steps to provide significant funding towards the achievement of the energy transition. COP21 to the UNFCCC held in Paris in late 2015 saw the announcement of major initiatives intended to foster a more rapid technological revolution in energy. Under the rubric Mission Innovation, US President Barack Obama and his counterparts from 19 other countries pledged to double their investment in clean energy R&D over the next five years, which would add about another US$10 billion annually. The countries participating in Mission Innovation include the biggest and most rapidly growing energy consumers (China, India, Indonesia and Brazil), countries with high penetration of renewables in their power sectors (Canada, Norway, Denmark, Brazil, Chile and Germany), and some of the largest oil and gas producers (not only the US but also Saudi Arabia, the United Arab Emirates, Mexico and Norway). In an unusually large-scale public–private partnership,

COP21 also saw the simultaneous announcement by Bill Gates and 27 other wealthy investors of the formation of the Breakthrough Energy Coalition, in which the investors commit to investing in the clean energy technologies developed under Mission Innovation to move them from the laboratory to the marketplace, and to tolerate longer timelines and higher risks than clean energy typically enjoys – a stated goal of "patient but transformational" investment (Sandalow 2015).

Global energy governance is about more than energy sources. Expanding the use of many green energy sources (hydropower, some types of solar, some wind facilities) also requires attention to cross-border connectivity and markets so that fluctuations in intermittent sources can be balanced out. This is particularly true when talking about green but relatively large-scale centralized energy sources such as concentrated solar, which could take advantage of the maturing technology for ultra-high voltage transmission technology at the regional level. The challenges are both technical and political, requiring alignment of regulation and markets.

There are a variety of efforts underway, particularly in Asia. The establishment of the non-profit Global Energy Interconnection Development and Cooperation Organization in Beijing in 2016 brought together officials and entrepreneurs from China, South Korea, Russia, and Japan with the avowed goal of linking grids to provide electricity from renewables (Hanley 2016). Whether the mechanics and politics of this vision are achievable remains unclear (Chang and Li 2013). Similarly, the ASEAN vision for power grid interconnection and energy trade, for example, may find that achieving meaningful integration is quite a challenge. ASEAN is still in the stage of beginning to model cost–benefit assessments of the new technologies and energy demands that would justify interconnections, and has yet to set priorities for which specific interconnections to invest in first. Most difficult of all will be addressing the institutional and legal barriers, and creating the market design to allow electricity trading. But it is possible to make progress: in some areas, such as the Nordic region and continental Europe, these things are happening.

Where Next: Evaluating Institutional Change as a Pathway beyond Gridlock

Global energy has changed dramatically in recent years. As Christoph Frei, Secretary-General of the World Energy Council, noted in 2015,

Large amounts of unconventional oil and gas are produced outside of OPEC countries, notably in North America; the renewables supply is building up in the sun-rich Middle East and Africa; the global demand centre is shifting from OECD to Asia; and technology at competitive costs is produced in countries with low labour costs including China and other emerging economies. This changing energy map has profound regional and geostrategic implications. International institutions related to energy, trade, or safety need to adapt or will fail to credibly pursue the tasks they were created to fulfil. (World Energy Council 2015: 3)

Moreover, ideas about what global energy governance should aim to achieve have expanded tremendously. There are now concrete and widely shared goals, in the form of Sustainable Development Goal 7 and the goals agreed at Paris in the December 2015 COP21. Multilateral processes such as the Clean Energy Ministerial and the International Solar Alliance are coming into their own or showing real potential. Some of the existing intergovernmental organizations dealing with energy, particularly the International Energy Agency, are making significant efforts to reconfigure themselves to keep up with rapidly shifting energy realities, as are other IGOs with broader remits that include energy-related issues. The G20 process, both through its explicitly energy-focused work (including the Energy Sustainability Working Group and the agreement to phase out fossil fuel subsidies) and in its finance track, is engaging ever more deeply in the fundamental issues of global energy governance.

Yet there is still a mismatch between agreements to make progress on various energy goals and governance mechanisms that make it possible for that progress to happen. Although the International Energy Agency is struggling heroically to provide those concrete mechanisms, it remains a tiny organization with limited resources, and cannot plausibly convert itself into a comprehensive overseer of the desperately needed changes in the global energy system. The G20 agreement in 2009 to reduce subsidies to fossil fuels unfortunately lacked any mechanisms to help countries deal with the technical, political, and economic challenges of making such reforms. Big sweeping recommendations are of much less use than concrete mechanisms.

And it is not clear how the various pieces of this dizzying array of initiatives, actors, and processes do or can fit together. At every stage of collective action – agenda-setting, negotiation, implementation, monitoring, enforcement – multiple authorities are putting forward demands. With so many relatively new and untested governance approaches underway, it is not clear which of the competing claims for legitimacy and authority will stand the test of time. And as fossil fuels continue to dominate current energy provision, zero-sum conflicts over these resources in locations from the Middle East to the South China Sea continue to threaten international peace and security, posing a significant global governance challenge.

Nor is it clear that the financing needed to achieve the SDG energy goals – which themselves are just stepping stones to a larger transition from a world in which 85 per cent of energy comes from fossil fuels – will materialize. According to World Bank estimates, for example, universal access to electricity and clean cooking fuels would require investment of about US$48 billion a year to 2030, roughly a fivefold increase (Neal 2012). To double the share of renewable energy in the global mix from 15 per cent to 30 per cent will require both direct investments and substantial policy and regulatory changes, including drastic cuts in fossil fuel subsidies.

Moreover, key issues are not addressed in any meaningful way. Despite considerable evidence of the causal connection between oil and conflict, both civil and interstate, no global governance process addresses the connection between oil and international security (Van de Graaf and Colgan 2016). And despite attention brought by the UN Principles on Business and Human Rights to the high level of human rights violations endemic in fossil fuel extraction, there is no "blood oil" counterpart to the "blood diamonds" structure of the Kimberly Process to certify whether oil that enters international trade has been produced in a way that protects human rights (Van de Graaf and Colgan 2016; Ruggie 2006).

Conclusion

Is global energy governance gridlocked? In part, no. Collective action is happening with regard to agenda-setting and negotiation involving most key actors. The combination of the 2015 Sustainable Development Goals and the 2015 Paris agreement on climate change together have codified an agenda that has been emerging for years: Global energy governance needs to simultaneously ensure the provision of basic energy services to everyone in a reliable and affordable manner, while simultaneously drastically reducing the carbon intensity of the sector. Existing institutions, from the IEA to the G20 to the UN, have responded with major initiatives. A plethora of wholly new organizations, networks, and ventures of all types have arisen in the past decade, such as the Clean Energy Ministerial, IRENA, the

International Solar Alliance, SE4ALL, and the Breakthrough Energy Coalition. Progress towards the creation of rule systems and institutions that foster a transition to sustainable energy for all is clearly happening.

But the paucity of concrete results to date suggest that some degree of gridlock remains, as impediments from inertia and vested interests are constraining the achievement of those goals. Most obviously, geopolitical tensions in the South China Sea and the Middle East make clear that the zero-sum mindset long associated with oil supply has not gone away. The G20's inability to make serious progress on removal of fossil fuel subsidies, despite agreement reached in 2009, is just one indicator of the difficulties of reformulating the fossil-based infrastructure and the financing systems that support it. Fossil fuel producers and others who benefit from the current energy system have fundamentally different interests, at least in the relatively short term, from those who want to foster a rapid energy transition.

Yet arguably GEG is responding to the multiple challenges of new fuel sources, issues, and technologies with a burst of institutional creativity. This fragmented system is not necessarily a problem, as long as the various bits are pulling in more or less the same direction. Global energy governance needs to facilitate nothing less than the complete transformation of what is currently a fossil fuel-based global economy – its production, transport, and built infrastructure. As is sometimes said of progress on the closely related issue of climate change, what is needed isn't a silver bullet, but silver buckshot – many changes driven by many initiatives, all aiming in the same general direction but striking multiple targets.

Fragmentation is not inherently a flaw in governance. Decentralized decision-making can allow expertise and local knowledge to be put to good use in solving specific problems. It is incoherence that is the problem. Policy incoherence has been a significant problem for energy. But in the past few years, there has been significant progress in developing a conceptual frame around which coherence could grow, despite the ever more fragmented institutional structures. As noted above, we have seen the beginnings of a set of common goals in the energy realm, developed in part through the UN Sustainable Development Goals process and in part through the climate negotiations. It is too soon to know whether efforts like SE4ALL to bring coherence to the fragmented energy governance scene will have significant impact.

Overall, pathways beyond gridlock clearly exist. Major powers and existing IGOs, from the G20 to the IEA to the UN, have shifted focus at least in part. New organizations (IRENA) and funding channels (Mission Innovation, Breakthrough Energy Coalition) are emerging. All told, we see meaningful momentum for multiple pathways beyond gridlock in global energy governance. These are not fixing the existing gridlock problems in fossil fuel governance. Instead, we see signs of many actors building on technological developments and on global consensus on the need for change as reflected in the 2015 Paris climate agreement and the SDGs. They are laying what could be the groundwork for bypassing fossils, creating a wholly new, far more decentralized and flexible set of systems for providing affordable, reliable, and clean energy services around the world. Momentum is not yet transformation. But the pathways are visible.

7

Humanitarianism

Stagnation, Fragmentation and Possibilities

Kyle McNally and James Orbinski

At its core, humanitarianism is concerned with providing assistance and protection to the most vulnerable people in the world in situations of war or crisis. Humanitarian action requires governance at the global and local levels. While humanitarianism as a concept and practice is difficult to define in concrete operational terms, and may be as old as humanity itself, it is possible to trace humanitarian action as a growing subject of global governance from the nineteenth to the twenty-first century. Humanitarianism can implicate virtually all sectors of global governance, sometimes in very direct ways (e.g. in the operations of the UN Office for the Coordination of Humanitarian Affairs (OCHA)), and at other times in indirect ways (e.g. via development banks, the UN Security Council, etc.).

Humanitarian governance is failing, especially at the global level. The most vulnerable groups are not receiving the assistance and protection they need, despite the potential for it to be delivered. This gap between what is possible and what is actual defines the humanitarian failures of the twenty-first century.

This chapter attempts to understand the "pathways through or beyond" gridlock proposed in the book's introduction. It begins by presenting a brief overview of humanitarianism as global policy, with an emphasis on governance at the multilateral level. The chapter then addresses the contemporary humanitarian context and takes forced migration of refugees and internally displaced persons as a specific focus of attention. It employs the *Gridlock* framework to consider how the challenges and failures in humanitarianism may be in line with broader systemic challenges of global governance as a whole. The chapter concludes with an account of potential pathways through or beyond gridlock – using examples of past successes and breakthroughs (however marginal) to understand what might lead to future progress and enhanced humanitarian action. The pathways out of gridlock considered here include (a) multiple, diverse organizations and institutions coalescing around common goals/norms, (b) innovative leadership as a reaction to gridlock, and (c) civil society coalitions with reformist states.

Humanitarianism as Global Policy

Humanitarianism is victim-centred, and grounded in an intention that seeks to ensure material assistance and political protection for the most vulnerable people in the world at any given time (see Terry 2002; Orbinski 2008; Barnett 2011). It has progressed throughout the postwar decades to become a core agenda item in the global governance system writ large (see Barnett 2014). Accordingly, it is useful to trace the development of humanitarian action since World War II, leading to the current landscape of institutions and actors at play today.

Rise of multilateral humanitarianism

During the Cold War, the principles of humanitarian action were largely endorsed and supported from within the Western-dominated post–World War II liberal institutional world order, and became recognized as global norms. These principles have been most clearly and consistently articulated by the International Committee of the Red Cross (ICRC) as Humanity, Dignity, Independence, Neutrality, and Impartiality. While normative, in many cases humanitarian action and its principles were honoured not in practice, but "in the breach." Also during this period, civil society organizations – especially Western-based transnational civil society organizations – blossomed from their early twentieth-century origins and emerged as dominant actors and partners with UN agencies both in humanitarian relief during war and in pursuit of development. The ICRC deserves special mention as a hybrid of both a multilateral para-statal organization and a civil society movement rooted in nationally based and supported associations. Notably too, the ICRC is the guardian and builder of international humanitarian law, which since 1864 can be characterized as an iterative process responsive to changes in the nature and practice of war and conflict.

In the post–Cold War period, under the American-led global political and economic system, state security concerns increasingly fused with humanitarian considerations. As countries saw the security implications of emerging infectious diseases and large, destabilizing refugee movements – and under pressure from largely Western-based but universally aspirant transnational civil society organizations – the broader political context increasingly took account of humanitarian concerns and issues. This shift gradually formalized through the emerging Human Security agenda of the 1990s and early twenty-first century (see Kaldor 2012). This agenda emerged in the context of the famine, civil war and ongoing state failure of Somalia, South Sudan and the Democratic Republic of Congo; growing intra-state conflict; war crimes, crimes against humanity and genocide in the former Yugoslavia and Rwanda; and the AIDS, tuberculosis and malaria epidemics which disproportionately affected the developing world but which also posed very real threats of varying types and degrees beyond.

Thus, convergent with state security interests, and in the wake of elevated humanitarian sentiment around a failure to respond to remediable large-scale human suffering in conditions of war, genocide and infectious disease, the UN Office for the Coordination of Humanitarian Affairs was formed following the Kurdish refugee crisis during the First Gulf War; the Joint United Nations Programme on HIV/AIDS (UNAIDS) was formed, as was the Global Fund for AIDS, Tuberculosis and Malaria; the Rome Statute was signed forming the International Criminal Court (ICC 2002); and the Responsibility to Protect (R2P) doctrine was promoted and soon adopted after the bombing campaign in Kosovo led by the North Atlantic Treaty Organization (NATO) (a campaign not legitimized by the UN Security Council). Humanitarianism thus became increasingly institutionalized, with new rules and organizations emerging. This process of institutionalization included both intergovernmental agencies (such as OCHA), but also non-governmental coalitions and networks that would help define humanitarian standards in contemporary context(s). Leading examples of the latter include the Sphere project (established in 1997), which brings together practitioners and attempts to set common principles and standards in humanitarian response; the Good Humanitarian Donorship framework, which seeks to enhance donor accountability; as well as the Centre for Education and Research in Humanitarian Action, which offers a range of trainings for actors in the humanitarian sector, to name a few.

The humanitarian system today is a complex network of intercon-nected institutional and operational bodies, with the core actors including UN humanitarian agencies, the Red Cross and Red Crescent movements, and a fluid but well-defined network of international NGOs and intergovernmental organizations. Most recent estimates suggest that there are 4,480 humanitarian organizations operating across the world (Stoddard et al. 2015). By 2014, the development and humanitarian sectors together accounted for more than US$18 billion of humanitarian assistance from national governments (at con-stant 2013 prices), spread across a vast network of recipient country governments, international organizations and civil society actors (Development Initiatives 2017). With the projected increase in con-flicts, natural disasters and epidemics, OCHA in 2013 recognized that there would continue to be a growing demand for a professional humanitarian workforce.

In sum, the growth of the humanitarian system and its gradual con-vergence with largely Western-led military and development agendas, and the burgeoning competitive humanitarian marketplace, have been concomitant and in many circumstances convergent with the postwar emergence of a legal human rights regime, the emergence of the United Nations and its humanitarian-oriented multilateral agen-cies, political decolonization movements, and the international devel-opment paradigm/project.

Contemporary Humanitarian Context

Although the international humanitarian system is larger than ever in terms of financial and human resources, it is manifestly failing to meet global humanitarian needs. New types of crises and disasters have meant more people in need, and have hampered response efforts in a situation with already limited humanitarian resources. In 2015, 125 million people in 37 countries were in need of humanitarian assis-tance or protection. Of these, only 88 million were getting any form of support, and much of this was well below established minimal norms and practices. While funding has increased and is more coordinated and accountable, there is a profound mismatch between growing needs and donor funds provided. OCHA's 2016 *World Humanitarian Data and Trends* report stated that overall needs and requirements increased, with funding requirements set at $19.3 billion and a 55 per cent funding gap (OCHA 2016). Given the trends found in the humanitarian sector, and in forced migration in particular, there is no reason to believe that the gap will not continue to widen in coming years.

Increasing refugee and forced migration flows, violent extremism, a rise in regional wars and conflicts as well as climate-related disasters have changed the global humanitarian landscape. In 2015 the ICRC said: "The incapacity of the international system to maintain peace and security has, among other things, had the effect of shifting the focus of international engagement from conflict resolution to humanitarian activities" (2015: 6); "The international humanitarian sector is at risk of reaching breaking point. The ICRC and other impartial humanitarian organizations are facing humanitarian needs on an epic scale, in an unprecedented number of concurrent crises around the world. The gap between those needs and the ability of humanitarian actors to meet them is impossible to bridge" (2015: 6).

Humanitarian needs in the world are changing and increasing. Emergencies today are regionalizing and affect larger numbers of people who require humanitarian assistance but whose principal need is humanitarian protection because they are directly targeted or are forced to migrate (Stoddard et al. 2015). Forced migration is intimately linked to violent conflict, but also to other often related issues such as health emergencies, poverty and starvation, climate-related migration, as well as development-induced displacement.

Forced migration

While a vast majority of forced migrants are in the developing world, with refugees and asylum seekers attempting access by land or sea to Europe by the hundreds of thousands, forced migration is now recognized as a global crisis. Thousands of men, women and children drowned in 2015 and 2016 while fleeing knowingly into dangerous Mediterranean waters. Having given over their safety to human smugglers, they sought refuge in an uncertain fate, from a known fate that is certainly repressive. Each dead person is the definition of a refugee. That this must be stated illuminates just how far humanitarianism and human rights have penetrated beyond the "Never Again" of the Holocaust. The *Economist* declared on its 27 April 2015 cover: "Europe's Boat People (are) a Moral and Political Disgrace" for Europe and the world. Its editorial stated that "after the crimes of the second world war, countries made solemn undertakings never again to abandon innocent people to persecution and conflict.... the plight of Europe's boat people...exposes the failings of countries with a duty to shelter them. In Europe that starts with a breakdown of ethics" (Economist 2015).

Forced migration is examined in the remainder of this chapter as a case study that may potentially illuminate *Gridlock* pathways, as well those pathways that might nudge humanitarian governance through or beyond the current governance challenges.

Those who are forced to migrate are typically designated as either refugees or internally displaced persons (IDPs). The former refers to those people who have been forced to flee their country because of persecution, war, or violence. A refugee has crossed an internationally recognized border because of a well-founded fear of persecution for reasons of race, religion, nationality, political opinion or membership in a particular social group (UNHCR 2010). By contrast, the term IDP refers to

> Persons or groups of persons who have been forced or obliged to flee or to leave their homes or places of habitual residence, in particular as a result of or in order to avoid the effects of armed conflict, situations of generalized violence, violations of human rights or natural or man-made disasters, and *who have not crossed an internationally recognized State border*. (OCHA 2004: 1, emphasis added)

These differences are significant and will be returned to in the sections that follow addressing how governance has developed in relation to these groups, including what constitutes legal and/or normative obligations to provide assistance and protection to said groups. Before going into the governance specifics, however, it is important to understand the scale of forced migration as a whole.

The most recent figures surrounding forced migration were compiled by the report of the United Nations High Commissioner for Refugees (UNHCR, the UN Refugee Agency) from June 2016, and the findings it portrays are dismal. In the words of UN Secretary-General Ban Ki-moon, they demonstrate not just a crisis of numbers, but also a crisis of solidarity (UNHCR 2016: 5). At the end of 2015, there were 65.3 million forcibly displaced people worldwide, more than at any time since the end of World War II (the period when global humanitarian institutions were formed under the aegis of the United Nations and in relation to the relatively long-established ICRC). This includes 21.3 million refugees, 40.8 million people internally displaced within their country and 3.2 million people still seeking asylum outside their country (2016: 2). To put this into perspective, "one out of every 113 people globally is forcibly displaced from their homes." An estimated 12.4 million people were newly displaced due to conflict or persecution in 2015. This included 8.6 million individuals displaced within the borders of their own country and 1.8 million newly displaced refugees. Children below 18 years of age constituted about half of the refugee population in 2015 (up from 41 per cent in 2009) (2016: 3).

The refugee crisis has brought worldwide attention to the issue of forced migration, nowhere more pronounced than for Europe since 2012 (see Frontex 2014). However, recalling the refugee-specific figures above, it is important to note that this is only one side of the forced migration coin, so to speak. Internal displacement – those people displaced but who have not crossed an internationally recognized border – are now more than double the number of refugees globally. These are individuals displaced, typically for the same reasons as refugees, and with the same needs as refugees, but, with little if any of the protection and assistance legally afforded to refugees because they have not made their way across a border (see section below). In many cases, they wait anxiously on the wrong side of this line in the sand, and therefore do not qualify for the same protections offered by international refugee law.

Adding to this complexity, displacement today takes many forms and is the result of diverse drivers and causes. As referred to above, violent conflict remains a, if not the, primary driver of forced migration, but it is not the only one. Those individuals that cross a border and seek asylum may do so because of economic strife and inability to feed themselves or their family. And yet, these individuals may not be granted the coveted refugee status and therefore become designated as "economic migrants." Alternatively, and increasingly, people may be displaced because of natural disasters – which may be linked to climate change. To be clear, the empirical link between climate change and migration is not linear, but rather a cascade effect of many variables. Yet many experts highlight this as a growing concern and a potential crisis of epic proportions (see Brown 2008).

In-depth analysis of the full range of these issues is beyond the scope of this current chapter. While some will be addressed more thoroughly by other authors in this volume, the point to be taken here is that the causes are diverse and can cascade and interact in complex ways to cause humanitarian crises.

Global governance of forced migration

Forced migration refers to the coercive or otherwise involuntary movement of peoples from their place of habitual residence (hence, displacement). As the humanitarian operations of global govern-ance actors and agencies grew in the postwar years, so too did their attention towards forced migration, with refugees being the primary focal point.

While there are certainly elements of refugee protection and assis-tance that pre-date World War II, the current governance regime finds its roots in the postwar institutional landscape. Indeed, the right to asylum is stated most simply in the Universal Declaration of Human Rights, Article 14, paragraph 1, where it is proclaimed that "Everyone has the right to seek and to enjoy in other countries asylum from persecution." The 1951 Convention Relating to the Status of Refugees set out the early, albeit limited, obligations of the international com-munity in providing assistance and protection to refugees, but the geographical and temporal limitations that were embedded in this Convention were removed in the 1967 Protocol Relating to the Status of Refugees. Put simply, the body of international refugee law that was developed called upon states to provide necessary protections and assistance to those fleeing persecution. This was inscribed in positivis-tic legal codes, but also became an embedded feature in the broader normative underpinning of the postwar institutional order.

Pierre Hassner provides one of the most compelling defences of this framework by stating that "It is precisely because [refugees] are citi-zens of nowhere that they are potential citizens of the world" (1998: 274). This is surely a noble principle that to a significant degree guided state and international behaviour in the postwar period. Notably, in the earliest days of the refugee regime this dimension of governance stood in relative isolation from many other areas of global policy (Betts 2010). However, as the postwar order developed and was codi-fied, refugee governance would come to overlap with various other sectors in significant ways until it became an entrenched feature of this institutional landscape.

While the refugee regime that developed in the wake of World War II began as somewhat of a governance silo, over time it would come to engage with various other governance regimes more and more, becoming a fully embedded and overlapping feature of global governance as a whole. What was once a silo of governance in many respects, now intersects with core security governance bodies such as the UN Security Council, mobility and labour organizations such as the International Organization for Migration, as well as human rights agencies and numerous legal mechanisms (see Betts 2010). Accordingly, and in line with the *Gridlock* theory, it is possible to see how refugee governance benefited from the postwar waves of institutional growth and codification. This is made even more complex by the fact that internal displacement policy is now also a central feature of forced migration governance. While Betts places IDP protection somewhere between the humanitarian and refugee regimes, in practice it also overlaps with at least the human rights regime as well. This is due to the fact that the international community has developed a set of norms aimed at enhancing the assistance and protection to IDPs, entitled the *Guiding Principles on Internal Displacement* (OCHA 2004). These principles splice together international humanitarian law, human rights law and refugee law (by analogy) in order to define more clearly the responsibilities of the international community, states and non-state actors in relation to IDPs (see below).

While the principles of humanitarian protection became embedded features of the postwar order, the practices of refugee assistance eroded over time as states became less and less willing to be active and benevolent partners in forced migration governance. Hassner captured well the ironic reality that developed in the post–Cold War era: "The most paradoxical result of this situation is that every humanitarian organization wants to broaden the definition of refugees, while every host country government wants to narrow it" (1998: 275).

Humanitarian Governance Failures: Forced Migration and Gridlock in Focus

Though the humanitarian system has evolved over the postwar period through to today, it is unfit to respond to current and future global needs for humanitarian assistance, and especially for humanitarian protection. "Gridlock" is one of the main reasons (though not the only one) for this failure. The "second-order" reasons articulated by Hale, Held and Young (2013) of multipolarity, harder problems, institutional inertia and fragmentation help illuminate some of the major issues in global governance of humanitarianism and forced migration today, with specific emphasis placed on harder problems as a primary driver and explanatory trend, with the other three included throughout as compounding factors.

Contemporary forced migration as a second-order cooperation problem

The *Gridlock* framework applied here is helpful in several key respects. First, it facilitates an analysis of contemporary forced migration governance challenges as "second-order" cooperation challenges, emerging from successive waves of postwar institutionalization. Second, it provides a set of underlying dynamics, each with their own set of causal mechanisms, that come together and explain what now inhibits more effective governance. Third, it allows for the interplay of these dimensions to be applied in an aggregated whole, creating greater coherence overall.

The United Nations system, reflecting the post–World War II global order, remains the main actor in global governance of humanitarianism and therefore also of forced migration policy. The UN structure and concomitant institutions were set up, in many ways, to preserve and perpetuate a global political order which was Western-centric and which forefronted Western interests (see Held 2004). While the mid-twentieth-century UN architecture after World War II has been somewhat adaptive, it has remained largely unchanged, especially in the context of humanitarianism. Accordingly, it now responds to twenty-first-century challenges with increasing incoherence, and impotence. At the very least, it is unable to respond because of structural constraints that stem from dominant powers retaining disproportionate control over policy and resources in the primary institutional settings. This may be understood as a form of inertia. On the one hand, it is possible to see institutional innovation, growth and adaptation; but on the other hand, a vast majority of these developments have occurred in the wider UN system – where institutional inertia is endemic.

Even with Kofi Annan's proactive 2001 UN Reform Agenda, building new or reforming old UN institutions never achieved meaningful implementation. For instance, the largest and possibly most powerful humanitarian agency, the UNHCR, was established in 1950 to deal with the aftermath of a European refugee crisis in the wake of World War II. It was initially established with the mandate of working for three years to solve the crisis, after which it was to disband (UNHCR 2017). Today, more than 60 years later, it continues to function, but now with a permanent and global mandate (see Hyndman 2000). The UNHCR's mandate, then and now, is about refugees per se. Yet, given the data presented above, it is clear that the forced migration challenges facing the world are drastically unbalanced, with those internally displaced far outstripping the number of refugees worldwide (IDMC 2015). Responding to this trend, the UNHCR has expanded its operational activities to focus increasingly on IDPs. In 1995 the UNHCR provided assistance/protection to only 4.3 million IDPs; by 2005 this number had modestly risen to 6.6 million; yet by 2015 the

UNHCR was assisting and/or protecting 37.5 million people internally displaced.

On the surface, this evolving profile of activity may present a promising picture. Indeed, the UNHCR does provide essential assistance and protection to millions of IDPs. But this is neither sufficient nor sustainable in the current model of forced migration governance. At the most basic level, the UNHCR's mandate has remained fundamentally the same. This makes the assistance and protection offered to IDPs uncertain, unpredictable and vulnerable to the whims of aggressor states, which are often the drivers of displacement in the first place. Despite the best of intentions, and the operational stretching of the mandate, the underlying strictures of refugee assistance and protection remain rigid and no longer in line with the reality of forced migration in the twenty-first century.

Given the scale and complexity of the forced migration crisis today, the current landscape of humanitarian crises can be described as a definitive "harder problem" within the *Gridlock* framework. The nature of forced migration has changed dramatically since the postwar UN institutions were created. In the 1950s, the legal definition of a refugee was established. This label, legalistic or not, became a symbol over the decades that would signal an international responsibility and obligation to help those making legitimate asylum claims. Recalling the obligations set out under international refugee law, there is an established standard for states and the international community at large to provide protection and assistance to people who are forced to migrate. While this principle remains intact, in practice it is lacking in critical respects.

Cohen and Deng argue that with the end of the Cold War, the incentive structure to accept refugee flows changed. Whereas before there was some incentive to accept asylum seekers as refugees, in the post–Cold War era this incentive diminished (1998a and 1998b). In particular, the bipolar tension between the US and the Soviet Union created a system wherein those fleeing Soviet rule or influence were assigned a kind of "ideological value," demonstrating the dominance and success of the West; a similar trend could be seen in Vietnam's 1.3 million "boat people" who sought Western asylum in the 1970s and 1980s (Economist 2001). In the absence of the bipolar tensions of the Cold War, increased air travel, and shifting patterns of conflict, the commitment to accept refugees diminished significantly.

In place of this commitment came a "litany of measures employed by such states to undermine the refugee protection regime during the last two decades such as visa requirements on the nationals of refugee-producing states, carrier sanctions, burden-shifting arrangements, so-called 'safe country' lists and forcible interdiction of refugees at frontiers and in international waters" (Bagshaw 2005: 74). This is now evident across the world, from razor fences lining the eastern European border, to Operation Sophia in the Mediterranean, to off-shore containment sites in Australia, and to cash transfers from Italy to Sudan to bolster border controls. While such "containment policies" abound, it follows that the displacement patterns observed today are increasingly characterized by internal displacement.

Until very recently the term refugee was casually used synonymously with IDP. Even US President George W. Bush referred to internally displaced persons as "internal refugees" (Orchard 2010). This conflation between refugees and those internally displaced is neither acceptable nor sufficient today. The plights and causal conditions of IDPs are now core to understanding the forced migration debate. While these are of deep concern for all practitioners involved in this area, they warrant little more than a passing mention in much of the popular discourse that is associated with contemporary refugee issues. And yet, as described earlier, the numbers of IDPs at the time of writing is more than double the number of refugees in the world (also IDMC 2015).

While "containment policies" proliferate, IDPs remain trapped, literally and figuratively, within the walls of state sovereignty and national authority. In this sense, forced migration is a definitive "harder problem." The problem has fundamentally changed since the immediate postwar years and is not solved by the refugee laws and policies established in the Cold War era. States have "pushed back" against forced migrants, and found ways to abdicate their responsibilities. In this sense, the current refugee crisis constitutes a second-order cooperation problem resulting from previous periods of successful institutionalization – in this context, defined by the entrenchment of refugee law that states now seek to circumvent.

For those willing, and indeed able, to cross an internationally recognized border, achieving official refugee status has become much more difficult. Germany, once a champion of refugee protection, has – along with much of Europe – sought to restrict the numbers of refugees permitted for resettlement (see Czuczka 2016). Similarly, the US is on a downward trend of assistance and protection provision, to be made more stark under a Trump presidency (Siegfried 2016). The result is a completely disproportionate distribution of refugees, with countries that are neighbours to a crisis shouldering an unrealistic burden in relation to those states often with greater resources (but lacking the political will) to provide adequate assistance and protection. For example, Turkey accepted 2.5 million Syrian refugees in 2015 alone (see UNHCR 2016).

This refugee crisis is, accordingly, one of the drivers for the growing crisis of internal displacement. And here, the nature of the problem is necessarily "harder" per se. What makes internal displacement harder, in particular, is the intractable issue of state sovereignty. As IDPs have not crossed an internationally recognized border, they remain under the purview of the states in which they habitually reside. In ideal scenarios, these are the states that are tasked with primary responsibility for providing assistance and protection to such populations; however, in practice, it is often the case that such states are in fact the aggressors and perpetrators of internal displacement in the first place (ranging from Syria to Sudan, from Kenya to Sri Lanka, and so on). The proscriptive dimensions of state sovereignty inhibit greater international community engagement. Despite the increased activity and attention paid to IDPs, theirs is a plight glaringly underserved and acutely vulnerable.

In addition to the challenges explained above, contemporary forced migration – both refugee based and in relation to IDPs – is made ever "harder" by the fact that new forms of displacement are emerging alongside violent conflict. Climate change is a case in point, representing a challenge already manifesting itself, but also a latent crisis looming on the horizon. Without delving into detailed analysis, some leading projections are stark: according to the UN Environment Programme, there could be 50 million "environmental refugees" by 2060 in Africa alone (Brown 2008). Even more profoundly, Christian Aid said in 2007 that close to 1 billion people could be permanently displaced by 2050, with climate change being a key driver in such forced migration (Brown 2008). What is already a harder problem for global governance bodies will surely only grow *harder* in the future.

There is no single understanding of humanitarianism in terms of gridlock. However, elements of gridlock are evident across humanitarianism as a whole and specifically in relation to forced migration, particularly concerning harder problems. It is also important to attempt an understanding of what has led to progress in the past, and particularly in a way that it might shine a light on what could be possible in the future. This is the focus for the next section of this chapter.

Pathways through Gridlock for Forced Migration

The *Beyond Gridlock* study has developed a set of "pathways" beyond or through gridlock that, despite representing only marginal progress to date, may anticipate potential pathways for greater progress in the future. It is insufficient to identify a set of prescriptive observations about what is needed if these are not grounded in the realm of what is possible. By linking the past and potential together, the speculative nature of these claims can be grounded and move beyond the realm of advocacy. Of the different pathways outlined in the introduction to this book, and operationalized throughout, three stand out as relevant for this chapter (see table 7.1):

Refugees and asylum seekers

It is important here not to overstate any progress in forced migration governance. That said, the theoretical contributions of *Gridlock* help us to understand the growth of global governance in this field, first as a

Table 7.1 Pathways out of gridlock in forced migration

PATHWAY	EFFECT	MECHANISM
Refugee governance		
Multiple, diverse organizations and institutions coalesce around common goals/norms	Realignment of UN mandates as well as plurilateral governance initiatives	M1: An additive and expansionary context M2: Diffusion/ entrenchment of common principles, norms, and goals
Innovative leadership as a reaction to gridlock	State leadership (e.g. Sweden; earlier, Germany)	M1: Gridlock provokes entrepreneurial responses (e.g. norm entrepreneurship)
Internal displacement governance		
Civil society coalitions with reformist states	Civil society leadership creating a normative framework for assistance and protection for IDPs	M1: Formation of coalitions across state–civil society boundaries

product of successive and successful waves of institutionalization (see above) by establishing international refugee law and entrenching the UNHCR in the multilateral order. Additionally, the normative underpinning of the postwar order created the governance space for established institutions to take on greater roles, and for new institutions to be created directly in response to forced migration and humanitarian issues (e.g. the creation of the OCHA, and the proliferation and growth of multitudes of civil society groups).

To the extent that progress may be identified in relation to refugee and asylum policies, the fact that the issue of forced migration has become a focus for many different organizations, and that it has been the source of re-energized activity for some, demonstrates the common and diverse base that is now focused on this issue. Forced migration in today's world has reshaped the activities of the UNHCR and has expanded the activity of many other UN agencies as well as of other relevant stakeholders. In this sense, there are common norms surrounding displacement which have come to inform wider policy, for both refugees and IDPs alike. For example, within the last ten years the World Bank has taken on issues of state fragility and resilience, and directly addressed forced migration (World Bank 2011b); the WHO, Food and Agriculture Organization, International Organization for Migration, and World Food Programme have all become cluster leads in the coordination of humanitarian response (OCHA 2017); and new norms – however imperfect – such as R2P have been developed, intimately linked to forced migration issues (Davies and Glanville 2010). In addition to the (inter)governmental actions and innovations focused on forced migration, a wide network of civil society organizations now also take this issue up as a primary concern, at times – even controversially so – working directly or indirectly with militaries and governments on the provision of assistance and protection. The additive and expansionary context that results from these changes signals potential for future actions that could bring more qualified actors into the governance of this issue.

There is no question that a broad base of multiple and diverse organizations has coalesced around the most basic common norms of humanity, assistance and protection for those forcibly displaced. It is impossible to calculate the untold counterfactuals of death, starvation and suffering if these actors had not been directly involved in the governance of refugee and asylum issues. Yet, such a broad and diverse coalition is neither fixed nor sufficient today. Indeed, this constantly shifting landscape, while signalling historical progress over time, has been unable to adequately deal with the needs of refugees today. Accordingly, this pathway represents an entry point for greater governance reform or reactivation for engaged stakeholders. Such a coalition may not need to become more diverse (especially in light of fragmentation concerns), but it does need to grow so that more stakeholders from the already wide spectrum are engaged, and committed to this issue.

In terms of forced migration, particularly focused on refugees, the role of leadership is also of utmost importance. The current (at time of writing) European migration crisis is a case in point. In the last two years, Germany stood at the forefront, making bold declarations about the numbers of refugees that it would and did accept. Angela Merkel carried this banner in many respects, joined by Sweden, demonstrating ambitious goals concerning the reception of refugees. Where singular instances of leadership can be identified, either by personal or state action, collective leadership in the European Union is lacking. More recently, Germany has reduced its commitment to a point where it is now in line with all other minimum EU standards such that the problem may inevitably be displaced onto Hungary, Greece and Italy (see Czuczka 2016). The one country that has maintained ambitious, albeit quiet, leadership on this issue is Sweden.

Sweden stands out as the foremost European country in its willingness to accept large refugee flows, relative to its population size. Despite popular concerns and spurious claims about employment (see Collier 2013 on concerns about migration and employment), Sweden has benefited from an influx of migration in meaningful ways. A recent study about Sweden's economy lists migration as one of the most important factors in re-energizing the local economy and leading to nation-wide economic growth (Witton 2016). In this sense, Sweden now takes the leadership banner from Germany on this issue. The factors underpinning such leadership are difficult to discern and beyond the scope of this chapter. Whether it is a combination of national resources, domestic political climate, or personal leadership influence, it is clear that leadership plays a significant role, deserving of greater research in the future.

As migration flows into Europe continue at a record pace (see Frontex 2015), and with a gridlocked multilateral system presently unable to provide the public good of assistance and protection to refugees in a systematic fashion, individual states take on greater significance and therefore open the door for state-based leadership to reshape this field. The EU has tried and failed to implement quota systems. As a result, countries like Italy and Greece shoulder a disproportionate burden in contrast to their European neighbours (EU Commission 2015). Yet even this does not begin to compare with the burdens experienced by Jordan and Lebanon. This is, perhaps, both driven and compounded by the rise of extreme right-wing politics across Europe (not to mention the US), which all too typically comes with the unsavoury tint of xenophobia. Accordingly, it will take bold and innovative leadership to counter this trend in both the short and medium term.

Internally displaced persons

On the other side of the forced migration issue stand IDPs – sharing many of the causes, traits and needs of refugee and asylum-seeker governance, but differing in some critical respects. In some ways it is easier to understand how global policy or globally relevant policies might affect would-be refugees. The laws are written, and the practice is prescribed. By virtue of crossing an internationally recognized border, a displaced person is eligible to apply for refugee status. Before they are granted said status, they remain asylum seekers. Should they be rejected, their status shifts to one of "economic migrant" or some other form of irregular migration classification. If a displaced person does not cross an internationally recognized border, they are most accurately understood as an "internally displaced person," and despite the fact that they might be living in the same UNHCR tents, facing the same challenges as refugees, they remain under the legal purview of the state in which they habitually reside and not protected under international refugee law (Phuong 2005).

As the patterns of conflict shifted in the post–Cold War era, and as attention shifted to the security of individuals (i.e. human security), the plight of those internally displaced became a greater priority in the international community (see Cohen and Deng 1998a; 1998b). Despite early leadership from some UN institutions (UN Economic and Social Council, UN Secretary-General's Office, UN Commission for Human Rights) (see Beyani 2012), the political will and action(s) of intergovernmental bodies proved unable or unwilling to address this issue in earnest without pressure and expertise from civil society, acting in concert with sympathetic states. The combination of Brookings Institution academics, Geneva-based Quaker representatives and Austria as an enabling supporter, with further research and programmatic evaluation into internal displacement, eventually led to breakthroughs in this area (Cohen and Deng 1998b). These civil society groups are largely credited with advancing the needs of IDPs in the multilateral system such that transformative action was eventually taken. However, the studies conducted and recommendations given would not have been advanced were it not for Austria pushing for the continuation of these activities (see Mooney 2005).

Notably, while civil society was directly involved at virtually all stages of this process, and propelled forward by the assistance of supportive states, this development took place in a permissive international context, and largely within the UN itself. The timing is also significant to note, as the express, early focus on internal displacement occurred within the span of ten years from 1989 to 1998. The results, in terms of governance itself, were profound. Not only was an internationally agreed-upon definition of IDP established – a contentious issue in its own right – but, as mentioned above, a set of *Guiding Principles on Internal Displacement* were also created. The *Guiding Principles* are a set of norms, based on human rights law, humanitarian law and refugee law by analogy, brought together into a common framework and either reinterpreted or restated with the purpose of filling the grey areas and gaps left by existing legal protections available to IDPs (Cohen and Deng 1998a). Moreover, the legal annotations for this document have continued, most recently updated in 2008, and the post of Representative of the UN Secretary-General has transitioned to its current form as the Special Rapporteur on the Human Rights of IDPs. Equally significant to note, this process represents a unique approach to governance, eschewing treaty-making as the preferred vehicle for change, in favour of adaptation and rearticulation of existing law, emboldened by soft-law norms (see Bagshaw 2005). This marks an approach to global governance that deliberately employs broad normative frameworks to influence the behaviour of all actors and agencies involved.

Here it is important to understand the stated progress in context. The institutional development recounted here certainly demonstrates something remarkable about governance, driven by civil society coalitions when supported by key states, but this does not necessarily mean improved outcomes. Since the implementation of the *Guiding Principles*, there have been mixed results across various implementation strategies in select countries (see Sánchez-Garzoli 2004). While the impact in terms of outcomes is beyond the scope of this chapter, this process and this example can serve as an example of past successes, reasonably demonstrating a potential pathway in the future, should necessary conditions be met.

What has been given above is a set of the leading and most relevant pathways for present purposes. Moreover, the prospect for improvement and enhanced governance, via the pathways considered, must be reasonable and grounded in past successes or breakthroughs. Each of the three "beyond gridlock" pathways here can be observed in the historical governance of humanitarianism and forced migration, and thus it stands to reason that in the right circumstances, with enough political will, such pathways may also provide guidance for future efforts – especially if they could be informed by systematic analysis such as that offered by this book.

Conclusion: Balancing Optimism with Pragmatic Futures

Humanitarianism as a concept is made ever more complex by humanitarian practice. As is the case with any normative theory, where ideas touch the ground the landscape is destined to be messy, full of contestation, and difficult to understand. In an effort to achieve a degree of analytical depth, this chapter began with consideration of humanitarianism as a whole, but narrowed its focus to forced migration – ranging from refugee policy to internal displacement governance. Looking at pathways out of gridlock, there is certainly some room for optimism when historical governance trajectories are understood in relation to present challenges. There is clear evidence that coalitions mobilizing around common norms, innovative or unique leadership, and active civil society groups working in concert with sympathetic states can create not only incremental improvements, but movements of progress and potential long-term change.

However, challenges abound. We cannot celebrate governance simply for governance's sake. The historical progress surrounding refugee governance does illuminate a robust, if also constantly lacking, international legal regime, engaging a multitude of actors and agencies seeking to provide assistance and protection. Yet, the refugee crisis in the contemporary global landscape is far from effectively managed and far from over. Similarly, despite progress in establishing global norms addressing the needs of internally displaced persons, much needed assistance and most especially protection today remains out of reach for tens of millions of refugees and IDPs. There may be some pathways out of gridlock, but they will likely be long ones.

8

Human Rights

Leveraging Compliance

Tom Pegram

The performance of global governance regimes across issue areas is increasingly beset by what scholars have termed the "governance dilemma" (Keohane 2001).[1] As noted in *Gridlock* (Hale, Held and Young 2013), second-order trends, brought on by deepening global interdependence, including multipolarity, harder problems, institutional inertia, and fragmentation, are combining to undermine international cooperation where it is needed most. This "gridlock" is compounded by the segmentation of domestic and international arenas and incomplete delegation, with few, if any, international organizations equipped with de jure or de facto capability (or legitimacy) to directly enforce international rules and standards. In response, critics warn that existing international organizations are "no longer fit for purpose," and that they are more a hindrance than an aid to advancing implementation of global public policy. Others raise legitimate concerns about the actual functioning of global governance institutions, even where they are influential in producing change.

The governance dilemma is particularly acute in the human rights domain, where competing interests among authorizing actors (individual states) introduce a high probability of "principal moral hazard," posing a threat to the integrity of the regime (Alston 2011). Principal moral hazard refers to the situation where effective regulation is dependent upon the cooperation of those actors who stand to gain least from faithful execution of the contract (Miller 2005). If principal–agent theory is preoccupied with negative behaviour on the part of the agent (shirking or slacking), principal moral hazard shifts our gaze to the principal: in this case, states that commit to United Nations human rights treaties with no intention of complying (Simmons 2009). In effect, the UN system has put the fox in charge of the henhouse. The travails of the UN human rights regime exemplify this dilemma, characterized by restrictive treaty mandates, limited financial and administrative resources, and a persistent compliance gap between human rights standards and practice in domestic jurisdictions.

That said, the assembling of a sophisticated international human rights apparatus, coupled with a significant expansion of resources, does pose a puzzle. As Ginsburg and Shaffer have pointed out, international human rights law presents a distinct context, entailing high sovereignty costs and few obvious benefits for government, given that it generally "does not involve collective-action problems or material externalities between states" (2012: 19). Traditional mechanisms that explain why states almost always follow international agreements in security or trade, such as reciprocity and retaliation, simply do not apply in the human rights field (Guzman 2008). The challenge becomes particularly acute at the domestic level, where implementation of policy directives typically confronts resistance from local bureaucrats and state officials.

This compliance problem has led some scholars to emphasize soft managerial techniques (for example, persuasion, learning, deliberation and transparency) to align interests and facilitate cooperative solutions (Chayes and Chayes 1993). However, others question the usefulness of management techniques in situations where compliance is most problematic (Downs, Rocke and Barsoom 1996). Confronted with egregious violations, functionalist rationales of interest alignment are rarely enough. This raises the important question: what to do when the limits of cooperation are reached? Human rights scholars have taken up this empirical question, exploring exit out of gridlock through diverse mechanisms, including socialization, intermediation, deliberative constitutionalism, and civil society mobilization (Simmons 2009; Pegram 2017; Goodman and Jinks 2013; de Búrca 2015). Nevertheless, the fundamental tension between functionalism (fostering interest alignment) and political empowerment (challenging structures of power) deeply informs human rights scholarship.

Drawing on the introduction to this book, the chapter surveys the current state of human rights scholarship and practice through an exploration of four potential pathways "through" or even "beyond" gridlock in the human rights domain, with particular attention to: (1) autonomous and adaptive institutions, and (2) plurality and diversity of actors and agencies around common goals/norms. In so doing, it highlights how human rights governance is emblematic of certain exit options from gridlock, especially mobilization of willing and able transgovernmental and transnational networks of non-state actors. This includes both civil society actors, as well as networks of national human rights institutions (NHRIs) and other official regulatory bodies, which have received growing attention of late (Pegram 2015).

This study shares the volume's interest in both positive and normative concerns. It is problem oriented, with a focus on pathways through which motivated human rights agents can succeed in carving out a zone of independent action. The focus here is on the functional question of which actors, mechanisms, and processes are central to ongoing efforts to expand the scope and intrusiveness of human rights norms. It also builds upon the premise of this project that pathways can be distinguished as routes "through" or "beyond" gridlock. This distinction is employed here to differentiate between a *reformist* concern with incremental change versus a *revolutionary* emphasis on wholesale transformations of power relations. It also brings the normative inquiry into focus: what kind of change is possible or desirable? In practice, conventional approaches to human rights change through multilateral forums, legal venues, and traditional activism more often resemble routes through, as opposed to beyond, gridlock. Efforts are geared towards achieving change through incremental progress, locking in institutional gains and mobilizing public opinion, a process which is incremental, contingent and vulnerable to reversal.

Frustration with incrementalism has given rise to wide-ranging critiques which view the international human rights regime as offering little more than palliative retributive justice, a superstructure ill-equipped and little disposed to achieving transformative political change (Hopgood 2014). From this critical standpoint, the pillars of human rights officialdom, in the form of international organizations, above all the United Nations, professional NGOs and state bureaucracies, unwittingly or not, serve the interests of a predominantly West-centric status quo, authorizing new hierarchies and legitimating existing inequalities within a structural reality of neoliberal globalization (O'Connell 2007). These scholars call for bold and fundamental transformations, emphasizing democratic controls and more radical forms of political mobilization. In effect, they call for pathways "beyond" gridlock. Notwithstanding the valid concerns raised by this critical strand of scholarship, this chapter suggests that it is important not to lose sight of the partial, but significant, gains made by ongoing efforts to "work human rights into the cracks of international society" in the shadow of interstate hierarchy (Vincent 1986: 3).

The chapter begins with an outline of governance arrangements in the human rights domain, including a survey of the many challenges human rights governance confronts. It then evaluates the extent to which the pathways out of gridlock identified in this project are evident in human rights governance and with what effect. The chapter concludes by reflecting on what the analysis means for advancing human rights policy objectives and overcoming multilateral gridlock more generally.

Governance Arrangements in the Human Rights Domain

Human rights governance bears the hallmarks of a globalized political arena, displaying multiple structures of authority, diverse forms of power, regime complexity, actor proliferation and, importantly, autonomous capacity for change. States remain prominent within human rights governance. Gridlock within multilateral and domestic fora, driven by a regulatory problem structure defined by principal moral hazard, poses a formidable impediment to cooperation in the human rights regulatory arena. However, the exercise and effects of state power in this domain have always been challenged and continue to undergo significant change, informed by emergent forms of private and hybrid authority which offer some inspiration for identifying pathways through and beyond gridlock.

The actors, mechanisms, and processes of global human rights governance have their antecedents in a desire to prevent massive violence and warfare in the post–World War II settlement. However, the remit has rapidly evolved to encompass a range of global policy challenges, from universal health provision to sustainable development. This expansion of normative scope poses a challenge, but also an opportunity to develop human rights as a programmatic effort in response to contemporary imperatives. Human rights provide one normative bedrock upon which to anchor a legitimate conception of governance, in the service of the global common good. Notwithstanding debate over their meaning and conceptual parameters, there is widespread acceptance that human rights norms are substantially important, reflecting pragmatic, deeply held shared concerns (Donnelly 2007). Human rights also provide basic operational norms (deliberation, participation, accountability, and so on) which may inform global governance activities across the full gamut of issue areas which impact upon human well-being.

The international human rights regime is codified in a dense array of treaties, institutions, networks and standards. If Ignatieff's claim that "we are scarcely aware of the extent to which our moral imagination has been transformed ... above all in a shared human rights culture" (1997: 8) strikes some as exaggerated, it is nevertheless hard to deny the extraordinary expansion and increased intrusiveness of global human rights norms in recent decades, especially in the legitimation of concern for the welfare of individuals and state behaviour regarding domestic human rights practices. We might add two further trends: first, an increased pluralism in norm entrepreneurs participating in an increasingly globalized governance system; and second, growing acceptability of norms of enforcement (broadly defined), as governance actors experiment with a multiplying array of direct and indirect compliance mechanisms focused on closing the "compliance gap" between standards and practice.

For much of the Cold War, human rights were consigned to the margins by ideological division, the dominance of sovereign states within multilateral fora, and limited opportunities for institutionalized cooperation. As a consequence, the UN human rights regime has historically been limited by the veto power of member states, restrictive treaty mandates, limited financial and administrative resources, and few non-governmental partners at bilateral, regional and transnational levels. A transformed ecology defines contemporary human rights governance. Propelled by the liberal internationalism of the 1990s and an operational shift towards implementation, architectural innovation has resulted in heightened scrutiny of states' human rights practices, ambitious and open-ended treaty mandates, the proliferation of dedicated institutional mechanisms at the multilateral, regional and local level, and enhanced access to UN procedures by non-state actors.

However, this ideational and procedural transition has not necessarily been smooth. The human rights imperative within a UN system historically geared towards harmonizing governmental interests is not easily squared. Article 100 of the UN Charter requires UN civil servants, including those who populate the Office of the High Commissioner for Human Rights (OHCHR), to formally maintain "neutrality." Prominent former UN human rights officials have questioned whether "neutrality" is possible or appropriate for a secretariat "that perceives itself as a trustee of human rights interests" (van Boven 2000: 148). Striking examples of this tension include UN field officers charged with failing to protect civilians during the Sri Lankan conflict of 2009 or to publicize violations committed by government forces (see United Nations 2012). It also informs the crisis which engulfed the OHCHR in 2015, with the suspension of Anders Kompass, a senior OHCHR official, for leaking allegations of child sexual abuse by French peacekeepers in the Central African Republic to French authorities (Laville 2016).

Along similar lines, the UN apparatus poses serious political and procedural obstacles to effective human rights governance. The Human Rights Council, the apex intergovernmental human rights forum, presents a mixed scorecard at best. It has often succumbed to regional bloc politics, autocratic states have exploited the forum to advance "traditional values," and the recent election of Saudi Arabia to the Council (allegedly assisted by the UK in a secret vote-trading deal) has stoked controversy (Bowcott 2015). Reflecting the zealous gatekeeper role of states within the UN system, the UN's intergovernmental Economic and Social Council, which officially accredits NGOs who wish to participate in UN procedures, has often made it difficult, if not impossible, for organizations dealing with sexual orientation, gender identity, reproductive rights, and minority issues to secure accreditation.

An officially endorsed liberal vision is perhaps most visible in the movement towards politically legitimating humanitarian intervention based on collective action – including the use of force – as embodied in the principle of Responsibility to Protect (R2P), and associated efforts to redefine threats to international peace and security that have pushed human rights compliance onto the agenda of the UN Security Council. R2P has been extensively analysed elsewhere, not least in *Gridlock* (Hale, Held and Young 2013). In practice, however, if the UN Security Council no longer rejects outright responsibility for situations of gross human rights violations, resistance on the part of member states to acting according to this emerging protection norm is the dominant trend.

The R2P doctrine reflects the tension at the heart of the UN Charter between sovereignty and human rights. The architects of the R2P norm may have sought to work within the UN Charter. However, R2P detractors argue that the norm (especially its coercive Pillar III envisaging enforcement action should a state manifestly fail to protect its population) lacks legal basis and infringes Article 2.7 of the Charter (non-interference within the domestic jurisdiction of any state). China and Russia have hardened their opposition to R2P following the Libya intervention of Spring 2011, with inaction over Syria further damaging the credibility of the doctrine. Coercive enforcement ostensibly in the name of human rights has been marred by selectivity (e.g. Libya), geopolitical calculation (e.g. South Ossetia), and failure to actually protect civilian lives (e.g. Kosovo and Syria).

The dysfunctionality of the UN Security Council when it comes to human rights is emblematic of the worst symptoms of multilateral gridlock. At root, this failure speaks to governmental resistance to the idea that human rights violations constitute a threat to national interest, framed in terms of international peace and security. Despite progress in advancing conceptions of human security, realpolitik frequently overrides cooperation. Proposals for reform of the UN Security Council are in deep-freeze and no UN standing military capability has ever been created. Similar pathologies afflict the International Criminal Court (Bosco 2014). If the court has made important advances, it nevertheless confronts significant enforcement challenges. Diverse strategic interest calculations among states have thwarted collective compliance action. Prosecution of sitting President Uhuru Muigai Kenyatta (2013–) collapsed in December 2014 due to non-cooperation by the Kenyan government. The South African government's failure to apprehend President al-Bashir of Sudan on an outstanding ICC arrest warrant in 2015 reinforces a worrying trend towards non-cooperation with the court. The ICC is also accused of imbalance, selectivity, delays, and mishandling of investigations (Hopgood 2014).

However, to pass judgement on global human rights governance based on intergovernmental inactivity and obstruction would be partial and misguided. Analytically, it denies a fuller appreciation of long-standing efforts by diverse public and private actors to respond to the transboundary challenge of human rights violations, frequently committed by states. Without denying Rengger's observation that "in order to [advance human rights] we have to give states and other agents more power, not less" (2011: 1177), it is important to be clear on the (potential) radical intent of the human rights project. As Reus-Smit (2011) argues, the fundamental normative justification for human rights is their role as "power mediators," seeking to empower the politically disadvantaged, irrespective of territorial boundaries. This inherently ideological and politically contested emancipatory project raises an important challenge to the (often implicit) functionalist collaboration narrative which informs much global governance scholarship and practice.

The Council on Foreign Relations (2013) sums up the effect of the international human rights regime pithily as "Heightened attention, uneven regional efforts, weak global compliance." On the face of it, this assessment may seem lenient. It is not hard to identify failures in multilateral governance which have contributed – often through inaction – to massive violations of human rights. A litany of major catastrophes has occurred in recent decades alone: Rwanda, the former Yugoslavia, and Syria, to name but a few. However, notwithstanding these prominent failures of multilateral governance, the issue of assessing "effectiveness" in global human rights governance is complex, largely due to the (possibly ungraspable) totality of activities underway.

On a more prosaic note, a 2013 Multilateral Aid Review conducted by the UK Department for International Development and partner agencies concluded that the OHCHR offered "adequate value for money." The report concludes by recommending efficiency savings and OHCHR reform priorities, including "cost and value consciousness," "financial resources management," "strategic and performance management," and "contribution to results" (DFID 2013: 26). The OHCHR is certainly not above criticism. However, it is important to note the normative assumptions which underpin such effectiveness metrics. Should "value for money" be the overriding concern? Structural reality also matters. Although human rights ranks, along with security and development, as one of the three pillars of the UN, the OHCHR has an annual budget of US$250 million, compared to US$1.3 billion allocated to security and US$1.1 billion to development. There is little love lost between the OHCHR and many UN member states at the sharp end of human rights criticism. In response, dedicated human rights agencies within UN structures have increasingly sought to bypass state consent by supporting and coordinating new forms of non-state and private authority.

If formal UN structures provide new arenas for experimentation in the shadow of interstate hierarchy, the question remains: with what effect? Within the scholarship, long-standing debate on the effects of the international human rights regime problematizes causal attribution. Are improvements in aggregate human rights outcomes simply second-order structural effects of democratization and/or reductions in interstate conflict (Davenport 1999)? Concern surrounding the disjuncture between human rights standards and domestic practice has animated a spirited debate in recent years (Hathaway 2002). In undermining the aspirational claim of universal human rights, this compliance gap presents a threat to the legitimacy of the project. In contrast to the somewhat Panglossian assessments of earlier scholars (Ignatieff 1997), for some contemporary observers, global human rights governance is failing (Hopgood 2014). In a particularly damning intervention, Posner concludes that human rights treaties "were not so much an act of idealism but an act of hubris" (2014: 148).

Much attention within an empirical human rights scholarship has focused on the effects of international human rights treaty commitments. A recent wave of research has examined specifically the influence of human rights treaty ratification on citizens' enjoyment of human rights (Hafner-Burton and Ron 2009). These studies generally find a negative correlation between international commitment and human rights practices. However, as one scholar observes, "this addresses a claim that human rights advocates seldom advance: that ratification in and of itself has a direct impact on respect for human rights" (Carver 2013: 7).

Interpreting correlational evidence on human rights effects raises difficult questions regarding causal identification, as well as the quality of data. However, the fact remains that for millions of people, basic human rights remain elusive. The global human rights system is least able to effect change in exactly those countries where human rights protections are most at risk. In "hard cases" like China, Iran, and Saudi Arabia, severe restrictions on domestic mobilization compound the enforcement paradox which lies at the heart of the international human rights regime. This has led scholars to suggest that international human rights treaties will have their greatest effect in partially democratic transitional settings between the polarities of stable democracy and autocracy, where pro-compliance mobilization is both meaningful, given local protection deficits, and not subject to violent repression by state authorities (Simmons 2009).

The analytical point is that a complex series of intermediate steps separate international instruments from human rights practices. For example, a negative correlation between international commitment and domestic practice could indicate that governments start persecuting their citizens after ratifying human rights treaties. However, this negative pattern could also appear if, following ratification, governments establish national agencies that monitor human rights violations more closely, and thus report more human rights violations. Treaty ratification does not necessarily set in motion an automatic process of domestic reform. Rather, ratification of a human rights treaty forms part of a prolonged and continuous process of political struggle focused on the domestic implementation of human rights norms. This cautionary note resonates with recent social scientific and sociological scholarship focused on explaining how human rights norms are actually instantiated in practice, and when and why they matter on the ground (Risse, Ropp and Sikkink 2013).

For many constructivist-inclined human rights scholars, predictive modelling of human rights effects is problematic, privileging a consequentialist paradigm and marginalizing consideration of indirect and process-based mechanisms of influence. As Dai (2013) reminds us, the most likely outcome of human rights treaty ratification is partial compliance. However, this is not necessarily inconsequential. The very existence of a gap between declared commitment and compliance may provide decentralized networks of pro-compliance actors with normative and/or material tools required to successfully pressure government. This proposition is borne out in a wealth of qualitative scholarship and practitioner literature (Brysk 2013).

Excessively focusing on legal instruments also risks essentializing human rights policy into a single "one size fits all" analytical framework. Specific institutional configurations of domestic human rights frameworks should be expected to vary according to the history and social traditions of diverse countries. It is the general acceptance of the basic norms of human rights which is important (Donnelly 2007). In turn, there is likely to be a range of institutional means (judicial, but also political, social, and cultural) towards the same ends – promotion and protection of human rights. Critically inclined scholars further challenge what they view as an elitist, northern and liberal bias permeating much human rights scholarship and practice (Hopgood 2014). Others problematize the reception of human rights norms in local jurisdictions, with a particular focus on the global South, highlighting processes of norm rejection, but also modification and negotiation (Engle-Merry 2006). In sum, this survey of the human rights governance regime demonstrates both its extraordinary expansion in recent decades and the severe challenges it confronts in fulfilling its function. It is incumbent upon those seeking pathways out of gridlock to calibrate expectations in light of context and in particular the challenges thrown up by this permanently challenged – and challenging – regulatory arena.

Pathways out of Gridlock

Since the reluctant acceptance by major powers (especially Great Britain and the Soviet Union) of the inclusion of human rights in the UN Charter, the international human rights regime has continued to face significant resistance from (some) state parties. As detailed at the outset, this introduces a distinct problem structure informed by "principal moral hazard." Human rights, in principle, do not privilege the interests of the authorizing actor (individual states), but rather those individuals at risk of abuse by those same actors. Regime dysfunctionality in general reflects this paradox, with the targets of human rights regulation often motivated to resist implementation. Nevertheless, it is not always so clear-cut. The human rights regime does have its supporters among state parties to UN treaties, not all of them the usual suspects, and the proliferation of national regulatory agencies and transnational advocacy networks is also a defining feature of human rights governance. This raises important questions surrounding where cooperation is taking place and among whom. Under what conditions can pro-human rights actors engineer a structural tilt in favour of cooperation? And when cooperation fails, what recourse remains to secure protection of victims of abuse?

To explore these questions, this section draws on the framework elaborated in the book's introduction to explore a number of potential pathways "through" or even "beyond" gridlock, focusing on the pathways identified in table 8.1: autonomous and adaptive international institutions, coupled with mobilization of motivated and capable domestic compliance constituencies. It also highlights alternative exit options which human rights governance exemplifies, especially the emergent power of transgovernmental and transnational networks of non-state actors.

As the project convenors note in the introduction, these pathways do not operate in isolation, opening up inquiry into how, and under what conditions, multi-actor systems can drive forward shared governance goals along parallel paths, achieving outcomes beyond the capabilities of any one actor. Human rights governance offers a valuable domain through which to trace out the extent to which specified pathways have prevented, diminished or circumvented gridlock. It also spotlights the potential for viable pathways to be closed off, as well as the adaptive response of human rights entrepreneurs to new opportunity structures.

Human rights implementation in many jurisdictions is a collective action problem defined more by power differentials than absolute gains, contestation rather than interest alignment. The optimism of liberal internationalism which informed the massive expansion of human rights governance machinery in the 1990s has taken a blow in recent years. A resurgent securitization agenda in the context of terrorism and drug-trafficking poses a powerful contextual challenge, with human rights defenders under unprecedented threat (Sherwood 2015). However, the scope and depth of human rights normative frameworks remain both flawed and remarkable, providing an authoritative

Table 8.1 Pathways through or beyond gridlock in human rights governance

Pathway	Effect	Mechanism
Shifts in major powers' core interests	Effective, if clearly tied to material benefits	Threat to international peace and security
Autonomous and adaptive international institutions	Effective, if credible signalling is important, issue area is "low politics," and multiple principals are divided	Norm expansion and codification (increased scope, precision and/or obligation) Procedural innovation, involving delegation to third parties
Plurality and diversity of actors and agencies coalescing around common goals/norms	Effective, if interest convergence among pro-human rights coalitions. Also availability of willing and able third party actors	Deliberation, peer review, transparency, accessibility to diverse interstate and transnational fora
Mobilization of domestic constituencies	Effective, if clearly tied to electoral benefits (instrumental), able to effect attitudinal alignment (managerial)	Elite agenda-setting by policy officials Strategic litigation in domestic legal systems Mobilization of public opinion

limit on the range of legally and morally permissible actions. In turn, human rights continue to be invoked by elite agenda-setters and incorporated into both foreign policy concerns and domestic policy. Senior government officials who have invoked human rights in their country's foreign policy, or continue to do so, include Jimmy Carter (US), Helen Clark (New Zealand), Robin Cook (United Kingdom), Nelson Mandela (South Africa), and Mary Robinson (Ireland).

Failures of the UN Security Council to act and the travails of the ICC may capture the headlines, but it is also important to reflect on some surprising progress in human rights within intergovernmental forums. The issue of torture prevention often provokes sensitivity on the part of government, given that torture violations generally implicate either directly or indirectly government as the responsible party. Individual governments have often proven reluctant to champion the Convention against Torture (CAT). Nevertheless, today, the anti-torture UN architecture is arguably the most intrusive apparatus within the human rights system. The Optional Protocol to the CAT (OPCAT), adopted by the UN General Assembly in 2002 and entering into force in 2006, mandates a global system of inspection of places of detention. The OPCAT focal actor, the international Subcommittee on Prevention of Torture, granted the authority to conduct field visits to arrive at its own independent assessment of state compliance, rightly self-identifies as "a new type of United Nations treaty body with a unique mandate" (United Nations 2008: para. 5). Such examples point to the importance of distinguishing between the regulator (state parties to the UN acting as a collective) and the targets of human rights regulation (individual states).

This example speaks to key components of the underlying strategic environment which informs human rights governance. Torture prevention norm entrepreneurs, above all non-governmental organizations, such as the Association for the Prevention of Torture, have mobilized to exploit the constructive ambiguities of the interstate system to foist their own progressive policy objectives onto government. As Alston (2011) has developed, high principal moral hazard may, counter-intuitively, actually lead to reduced formal oversight as governments intentionally insulate the agent, in this case the Subcommittee on Prevention of Torture, in order to signal credibility. In turn, torture, due to its normative salience, may provoke disagreement within a collective principal, with pro–human rights governments seeking to secure deeper agreement in the face of opposition from their peers. It is also worth noting that human rights is generally not regarded as "high politics," with powerful governments less exercised about imprinting their preferences onto agreements which do not impinge on core interests. This argument is consistent with Hawkins's observations on the CAT negotiations where "Sweden, and later the Netherlands, provided most of the initiative to keep the negotiation moving forward, and the US did not make the treaty a priority" (2004: 797).

One of the most significant pathways of impact in human rights governance is the articulation of an increasingly intrusive global architecture into domestic politics. The distributional power implications of IGO empowerment of third party actors within domestic jurisdictions should not be underestimated. UN IGOs thus may intervene directly on matters of human rights protection. For example, the UN refugee agency, the UNHCR, recently sought and was granted permission to appear in a High Court challenge contesting the Australian government's treatment of asylum seekers (Reuters News

2014). Although the challenge was ultimately unsuccessful (UNHCR Canberra 2016), UNHCR's actions alongside local advocates serve as a focal point for contestation and ongoing mobilization. There is a large body of evidence which demonstrates that legal interventions, shaped by human rights law, have contributed to human rights gains (Yamin and Parra-Vera 2009).

Intervention by human rights IGOs in domestic political processes has also often been exercised indirectly, through empowerment of local pro-accountability actors. Although denied treaty status, the Helsinki Accords, negotiated in 1975, are widely viewed as having had a powerful domestic mobilization effect in parts of the Eastern European Soviet bloc (Finnemore and Toope 2001). This speaks to the broader point of domestic mobilization effects – both direct and indirect – of human rights discourse. In recent years the human rights regime has begun to functionally integrate non-state actors and subdivisions within the state into core governance roles within international regulatory frameworks. In perhaps the biggest shake-up of traditional treaty law paradigms in recent years, both the OPCAT and the Convention on the Rights of Persons with Disabilities formally delegate monitoring and implementation functions to domestic mechanisms (Pegram 2017).

IGOs constitute an important resource for transnational and transgovernmental human rights networks in terms of standard setting, capacity-building, network facilitating, and membership granting (Martens 2004). Indeed, the UN has played a pivotal role in the extraordinary proliferation of national human rights institutions from approximately 21 offices in 1990 to 108 today (Goodman and Pegram 2012). Distinct from NGOs, NHRIs are independent, but state-funded, regulatory agencies created to protect human rights. Their explicit mandate to engage with external actors has been important, providing individual institutions and their transgovernmental peer network with material support, as well as legitimacy within international governmental structures (Pegram 2015). Growing interaction is occurring within UN and regional IGOs, with NHRIs potentially serving as independent, if state-based, human rights receptor sites for norm transmission and implementation. As domestic agencies they are well placed to tailor solutions to local settings (Carver 2010). This intermediary function is particularly pertinent to areas displaying high sovereignty costs. Of course, the extent to which any one national mechanism actually serves to effectively steward norm implementation in line with IGO objectives is an empirical question.

If human rights IGOs have assumed a margin of independent action, criticism is also rightly directed at strategic and accountability deficits on the part of an excessively vertical UN bureaucracy itself, as well as other agents operating within an increasingly globalized pro–human rights accountability network (Hopgood 2014). The UN system remains a key focal point for global human rights governance. The renovation of the UN's Human Rights Council (HRC) in 2005 has had some notable successes, in particular the novel Universal Periodic Review procedure and new modalities for non-state actor participation. However, it is the Office of the High Commissioner which serves as the focal point for system-wide coordination. The OHCHR has struggled to reconcile its mandate with its status as part of the overall UN secretariat in the shadow of its proximate political body: the HRC. The task of navigating this fraught political space has largely fallen on the leadership of the High Commissioner, most notably Mary Robinson (1997–2002). Public confrontations between independent-minded High Commissioners and rights-violating governments are frequent. Powerful states have been accused of engineering the departure of courageous High Commissioners (Burkeman 2002).

Government and IGOs may choose to bargain, collaborate or delegate through independent agencies. But non-governmental actors are not just passive opportunity structures for solving interstate coordination problems. For example, principal moral hazard raises the possibility of the International Criminal Court being "designed to fail." Notwithstanding conflicting interests among its authorizing actors (Assembly of State Parties), the ICC – and in particular the Office of the Prosecutor – cannot be simply labelled as a paper tiger. Importantly, the ICC represents an important ceding of authority to independent judicial structures. At the same time, it is material to note that states retain significant control over core governance functions, most visibly resource allocation and enforcement of judicial orders. As David Bosco (2014) details, the court has worked hard to develop a fragile modus vivendi with the US government.[2] However, the decision by the Office of the Prosecutor in 2015 to open a preliminary investigation into the Gaza conflict of 2014 was met with surprise, being widely viewed as intruding into core geopolitical interests of powerful governments, not least the US. The outcome of this development, specifically whether the Office of the Prosecutor decides to proceed with a full and formal investigation, may prove to be a watershed moment for the court.

As multi-level governance in the human rights domain becomes more complex, it is important to probe more deeply into how diverse actors are connected to centres of state authority. The relational boundaries and division of capabilities among actors often remain unclear in stock theoretical frames such as principal–agent theory. In new areas of regulatory scholarship, scholars have begun to demonstrate how IGO linkages shape "the capabilities, the governance goals and even the very existence of transnational organizations" (Abbott et al. 2015: 7). However, when applied to the human rights domain, such influence may also flow in the opposite direction, with intermediaries potentially serving as self-interested actors or vectors for governmental influence over IGOs. Notwithstanding the potential for capture, the proliferation of schemes of transformation, governance, and regulation, anchored in the language of human rights, shows little sign of abating. In turn, technological innovation has created fertile conditions for unprecedented transnational mobilization among pro–human rights networks, as well as increasingly sophisticated and stringent monitoring.

It is also important to reflect on the multiplier effect of robust regional human rights protection systems, especially in the Americas and Europe. It is not only government which engages in forum shopping. Non-governmental human rights actors have also proven adept at scaling up their authority through inter- and intra-regime forum shopping across levels. This may involve NGOs drawing upon regional protection systems for protection, for example by lobbying the Inter-American Commission to issue precautionary measures in defence of vulnerable individuals (Engstrom 2015). Regional human rights systems play an important role in mediating between global norms and regional diversity and traditions. The European and Latin American systems are particularly notable for advancing norm creation and, importantly, judicial enforcement of regional human rights standards. The European Convention on Human Rights is described by Janis, Kay and Bradley as "the most successful system of international law for the protection of human rights" (1995: 3), having exercised a profound influence on European public law.

Non-governmental actors have not only directly accessed regional legal systems, they have also sought to use regional systems as a springboard for vertical norm collaboration. Regional country blocs have on occasion aligned with non-governmental actors to advance human rights standards at the UN. For example, the negotiation of the Convention on the Rights of Persons with Disabilities has been described by observers as extraordinarily transparent and participative. The EU bloc worked alongside NGOs, especially disability rights organizations, to establish what de Búrca (2015) defines as the first experimentalist human rights agreement (displaying features of revisability, stakeholder participation, open-ended norms, and transparency). Notably, in contrast to the OPCAT, "the disability rights agenda was not a politically high-profile or a particularly divisive issue" (de Búrca 2015: 321). In mapping pathways through gridlock, analysts would be well advised to also be attentive to problem structure variation *within* as well as across substantive regimes such as disability rights and torture prevention.

Non-governmental actors are often engaged in the promotion, monitoring, and ongoing interpretation and revision of human rights standards (Engle-Merry 2006). Their role may be bolstered by substantive and technical expertise in their respective policy fields. However, substate actors may also be empowered to generate binding and voluntary standards, or recommendations of their own accord. The mobilization of such third party actors introduces an important endogeneity, with intergovernmental organizations such as the UN seeking to imprint their preferences by proxy onto governing rules ex ante across regulatory jurisdictions, not only once regulation is in place. In turn, soft international standards may subsequently be "hardened" through incorporation into domestic legal frameworks.

The informal or political activities of substate actors in driving forward legislative reform are consequential in this regard and potentially transformative. There has been widespread incorporation of substantive and procedural human rights norms into domestic constitutional texts. Even more consequentially, countries have established organizational structures *ex nihilo* – such as national human rights institutions – increasing the potential for unintended consequences. In tracing out possible pathways beyond gridlock, this section highlights efforts to advance compliance based on consensus but also compliance, with the ICC symbolizing the boldest inroad yet into the protected domain of state sovereignty. But it is the embedding of human rights norms and structures within domestic political systems which perhaps offers the greatest promise of advancing human rights implementation, empowering local actors to defy multilateral gridlock.

Trends and Prospects for Overcoming Gridlock in Human Rights Governance

As social scientists know well, in politics demand does not translate automatically into supply. Even where legal frameworks exist, power often rules. It is therefore rarely enough to rely on functionalist rationales underpinned by interest alignment. This dilemma deeply informs human rights governance. The rapid diffusion of human rights and other liberal norms and the deepening interdependence of cross-border activism bely the relative absence of governance mechanisms capable of effectively holding public and private power-holders to account. The scale of future challenges is formidable, including the impact of new technology, in particular the internet, genetic technology, and, of course, the challenge of safeguarding our environment.

But the human rights regulatory challenge has always been hard. After all, the transnational regulation of domestic state conduct is a deeply challenging policy goal. Moyn (2012) calls for a political pragmatic turn among human rights scholars and practitioners away from the notion of human rights activity as non-political or purely moral action. The extent to which this stylized view of the "purity of the struggle" ever really held sway may be disputed. However, one crucial first-order task is surely a clear-eyed reappraisal of problem identification in human rights regulation.

In this sense, it is not just that the problem has got "harder," but that we are more attentive to the contours and magnitude of the problem. And it is not just that the problem structure of human rights regulation is itself challenging, but that there is also significant variation in problem structures across different sets of rights. Perhaps one of the most challenging domains is achieving effective implementation in the field of health rights. Although referenced in various international bills of rights, no global framework convention on health exists and the sector is riven with deep-seated divisions of both a normative (e.g. prioritizing targeted intervention versus holistic health systems) and sectoral nature (e.g. the extraordinary hybridization of the political ecology of global health in recent decades). This stands in stark contrast to torture as a distinct problem structure, displaying an unusually high degree of norm precision, normative salience and universal prohibition under *jus cogens*, principles of international law that cannot be set aside.

If global human rights governance scholarship is to take policy delivery seriously, a more forensic understanding of multi-level governance problem structures is also required. The formal structural dimension remains a popular way to tame global system complexity, most evident in the liberal preoccupation with regulation. However, it is important not to overlook the dynamic effects of regulation (or its absence) as we enter an ever more plural landscape of structural overlaps and normative orders. Consideration of structural overlaps demands that we are attentive to the site of gridlock. Human rights governance exemplifies efforts to bypass multilateral gridlock and connect rapidly decentralizing global regulatory networks to the political realities of violations on the ground.

The challenge of advancing a rules-based human rights system in a plural landscape of normative orders can be seen in efforts to embed human rights into global business practices, a realm where the forces of globalization are constantly reshaping the scale of governance challenges, the sources of control and influence, and the subjects of control. As Abbott and Snidal pointedly note, "states have denied virtually all [international organizations] direct access to private targets and strong regulatory authority" (2013: 96). Asserting human rights regulation into a realm of global governance historically resistant to conventional notions of public law and the common good is a tall order. However, it may be vital if human rights is to respond to the ethical challenges facing the world today, including economic inequality. At a structural level, a shift towards rights governance of business practices requires a deeper understanding of how private power is exercised across scales.

Human rights rule frameworks may be devised by government delegations in New York or Geneva, but closing the implementation circle of policy administration and execution will be dependent upon operationalizing national or even subnational instruments, such as legal sanction, popular mobilization, informational campaigns and regulation. This chapter has highlighted a fundamental tension between functionalist (interest alignment) and political empowerment (challenging power structures) approaches to securing human rights gains. Cooperation may get us a long way along the road. The UN Guiding Principles on Business and Human Rights are a laudable effort to embed human rights into business practice through voluntary standards (United Nations 2011). However, its detractors point out that such initiatives do little to advance the hard-edged dimension of enforcement when confronted with egregious violations. Conversely, the ICC is an extraordinary development, an apex international enforcement venue for prosecuting mass-atrocity crimes. However, a mandate to pursue formal justice on behalf of the most politically disadvantaged in society is a deeply challenged objective. More radical forms of political empowerment and legitimation by ICC supporters will likely be necessary if the court is to navigate its political environment effectively.

Conflicting findings regarding the overall influence of the UN-centred regime and myriad mechanisms have provoked a lively debate, leading some commentators to conclude that the international system is beyond saving. Whether the existing regime is willing or able to facilitate pathways "beyond" gridlock in human rights governance, understood as a wholesale transition in power relations, is debatable. However, pathways "through" gridlock, even if uneven, contested and partial, may still be significant, especially for victims of human rights abuse. This is reflected in the words of Olusegun Obasanjo, one of Amnesty International's most high-profile adopted political prisoners, who likened the effect of the organization to "water on stone" (Power 2001). This chapter has sought to expose some of the smaller incremental steps which often go unnoticed, but may cumulatively pave the way towards significant change.

9

Health

New Leadership for Devastating Challenges

Garrett Wallace Brown and David Held

It is commonplace to argue that the cooperative properties of global governance have not kept pace with the growth and associated challenges of globalization. Many scholars and policymakers often claim that the current multilateral order is "unfit for purpose" (Goldin 2013) and that cooperation has failed to offer reliable crisis management (Broome, Clegg and Rethel 2015; Gill 2015; Held and Roger 2013). Even Chinese President Xi Jinping, addressing the opening ceremony of the G20 in 2016, has noted that the world is "increasingly unable to deliver long-term solutions for sustainable coexistence." The predominant view of global governance is that global cooperation is in a "permanent deficit" (Lamy and Goldin 2014), that this condition represents a "governance dilemma" (Keohane 2002), and that effective governance has become increasingly "gridlocked" (Hale, Held and Young 2013).

In relation to global health governance, assigning such a negative prognosis is not straightforward. This is because global health governance has in many ways witnessed something of a governance boom over the last 16 years with many positive effects (Youde 2014). Global health has had an explosion of new international health actors, development assistance for health (DAH), multisectoral bodies, private foundations, private–public partnerships, bilateral initiatives, multilateral initiatives and new policy directives channelled through traditional United Nations mechanisms. Since the year 2000, global health governance has seen the establishment of key global health institutions and governance mechanisms, such as the Global Fund to Fight AIDS, Tuberculosis and Malaria (GFATM), Gavi, the Vaccine Alliance, and the 2005 International Health Regulations (IHR), as well as the addition of a number of major private organizations such as the Bill and Melinda Gates Foundation. With this increased interest in health came new promises for aid delivery and global health "partnerships," which were articulated through the health policy components of the Millennium Development Goals (MDGs), the Paris Declaration on Aid Effectiveness, its reiterations in Accra and Busan, and now within the Sustainable Development Goals (SDGs). In terms of funding, between 2000 and 2013 annual DAH tripled from US$10.8 billion to US$31.3 billion, signifying an annualized growth rate of over 11 per cent (IHME 2015).

Nevertheless, despite the growth in DAH and increased calls within the MDGs and SDGs for a coordinated global cooperation in health, it would still be overly enthusiastic to claim that the overall condition of global health cooperation has improved to the point where global health governance is substantially "fit for purpose," or that global health outcomes adequately reflect the growth of global health actors, DAH and the health risks associated with globalization. Accordingly, although global health governance is unlike some other policy sectors – in that it has witnessed substantially increased activity – it still suffers from its own unique symptoms of gridlock. For example, although there have been some successes in meeting MDGs 4 and 5 (to reduce child mortality and improve maternal health), the consensus is that the goals went largely unmet (UN IGME 2013). In addition, as in the case of Ebola and the rise of extensively drug-resistant tuberculosis (XDR-TB), the increased number of institutions and funding streams do not translate into a sufficiently quick response, enhanced coordinated governance, or decisive global health leadership. Furthermore, despite increased DAH, it is still the case that most DAH funding is allocated to select diseases, mainly AIDS, tuberculosis and malaria, which often results in underfunding for what are known as the "neglected diseases." Moreover, although there have been excellent efforts to form partnerships within such frameworks as Gavi and the GFATM, the verdict on the long-term success of these pockets of targeted cooperation remains contested, since there is evidence to question whether these initiatives have translated into long-term health system strengthening or sustainable health delivery mechanisms (Coyne and Williams 2014; Swanson et al. 2015). When considered at the macro-level, there clearly remains a significant gap between overall increases in institutional growth and DAH and the implementation of policy that delivers effective healthcare, a point that has led some to argue that current practice fails to improve global health outcomes overall

(Coyne and Williams 2014; Swanson et al. 2015). What this suggests is that despite all the growth in health expenditure and attention, global health cooperation remains significantly underperforming.

Against this background, it is possible to locate key indicators symptomatic of global health gridlock as well as a number of recent pathways that suggest there are avenues through it. The gridlock heuristic highlights how the meteoric growth of global health governance since the year 2000 created a condition in which effective global policymaking is increasingly compromised due to rising transaction costs and policy coordination problems, exacerbated by an increased number of health actors that must operate within a narrow policy bandwidth. Viewing current global health governance through the lens of gridlock sheds light on the fact that global health cooperation today is underperforming not simply because it is very difficult to solve many global health problems, but because previous phases of global health mobilization have been incredibly successful in creating a large number of global health actors and programmes, which, in turn, have produced unintended consequences that now complicate the coordination and problem-solving capacities of the health regime complex as a whole. Yet, as we explore later in the chapter, there are also a number of potential avenues to increase cooperation and move through gridlock, despite the fact that global health governance, as a whole, still remains far from being "fit for purpose."

The aim of this chapter is to better understand the role of gridlock within global health as well as to locate potential mechanisms through and beyond it. Accordingly, the chapter first provides a mapping of global health gridlock. Second, it will explore three pathways "through" gridlock. Although there are potentially many avenues *through* and even *beyond* global health gridlock, this chapter will specifically focus on three key pathways that offer the most promising avenues in current global health governance: (1) a realignment of major power interests around global infectious disease control; (2) a plurality of actors around common International Health Regulations and SDG principles; and (3) a reinvigorated trend of innovative leadership by G7 countries and their institutional partners.

Pathways to Gridlock in the Global Health Regime

In an effort to understand global health gridlock and potential avenues through it, it is useful to identify four pathways to gridlock in global health governance: rising multipolarity, institutional inertia, harder problems, and institutional fragmentation (Hale, Held and Young 2013). Each pathway can be thought of as a growing trend that embodies a specific mix of causal mechanisms related to global health governance. These pathways, when examined as a whole, often inter-relate and conjoin to limit cooperative and effective problem solving and thus represent key barriers for the construction of more effective global health policies.

Global health gridlock and growing multipolarity

The total number of states has increased substantially over the last 70 years. More importantly, the number of states that must politically engage on a given issue – that is, the states without whose cooperation a global problem cannot be adequately addressed – has expanded by similar proportions. When the World Health Organization (WHO) was founded in 1948, it had 61 members. Today, it has over 190 which have to come together to agree on policy initiatives and implementation. Integrating the views of actors at different stages of development, with distinct but varying alignments, not to mention shifting inter-ests, is extremely challenging and often difficult to achieve. The WHO has to achieve consensus between its 194 countries if policy is to be agreed and, accordingly, the weaving of coherent policy outcomes is often impossible (Kickbusch and Reddy 2015).

During the Cold War, competing interests were largely articulated through the struggle between the US and the Soviet Union. Today alignments are much more complicated as many of the developing countries have grown significantly in recent years and have become major investors and shareholders in the global health industry. As a result, power differentials are more diffused and donor/recipient relations no longer simply map on to the West/South divide. For example, new emerging powers such as Brazil, Russia, India, China and South Africa (BRICS) are having greater influence on global health policy (Harmer and Buse 2014). In addition, the BRICS are able increas-ingly to exert influence on WHO decision-making (Gautier et al. 2014) to provide access to medicines outside of traditional markets (Yu 2008), to offer alternative sources of DAH (Chan 2011; Cabral, Russo and Weinstock 2014), and increasingly to represent an alternative to Western "business as usual" in global health (Bax 2014; Bond and Garcia 2015).

This increased multipolarity has in many ways helped to undermine WHO authority, since many influential states place more stringent conditions on the WHO and/or seek alternative policy mechanisms outside the UN system. For example, the WHO used to receive three-quarters of its financing from assessed contributions levied on members. However, a change to a zero real growth policy for its regular budget in the 1980s has meant it now only receives one-quarter of its budget from member contributions and is dependent on extra-budgetary ring-fenced "pet project" funding from donors to fill an increasingly shrinking budget (Sridhar and Gostin 2011). As the money flows to bilateral or other multilateral initiatives, WHO authority dissipates, with numerous organizations like the Institute for Health Metrics and Evaluations, the Bill and Melinda Gates Foundation and Médecins Sans Frontières/Doctors Without Borders able to command greater epistemic authority (Shiffman 2014), financial influence (Frenk and Moon 2013) and response effectiveness (Chonghaile 2015). Although these new institutions might represent one possible pathway "through" gridlock, a real consequence of this development is also that many more countries and their organizational favourites (which represent a diverse range of interests) must agree in order for long-term and more effective global cooperation to occur.

Institutional inertia and global health gridlock

The 1945 postwar order succeeded in part because it incentivized great power involvement in key institutions. From the World Health Organization, to the United Nations Development Programme, to the establishment of UNAIDS, to the programmes of the World Bank – key pillars of the global order explicitly granted special privilege to the countries that were wealthy and powerful at the time of their creation (Barnes and Brown 2011; Hale, Held and Young 2013). This hierarchy helped to secure the participation of the most important countries in global health governance. Today, the gain from this trade-off has shrunk while the costs have grown. As power shifts from the West to the East (the rise of China), the North to the South (with the rise of the BRICS), or from the G7 to the G20, a broader range of participation and coordination is needed on nearly all global issues if they are to be dealt with effectively.

As suggested above, under increased conditions of multipolarity it is becoming increasingly difficult for the WHO to find the authority and resources required to sustain a clear leadership role in global health. Negotiating its way through a landscape of shifting interests, and in an era where collective global action was frowned upon in the face of market triumphalism, it was difficult for the WHO to manoeuvre successfully and reshape the organization in a way that was both responsive and effective. As Kickbusch has observed:

> over the last 30 years or so, the WHO member states – despite continuous verbal commitment to reform – have weakened their organization through significantly reducing its budget, refusing to change its regional structure and not being able to agree on the key mandate and functions of the organization. Many of the policy processes enshrined in the constitution – such as the Executive Board and the World Health Assembly have become dysfunctional; agendas are overloaded, meaningful debates are not easy and consensus based decisions are ever more difficult to achieve. (Kickbusch and Reddy 2015: 839–40)

The WHO has all too often become a victim of its members' interests at just the time when it needed more independent authority to act decisively. What has happened, specifically in the case of global health, is that many countries now pursue their interests elsewhere in a largely under-coordinated manner with cooperation often being more about aligned interests than finding long-term solutions to global health needs (Barnes and Brown 2011; Bruen and Brugha 2014; Brown 2015b; Kickbusch et al. 2013). This has resulted in a series of negative externalities in global health. For example, those with power hold onto asymmetrical influence through mandatory legal mechanisms like the Agreement on Trade-Related Aspects of Intellectual Property Rights (TRIPS) and TRIPS-plus (Muzaka 2011) and/or through more subtle "soft-power" conditionalities insisted on by donors in association with performance-based funding (Barnes, Brown and Harman 2015); or settle on health priorities that can get broad global support in general terms (like the MDGs), but that leave the details of turning normative rhetoric into a decisive political action still wanting (Kickbusch et al. 2013).

Harder problems and global health gridlock

As interdependence deepens, the types and scope of health-related problems around which countries must cooperate has evolved. Problems are now both more extensive and more intensive, and this increases the challenge of effective infectious disease control. Infectious diseases and threats such as Ebola, H1N1 (swine flu), H7N9 (bird flu), MERS-CoV (novel coronavirus), Zika, antimicrobial resistance (AMR), and XDR-TB have grabbed headlines not only because of their potential global threat, but also due to past and existing confusion surrounding how global responses to transborder infectious diseases are organized (Senthilingam 2015). Globalization also poses challenges for combating non-communicable diseases, such as heart disease, which are on the increase as Western lifestyles are mirrored within developing countries (Micha et al. 2012).

Moreover, the "social determinants of health" can be negatively impacted by global factors such as financial crises and unequal economic market conditions (Labonte et al. 2009). There are also major issues stemming from the impact of climate change, which has been predicted to lead to an increase in diseases such as malaria, diarrheal diseases, infectious disease such as HIV/AIDS as well as an increase in serious cardiorespiratory difficulties (IPCC 2014). In fact, there is significant evidence that this impact is already being felt, especially in the poorest countries (Hansen et al. 2013; Chen et al. 2013). The problem is that in order to meet these challenges, health diplomacy must navigate a host of social, environmental, and cultural subjects, such as intellectual property, health and environmental standards and financial responsibility – about which countries and international organizations often disagree sharply.

Fragmentation and global health gridlock

The institution-builders of the late 1940s operated in a far less crowded organizational space with only limited institutional path dependencies like the League of Nations Health Organization, the Office International d'Hygiène Publique and the Pan American Sanitary Bureau to absorb into policy coordination. But efforts to cooperate internationally today occur in a dense institutional ecosystem shaped by large-scale and multivariate path dependency. The exponential rise in both multilateral and transnational organizations has created a more complex multi-level and multi-actor system of global health governance. For example, in 1909 the total number of intergovernmental organizations in existence was 37. In 2014, the global health sector alone accounts for 3,401 registered international institutions, associations and associated organizations (Union of International Associations 2014). What is astounding is that this number does not include all bilateral health programmes, such as those offered by the US Agency for International Development (USAID) or the President's Emergency Plan for AIDS Relief (PEPFAR), and further excludes many specific programmes by multilateral international bodies that may have significant bearing on health policy, such as the World Bank and the UN Children's Fund (UNICEF). This condition is further exacerbated and enhanced by the increase in multipolarity outlined above, since fragmented institutions often become avenues for more traditional forms of state brinkmanship and compliance avoidance.

Within this dense web of institutions mandates can conflict, interventions are frequently uncoordinated, and all too typically scarce resources are subject to intense competition. In this context, the proliferation of institutions can lead to dysfunctional fragmentation, reducing the ability of multilateral institutions to provide public goods. When funding and political will are scarce, countries need focal points to guide policy (Keohane and Martin 1995), which can help define the nature and form of cooperation. Yet, when international regimes overlap, with multiple funding streams, these positive effects can be weakened. Fragmented institutions, in turn, can disaggregate resources and political will, while increasing transaction costs.

This is an acute problem in global health since nearly all initiatives in high-burden countries are funded by multiple sources. These sources have their own monitoring, accounting and evaluation systems that are often not compatible with one another and/or with local systems. With more health actors come more meetings and evaluations, which are widely reported as one of many capacity restraints faced by already weakened health systems (Barnes, Brown and Harman 2015). The increased number of actors can also lead to an inefficient division of labour, where actors such as the WHO, Global Fund, PEPFAR, UNAIDS, USAID, the BRICS, World Bank, the Gates Foundation and the Clinton Foundation (to name only a few) often produce parallel programmes or disjointed vertical health silos that have not generated overall system strengthening in high-burden countries (Swanson et al. 2015; Montagu and Yamey 2011). Although this is not always the case, and there are success stories (see below), the problem is that there is undoubtedly a marked level of fragmentation within global health policy, which can lead to diffused responsibility, unclear accountability chains and the potential for certain actors to escape or undermine global norm constraints and progress.

Through and beyond Global Health Gridlock

Although different pathways can carry more significance in some health sectors than in others, the rapid growth in global health governance since 2000 has in many ways generated a condition in which effective global policymaking is increasingly slowed or stalled due to heightened transaction costs and policy coordination problems. While current practice overall does not represent a condition of gridlock, in the sense of the full paralysis of policymaking, it is still the case that many areas are exhibiting features of gridlock. That is, a series of second-order cooperation problems arising from previous phases of success in globalization and increases in global health response now complicate effective problem solving as well as long-term reform at the global level.

Nevertheless, some recent positive trends signal pathways *through gridlock* within the global health regime. Three pathways stand out as particularly germane to global health: (1) a realignment of major power interests around global infectious disease control; (2) plurality around common principles like the IHR and SDGs; and (3) renewed trends of innovative leadership by the G7 and its institutional partners.

Global pandemics and shifts in major powers' core security interests

There has been widespread consensus that "the Ebola epidemic was a wake-up call for all of us." This statement, jointly made by Angela Merkel, Barack Obama and David Cameron at the 2015 G7 Summit in Germany, reflects growing concern about the ability of countries and global institutions to respond effectively to the next global outbreak (Brown 2015b). For example, the Ebola epidemic killed over 11,000 people, infecting over 27,000, and there is widespread recognition by the health community that the WHO (and global health governance more broadly) was poorly prepared to fight the outbreak. Particularly, it is widely held that there was a very slow global response to Ebola, that there was ineffective surveillance of the virus despite long-standing knowledge of its potential threat, that the alarm was not raised soon enough, that there was a general lack of health leadership across all sectors, a lack of coordination and emergency funding, and that there is a general lack of treatment and vaccines in relation to most diseases that represent global threats, including but not just Ebola.

As part of this post-Ebola "call to arms" two new global financing mechanisms were introduced in 2015 to support health emergency responses. These are the WHO's Contingency Fund for Emergencies (CFE) and the World Bank's Pandemic Emergency Financing Facility (PEF). In essence, the CFE was the by-product of continued discussions around the International Health Regulations and was adopted at the 68th World Health Assembly. As part of a more coordinated global emergency response strategy, the CFE aims to fill the gap between the first 72 hours of a declared health emergency and the time at which resources from other financing mechanisms begin to flow. The CFE covers all countries regardless of income in order to prevent an infectious disease from escalating into a "public health emergency of international concern," as defined in the IHR, as well as to respond to other Grade 3 events with substantial public health consequences, whether disease related or not. The fund is triggered by national request and the level of funding is decided on a case-by-case basis (from a US$100 million fund), which can include funding for personnel, information technology and information systems, medical supplies, and field and local government support. Since its creation in 2015, the CFE has disbursed US$8.5 million for a range of interventions related to the Zika virus in South America, yellow fever in central Africa, and drought-related food insecurity in Asia. Undoubtedly the CFE shows signs of promise, yet the programme is still in its infancy and its success will be determined by how well it continues to be funded, and how well it is implemented as a global first response.

The PEF was established after the final 2015 G7 communiqué in Germany and is currently in its final design phase at the World Bank with an expected launch at the end of 2017. It was proposed by the G7 as an insurance mechanism that seeks to support and follow up measures in emergencies after initial CFE funds have been mobilized. It aims to do this by providing a surge of post-CFE funding for response efforts to prevent infectious disease outbreaks from becoming costly pandemics with a high global death toll. It notes, for example, epidemic risks from new orthomyxoviruses (new influenza pandemic virus A, B and C), coronaviridae (SARS, MERS), filoviridae (Ebola, Marburg) and other zoonotic diseases that can be transmitted from animals (Crimean-Congo haemorrhagic fever, Rift Valley fever, Lassa fever).

The total level of funding for the PEF is estimated to be up to US$500 million per outbreak. In many ways, this financial mechanism signals a significant response by major powers to the immediate failures associated with Ebola and thus represents a potentially powerful pathway through gridlock in fighting major disease outbreaks. The PEF will be financed through two delivery "windows" initially underwritten by G7 countries: an insurance mechanism for funds up to US$500 million, and an immediate cash injection between US$50 and US$100 million. In creating an insurance mechanism, the G7 and World Bank have suggested that the PEF will create a new market for pandemic insurance that will bring "greater discipline and rigor to pandemic preparedness and incentivize better pandemic response planning." In addition, the World Bank anticipates SDG 3.8 (universal health coverage, see below) enhancement since it is foreseen that the PEF will "stimulate efforts by countries and development partners to build better core public health capabilities for disease surveillance and health systems strengthening, toward universal health coverage" (World Bank 2016). Prima facie, this statement does suggest that the PEF should link into more long-term health system and capacity strategies, thus signalling a potentially robust move through multipolarity and fragmented gridlock. Yet, specific targets for measuring these aims for greater discipline and emergency preparedness have not yet been publicized and without clear enumeration it is hard to see exactly how the insurance scheme will promote health system strengthening (HSS) of the sort that is recommended by both the IHR and the SDGs.

Although these new financing mechanisms are designed to fill important gaps in overall global emergency preparedness and demonstrate a level of coordinated interest by major powers, they also raise a number of questions regarding how they might provide a more comprehensive pathway through gridlock. First, these initiatives are the products of two very different global health governance processes, with the CFE being a product of the World Health Assembly and the PEF being underwritten by the G7 via the World Bank. Although both initiatives seek to respond to the failures in confronting Ebola and, hence, to a significant consequence of gridlock, there are concerns that they are not sufficiently joined up in terms of how they link to already agreed IHR commitments as well as how they will draw from, and build, SDGs' response capacities within regions and countries. Again, it is important to note that only the CFE has a formal relationship with the IHR and thus its catalogue of internationally agreed interventions. The CFE was set up within the context of an IHR recommendation, and located within the wider WHO Health Emergencies Programme, as confirmed at the World Health Assembly in 2016. Therefore, unlike the PEF, it enjoys a level of global legitimacy, since it is available to all WHO member states, covers the full spectrum of cross-border public health risks enumerated in the IHR, and is managed under the funding rules and institutional frameworks of the intergovernmental body.

Second, there are concerns about whether the "securitization of health" (with particular emphasis on infectious disease control) within the motivational logic of the major powers can sufficiently address the broader health risks associated with globalization. This is because "securitizing health" prioritizes surveillance and containment, which many argue does so at the expense of more long-term and effective strategies that focus on prevention, detection and care via strengthened health systems (Rushton 2011; Rushton and Youde 2014). For example, the PEF, unlike the CFE, which covers Grade 3 emergencies, does not specifically mention funding for health emergencies related to non-infectious disease, such as chemical poisonings or climate disaster. As a result, it remains unclear, as well as unlikely, that these sorts of health-related emergencies would be covered under PEF guidelines. The implication is that these initiatives can at the moment be seen to represent only an investment in the securitization of global health by the G7 major powers, with their limited focus on surveillance and containment of infectious diseases, versus the broader health initiatives required for reaching the SDGs beyond gridlock.

Third, although the PEF initiative will no doubt have an impact on creating more effective health responses, there are concerns about the "global" reach of the PEF. Unlike the CFE, only countries eligible for financing from the International Development Association (IDA, the World Bank's fund for the poorest countries) can be beneficiaries of the PEF. This then raises a number of questions about coverage in areas where disease risks remain high. As one example, India is no longer eligible for IDA and thus will remain uncovered by PEF under its current design. This is despite the fact that India continues to have a high disease burden rate as well as significant global health security risks, as evidenced by high numbers of cases of XDR-TB and other forms of antimicrobial resistance such as methicillin-resistant Staphylococcus aureus (MRSA). As mentioned above, the PEF is not included as a significant element within the WHO Health Emergencies Programme, and is mentioned only as a fund that the CFE should be careful not to replicate. This raises concerns since it is the stated aim of the Health Emergencies Programme for the WHO to be the sole coordinator for global emergency response and to limit fragmentation of development assistance for health. As a result, it is unclear how well the PEF can effectively cover health emergencies in all cases and where health emergency relief can reliably be acquired in non-IDA cases (such as in India). Although a tightly aligned CFE and PEF could provide an effective avenue beyond gridlock, there is also potential for further fragmentation between the two misaligned initiatives.

Due to current policy ambiguities it is unclear whether both financial mechanisms can be seen as complementary additions to longer-term global strategies to build preparedness capacities and strengthen overall global SDG responses. In addition, it is uncertain whether PEF will garner widespread "buy in" and compliance as the G7 mandate moves forward. This is largely due to lingering doubts about PEF's global representativeness, the fact that it is located outside the IHR, and because of its perceived lack of political legitimacy. Therefore, as it stands, these emergency mechanisms only represent a possible pathway through gridlock. However, if they remain partly disconnected, and add to the fragmentation of efforts, they could also provide ripe conditions for continued gridlock and underperformance in global health.

Coordinating plurality around the IHR and SDGs

As the introduction to this volume notes, pathways to or through gridlock rarely operate in isolation. The relationship between major power interests, global health security risks, health regulations, health goals and health outcomes are, as illustrated above, often interlinked within global health governance. As part of the health security discourse it is often recognized that many health systems remain too weak to prevent, monitor, track and respond to emerging global threats. It is not surprising, for example, that Ebola was most prevalent in African countries that had weak health systems. Many health experts have long argued the importance of better implementing the IHR as well as for renewed efforts to strengthen regional and national health capacities around a set of common goals like the SDGs. For many, including major powers in the West, there is now an understanding that long-term health security is dependent on health system strengthening and increased global governance capacities, and that there is currently a deficit in this regard. This concern has been compounded recently by the fact that many diseases continue to be "neglected" throughout all levels of health governance and, thus, get inadequate attention until it is often too late to avoid large-scale and highly expensive responses. In particular, over the last five years there has been a new policy focus on a diverse set of WHO-recognized neglected tropical diseases that thrive mainly among the poorest and in the most unprepared health systems. It is estimated that the 17 main examples of these neglected diseases affect more than 1.4 billion people and are endemic in 149 countries. In this way, the scope of potential risks is global.

As a policy response, there have been increasing calls by global health actors for more robust health regulations and strategy targets. In line with the framework presented in this volume, it is possible to understand specific efforts within global health policy to coordinate multiple and diverse organizations around a common set of goals and norms. Although there have been a number of promising and successful policy efforts (such as the Framework Convention on Tobacco Control), there have been two particularly promising cooperative efforts around acceptance and implementation of the IHR as well as positive norm diffusion associated with the newly adopted Sustainable Development Goal 3.8, which focuses on universal health coverage (UHC).

The International Health Regulations were adopted by member states in the World Health Organization on 23 May 2005. They require that all countries have the ability to detect, assess, report and respond to potential public health emergencies of international concern at all levels of government, and to report such events rapidly to the WHO to determine whether a coordinated, global response is required. Under the agreement, countries were given until 2016 to prevent the spread of risk by developing core capacities to determine the control measures required, provide logistical detection capability, create investigative mechanisms, boost internal and external communication capabilities, and create robust national response plans (WHO 2015a).

The main coordinating feature of the IHR, and thus the regulations' main mechanism for steering policies through gridlock, is the requirement that all state parties must have established the minimum public health core capacities by June 2016. From self-assessment reports sent to the WHO in 2015, many countries have made progress since 2012, most notably in surveillance and laboratory capacities, in legislation and in human resources (WHO 2015a), including through an Integrated Disease Surveillance Response (WHO Africa 2015). In this way, the IHR have provided a consistent policy focus to align multisectoral actors and regulate compliance. However, less progress has been reported regarding emergency preparedness, in capacities at points of entry to countries, and in dealing with chemical and food safety risks, suggesting poor preparedness in dealing with a wide range of public health risks (SEATINI, TARSC with Limpopo 2016). What this suggests, in terms of movement beyond gridlock, is that although common norms, regulations and goals have the ability to generate common policy drivers and outcomes, the effectiveness of those outcomes still relies on consistent reinforcement via financial and technical cooperation. The fact that the IHR have only been partly met suggests that, despite widespread normative agreement, a more concerted effort to promote all aspects of IHR compliance is still needed. Without this, the IHR might lead to continued underperformance and gridlock, specifically as PEF and other non-aligned programmes scale up.

In order to mitigate gridlock it is necessary to strengthen the implementation of the IHR so that they can act as the primary framework in the global health security agenda. As part of this the IHR will require better short-, medium- and long-term strategies and targets that work in a complementary manner, with funding directed to the full set of implementation capacities as well as more emphasis on sustainable funding for longer-term strengthening of health systems. Adopting this approach could offer new avenues through gridlock in the long term, since a strength of the IHR is that they are not limited to addressing emergencies after they have started, but are also intended to build public health capacities to detect, prevent and control diseases. As a policy umbrella, other global health security measures could be aligned to the IHR (see concerns with PEF above), and to measures in countries and regions, to build systems to detect, prevent, manage and respond to public health risks and emergencies. This would not only increase coverage, but also effectiveness.

In terms of providing additional overarching policy uniformity, one of the great innovations of the Sustainable Development Goals initiative is that it situates all global development activities within its 17 development goals and 169 targets. In this way, if taken seriously, the potential for institutional pluralism to act as a mechanism for gridlock could be diminished by the SDGs. This unifying element is enhanced by the recent adoption of SDG 3.8, which enumerates universal health coverage as the primary organizational norm. The norm is defined as the objective that "all individuals and communities receive the health services they need without suffering financial hardship. It includes the full spectrum of essential, quality health services, from health promotion to prevention, treatment, rehabilitation, and palliative care" (WHO 2015b).

It is too soon to determine the positive affects of the SDGs on global health policy coordination and its ability to counter gridlock. Nevertheless, there are a number of positive signs suggesting that the SDGs, and in particular UHC, could provide what Keohane and Martin (1995) have described as a necessary focal point for more coordinated global cooperation. First, unlike the MDGs, the SDGs have had a long and inclusive deliberative process that included an Open Working Group of 70 countries, a series of UN-sponsored "Global Conversations," 11 thematic consultations, 83 national consultations and several door-to-door surveys so as to capture population preferences. As a result, the SDGs enjoy a sense of perceived legitimacy and self-legislation, which should translate into improved compliance and implementation. Second, there is agreed recognition about the failures of the MDGs and there has been an upsurge in political will not to repeat past mistakes. Third, there is significant evidence suggesting that a majority of countries are already incorporating the SDGs into their national health strategies, which illustrates that the SDGs are already delivering some of their planned coordinating effects. Fourth, although the SDGs are clearly overly ambitious in terms of scope, they do help to sharpen development aims by framing them against 169 measurable targets. As part of this performance-based model, it will be easier to track progress, locate policy and resource gaps, and to demand accountability in cases of non-compliance (for both developed and developing countries). Fifth, as will be discussed in the next section, the SDGs – and particularly UHC – has been diffused and adopted by the major powers and key institutions as a master concept and norm. For example, UHC has been explicitly stated as the guiding norm in global health development by key institutions such as the G7, G20, G77 (developing countries), the World Bank, the GFATM, Gavi, PETFAR, the New Development Bank, the BRICS, the EU, USAID, African Union, ASEAN, all UN agencies, the Bill and Melinda Gates Foundation, and many more. Sixth, the link between the SDGs, UHC and health system strengthening is being driven by key global health leaders as well as by a majority of developing countries (see below). This starts to address a main failure in MDG thinking, but also sharpens long-term health development aims that seek to end dependency cycles and underperformance in development assistance for health. In this respect, there are promising signs that the SDGs will at least enjoy faster and more sustained effect than the MDGs, which could alleviate disjointed multipolarity, underperformance and policy fragmentation.

New global health leadership by the G7 and associates

As stated above, pathways through gridlock overlap and there are often multifarious policy interplays between the motivational interests of major powers, the norms and institutions created to secure those interests, and the diffusion of those norms across sectors. Moreover, these governance pathways are often intersected and influenced by specific global health leaders who can produce innovations within existing pathways or construct new pathways to fill existing deficits. These leaders can be motivated by shifts in self-interest in alignment with others or by broader recognition of the need for norm entrepreneurship in the face of collective action problems. In global health it is possible to witness an increased number of new and old actors assuming leadership roles in an effort to navigate through existing health gridlock.

In terms of non-traditional leadership, the last ten years have seen the rise of influential global foundations such as the Bill and Melinda Gates Foundation and the Clinton Foundation. Although there are meaningful debates about whether organizations like the Gates Foundation have disproportionately positive or negative authority in global health policy, it is impossible to ignore the massive funding provided by these foundations as well as their ability to provide epistemic leadership. In the case of the Gates Foundation, its leadership in global health has led to the creation of the Institute for Health Metrics and Evaluations, and it has become the largest donor to the GFATM during the financial crisis and a key broker in a number of key health initiatives centred around evidence-based policymaking in health.

Although innovations associated with non-traditional leadership sources can be effective, it is still the case that most global health innovations are driven by powerful states and their collective coordinating and financial power. For example, there is a long tradition of G7 leadership giving a vital injection of political and financial support to global health. Perhaps the best illustration of this is from the 2000 Summit in Okinawa, where the then G8 (G7 plus Russia) agreed to support the establishment of the Global Fund to Fight AIDS, Tuberculosis and Malaria. In Japan the G8 stated that diseases like HIV/AIDS, malaria and TB were having large-scale negative effects on global economic growth, development and health security. In order to curb these threats, the G8 facilitated the creation of the Transitional Working Group to design the new institution, while also pledging an initial funding round of US$10 billion to help launch the institution's funding efforts. This act of leadership has had profound impacts on global responses to infectious disease (although adding to fragmentation). According to the GFATM, the estimated result of this particular leadership injection has been the saving of 20 million lives since its establishment in 2002, with over 2 million lives predicted to be saved each year. Moreover, the Global Fund's efforts within participating countries has equated to a 40 per cent decrease in new HIV/AIDS cases, a 29 per cent reduction in tuberculosis, and a 48 per cent decrease in new malaria infections since 2002 (GFATM 2016). Although a direct causal connection between these reductions and the interventions of the GFATM is difficult to determine (due to the fact that national programmes also play a huge role), it is clear that the GFATM has made a significant contribution to improving population health.

More recently, as a direct response to the failure to meet MDG goals 4 and 5, the G7 provided the catalyst for the creation of the Global Financial Facility (GFF). Designed as a financial component to the SDGs, GFF was announced in September 2014 to help close the funding gap for reproductive, maternal, newborn, child and adolescent health. In order to enhance greater collaboration, the fund is delivered through the World Bank, but in compliance with the UN Secretary-General's Every Woman Every Child Global Strategy 2.0. As part of the GFF, a total of 62 high-burden, low- and lower-middle-income countries are eligible to receive grant resources. As of now, the GFF is phasing in its operations, beginning with an initial set of four "frontrunner" countries – Democratic Republic of Congo, Ethiopia, Kenya and Tanzania, with Bangladesh, Cameroon, India, Liberia, Mozambique, Nigeria, Senegal and Uganda announced as the second wave of GFF countries to be funded from 2016. Countries are eligible for between US$10 million and US$60 million over a three- to four-year period.

Again in an attempt to move through gridlock and correct past failures in the response to diseases like severe acute respiratory syndrome (SARS) and Ebola, the G7 in 2016 reaffirmed the WHO's central role in coordinating rapid and effective responses to public health emergencies, as well as restating the G7's commitment to the Global Health Security Agenda (GHSA), which represents a partnership of over 50 countries to promote health security at both the global and national level through collective resource mobilization. As part of the overall health security agenda, the G7 urged the WHO to implement rapidly its emergency reforms, including the full roll-out of its One WHO approach, as well as calling on the international community to support the WHO's new CFE, which enables an injection of money and technical expertise within 24 hours of a declared emergency. The G7 has also assigned the creation of PEF to the World Bank, as noted earlier, and invited the international community to further lend their financial and technical support to PEF. In a welcome shift of discourse, the G7 has now also made an explicit request for better alignment of the CFE and PEF initiatives, in order to protect against gridlock by creating a more comprehensive and coordinated global health architecture.

In response to similar concerns to those raised in the sections above, there are also renewed efforts by the G7 to link the IHR explicitly to the GHSA as well as to key health-related initiatives, such as the Joint External Evaluation tool, the Food and Agriculture Organization's food nutrition efforts, the new WHO Health Emergencies Programme, and the World Organisation for Animal Health. In addition, the G7 is backing antimicrobial resistance programmes as part of GHSA by promoting and financially stimulating efforts associated with the One Health Approach, and its connection to the IHR, the 2016 High Level Meetings on AMR at the United Nations, the EU Ministerial One Health Conference, the Tokyo Meeting of Health Ministers on AMR, and the GHSA AMR Action Package. Although it is too soon to determine whether leadership here will help move beyond gridlock by linking various health security streams, these meetings do offer the opportunity for creating more robust and cooperative strategies.

In making a clear link between the IHR and other health security activities, the G7 has suggested that the IHR are a key mechanism for better organizing global health governance. This has significant meaning since by promoting the IHR the G7 has effectively advanced a policy mechanism that has traditionally generated a high level of "buy in" from the World Health Assembly, the 196 signature countries, as well as a majority of high disease burdened communities. In addition, in the face of widely recognized disease response failures, the IHR represent a crucial detection and prevention mechanism that, in principle, strengthens protective measures against pandemic diseases. What this potentially signals, when viewed optimistically, is a move towards a more legitimate alignment of global health policies, in which the internationally agreed IHR can help steer and legitimate ongoing global health policies through gridlock.

Yet, perhaps the most significant leadership move through potential gridlock relates to the G7's recent recognition of the importance of universal health coverage at the Japan 2016 Leaders' Summit and its necessary connection to health system strengthening. What is most promising in terms of breaking gridlock is the fact that the G7 positioned UHC as the overarching normative framework in global health. This was done by bringing key global health initiatives under the umbrella of UHC as a master concept. For example, the G7 positioned the work of both the WHO and the World Bank as essential representatives of a UHC approach to health. In doing so, the G7 also listed key new initiatives such as the GFF as needing to fit into an overall UHC framework. What is perhaps most promising in terms of global health effectiveness is the fact that the G7 has also linked the GHSA to the health systems strengthening approach, which stresses a long-term global health strategy from the ground up and affirms that security and health systems are co-constituted (Brown and Stoeva 2014). As the official G7 Leaders' Summit Declaration states:

> we reiterate our commitment to enhance our support and coordination to strengthen health systems, especially in developing countries, to make them more resilient, inclusive, affordable, sustainable, and equitable ones. To this end, we emphasize the need for a strengthened international framework to coordinate the efforts and expertise of all relevant stakeholders...we support the establishment of *UHC 2030* that seeks to ensure the International Health Partnership (IHP+) principles...and to promote and catalyze [through establishing a UN envoy] efforts towards UHC across different sectors. (G7 2016: 11–12)

The implications of this leadership position on UHC are potentially dramatic. First, by presenting UHC as a master concept in global health, the G7 has effectively signalled its "buy in" to SDG 3, as well as to its most ambitious target for UHC. Second, in doing so, the G7 endorsed the UCH 2030 Alliance, which will create a political and coordinated forum that can deliver on SDG 3.8. By backing this initiative, the G7 solidified the Alliance's role as a key international health partner and further gave the forum the needed authority to help manage the complexities of global gridlock. Third, the emphasis placed on "country-led" health system strengthening as a means to effectively deliver UHC is also important to note. Although it is too early to tell, G7 commitments could represent the kind of normative shift that many global health experts have been arguing is needed to move beyond gridlock. Finally, it is necessary to underscore the significance of linking HSS to long-term health security, since a failure to do so in the past has often been a source of criticism – where health security favours surveillance and containment rather than HSS, which itself favours long-term preventative strategies aimed at removing future threats through strengthened health systems (Rushton 2011; Brown and Stoeva 2014). Although it is clear that health security is still the dominant motivator for the G7, and there are still concerns about the role of PEF within the IHR and SDGs (see above), it nevertheless could represent a significant first step towards a more sophisticated and comprehensively long-term global health strategy through and beyond gridlock.

However, there remain reasons to be cautious. First, although the G7 supported better coordination through the UHC 2030 Alliance, they have not yet offered financial support. Second, in relation to AMR, the G7 has remained lacklustre in promoting cooperative research and development opportunities. One argument for this reluctance relates to traditional issues surrounding intellectual property rights and concerns for the protection of G7 corporate interests. Although this reading might be overly cynical, it remains the case that the G7 has only been vaguely willing "to consider potential for new incentives to promote R&D," stopping far short of providing any tangible leadership or financial commitment. At present, the exception has been Britain, which pledged over £300 million to finance national and global support for exploring new collaborations and research in AMR.

Having said this, it would, all things being equal, be churlish to overlook the G7's positive leadership role in global health since 2000 as well as its seemingly re-energized efforts to better coordinate global policies since 2014. In particular, the G7 shows revitalized interest in embedding the language of UCH into the global health lexicon, thus providing additional opportunities through gridlock via common norms and goals. In this way, renewed leadership in global health by G7 countries offers some needed pathways through gridlock while suggesting that once again, as with the creation of the GFATM in Okinawa in 2000, the G7 can lay the seeds for more fit-for-purpose global health policy. The key, however, is making sure that these new global health initiatives take stock of past fragmentations that resulted from rapid and uncoordinated growth, so that they are joined up and guided by a limited number of rules that promote coordinated follow-through politically and financially.

Conclusion

In many ways the three pathways above represent potentially powerful mechanisms through gridlock. Although there is still much more that needs to be done in order to unravel existing gridlock – in particular to limit counterproductive competitiveness in development assistance for health and unclear institutional jurisdictions – there are some promising signs. The key is to recognize that expansive sectorial growth in global health without meaningful coordination can disrupt and undermine the effectiveness of global health policy. As a result, there needs to be recognition of the importance of better partnerships not just more partnerships, since more does not always equal better (Barnes and Brown 2011). Recognition of gridlock can help us to search for a politics beyond gridlock and to strengthen current initiatives that provide realistic pathways through it. In addition, by applying gridlock as a heuristic device we are able to assess critically new efforts to coordinate global health policy (such as between IHR, PEF and CFE) as well as highlight potential areas of under-coordination that could exacerbate existing underperformance.

Understanding conditions of gridlock and avenues through it represents a hugely significant and important task. In global health governance this becomes particularly true as we embark on the monumental task of achieving the SDGs while also facing acute health challenges such as the rise of AMR, the health effects of spreading Western diets, increasing climate-related disease, and amplified social determinants of health associated with growing global inequalities. Thus, it is only by recognizing the conditions of gridlock and by creating pathways through them that global health policy will be able to tackle the health-related collective action problems that threaten our planet (Bruen and Brugha 2014; Brown 2015a; Kickbusch et al. 2013; Ooms 2014).

10

Climate Change

From Gridlock to Catalyst

Thomas Hale

Ecologists describe the present age as the Anthropocene to mark the unprecedented reality that the actions of humans now represent the single greatest influence on the Earth's natural systems. No issue exemplifies this shift better than climate change. As carbon dioxide and other gases from industrialization and changes in land use progressively saturate the atmosphere, solar radiation is trapped close to the Earth's surface, warming the climate and disrupting many of the natural systems on which we depend. This physical process creates an unprecedented level of political and economic interdependence. It is no exaggeration to note that nearly every action taken by nearly every individual around the world today has an effect on the climate that every other individual on the planet, as well as future generations, must inhabit.

Such intense interdependence creates a classic dilemma of collective action and therefore a need for international cooperation. We would all be better off moving towards a low carbon world, but we all have a selfish incentive to let others lead the way. Worse, those who stand to lose most from climate change – individuals and future generations in underdeveloped countries close to the equator – possess little political power compared to those who benefit most from inaction: the countries, economic interests, and individuals that exploit the most fossil energy. This last category includes, essentially by definition, many of the wealthiest and most powerful countries and interest groups in the world.

It is therefore unsurprising for social scientists that the politics of climate change, at all levels, has more often than not remained stuck in various forms of gridlock (Victor 2011a). Indeed, the multilateral climate regime was a significant motivating case and source of theoretical inspiration for *Gridlock*. Writing in the aftermath of the 2009 Copenhagen Summit, at which countries failed to agree a successor to the Kyoto Protocol, Hale, Held and Young (2013) noted how the climate regime was beset by all four of the gridlock trends: rising multipolarity, harder problems, institutional inertia, and fragmentation.

The time has come to review that diagnosis. Since the 2009 Copenhagen Summit, and, indeed, since *Gridlock*, the climate regime has evolved in extraordinary ways (Bäckstrand and Lövbrand 2016). It has become less intergovernmental and more national, subnational, and transnational, meaning that emphasis has shifted from intergovernmental treaty-making to national policies, as well as the actions of sub- and non-state actors and transnational networks that link various actors across borders (Falkner 2016; Hale 2016; Keohane and Oppenheimer 2016). The 2015 Paris Agreement cemented this shift from a "regulatory" regime that seeks to negotiate binding limits on emissions, to a "catalytic" regime, which seeks to create conditions under which countries and other actors make progressively more ambitious commitments to reduce emissions and build their resilience to changes in the climate, while the multilateral system provides a framework to scrutinize and support such actions. The logic of this "pledge and review and ratchet" system is to create an upward spiral of ambition in which action in the short term begets not free riding but tipping points in both political and economic systems that facilitate even more ambitious actions in the future. This fundamental shift in the nature of the regime represents an extraordinary case of multilateral adaptation and innovation in the face of gridlock.

Can it work? It is far too early to know. At the time of writing, many details of the new regime, such as how the review process will work, are still being negotiated, and the election of Donald Trump in the United States has put into question the role of the world's second largest emitter. Current pledges, if fulfilled, likely put the world on track to somewhere around 3 degrees of warming in the twenty-first century, a massive improvement over the 4 or 5 degrees that would have resulted from business-as-usual, but still 50 percent above the 2-degree target countries have committed to and double the aspirational target of limiting temperature changes to 1.5°C this century. To achieve that goal, net emissions will have to fall to zero in the middle of this century – that is, near total decarbonization of the world economy over the next three to four decades. Even then, significant "negative emissions" technologies – removing carbon permanently from the atmosphere – will likely be required, and perhaps even more radical forms of geoengineering.

If the world is able to achieve these goals over the next decades, or even to make substantial progress towards them, then the way the climate regime shifted from a regulatory to a catalytic model over the last several years will figure as one of the great political successes of the twenty-first century and a decisive move beyond gridlock. If progress is instead limited, history will see the shift as, at most, a second-best, incremental advance.

Because the larger question of effectiveness remains unanswerable, this chapter seeks to explain the changes that *may* come to be seen as pathways beyond gridlock. How and why did the regime shift so dramatically? While these questions will surely require more detailed empirical research than space permits, this chapter draws on several of the pathways beyond gridlock to sketch some initial answers. It is structured as follows. The next section traces the multilateral regime's descent into gridlock from its creation in the early 1990s to its nadir around the 2009 Copenhagen summit. Each of the gridlock trends is clearly at work in this process. The third section then follows the surprising evolution of the regime from Copenhagen to the 2015 Paris conference, describing the shift from a regulatory model to a catalytic one. The fourth section explains how several of the pathways beyond gridlock that animate this book help to explain this shift, and may prospectively shape the effectiveness of the new regime. It focuses on shifts in major powers' interests, a plurality of institutions and actors cohering around a common goal, technical groups, innovative leadership, and the mobilization of domestic constituencies. The concluding section returns to the larger questions of effectiveness that will confront the regime going forward, and considers future issues.

The Descent into Gridlock over Two Decades of Climate Diplomacy

The climate regime emerged at a high point in optimism regarding multilateral governance of the environment. In 1972, hundreds of countries met in Stockholm for the United Nations Conference on the Human Environment. They declared global environmental challenges to be a central concern of human welfare and world politics, and created the United Nations Environment Programme to drive scientific and policy coordination. Over the next two decades, countries agreed a steadily growing number of international treaties to manage international environmental concerns, ranging from cross-boundary air pollution, to the trade in endangered species, to tropical forests. The 1989 Montreal Protocol, which set limits on the production of ozone-depleting substances, enforceable via trade sanctions, was seen as a particularly ambitious and successful example of multi-lateral treaty-based cooperation on a crucial global environmental concern.

Despite such successes, the condition of the global environment continued to worsen, and attention increasingly focused on more systemic global issues like biodiversity, forests, and climate change. At the same time, the 1987 UN report *Our Common Future*, which coined the term "sustainable development," emphasized the linkages between environmental protection, human welfare, and economic growth.

Countries therefore decided that global efforts to protect the environment needed to be consolidated and to be pushed to a higher level of scale and ambition, and so organized, on the twentieth anniversary of the Stockholm conference, the 1992 UN Conference on Environment and Development in Rio. The so-called Earth Summit set out an ambitious programme, summarized as Agenda 21, launching new multilateral negotiations around a wide range of issues including biodiversity, global forests, desertification, and climate change.

Emerging from Rio, the 1992 UN Framework Convention on Climate Change promised to achieve "stabilization of greenhouse gas concentrations in the atmosphere at a level that would prevent dangerous anthropogenic interference with the climate system." It was explicitly designed on the model of the ozone regime, in which an initial framework convention (in the case of ozone, the 1985 Vienna Convention for the Protection of the Ozone Layer) was intended to provide a base for further protocols that would create specific and enforceable obligations to reduce emissions. After all, if the model had worked for ozone-depleting substances, why not greenhouse gases? Also following the ozone regime, the UNFCCC drew a bright line between developed countries, named under Annex 1 of the Convention, and developing countries, with the former expected to take the lead in reducing emissions under the principle of "common but differentiated responsibilities and respective capabilities."

Negotiations then began to translate the ambitious goal of the UNFCCC into specific reductions commitments. These efforts led to the 1997 Kyoto Protocol. After intense negotiations, developed countries committed to reduce emissions by an average of 5 per cent below 1990 levels. Developing countries did not take on any emissions reductions obligations, but were able to participate in various "flexibility mechanisms" in which developed countries could fund emissions reductions in developing countries and count the resulting carbon savings against their own targets.

Though the Kyoto targets were not particularly ambitious, they were seen as an important first step. However, before the Protocol had even been agreed its effectiveness was thrown into question as the United States, the world's largest emitter at the time, rejected it. The United States Senate, in a 95–0 vote, passed a non-binding but highly symbolic resolution to reject any treaty that did not include reduction commitments for developing countries. And by the time the Protocol reached the ratification threshold to actually enter into force, in 2005, the growth of China, India, and other developing countries was rapidly rendering the Protocol less and less significant. Meeting in Bali in 2007, countries therefore decided to negotiate a new protocol by the time they met in Copenhagen in 2009.

But the political fissures that had hampered Kyoto's effectiveness had metastasized in the intervening years. The United States, facing a highly sceptical Congress, disagreed with Europe and others over the legal form a successor to the Kyoto Protocol should take. Least developed countries struggled to secure meaningful commitments to increase their capacity and resources to adapt to climate, despite a pledge from Secretary of State Hillary Clinton that wealthy nations would "mobilize" US$100 billion of climate finance per year by 2020. And perhaps most significantly, no consensus existed on how to interpret the principle of "common but differentiated responsibilities." Despite months of negotiations, developing countries insisted that responsibility for reducing emissions lay with rich countries, which had contributed far more to the problem historically, while developed nations refused to accept a deal that required no commitments from emerging economies. Compounding these structural difficulties, the 2009 economic crisis distracted diplomatic attention from climate change, while some diplomatic missteps by the Danish host government undercut the negotiation process. The Copenhagen conference therefore ended in acrimony, the only substantive outcome of significance a series of national pledges about future emissions reductions made by around 60 countries.

The first decades of the climate regime therefore trace a steady descent into gridlock. It is worth highlighting how the four key gridlock mechanisms hamstrung cooperation around climate.

Multipolarity   In some ways, the grim math of climate change pits what is needed against what is fair. Rich countries are rich in large part because they have enjoyed the benefits of carbon-powered industrialization over the last 150 years. On average, their citizens continue to emit more greenhouse gases per capita than people in poorer countries. Even though in most wealthy countries today emissions have gone down or at least plateaued (in part due to strong environmental policies and increasing efficiency, and in part due to deindustrialization), their historical emissions are what has brought the climate to its current precarious state. Projecting into the future, however, it is largely emissions from poorer developing countries, which now comprise over half of global emissions, that will tip us into crisis in the decades to come. These countries, some of which have only just begun to reap the economic benefits of industrialization, ask why they must limit their own growth to solve a problem they did not cause. The resulting conflict creates a political fault line that has plagued climate negotiations ever since countries sought to give meaning to the idea of "common but differentiated responsibilities and respective capabilities." In 1992, when the rich world accounted for the lion's share of global emissions, it seemed likely that this phrase could be operationalized through some compromise that gave developing countries additional time and technological and financial support to reduce emissions. After all, such two-track systems had worked well for previous environmental issues, such as ozone. The 1997 Kyoto Protocol attempted to create just such a system, by only requiring wealthy countries to reduce emissions. In subsequent years, however, the growth of emerging economies transformed countries like China, Brazil, India, and Indonesia into climate "superpowers," without whose cooperation no solution will be possible. Under these conditions of multipolarity, a Kyoto-style treaty applicable to all major emitters (especially the United States and the larger emerging economies) proved impossible.

Institutional inertia   Inertia worked alongside multipolarity to gridlock the climate regime in several ways. First, procedural wrangling at the first Conference of the Parties prevented countries from adopting formal rules of procedure for the UNFCCC, such as voting rules. Instead, consensus emerged as the de facto rule for decision-making, meaning that a single country can potentially stall the entire process. Once set, these rules have proven impossible to update, leaving the UNFCCC saddled with an awkward set of procedures that often delay negotiations. Second, and even more importantly, the sharp bifurcation drawn in the early years of the regime between rich and poor countries, noted above, was quickly outpaced by reality. By creating two static categories of countries, instead of tying "differentiated responsibilities and respective capabilities" to objective measures like emissions or wealth, the regime created artificial categories that then became politically important to defend. Third, the entire approach the regime pursued for decades – the regulatory model of a "global deal" – was based too closely on other environmental issues, and especially ozone, when climate in fact represented a far different and more complex sort of policy challenge (Rayner and Caine 2015). This "cognitive inertia" among policymakers, activists, and experts arguably became an important barrier to innovation in the face of gridlock.

Harder problems   Climate is a complex problem, relating to multiple interacting physical, social, political, and economic systems that are each categorized by significant degrees of uncertainty. Unlike other environmental issues, it requires a fundamental shift in the basis of the modern economy that has spread around the world since the Industrial Revolution. Decarbonizing the entire world economy in a few short decades, while also delivering rising standards of living to a rapidly expanding global population, is perhaps the most difficult task humanity has ever set for itself. Climate policy therefore extends far beyond the realm of diplomacy to penetrate core aspects of domestic politics and even the daily life of individuals.

Fragmentation   As *Gridlock* argued, the climate regime has come to encompass not just the UNFCCC but a bewildering array of intergovernmental institutions, transnational governance initiatives that link sub- and non-state actors across borders, national and local policies, and other arrangements (Keohane and Victor 2011; Bulkeley et al. 2014). Just at the multilateral level, nearly every major international institution today now engages on the issue in some capacity. The conditions were thus ripe for the unproductive institutional conflict, forum shopping, redundancy of efforts, dissipation of political will, and other negative dynamics that affect some fragmented regimes. After the Copenhagen Summit, with the legitimacy and perceived viability of the UNFCCC process at a historic ebb, corrosive fragmentation was a real possibility. However, in an extraordinary act of adaptation and innovation, the regime has been able to reinvent itself in a way that seems to make fragmentation a virtue. We turn to this shift now.

From Copenhagen to Paris: Shifting from a Regulatory Regime to a Catalytic Regime

After Copenhagen, many observers re-evaluated their expectations about what could be achieved through the UNFCCC process. They shifted attention instead to climate policy in other spheres and at other levels (Falkner, Stephan and Vogler 2010). For example, national policies in key countries were a major focus, especially in the United States where Congress actively considered – and fell just a few votes short of passing – a "cap-and-trade" bill (which would have limited emissions through a market-based mechanism) in the year after Copenhagen. Second, countries increasingly discussed climate change in other intergovernmental fora, such as the G20 or the Major Economies Forum, a negotiating venue of the largest emitters that was created in 2009. Third, attention also grew around the actions being taken by cities and other subnational governments, as well as private companies, either individually or collectively via transnational networks (Hale 2011; Hoffmann 2011; Bulkeley et al. 2014). This "groundswell" of bottom-up climate action had been building over decades, but many observers began ascribing special importance to it as a potential substitute for the lack of an intergovernmental treaty following the perceived failure of Copenhagen.

Despite this growing diversity of institutional fora, the UNFCCC process proved to be more resilient than some had thought. In 2010, meeting in Cancun, Mexico, countries took a number of modest but positive steps: officially recognizing the ad hoc national pledges that had emerged post-Copenhagen and setting the goal of limiting temperature changes to 2°C in this century. This goodwill, enhanced by determined and skilful diplomacy from the Mexican government and reinforced at a meeting in Durban, South Africa, the following year, translated into a commitment to try yet again to come to a global deal, with countries giving themselves a deadline of December 2015, at their meeting in Paris, to deliver a new agreement on climate change.

However, as negotiations proceeded over the subsequent years, it became clear that the Kyoto "global deal" approach – modelled on previous environmental treaties like the Montreal Protocol – would not be possible. First, the United States was adamant that the new agreement should not create new legal obligations that would require ratification by the US Senate, which was seen as an insurmountable hurdle. Second, with continued growth in emerging economies, it was implausible to maintain the idea that no new obligations would be required from China (now the world's largest emitter), India, Brazil, or similar nations. At the same time, the expanding range of actions being taken by some leading countries, cities, regions, and private companies – coupled with rapid advances in renewable energy technologies – showed that the problem was perhaps less intractable than previously thought. Many actors sought to build a new narrative around "green growth," arguing that shifting away from fossil fuels could be done economically, and indeed bring positive benefits beyond limiting future changes in the climate.

These moves found their way into the multilateral negotiations, both in the positions countries adopted and in the strategic leadership of key UN officials – principally the UNFCCC Secretariat and the UN Secretary-General's office – who were eager to maintain the relevance of the multilateral process by adapting it to a new reality. Clearly a new type of treaty would be required. And so diplomats, experts, and activists began to explore how a new climate treaty could best build on and strengthen the more fragmented and "bottom-up" system that had begun to emerge post-Copenhagen. Two key shifts stand out.

First, it was clear that the treaty could not contain the kind of globally agreed reduction targets for individual countries, inscribed in international law, that had formed the backbone of Kyoto. The United States had made it very clear that such a treaty would require Senate ratification, and therefore prevent the US from participating. While this intransigence caused considerable consternation in Europe and among least developed countries, which emphasized the importance of legally binding commitments, the US position was not very distant from that of China, India, or other large emerging economies. If these countries were going to take on obligations under the new treaty – which, given their low levels of historical emissions and continuing levels of poverty, they considered to be a major concession – it would be inconceivable that such obligations would take the form of internationally imposed emissions targets. A more nationally driven process would be required to protect sovereignty.

At the same time, the experience of Kyoto showed that legally binding targets were not always worth very much in practice. The United States, of course, had nominally agreed to a legally binding target but never actually joined the treaty. And other countries that did join, like Canada, simply exited the treaty once it became clear they would not meet their target, therefore avoiding any penalties. Without a credible enforcement mechanism, it was unclear exactly what benefit "legally binding" targets brought to the treaty, while the cost seemed to be the exclusion of the world's largest emitters.

The regime therefore had little choice but to build upon the de facto "pledge and review" system that had emerged from Copenhagen (and which in fact harked back to key provisions of the original 1992 treaty that created the UNFCCC). Countries agreed to submit pledges stating what steps they would take in the future to limit climate change, though substantial disagreement existed over the form, content, and level of ambition the pledges should reflect. Countries also agreed to progressively increase pledges over time, and to create some form of review process to measure progress towards implementation and the adequacy of various national pledges in serving the larger goals of the Convention. The obligation to submit pledges, review them, and ratchet them up would be legally binding, but the content of the pledges would be set by each country for itself. So the way the climate regime tries to solve the collective action problem was flipped on its head. Instead of negotiating how much each country would contribute to the collective good ex ante, countries were asked to set their own contributions and then progressively scrutinize and revise them ex post.

The second major shift in the regime was perhaps even more radical. At the same time as governments were developing the "pledge, review, and ratchet" model, a number of actors began seeking to bring actions beyond the UNFCCC and national governments, especially the increasingly ambitious steps being taken by sub- and non-state actors, closer to the intergovernmental process. In September 2014, UN Secretary-General Ban Ki-moon organized a Climate Summit in New York, inviting not just heads of state but also mayors, CEOs, civil society groups, and others. All actors, state, non-state, and substate, were encouraged to make ambitious pledges. The Secretary-General's office had also been working for several months ahead of the summit to orchestrate dozens of initiatives bringing together various actors around specific climate goals. These included the New York Declaration on Forests, which sought to eliminate deforestation by 2030, and the Compact of Mayors, an alliance of various global city networks intending to radically reduce emissions at the municipal level, which account for some 70 per cent of global emissions.

This opening of the regime to other kinds of actors was reinforced at the 20th Conference of the Parties, meeting in Lima in December 2014. The UNFCCC and the Peruvian host government launched the Non-state Actor Zone for Climate Action (NAZCA) portal, an online tool to track and aggregate information on the actions being taken around the world by sub- and non-state actors, both individually and through joint initiatives (UNFCCC 2017). Shortly thereafter, with COP21 in Paris approaching, the UNFCCC Secretariat, the UN Secretary-General's office, and the governments of Peru and France created the Lima-Paris Action Agenda, an unprecedented attempt to orchestrate further commitments and initiatives from all actors and all sectors, and to make this groundswell of activity an official part of the December 2015 Paris conference. While some actors feared that emphasizing such actions might somehow let countries off the hook or undermine sovereignty, the growing "catalytic" logic behind the new regime saw sub- and non-state action as both an important source of reductions above and beyond national commitments, and a way to build constituencies for further climate action in the future (Chan et al. 2015).

While these shifts to a more "bottom-up" regime were well in evidence in the years before the 2015 Paris conference, many observers were surprised at how strongly they emerged in the Paris Agreement and other outcomes of COP21. Three outcomes are particularly notable.

First, Paris gave additional clarity and ambition to the goals of the regime. For the first time, it set the target of achieving greenhouse gas neutrality as soon as possible in the latter half of this century. While scientists have long argued that this would be required, Paris was the first time countries committed themselves to this extraordinarily ambitious goal. Moreover, pushed especially by the island states and other most vulnerable countries, the Paris Agreement sets an aspirational goal of limiting temperature changes to 1.5°C, not 2°C as previously agreed.

Second, the Paris Agreement was successful in securing, for the first time, emissions reduction pledges from nearly every country in the world, including all of the major emitters. Together these pledges could reduce greenhouse gases by 4–6 billion tons by 2030, enough to keep temperature changes to perhaps 2.7–3.4°C. Moreover, countries agreed to submit new pledges every five years, which are required to be at least as ambitious as previous efforts. While countries also agreed to create a system to review implementation of these pledges, many crucial details of how that review will work were left to subsequent negotiations.

Third, the Paris Agreement explicitly calls upon "non-party actors" – cities, companies, and others – to increase their climate actions, and creates a framework to review and support such actions going forward. The Lima-Paris Action Agenda came to include some 10,000 commitments from dozens of initiatives. Several studies released around the conference, looking only at a few of the initiatives, found their emissions reduction potential to be somewhere around 2.5 to 4 billion tons by 2020, in the same order of magnitude as the national pledges (Galvanizing the Groundswell of Climate Actions 2015).

The Paris Agreement therefore represents a massive shift in the regime's approach to mitigation, moving from the regulatory "global deal" model to the bottom-up "catalytic" model. That said, it is important to note that the regime remains deadlocked in other areas where the interests of rich and poor countries are more explicitly zero-sum. Two areas stand out in particular.

First, the question of finance. While developed countries had pledged to "mobilize" US$100 billion in assistance to developing countries per year by 2020, countries have yet to agree on how to measure or assess progress towards this goal. Developed nations have emphasized how public funding can "leverage" private financial flows, while developing countries have called for increased direct financial support, and noted that the actual disbursement of funds for climate finance tends to lag significantly behind pledges to do so. Meanwhile, climate finance has grown steadily, but not yet at the exponential rates that most experts believe are needed to drive a rapid transition to low carbon energy. The Paris Agreement broke little new ground on this crucial issue, though it did crucially open the window to greater South–South financial flows.

Second, vulnerable nations pushed hard in recent years to secure forms of risk management and compensation for the damage they are already suffering from climate change. Island states in particular emphasized that large emitters are responsible, and perhaps even legally liable, for damages attributable to climate, for example from extreme weather. But because this issue was anathema to developed countries, and the United States in particular, little was done at Paris except to agree to keep discussing the issue.

In sum, the Paris Agreement and associated shifts reflect significant innovations in the climate regime. How can we explain them?

Which Pathways Are Driving This Change?

Four of the seven pathways beyond gridlock seem particularly relevant to the shifts in the climate regime, and a further one is crucial as a prospective pathway the Paris Agreement may create in the future. Consider each in turn.

Technical groups with effective and legitimate processes

A little appreciated, but hugely important, element of the climate regime is the Intergovernmental Panel on Climate Change (IPCC). Created by the World Meteorological Organization and the UN Environment Programme in 1988, the IPCC is both a scientific and intergovernmental body. Its role is to summarize and clarify the state of scientific knowledge on climate change and its effects in order to inform policymaking. At regular intervals, thousands of scientists from around the world review the entire corpus of scientific literature on key areas of climate change (e.g. on mitigation, adaptation, etc.), and publish lengthy reports that lay out what is known about the problem, as well as the level of uncertainty around existing knowledge. A "summary for policymakers" is produced for each report, which must be reviewed and approved by diplomats of the 195 countries that are members of the IPCC. The IPCC is thus largely a scientific body, but with intergovernmental oversight.

Because environmental challenges often involve technical complexity and significant degrees of uncertainty, scientific review bodies of this nature are common in global environmental policy, though the IPCC is larger and more institutionalized than most. Policymakers rely on scientists to tell them what effects climate change is likely to have and how they can best address the problem. This information is also crucial for shaping how the public and the various interest groups that advocate for or against action on climate change behave on this issue, and therefore has important political effects. Of course, scientific information is only one input into the policy preferences that individuals, interest groups, and countries ultimately come to hold (ideology, parochial interests, and other factors matter as well, often more). That said, the growing scientific consensus on climate change and its impacts has decisively shaped actors' preferences and the larger discourse around climate change. While not sufficient to push the regime through gridlock, it seems likely that growing scientific consensus on the urgency of acting was a necessary condition for the evolution of the climate regime.

The IPCC has been the lynchpin of this process. By employing a relatively transparent and scientific review process, the IPCC has established credibility as a legitimate and authoritative voice on climate science. In some ways this credibility has been enhanced by the intergovernmental seal of approval that is conveyed with its assessments, in that governments go on the record as formally approving the conclusions reached by the scientific process. At the same time, the governmental approval process also introduces an element of politics and negotiation that has, if not undermined the reports' scientific validity, at times affected what they choose to emphasize or elide. On average, however, this multilateral scientific body has shown how an inclusive, transparent, and science-based process can support an effective regime even in the face of gridlock. While the IPCC of course could not force governments to act, it is hard to see how they could have acted without it. Indeed, several elements of the Paris Agreement draw directly on the IPCC's reports. Most critically, the long-term goal established in the Agreement to ensure that no more greenhouse gases go into the atmosphere than come out (through carbon sinks and other natural processes) by the second half of this century is taken directly from the IPCC's Fifth Assessment Report.

Shifts in major powers' core interests

One of the most striking shifts after Copenhagen was the evolution of climate policy in the United States and China, the world's largest emitters, which together contribute nearly 40 per cent of global emissions. While both had historically resisted taking on international obligations, President Obama had personally intervened in the Copenhagen talks at the eleventh hour to attempt to force a deal, and was widely perceived as having been snubbed by China, which sent a relatively low-ranking official to negotiate with the American President. Both sides blamed the other for the resulting impasse.

But in the years after Copenhagen, the politics of climate shifted in both countries. In the US, Congress nearly passed a national cap-and-trade bill in 2010, failing by just a few votes. The subsequent election then put both houses of Congress under the control of the Republican Party and so removed any further possibility of Congressional action. For a number of years it seemed that US climate policy would remain confined to progressive US states. But then, after Obama won re-election in 2012, the US Administration developed an aggressive national plan that relied solely on executive authority.

The centrepiece of this effort was the Clean Power Plan, an executive directive, first announced in June 2014, to limit carbon pollution from power plants under existing regulatory authority under the 1990 Clean Air Act. The regulation required power plants to progressively lower emissions to a point that would effectively prohibit coal as a source of power. This unilateral executive action built on a previous agreement on fuel efficiency standards for cars that the Obama Administration had put forward in 2009. It is worth noting that this new push coincided with the vast expansion of natural gas and oil production in the United States as hydraulic fracturing ("fracking") technology reached maturity. The existence of a cheap, reliable, domestic replacement for coal no doubt enhanced the US Administration's determination to regulate power plants.

Meanwhile, in China, similarly stark changes were altering the government's views on climate policy. While air pollution has long afflicted China's cities, the issue became significantly more salient among the Chinese public following a dispute between the Chinese government and the US Embassy in Beijing in 2010, which had been publishing pollution metrics online that contradicted official numbers. Over the next years, as the government's reporting on the issue became more transparent, air pollution became a central concern of the urban middle classes and thus a top priority for policymakers.

These changes in politics and policy at the national level in both countries fed into, and were reinforced by, proactive bilateral engagement between the US and China. This engagement was initiated by the United States, though it served both countries' interests. For the Obama Administration, Chinese cooperation was essential to thwart the Republican charge that the United States should not act unless other major emitters – especially economic competitors – did so as well. For China, which increasingly found itself at odds with the United States on, for example, regional security issues, cooperation with the US on climate change provided a useful way to demonstrate goodwill without sacrificing core national interests or appearing to bend to US pressure. After months of negotiation, the US and China made a joint announcement in November 2014 that they had come to a bilateral understanding to reduce emissions, with the United States reducing emissions 26 to 28 per cent below 2005 levels by 2025, and China agreeing to peak its emissions by 2030 and generate 20 per cent of its power from renewable sources by 2020. This unexpected announcement from the "G2" a year before the Paris Summit helped to reassure other countries that their own contributions would not be for naught. And while US–China cooperation on climate helped reassure domestic and international audiences, it also prompted some healthy competition. After the United States announced US\$3 billion in climate finance for developing countries, China followed some months later with a US\$3.1 billion pledge.

In sum, both domestic politics in the US and China and bilateral relations between them generated increasingly pro-cooperation policies and strategies by the major powers. Critically, however, such shifts are neither inevitable nor permanent. The election of Donald Trump in the United States promises to significantly reverse climate policy in the United States, though the rollback of federal action will be drawn out in lengthy legal battles and partially compensated for by increasing action at the state and city level. A broader question is how China and other major emitters react to a reversal by the United States. Will they slow down their own efforts, or does the new "bottom-up" logic of the regime reduce the need for reciprocal concessions?

Multiple, diverse organizations and institutions coalesce around common goals/norms

For many years, institutional pluralism in the climate regime was regarded by many as a negative consequence of gridlock. One of the great innovations of the Paris model, instead, was to embrace the diffusion of climate policy to multiple fora and to situate the UNFCCC as a central node in an increasingly complex governance ecosystem. As noted above, this occurred in several ways. First, the UN processes recognized and celebrated the importance of sub- and non-state actions through events and programmes like the September 2014 Secretary-General's Summit, the Non-state Actor Zone for Climate Action portal, or the Lima-Paris Action Agenda. Second, governments and UN bodies actively worked to initiate, support, shape, and otherwise orchestrate a panoply of initiatives involving all kinds of actors. Third, in Paris governments took steps to create an ongoing framework to support and enhance such actions and initiatives going forward, now referred to as Global Climate Action. Governments agreed to continue the Action Agenda, appointed two "champions" to spur even more actions and initiatives, established an annual high-level event at which sub- and non-state actors would be asked to report on progress, and linked the groundswell of action to the UNFCCC process for helping countries identify practical policy solutions. While it remains to be seen how effective this framework is in delivering on the promise of the groundswell of climate actions, it represents a conscious attempt by the UN system to improve upon the 2002 Johannesburg and 2012 Rio Summits (respectively, the 10-year and 20-year anniversaries of the 1992 Earth Summit), at which numerous partnerships for sustainable development were launched, with many never delivered upon.

There are also increasing signs of coherence among the sub- and non-state actors within the regime. The major networks of cities, businesses, and subnational regional governments have either merged together or partnered in umbrella initiatives like the Global Covenant of Mayors for Energy and Climate, the We Mean Business coalition, the Compact of States and Regions and the Under 2 Coalition. Many of these initiatives have explicitly linked to the intergovernmental regime by taking on the 2° or 1.5°C temperature goals as their own objectives.

These changes were possible in large part because the relationship between different institutional levels and fora can be thought of differently under the "regulatory" model and the "catalytic" model. Under the former, in which states take on international legal obligations to reduce emissions, sub- and non-state actions can seem like a way for states either to avoid their obligations or, at best, to substitute for lacklustre national policies. In a bottom-up model, in turn, it is possible to see climate actions at different levels as more complementary. To the extent that national and sub- or non-state or transnational actions overlap, the latter serves as a means of implementation of the former, helping countries reach the pledges they have made (and giving those pledges more credibility should national policies waver). Where they do not overlap, sub- and non-state actions help to close the emissions gap and bring the world closer to the ultimate goal of decarbonization. While careful disambiguation of who reduces what is required for situations in which strict accounting is needed (e.g. in carbon trading or offsetting schemes), in general the logic of the "bottom-up" approach sees the efforts of all actors as contributing to an upward spiral of action and ambition.

Innovative leadership as a reaction to gridlock

After 20 years of seeking a global deal along the lines of the Kyoto Protocol, shifting to a new model for the regime required significant agency and leadership. As noted above, for many negotiators, activists, and observers who had spent a significant portion of their professional lives in the negotiating halls of the UNFCCC, the "cognitive inertia" around how to structure the regime ran deep. Bold leadership was therefore required to envision a new model for climate governance and build coalitions to support it. Several important examples stand out.

First, two UN officials were particularly important in pushing a new model for the regime: UNFCCC Executive Secretary Christiana Figueres and UN Secretary-General Ban Ki-moon. Figueres took on leadership of the UN climate secretariat in the months after Copenhagen, hardly an auspicious time. An unconventionally dynamic and passionate UN official, Figueres tirelessly communicated a narrative of relentless optimism, reasoning, "I have never know anyone to be motivated by bad news." She was also instrumental in embracing action by sub- and non-state actors, starting a Momentum for Change initiative to highlight inspiring examples of climate action and creating a "groundswell" team in her office to engage with all kinds of actors in all sectors. Similarly, Secretary-General Ban was also keen to make a successful agreement on climate change part of his legacy, taking the bold and unprecedented step of hosting the September 2014 conference. In the same vein, the government of Peru, and particularly Environment Minister Manuel Pulgar-Vidal, deserves significant credit for championing the role of non-state actors in climate solutions and bringing them closer to the UNFCCC process through the Lima COP.

Second, many sub- and non-state actors asserted their growing role in the process with significant force. As mayor of New York, Michael Bloomberg injected significant effort into the C40, a network of mega-cities around the world tackling climate change, which he chaired. After leaving office, Bloomberg was appointed the UN's Special Envoy for Cities and Climate Change, and his foundation spent heavily to strengthen global city networks. Two consecutive governors of California, Arnold Schwarzenegger and Jerry Brown, played a similar role, signing Memorandums of Understanding to cooperate on climate change with states and provinces around the world and creating global networks to bring other subnational governments to the forefront of climate action. In the private sector as well, foresighted and outspoken CEOs like Paul Polman of Unilever were instrumental in convincing large companies to take steps to reduce their emissions and actively lobby governments to follow suit.

Third, while the role of the major powers was no doubt a necessary condition for the shifts of the regime, smaller players also played a role in some key aspects. For example, the Alliance of Small Island States built a coalition of progressive countries that was able to achieve certain policy outcomes. The most dramatic example of this effort was the High Ambition Coalition, a block of nearly 100 countries – including the US, the EU, and Brazil – that united to endorse the aspirational goal of 1.5°C. Veteran negotiator Tony de Brum, the Foreign Minister of the Marshall Islands, drove the creation of this coalition, which came to play a significant role in the diplomatic pressure both the United States and Europe applied to the emerging economies in the final days of the Paris conference.

Fourth, civil society groups, and particularly the large international environmental NGOs, played a decisive role in encouraging, supporting, and lobbying all of the other actors.

Finally, but crucially, the French government played a very important role as the host of COP21 by mobilizing its entire diplomatic corps to build support for a successful outcome in Paris over the entire proceeding year. Foreign Minister Laurent Fabius and climate ambassador Laurence Tubiana earned widespread acclaim for shepherding the negotiations through the critical last days, avoiding the stumbles that had plagued Copenhagen.

Mobilization of domestic constituencies for cooperation and compliance

Looking forward, the Paris Agreement places significant hope on one of the key pathways through gridlock: the ability of international institutions and multilateral processes to mobilize and strengthen pro-cooperation interest groups within countries that can shift governments to increasingly cooperative behaviour over time. The Paris architecture requires countries to make new pledges every five years, but has no formal mechanism for requiring countries to make those pledges sufficiently ambitious to, in aggregate, address the problem. Instead, it relies on the catalytic logic that action in one area will reassure others and inspire further action in other spheres, creating an upward spiral of collective action.

The Paris Agreement creates several features that seek to enhance its ability to mobilize domestic constituencies in this way, though many details as to how they will operate remain to be decided at the time of writing.

First, the requirement that countries submit a new pledge every five years creates an important "hook" around which domestic constituencies can mobilize. In the lead-up to Paris, many civil society groups and other actors mobilized at the domestic level to ensure their country's contribution was as ambitious as possible. Many governments, such as India and Chile, engaged in large consultation processes with experts, industry groups, civil society, and others to help them determine the extent and nature of their contributions. By requiring countries to revise their pledge every five years, the Paris Agreement is likely to engender many more such processes, creating a ready forum in which domestic constituencies can be mobilized to support international cooperation.

Second, the Paris Agreement creates three kinds of review processes: individual review of countries' implementation of their pledges; aggregate review of collective progress towards decarbonization and other targets set out in the Agreement; and a "facilitative, non-punitive" compliance mechanism that aims to help laggards meet their obligations (van Asselt et al. 2016). While the format for these processes is still being negotiated at the time of writing, some observers have argued they should follow the model of human rights reviews and allow for the participation of domestic civil society groups or other non-state actors. To the extent that the international process can lift up and elevate the voice of such groups, it increases their ability to push their governments for effective compliance with their national targets.

Finally, as highlighted above, the Paris architecture explicitly calls on cities, companies, and other actors to increase their efforts on climate, and creates various systems to recognize and catalyse them, like the Global Climate Action Agenda, the High Level Champions, the Non-state Actor Zone for Climate Action portal, and regular High Level Events at COPs. In this context, sub- and non-state actions and transnational initiatives feed into the catalytic logic of the post-Paris regime in more indirect ways. First, they can help to experiment with new approaches to addressing climate, and then diffuse innovations globally, creating a knowledge base, technologies, and a set of practices and models that make it easier for all actors to take more ambitious actions in the future (Hoffmann 2011). Second, increasing sub- and non-state actors' climate actions builds new and stronger constituencies for climate action in the future. As the number of cities, companies, and other actors invested in low carbon infrastructure and business models increases, political support for such measures grows. Once proponents of climate action reach a critical mass inside a country, it is likely that national policies will become more ambitious as well. Transnational networks of sub- and non-state actors therefore represent a way to reach inside the black box of domestic politics.

Beyond Gridlock in Climate Change?

It is perhaps fitting that climate change, the issue most quintessentially emblematic of the challenges of complex interdependence, is such a critical case both of gridlock and pathways through or beyond gridlock. The shifts in the climate regime were not foreseen, either in academic theories or in practitioner accounts, even a few years ago, making the issue a fascinating laboratory for the study of how we can manage global interdependence in the twenty-first century. Further work will be needed to understand and explain the shifts in the regime described above. Even more importantly, future work will need to assess the effects and efficacy of the new regime in order to understand whether the innovations described in this chapter are truly pathways through and beyond gridlock, or not.

The election of Donald Trump in the United States provides an early and stark test of the new logic of cooperation that Paris embodies. Will a reversal of policy in the United States lead other nations, but also sub- and non-state actors, to abandon or slow their efforts to address climate? Or does this distributed model of global governance provide exactly the kind of political resiliency needed to weather sudden shocks? Again, it is too soon to tell, but it is hard to imagine a rigid regime modelled on the Kyoto Protocol surviving an American Administration hostile to climate policy, just as Kyoto itself was hamstrung by the Bush Administration. There are thus reasons for cautious optimism.

As the regime develops, it is likely to come to encompass new issues that may further alter its structures, or consign it back to gridlock. First, as discussed above, the Paris Agreement has not laid to rest two critical areas of gridlock in the climate realm: the issue of how much financial support rich countries will provide to poor countries, and the compensation, if any, large emitters will make to those already suffering loss and damage from climate change. Both of these areas, typically framed as adversarial, zero-sum conflicts, have significant potential to gridlock future negotiations. Further into the future, and especially if mitigation efforts proceed slower than hoped and research increasingly leans to the more pessimistic warming scenarios, new problems may arise. Countries could begin to physically alter the climate in ways to forestall warming, for example by injecting sulphates into the upper stratosphere in a way that simulates a large volcanic eruption and thereby prevents solar radiation from warming the Earth. Such geoengineering technologies are still in their infancy, but could potentially introduce difficult political conflicts into the climate realm by altering local weather patterns, ocean acidity, or other natural processes in ways that benefit some countries but harm others. Should the climate regime come to encompass these more conflictive political issues, it seems likely that gridlock may return.

11

Cyber Security

Gridlock and Innovation

Lucas Kello

Governance under conditions of international anarchy does not emerge naturally.[1] Rather, it is the outcome of the will and the power of the sovereign units which take it upon themselves to impose stable expectations out of uncertainty, behavioural regularity out of inconsistency, a legitimate political framework out of incessant subversion – in short, order out of chaos. It relies on three factors. The first is agreement among the main units on the problems whose solutions merit collective attention, as opposed to those the units wish to address singly. The second is a unity of basic priorities among the players, for if their preferences clash and the complementarity of interests is weak, the existence of urgent problems is an assurance of contention, not cooperation. The third is the presence of adequate institutional instruments – formal or informal – to clarify, monitor, and if necessary enforce the behaviour necessary to attain shared priorities. Only then can there be stable governance: a regularized mode of conduct that the units accept as legitimate and whose violation, therefore, would signalize a breakdown in the international order.

All of these precursors of global governance have so far proven difficult to attain in the cyber domain. States, especially large ones, disagree on which problems of cyber security merit a multilateral solution; they pursue divergent priorities in seeking to resolve them; and they have few effective institutional mechanisms to regulate their mutual dealings even in areas of high common priority, such as the avoidance of cyberwar – or a highly destructive cyber attack that is comparable in the scale of destruction to a traditional act of war.[2]

This situation has resulted in a state of intense global gridlock on cyber issues.

This chapter examines the sources of and possible solutions to cyber gridlock. First, it is important to define what the study covers and what it omits. The study focuses on cyber governance, or the management of problems of cyber security – especially cyber attacks and cyber espionage. Thus it is not a study on internet governance, a much broader topic that involves the regulation of the globe's vast computer network infrastructure. Cyber governance may significantly influence but does not encompass internet governance, of which it is only one area. The meaning of cyber governance is often not clear. One study, for example, describes it as "the challenge of securing the essential shared infrastructures of Internet governance" (DeNardis and Raymond 2013: 4). By emphasizing the role of infrastructure, however, this definition implies a focus on the physical components of cyberspace – the technical plane of action comprising routers, servers, user nodes, etc. Yet cyber governance also encompasses, sometimes primarily, the protection of operations and interests residing *outside* cyberspace but reliant on it for their proper functioning. For the purposes of this chapter, cyber governance concerns the resolution of problems in both of these realms. That is, it entails two broad senses of the term "cyber security": the protection of machines and networks or the integrity of their data from hostile action; and the protection of political, economic, and social interests from threats travelling via machines as code. The segmentation of these two security aspects is important, because they represent a major line of contention among large states in the prioritization of cyber issues. Problems of cyber governance concern not just the security of cyberspace but also the protection of interests in the cyber *domain* – a human and political realm of activity.

The body of academic work on internet governance is large and spans various disciplines (Mueller 2002; Mueller et al. 2007; DeNardis 2009; Mueller 2010; Nye 2014). The narrower question of cyber governance, by contrast, has received less attention among scholars, especially those working in the discipline most directly affected by the consequences of its shortcomings: international relations. Although a number of important works have explored specific aspects of the topic, such as deterrence theory (Libicki 2009; Morgan 2010; Lupovici 2011), few have examined its sources and manifestations in the broader political context of international anarchy (Choucri 2013). This scholarship gap is symptomatic of a deeper but slowly waning reluctance among international relations scholars to integrate cyber issues into their discipline's intellectual agenda (Kello 2013). This chapter, then, seeks to help fill an important gap in scholarship by analysing cyber gridlock as a new set of problems that is rooted in much older, but evolving, tendencies of security competition among sovereign states.

This chapter argues that the sources of cyber gridlock are deep and varied. They involve problems of cooperation at the two basic levels discussed in this book. "First order" problems of cooperation arise from geopolitical contentions among large powers such as the United States, Russia, and China, which disagree on the very meaning and priorities of cyber security. "Second order" problems emerge out of historical trends of interdependence whose challenges cyberspace aggravates. The rapid expansion of cyberspace, and especially the internet, has given a technological impetus to economic and social interactions across state borders. "Interdependence among societies is not new," observed Robert Keohane and Joseph Nye at the time of the internet's explosive growth in the 1990s. "What is new is the virtual erasing of costs of communicating over distance as a result of the information revolution" (Keohane and Nye 1999). Greater interconnectedness, in turn, creates new challenges in securing the underlying technology, which provides a medium in which threats can propagate among machines almost cost free. A further difficulty – perhaps the gravest of all – is power diffusion, or the gradual erosion of state power. The forces of diffusion in the cyber domain are similar to those of globalization: new communications technologies and transportation links that reduce the costs of transnational interactions (Held and McGrew 1999; Krasner 1999; Hummels 2007; Rosecrance 2013). The erosion of state power is a broader global trend; it afflicts multilateral governance in other domains examined in this book, such as terrorism and health. But the phenomenon is perhaps most acute in the cyber realm, where the barriers to entry are the lowest relatively (Nye 2011; Kello 2013).

The reasons for the persistence of cyber gridlock, then, are both political and technological. For one thing, they are rooted in the timeless problems of anarchic international politics that spill over into the new technological domain: the attempt by large powers to harness cyberspace as a tool of global dominance; the divergent priorities that each pursues in neutralizing cyber threats; and the difficulties of adapting international bodies to regulate behaviour in ways that the main players can agree upon. For another, the related technology itself is a problem: it changes faster than policymakers and analysts are able to interpret, much less regulate it.

The chapter also draws on the gridlock "pathways" framework developed in the introduction to this book in exploring three prospective approaches to breaking the impasse of cyber governance. These pathways are of three broad kinds. The first involves the role of innovative leadership (pathway 7) in cultivating rules and norms of restraint to prevent major cyber incidents. The second pathway concerns a classic problem of international cooperation among major powers with divergent interests (pathway 1): how to develop rational measures of conflict control to prevent or regulate unwanted escalation of a crisis under conditions of acute anarchic uncertainty. The third pathway relates to power diffusion and the role of technical groups (pathway 3): how to absorb new relevant players such as proxy militia groups and private technology firms into a states system that struggles to house them. These pathways have only just begun to emerge, but they indicate possible solutions to seemingly intractable problems.

The Cyber Threat: Origins of the Problem

The problems of cyber governance are young, but the underlying technologies of cyberspace are old. The concept of computing originated in the mid-1930s, when English computer scientist Alan Turing first laid down its principles (Turing 1937). The first computers – colossal machines whose computing power was almost negligible compared with today's potent handheld devices – emerged soon after, during World War II. Military engineers applied them to solve urgent problems of military tactics, such as the calculation of naval fire or the decryption of German cyphers. Since then, engineers have applied computer technology to achieve a growing array of economic and social ends – the prediction of climatic patterns, the reduction of financial transaction costs, the collection of citizen data by governments, and so on. Yet the notion that one could use code to manipulate the functions of machines – and thereby affect functions and interests they support – was for a long time ingenious speculation. For several decades, cyberspace existed in the absence of major public concerns about cyber security.

Concerns began to materialize with the emergence of the internet, or the "network of networks" of computers linked at the information level (Clarke and Knake 2010). Created in 1969, the Advanced Research Projects Agency Network (ARPANET), as the internet was initially called, transformed not only the reach but also the nature of cyberspace.[3] The new technology enabled machines and their human operators to communicate with each other remotely; it unleashed machine functions from traditional geographic restrictions. Governance questions arose almost immediately. These questions were at first largely technical: By what method would machines identify themselves to each other? How would data travel between them? During the 1970s and 1980s, debates over the internet's design principles consumed much thinking within the small, esoteric, and self-governing community of scientists who used the network. In 1974, internet pioneers Vinton Cerf and Robert Khan proposed two sets of protocols: Transmission Control Protocol/Internet Protocol (TCP/IP) – one that would parcel out and transmit data content as streams of packets, another for use as a "gateway" that would read envelopes of data (Cerf and Kahn 1974; Naughton 1999). When in 1982 the ARPANET split into civilian and military (MILNET) networks, the loosely governed community of scientists who set the ARPANET's technical standards decided that henceforth, civilian communications would employ these two protocols. Adherents of the main competing protocol, the Network Control Program, resisted the move, but relented after Cerf threatened to cut off their connections. A singular act of coercion, then, defined the internet's basic protocols for the indefinite future.

Later, these early design decisions provided the technical basis for the inherent insecurity of internet communications. The TCP/IP protocols prioritized the successful delivery of packets over accounting of the sender's identity and their content. David Clark explains: "since the network was designed to operate in a military context, which implied the possibility of a hostile environment, survivability [of communications] was put as a first goal, and accountability as a last goal." But the non-military functions, including commercial activity, that today predominate in the network "would clearly place these goals at the opposite end of the list" (Clark 1988). That it would have been better if the founding architects had prioritized accounting over delivery is something about which many computer specialists would agree. But in a world in which so many social and economic activities rely on the original architecture, this is a statement of retrospective lament and not of current possibility. Thus, without knowing how to think about authentication, the internet's insular community of custodians – in Nye's words, "a small village of known users" (Nye 2014) – wielded the powers of creativity and coercion to establish a universal communications syntax, one that enabled a "consolidation period" during which the internet grew to connect tens of thousands of users. All the while, the network's founding architects struggled to think about how to do "accounting" over it (Naughton 1999; Clark 2016).

Then, the problems began. In November 1988, the first significant malware incident – the "Morris worm" – occurred. The product of a curious graduate student at Cornell University striving to measure the size of the internet, the Morris worm travelled the network to impair thousands of computers inadvertently. The worm's direct effects were significant: it rendered several thousand machines inoperable until disinfected. Its indirect effects were greater still: it prompted network operators to segment entire sections of the tens of thousands of machines on the internet for a period of several days (Stoll 1989). The incident revealed the difficulties of securing machines against malware and demonstrated the awesome speed by which such threats could propagate via the internet.

Heedless of these emergent dangers, the internet underwent an explosive expansion in the decade that followed. In 1990, Tim Berners-Lee, a British computer specialist based at the European Organization for Nuclear Research (CERN) in Geneva, Switzerland, designed the world's first browser software, thus establishing the conceptual and technical rudiments of the World Wide Web – the global system of "hyperlinked" machines that delivered internet technology to millions of private homes and businesses. A line in the Web's original proposal identifying necessary "future paths" portended the dangers to come: "A serious study of the use and abuse of the system, the sociology of its use" (Berners-Lee and Cailliau 1990).

Then, in a realization of this insight, the problems grew graver. The cyber threat rapidly became not just a technical but also a political and societal problem. During the early twenty-first century, a succession of harmful incidents heralded problems of a larger magnitude – the convulsion of financial and governmental infrastructures in Estonia in 2007; the paralysis of the national bank and communications systems of Georgia in 2008 (while the country suffered a Russian military incursion); and perhaps most spectacularly, the physical destruction of almost 1,000 uranium enrichment centrifuges in the nuclear facility in Natanz, Iran in 2009 (Falliere, Murchu and Chien 2011). The Natanz incident revealed an important truth: although malware cannot use the internet to compromise machines in the cyber archipelago, attackers can still bridge the "air gap" in other ways, such as by infecting the devices of systems operators that in turn infect the target machine complex.

At last, national security planners began to awake to the reality of the cyber threat. Since at least 1993, observers had warned of its dangers with the dire slogan: "Cyberwar is coming!" (Arquilla and Ronfeldt 1993). Few heeded the call until the Estonian crisis – a demonstration of technological potential as significant for the cyber age as the explosions over Hiroshima and Nagasaki were for the nuclear era. In 2007, no country had a dedicated national cyber-security strategy; in 2016, dozens of countries have one. Before the attacks on Estonia, no Western intelligence agency regarded the cyber threat as a major national security concern. Presently, they rate this threat among their foremost if not their most pressing concern (Obama 2009; HM Government 2010; Président de la République 2013; Clapper 2013). Elemental questions of security doctrine and governance converged upon the world of diplomacy. How can nations deter each other from carrying out major cyber attacks? Does the law of armed conflict apply to the regulation of such conduct? What measures can mitigate the intensity of a cyber conflict following a failure to prevent it? How can a nation stem the proliferation of attack tools whose transmission can be costless and instantaneous because the payload is an intangible?

In sum, the question of cyber governance is very new if one considers not the origins of the underlying technology, which is as old as Turing's transforming invention, but its effects on the behaviour, laws, institutions, and competition of states and other actors in the international system – that is, if it means not merely the regulation of cyberspace, a technical plane of action, but also of the cyber *domain* – a social and political plane (Lindsay and Kello 2014).

Against this backdrop of ongoing technological dislocation, global cyber governance is acutely necessary for two main reasons. First, the security of cyberspace has become a condition of the survival of modern society (Kello 2017). Almost no aspect of contemporary public or private life is beyond the reach of Turing's machines. In the developed world, and increasingly in developing countries, cyberspace permeates almost all essential infrastructures, from financial systems to public and private health systems to transportation systems to voting machines to the so-called Internet of Things, or the explosive growth of the internet into everyday objects (Brenner 2011). Digital dependency creates vulnerabilities that adversaries are able to exploit for political or strategic purposes. Second, the technologies of harm are becoming more potent. The threshold of proven direct effects has expanded since the "Stuxnet" worm hit the Natanz facility in 2009. Cyber artefacts have also incapacitated tens of thousands of machines at the world's largest oil firm (Saudi Aramco in 2012) and impaired three-quarters of machines and networks at a major multinational firm (Sony Pictures Entertainment in 2014). Scientists and security planners warn of more severe consequences to come (Geers 2009; Johnson 2016; Monaco 2016).

The Sources of the Problem: Power Transition and Growing Complexity

The discord and hostility that pervades in the new domain has prompted various attempts to govern it through multilateralism. None of these efforts has gone far. The failure and persistence of gridlock has two sets of reasons.

One concerns the first-order challenges of cooperation. Most notable among these is growing multipolarity, a problem that in the cyber domain has two faces. The first is the general realignment of power in the system. The waning of US hegemony and the rise of new centres of power, especially China and Russia, strain the global governance framework. It was once possible to say of the new domain that its structure reflected the preponderance of influence and its ethos embodied the political values of the world's sole superpower. US engineers, as we saw, invented the internet (although an Englishman catalysed its social diffusion). For almost two decades, the Internet Corporation for Assigned Names and Numbers (ICANN), an important regulatory body that assigns top-level numeric addresses to web domains, operated under a contract with the US Department of Commerce before transitioning in October 2016 to a global, multi-stakeholder arrangement involving representatives from government, civil society, and industry (Klein 2002; King 2004; Drissel 2007). Almost everywhere across the globe that the internet spread, aspiring liberals saw in it a medium to propagate their values and system of government – a great technological current of democratization that would solidify and extend the project of the ancient Greeks in the form of a new "electronic republic" (Grossman 1995).

Reality, however, has changed. Among the world's rising powers are the authoritarian nations of China and Russia, which, along with middling powers with autocratic tendencies such as Iran and Turkey, perceive the internet as a threat to the longevity of their ruling regimes. The political threat to them is one that Secretary of State Hillary Clinton enunciated in 2010 as a matter of US foreign policy: "We want to put these [internet] tools in the hands of people who will use them to advance democracy and human rights," emphasizing in particular the prospects for democratization in China (Clinton 2010). Concerned by the internet's subversive potential, these rising nations have taken steps to impose strict censorship on its use or to create "national" intranets – an assault on the technology's foundational purpose of unleashing information flows, an objective that China and Russia increasingly coordinate to impede within their territories (Soldatov and Borogan 2016).

Clashes over the freedom of the internet reflect a deeper disagreement among the major powers on the very meaning of cyber security. Western powers such as the United States, Britain, and France define it primarily as the proper operation of computer systems on which the survival of essential economic, social, and governmental functions depends. The censoring nations, by contrast, emphasize "information security," or the protection of information flows within domestic society, primarily to preserve the regime survival (King, Pan and Roberts 2013; Reuter and Szakonyi 2015). Western governments acutely concerned about threats to their vital infrastructures find that the Chinese are far more concerned about controlling the flow of ideas than protecting against malware attacks.

Such fundamental disagreement on the basic priorities and very meaning of cyber security has impeded broader efforts to establish international regimes of rules and norms of conduct in the cyber domain (Goldsmith 2011). In 2010, for instance, a proposal for a global cybercrime treaty, which covered issues from child pornography to high-impact attacks, floundered as the United States, the European Union, and Canada failed to agree on priorities with Russia, China, and a number of developing countries. At present, only a single, regional treaty exists to regulate cyber conduct, the Council of Europe's 2004 Convention on Cybercrime, which does not, however, proscribe states' strategic actions – explaining why large European powers allow the treaty to exist at all.

Another manifestation of multipolarity concerns the technology itself: the proliferation of cyber arms proceeds unabated. Not only the major powers but also lesser powers have this new capability. Military and intelligence analysts estimate that more than one hundred states possess or are assembling virtual weapons stockpiles (Lynn 2010). The large powers, to be sure, possess the most potent arsenals. Notably, in 2009, the United States established a cyber command to augment its military's offensive capabilities, which it has used, for instance, against the computer infrastructure of the Islamic State in Syria. In 2013, the United Kingdom became the first country to disclose the existence of an offensive cyber weapons programme when Defence Secretary Philip Hammond declared that his government was "developing a full spectrum military cyber capability, including a strike capability"

(Blitz 2013), which also found its way to Syria. These nations appear to have the intelligence and other resources to mount highly sophisticated and destructive operations – hence their technical moniker, "advanced persistent threats" (APTs). Yet while lesser powers remain weaker in relative terms, they are steadily climbing the absolute ladder of capabilities. Take, for example, Iran. Not only does the government surveil its own citizens, but it has also penetrated and disrupted the networks of foreign governments and private firms. As Martin Libicki reported, since 2012 Iran has mounted repeated distributed denial of service attacks (which work by flooding web services with simultaneous requests for information) against US banking websites, impaired thousands of machines at Saudi Aramco, and incapacitated the computers of the casino and resort firm Las Vegas Sands (Libicki 2015).

As the number of relevant offensive players rises, so does the diversity of priorities among them; therefore, the transactional costs of governance continue to grow. What in the intimate league of nuclear powers is a straightforward business of agreeing to rules of conduct is in the cyber domain an intricate affair. Diversification of the player pool has strained the political legitimacy of existing global structures. The institutional framework has fractured along regional lines. Regional initiatives on cyber conduct are numerous: for example, the aforementioned Convention on Cybercrime in Europe; the cybercrime treaty among members of the Commonwealth of Independent States; the Agreement on Cooperation in the Field of International Information Security within the Shanghai Cooperation Organization; and the Convention on Cybersecurity and Personal Data Protection in the African Union. Each of these groups provides a forum in which the members can realize their own competing visions of rules of cyber conduct.

Here, the two trends of multipolarity converge. As the regional frameworks fall under the influence of their respective centres of power, opportunities to establish global governance fade. But while regional efforts at cyber governance present obstacles to the development of global fora, they nevertheless help to produce partial governance solutions. Security organizations such as NATO and the Organization for Security and Co-operation in Europe (OSCE) are best poised to elaborate frameworks for the prevention and limitation of hostile cyber actions involving their own member states. The European Union, with its formidable "civilian power," is well positioned to promote a rules-based governance structure to stem the indiscriminate use of cyber exploitation, or intelligence gathering, as a foreign policy instrument. The Lisbon Treaty's "Solidarity Clause"

(Article 222 of the Treaty on the Functioning of the European Union, consolidated version) on natural or man-made disasters such as terrorist attacks provides a legal basis for articulating such duties. The political legitimacy of governance structures, in brief, is fleeing from global to regional institutions.

A second bane of multilateral governance efforts are the second-order problems of cooperation: cyber issues have become more intricate – or in the sense developed by this book, the problems are "harder." Three elements of complexity deserve our attention. One, again, is the technology: it is difficult to understand, much less control. Efforts to limit the damage of new weapons have a long history in international diplomacy. The nuclear powers, for example, restrained the technology by imposing treaty limitations upon it. In 1963, they signed the Partial Test Ban Treaty, which prohibited all nuclear detonations above the ground. A flurry of other accords ensued in just the following decade. To be sure, the nuclear arms control regime did not reduce nuclear stockpiles, halt their proliferation, or limit their use in wartime (Evangelista 1999). But while the regime did not seriously impede the superpowers' development of small-yield tactical weapons, it slowed the development of some new classes of nuclear weapons (US Intelligence Board 1966). Consequently, nuclear warheads today are not much different or more powerful than they were in the 1970s. Furthermore, some recent innovations in nuclear weapons technology have tended to reduce the yield and potential collateral effects of its use. For instance, the US revitalization of the B61 bomb, originally designed in 1963, will reduce its yield by as much as 50 times the explosive power of the bomb detonated over Hiroshima (Broad and Sanger 2016).

The technological freeze of international law, however, does not apply easily to the cyber domain. The chief prerequisite of successful cyber arms control is cyber arms verification. It confronts enormous challenges. The intangibility of the weapons, which exist as information stored in the form of electrons, complicates their detection. Parties who agree to a meaningful reduction in arms cannot be certain that one of them will not breach the arrangement until it is too late to neutralize the threat of more powerful arms. Weaponized code can be stored in almost any digital device; thus it is impossible to verify the absence of weapons. Moreover, it is hard to know what weaponized code even looks like. The presence of a malicious artefact may only become known after the activation of its payload. Even if inspectors gained precise knowledge of the totality of an adversary nation's cyber arsenals, it may be impossible to measure their destructive capacity, because the measurement process itself would require knowledge of the underlying vulnerabilities in the target system that the weapon was designed to exploit; this knowledge, however, the adversary may conceal. A further complication relates to test bans. Testing in a simulated environment is essential to establish that a new cyber weapon can achieve its intended tactical effects. Before delivering Stuxnet to the Natanz nuclear facility, the worm's handlers first tested its effects against a replica of the plant's industrial control system. The test itself was air-gapped; no visible signatures outside the simulated environment were reported. Detection of cyber arms development, therefore, is much harder than in the nuclear and other physical realms of conflict. Even if simulated tests could reveal the direct effects of a new weapon to a high degree of certainty, the indirect effects may be impossible to model. For in a highly complex and globalized economic system, the cascading effects of a major cyber attack may affect multiple sectors and jurisdictions. Stuxnet was superbly customized: it infected thousands of machines in many countries but affected only the Siemens-built industrial controller at the Natanz plant. But imagine that the artefact had been poorly customized. Imagine, for instance, that it had been designed to exploit vulnerabilities in the controller's Windows-run engineering stations. Such a poorly customized artefact could have achieved a wide range of indiscriminate direct effects against many ordinary and personal machines.

For all these reasons, no international limitations presently exist on the production of offensive code. No such regulatory framework has yet been foreseen. By many accounts, the weapons will continue to grow in potency – even as scientists and strategic planners struggle to model their behavioural properties and harmful effects.

Another source of complexity concerns the expanding spectrum of cyber events. The methods of hostile action are becoming more ingenious and their indirect effects more powerful – even as they fall short of legal definitions of war and measures to control it. They involve not only directly disruptive behaviour, but also the subversive techniques of political subversion, such as the Russian practice of *kompromat*: the release of sensitive information about a public official or organization that is timed specifically to influence and possibly alter the shape of an adversary's foreign policy and even its government (Kello 2017). Examples of this behaviour include the public disclosure of the content of seized emails from officials at the US Democratic National Committee as well as the hacking of machines in the offices of German legislators and political parties, which some observers describe as an attempt by the Kremlin to influence the

2016 US presidential election and the 2017 German national election respectively. Consider, also, China's theft of the engine and stealth radar designs of the F-35 aircraft – the most expensive weapons programme in US history. The seized data reportedly enabled China to produce, at lower cost and more rapidly, a rival and by some accounts superior plane, the J-31 (Majumdar 2015). According to Director of the National Security Agency and the chief of US Cyber Command General Keith Alexander, the theft and replication of US technological prowess via cyberspace amounts to "the greatest transfer of wealth in history" (Rogin 2012).

Officials and strategic thinkers struggle to make sense of these developments. Much of cyber activity is neither recognizably war nor recognizably peace. Rather, it falls between the definitional bounds of these two binary concepts without neatly satisfying either one. It does not fit the definition of war, although it may do greater damage to national and economic security than even some acts of war could achieve. Nor does it match the criterion of peace – if peace means not merely the absence of war but also a tolerable situation of competition among states coexisting in anarchy to which governments can generally aspire. The incessant and non-violent hostilities in the new domain represent instead what one might call a state of *unpeace* (Kello 2017). Revealingly, comments of public officials and writings of analysts abound with statements conflating the meanings of war and peace: "Russia and China see cyber operations as a part of a warfare strategy during peacetime" (Barroso, Fallin and Foxx 2016) or "warfare during peacetime" (Van de Velde 2016). Such "mid-threshold" cyber activity defies established security and conflict models as well as legal categories of thinking. Because it is a form of espionage, cyber exploitation is not prohibited by international law. By contrast, a high-impact cyber attack could rise to the level of use of force or even an armed attack under existing treaty obligations. The ongoing lag in conceptual adaptation hinders the development of viable strategies to secure critical computer systems as well as the design of international agreements on rules and norms of cyber conduct.

A third source of complexity is power diffusion. Although the high spectrum of cyber action necessary to damage physical infrastructures remains the preserve of the most capable states, private culprits can nevertheless cause significant harm with the new capability. For instance, hacktivists conducted the attacks on Estonia and Georgia (Cyber Consequences Unit 2009). They may also have been responsible for the interruption of global internet services in October 2016 (Romm 2016). These actors can attack for motives and aims that are subversive of national or international order. In the Estonian crisis, for example, politically motivated Russian citizens sought to punish the Estonian government for relocating a Soviet war memorial from the centre of Tallinn. These agents can also instigate a diplomatic crisis; the attacks against Estonia, for instance, prompted officials in Tallinn to consider invoking NATO's collective defence article.

The universe of relevant culprits is diverse: political hacktivists, private firms, militant groups, criminal syndicates, and so forth. The absolute price for mounting offensive actions is falling owing to the growth of markets for "zero-day" vulnerabilities (vulnerabilities that are known only to the attacker or that software vendors have not yet patched) and the expansion of the network surface in society, such as the Internet of Things (Harris 2014; Economist 2013). Opportunistic attackers can study and emulate the "design principles" of observable sophisticated operations such as the Stuxnet worm. Ralph Langner, the security specialist who deciphered the worm's tactical purpose, explains: "Now that Stuxnet is in the wild, you don't need to be a rocket scientist [to reproduce it]. You've got a blueprint of how to do it" (Sanger 2012). Government officials warn about the potential for a major cyber attack by terrorist groups such as Islamic State, which possesses state-like resources and has demonstrated savviness in the use of information technologies. Certainly, it is too much to claim, in the words of security entrepreneur John McAfee, that "arsenals of bullets, bombs, tanks, planes, boats, missiles and our nuclear capabilities" will become obsolete in future conflicts against terrorists (McAfee and Loggia 2015), but these groups have a proven desire to acquire cyberwar capabilities. "[Islamic State] are already using the internet for hideous propaganda purposes; for radicalisation, for operational planning too," Britain's Chancellor of the Exchequer George Osborne recently warned. "They have not been able to use it to kill people yet by attacking our infrastructure through cyber attack. They do not yet have that capability. But we know they want it, and are doing their best to build it" (Osborne 2015). Similarly, US Assistant Secretary for Infrastructure Protection Caitlin Durkovich warned US company executives that Islamic State "is beginning to perpetrate cyberattacks" against critical infrastructures, albeit unsuccessfully – so far (Pagliery 2015). Militant groups present an irresolvable challenge to governance structures: because they are motivated by extremist ideologies, they will repudiate the traditional rules, norms, and institutions that govern the use of force in the international system. Private firms present further problems. Increasingly, they are acquiring "strikeback" technology that enables them to carry out a proactive defence in external networks, such as the insertion of beacons to detect attack capabilities or the outright incapacitation of attacking machines (Timberg, Nakashima and Douglas-Gabriel 2014). Even if non-state capabilities remain at current levels, their upper threshold of proven effects is high enough to affect core interests of national security.

States, moreover, are no longer the sole or, in some respects, even the most relevant security providers. In many Western countries, the government depends on privately owned computer infrastructures for some of its most basic functions. Ninety per cent of government communications – including some military traffic – travels via private networks. Private technology firms own and control the vast major-ity of the enormous amounts of data that citizens generate in their private lives. In the aftermath of the mass shooting in December 2015 by two Islamic State sympathisers in San Bernardino, California, Apple declined to assist the FBI in unlocking one of the shooter's crypto-graphically sealed iPhones, which authorities believed held data that were crucial to their investigation (Cook 2016). Remarkably, and for a while, a private company was in a position to dictate to the most powerful government in the world which of two seemingly opposed public goods, public safety from terrorism or individual privacy rights, should prevail.

In important areas of security, then, the government cannot operate with full latitude because it lacks access to private data or other resources that it requires for its cyber operations, domestic or foreign. Large technology firms such as Apple can enable or deny this access, often in defiance of policy and law. The task of integrating these players into conventional multilateral structures faces the constraints of institutional inertia and path dependency. So far, institutional and normative efforts in the prevention and limitation of major cyber attacks have unfolded within traditional diplomatic fora – the First Committee of the UN General Assembly, the OSCE, and the Council of Europe. These intergovernmental arenas often neglect to involve rel-evant non-state actors because they are not recognized state players. Moreover, the formal and informal agreements that emerge from such fora are not always relevant to the interests and capabilities of industry and other private actors.

Prospective Pathways through Cyber Gridlock

We arrive now at the most delicate part of the analysis: identify-ing possible pathways to break through the impasse of cyber govern-ance. The exploration above of the sources and manifestations of the present situation describe a challenging but not wholly insuperable state of gridlock. Our task here is to define how nations may operate within the limits of this situation or else search for new departures in statesmanship. Three pathways are visible, if only dimly.

One involves innovative leadership in the normative domain. The introduction to this volume noted that the very complexity and persistence of gridlock can instigate – in exceptional circumstances – new forms of agency in overcoming it, forms that do not involve structural or institutional mechanisms, but, rather, the efforts of individual actors on the world stage. The discussion noted in particular the important role that specific leaders can play as "norm entrepreneurs" who seek to foster a new set of beliefs that can alter other actors' preferences and behaviour, such as the campaign to enshrine the Responsibility to Protect as a moral duty of statecraft or the push to establish the International Criminal Court to prosecute war criminals (Welsh 2009; Acharya 2013). A similar mechanism of innovative leadership may give rise to normative restraints that help to prevent major cyber incidents.

This brings us to the question of the "just war" theory. Concerns over the prevention of certain forms of conflict are almost as old as conflict itself. The moral tradition of thought that underpins the contemporary law of armed conflict traces its roots to St Augustine in the fifth century (Solis 2016). It identifies the legitimate reasons for which a party may initiate aggression – preventive war to preserve a balance of power among major contenders, pre-emptive war to avert an imminent strike, humanitarian intervention, and so on – and it sets principles of restraint within a conflict, chiefly proportionality and discrimination (Walzer 2015).

Application of the just war theory to the technologies of conflict has a long history. Individual political and religious figures featured prominently in it. For much of the period between the twelfth and sixteenth centuries, popes and kings banned the use among Christians of the crossbow, a technology that many people then regarded as unholy. "We prohibit as anathema the murderous art of crossbowmen and archers, which is hated by God," declared the Second Lateran Council in 1139. The primary motivation behind the ban may have been more worldly than godly: a desire to preserve the chivalrous order of mounted knights that was imperilled by bows and arrows in the hands of foot soldiers. But despite its broad evasion by contemporaries, the extent and duration of the prohibition reveal a concerted attempt to limit the use of technologies of war. Similar moral frameworks appeared in modern times. The Geneva Protocol of 1925 prohibited the use in war of "asphyxiating, poisonous or other gases, and of bacteriological methods." More general limitations followed in the form of the Biological Weapons Convention of 1975 and the Chemical Weapons Convention of 1997. As Richard Price and Nina Tannenwald (1996) have argued, the pattern of non-use of nuclear and chemical arms is explained by "the development of prohibitionary norms that shaped these weapons as unacceptable 'weapons of mass destruction.'" Although no equivalent treaty prohibition against the use of nuclear weapons exists, a similar normative taboo may explain the pattern of non-use of nuclear weapons since 1945 (Tannenwald 1999; 2005).

A similar normative framework of non-use may constrain the virtual weapon. Insofar as a cyber attack could inflict significant physical damage and loss of life, the principle of "just cause" applies to prevent it in many instances. Although the top-tier nations diverge widely in their views on internet regulation, they share broad interests in the prevention of cyberwar against each other. Indeed, the world has not yet witnessed a true act of cyberwar. Analysts do not fully comprehend the reasons for its absence. Certainly, as we saw, technological impossibility is not the cause. Rather, the reasons may at least partly involve normative leadership.

One possible mechanism of this kind involves leaders' use of traditional international bodies such as the United Nations to foster norms of cyber restraint. Since 2010, a UN Group of Governmental Experts (UNGGE) on Developments in the Field of Information and Telecommunications in the Context of International Security comprising diplomats from large nations such as the United States, Russia, and China has been working on the development of such norms. The effort traces back to a draft resolution presented by Russia's foreign minister Igor Ivanov to the UN Secretary-General in 1998, which expressed concern about the "military potential" of information technology and the danger it poses to "international stability and security" (Streltsov 2007). After a series of initial setbacks, owing partly to the desire of US officials not to impose limits on a domain of conflict in which their country was a pre-eminent player, the group achieved a breakthrough consensus on the need to foster a "global culture of cyber security" (UN General Assembly 2003). The US and Russian representatives – Michele G. Markoff and Andrey V. Krutskikh, respectively – played a crucial role in bringing the disparate group of 20 representatives to a consensus view (Maurer 2011). A subsequent UNGGE in 2012–13 achieved another interpretive landmark: an agreement that existing international law, particularly the UN Charter's

Articles 51 and 2(4), which regulate "armed attacks" and "the use of force," applies to the new domain (Psaki 2013). A further round of discussions concluded in 2015. Its mandate was to provide insights on how, exactly, international law applied to prevent a cyber conflict (Markoff 2015). Among its various "voluntary, non-binding norms," one stands out: the recommendation that states not conduct offensive activity that "intentionally damages critical infrastructure or otherwise impairs the use and operation of critical infrastructure to provide services to the public" (UN General Assembly 2015) – in short, an injunction against strategic cyber attacks that impair governmental functions.

A similar mechanism of norm creation would strive to promote constraints against cyber attacks that produce collateral damage. The moral object of this aim – individual human beings – reflects the original purpose of the just war theory: the protection of non-combatants from hostilities among warring parties. Top officials in the US and other governments have stated that just war principles apply to the new domain. "[A]ny US military [cyber] operation must comport with the principles of military necessity, discrimination, and proportionality," stated Keith Alexander. "These legal principles are addressed during the planning and operational phases of all military operations," he continued (US Senate Armed Services Committee 2010). Legal scholars broadly accept the view that prohibitions against targeting civilians apply to cyber attacks – but only if the attacks' consequences fulfil the criteria of armed attack (Lewis 2010; Schmitt 2013). Nevertheless, governments have shown restraint in the use of weapons that would likely have fallen well below this threshold. For instance, US presidents decided not to employ offensive cyber weapons in two notable instances: President George W. Bush in disrupting Iraq's financial infrastructures prior to the invasion of that country in 2003, because the attack could have incapacitated banks in Europe (Smith 2003); and President Barack Obama in disabling Libya's air defences in preparation for the NATO air campaign to depose Muammar Gaddafi in 2011, because the operation could have affected civilian networks in that country (Schmitt and Shanker 2011).

This normative life cycle faces doctrinal and analytical hurdles. Some observers perceive the virtual quality of cyber attacks so far as an asset (Liff 2012). It enables states to achieve the strategic and political aims of war while avoiding its violent physical consequences. Paradoxically, then, the normative pressures for mid-threshold cyber action may grow rather than diminish. Moreover, there is no consensus among analysts on the precise thresholds for an armed attack or a use of force in the new domain; much less is there agreement on proportionate responses to it. Thus leaders may not know where, exactly, to draw the red line, except at the most obvious place – large-scale death and destruction, which many observers believe cyber weapons can cause despite their intangible nature. Yet if the record of "no first use" continues, it may one day give rise to a prima facie presumption of non-use. Leaders could reinforce this presumption by publicly pledging to abide by it. Moreover, if they make public their decisions not to initiate cyber attacks that they expect will fall below the thresholds of use of force or armed attack, then the moral logic of the presumption may one day restrain such actions, too.

Until such a time, the most plausible explanation for non-use will be rational rather than normative: deterrence. It involves two mechanisms: deterrence by punishment, in which the promise of severe retaliation, including by conventional military force, induces adversaries not to attack (Libicki 2009; Morgan 2010); and deterrence by entanglement, whereby the unknown risk of "blowback" arising from the global interconnectedness of computer systems discourages their disruption (Nye 2017). (Deterrence by denial, which works by reducing the gains from offensive attack, is harder to achieve because APTs are very difficult to neutralize.) Some second-tier nations, however, may not be easily integrated into deterrence logics. Of particular concern is North Korea, a known perpetrator of major cyber attacks (such as the Sony Pictures hack), whose unstable leadership often conducts defence policy for subversive aims that are directly contrary to rational expectations.

A second and third governance pathway involve the prevention not of conflict, but of unwanted escalation following a failure to deter it. Let us recognize the difficulties of preventing a major cyber conflict. Let us assume for a moment that it will occur – even at the high end of the spectrum, where so far norms of restraint or deterrence or both have worked. Escalatory risks in such a scenario will be high. Yet it may still be possible to regulate the intensity of the conflict and reach a termination.

One possible pathway towards conflict stability involves stronger intergovernmental communication and signalling to reduce uncertainty and miscalculation. This pathway, it is important to note, relates to a classical avenue of international cooperation: the process of strategic learning among major powers coexisting under conditions of anarchic uncertainty – thus it does not fit neatly within the framework of pathways developed in this volume. It nevertheless merits attention. The cyber question, as we saw, is a new area of international security; the learning process that in other domains has enjoyed decades of development is in the new domain still at an early stage. Although the pathway of interstate conflict stability is "old," in the cyber domain it offers new potential benefits.

Perhaps the most important communication and signalling pathway concerns the risk of escalation from the cyber to the conventional domain. This risk inheres in prevailing US and British strategies, which advocate the "equivalence principle," or the notion that the victim of a major cyber attack reserves the right to retaliate with an armed attack. The principle strengthens the logic of punishment; it also creates dangers of rapid escalation following a failure to deter (Kello 2014–15). To an adversary, a cross-domain reprisal may seem excessive, prompting an escalating counter-response. A clear public declaration of "conversion tables" specifying the upper limits of equivalence could avert a miscalculation about where they reside. It may also reduce this danger by removing adversaries' temptation to probe the limits. This approach suffers the drawback that it may invite "up to the line" attacks. But the declaration need not be precise; merely an indication of the general thresholds of equivalence may suffice to dissuade an adversary from engaging in strategic exploration. This is particularly true if the principle applies to new forms of action where the limits are unclear, such as a *kompromat* operation that causes enormous political and reputational harm to a nation without inflicting physical harm.

Efforts to achieve greater clarity on escalation should build on the activities of the OSCE, which has made some progress in identifying intergovernmental confidence-building measures (OSCE 2013). These measures so far are largely symbolic. They involve voluntary information-sharing on national organizations, strategies, and policies as well as the establishment of contact points to mitigate uncertainty and misperception in a crisis. The measure proposed here would go further by clarifying clearer boundaries of cross-domain escalation. Although the OSCE offers a promising vehicle of conflict stability, it suffers the general limitation of all regional security organizations: it draws in regional contenders while leaving others largely at the wayside (MacFarlane and Weiss 1992; Lake and Morgan 2010). A plausible argument can be made that the organization can clarify some of the ambiguities of crisis stability, such as unclear signalling procedures, which may diminish the contenders' ability to control a crisis even when they want to avoid escalating it, that exist in Russia's relations with Western powers, but it may not add much to the resolution of uncertainties among these players and non-European powers – China or Iran, for example – that do not participate in the forum as "partner" nations.

Another pathway of crisis control is about power diffusion: how to achieve consensus on a common set of rules among a diverse universe of relevant actors, many of whom the conventional instruments of diplomacy do not regard as legitimate players. These actors range from proxy militia groups to technology firms to specialized bodies. In cases where the players are technocratic groups, they can positively influence global governance. ICANN, a technocratic non-profit organization once closely tied to Washington, recently privatized the distribution of internet domain names, thereby shielding this crucial function from the political pitfalls of global debates about internet freedom and state surveillance (a concern that intensified in the aftermath of the revelations in Edward Snowden's leak of thousands of US National Security Agency documents). But if the players are ideologically or politically motivated, they may destabilize interstate dealings. Consider, for example, proxy militias. They offer governments a tool of plausible deniability in an attack – indeed, Russia's relationship with such groups seems to have grown closer since the Estonian crisis (Bennett 2015). But these actors may cause unwanted escalation if they decide to crash foreign computer systems without their government's direction or sanction. Low barriers to entry, then, ensure that all future cyber conflicts present a danger that these private actors will intensify the showdown in ways that are difficult for states to predict and manage.

The answer to this problem lies in fostering closer ties between the public and private sectors. This may be achieved in at least two ways. One is by way of closer civil-military relations: for example, the establishment of voluntary paramilitary cyber units, such as Estonia's Cyber Defence League (*Küberkaitseliit*), a civilian defence organization that supports the regular armed forces; or conscription, as in Israel's Unit 8200, whose ranks include drafted servicemen and women who, after an initial term of service, enter the Army reserves. Paramilitary formations of this sort may enable governments to achieve at least some of the benefits of civilian partnerships, such as greater access to technological resources, while at the same time avoiding their escalation dangers in a crisis. In both approaches, civil-military integration may have the effect of "sanitizing" private culprits; that is, it could convert unruly hacktivists into loosely organized technical units operating under the state's partial oversight. Although the state may not fully control the units, it may at least monitor and guide the activities of their members more closely than in arrangements where they are formally unaffiliated.

Second, integration of the state and civilian sectors could also cover the security providers – that is, large technology firms. These firms reside beyond the traditional apparatus of diplomacy. At the same time, they may be instrumental to its proper functioning in a time of crisis. North Korea's cyber attacks against Sony Pictures were a problem primarily for Washington, where the company is based, but also for Tokyo, the home of its parent firm. The Japanese government played down its role in this incident. Company executives appeared to have coordinated their response primarily with Washington. But they could have chosen to pursue an independent course of action: for example, a defensive probe of North Korean networks to determine whether further imminent attacks awaited – an activity that some US government officials have publicly hinted they may tolerate despite its illegality (Lynch 2016). If detected by Pyongyang, the activity may have caused inadvertent diplomatic problems for Washington and Tokyo. And what is the role of firms such as Facebook and Twitter in the multinational effort to combat terrorist groups' use of social media to recruit, activate, and direct fighters across state frontiers? A world in which large firms, nations, and international organizations exchange informal but permanent "ambassadors" may no longer be a wild figment of the imagination.

Conclusion: Transitional Problems, Harder Problems, and the Merging of Systems

Gridlock does not affect all areas of world politics equally. In the cyber domain, it impedes governance acutely. The record of failure in this area far exceeds the record of success.

We can see several factors at work undermining efforts to impose order on chaos. The accelerating transition to a multipolar world aggravates first-order problems of cooperation. Large nations cannot agree on which core areas of activity merit a global solution; they disagree on basic priorities for action. In contrast to the Western powers, Russia and China pursue a conception of security that prioritizes the defeat of pernicious ideas that threaten autocratic regimes over the defeat of pernicious code that imperils machines. The problem of multipolarity also manifests in another way: the ease of proliferation of cyber instruments gives impetus to the fragmentation of power by empowering militarily weak nations; smaller powers are able to pursue strategic ends in cyberspace that traditional geopolitics previously denied them. As the structure of power fragments so, too, does the political framework splinter. The world's regions have made the greatest strides in regulating antagonisms in the new domain, as evidenced by the piecemeal efforts of the Council of Europe, European Union, and Shanghai Cooperation Organization. But in a world where the centres of power increasingly draw cooperative agreements in their own image of security, the success of the regions will mean greater trouble for a meaningful global arrangement.

Second-order problems also fill the picture of cyber gridlock. The related technology's intangible nature complicates the task of monitoring and limiting its development. The spectrum of harm, meanwhile, is expanding beyond the ability of analysts to fit it into familiar legal, diplomatic, and military doctrines. Much of cyber activity is neither war nor even peace. Yet the costs of "unpeaceful" activity have grown intolerable. It imperils the economic and national security of advanced industrial nations which struggle to adapt regulatory frameworks to prevent it.

Hardest of all is the problem of power diffusion. Cyberspace has produced a chaotic and uneven collision between the classic states system and the sprawling global system of private and transnational actors. These actors increasingly challenge the supremacy that states have customarily enjoyed in the management of their own security relations. The new entrants on the international scene hold some sway over interstate dealings and compete for influence with states and among themselves.

It is not easy to resolve this dysfunctional picture. Possible pathways to break through the deadlock nevertheless exist. Three are notable. One concerns innovative leadership: governmental elites may work together within existing multilateral fora to develop rules and norms of cyber conflict; or else they may set an example by unilaterally pledging to affirm desired norms where these are weak or unclear. Restraint against cyberwar and indiscriminate attacks are possible; it is hard to imagine that states, even the main contenders, would not want to build them. But it is misguided to act in the present as if the future had already resolutely arrived. The experience of previous eras of technological revolution shows that moral controls on the means of conflict emerge after a paradoxical combination of tragedy and moderation. It may yet take a catastrophic cyber attack, about which intelligence agencies have long warned, to carve out lasting habits of restraint – an a priori assumption of no first use for example.

Meanwhile, what is required is an appeal to the self-interests of the units in containing a conflict when pressures compel its intensification. Here, two prospective pathways emerge. One involves interstate strategic learning – a classical approach to conflict stability which, though old in other contexts, and thus outside the main framework of this book, offers new governance benefits in the current domain. Measures to promote learning and to reduce uncertainty and miscalculation about players' intentions and their willingness to carry them out may benefit from existing institutions such as the OSCE, which have proven slow but ready to adapt the mechanisms of interstate conflict control to the unprecedented challenges of our times.

Another pathway concerns the issue that demands the greatest ingenuity in statesmanship: power diffusion. The dangers of crisis acceleration and the requirements of crisis response make it imperative to integrate non-traditional players such as proxy militias and private firms more tightly into the Westphalian mould. This pathway through gridlock relates to a central theme of this volume: how to achieve consistency of rules and behaviour among the expanding universe of relevant private actors. No intergovernmental arrangement is so fine that it can afford to neglect the diverse and – to the inhabitants of the old system – peculiar realm of private actors. What is involved here is not a reversal of the collision between the Westphalian and the global systems but a gentler merging – in a word, convergence.

12

Weapons of Mass Destruction

Incremental Steps

Michael Clarke

More than most political regimes and structures of organization and control, those concerned with a state's essential security are both "an anomaly and an enduring practice in international relations" (Cronin 2003: 1). Neo-realist theories have always had difficulty in accommodating the persistence of various organizing regimes in global politics, but have felt on safer ground in being sceptical about regimes to control nuclear proliferation and other manifestations of weapons of mass destruction (WMD) (Davis 1993). Here, there is an operating principle that the high politics of national security will always predominate and that when international regimes to control the spread of WMD are in existence, no matter how deeply rooted they may seem to be, they are so only through the permissive framework that the national security policies of the great powers are prepared to grant (Bull 2003: 178; Waltz 2010: 102).

Such neo-realist explanations appear to have been given greater substance by the evident gridlock that has befallen the regime structures that have sought to deal with WMD proliferation. "Great power politics" and the emergence of autocratic and demagogic leaders across the world in recent years appear to have diminished the authority and attraction of international and cooperative approaches to handling global problems. National interest motivations seem to have predominated over "international public good" motivations in the WMD realm. But neo-realists should be cautious in drawing too many conclusions from the last 15 years of increasing gridlock. These years should be set against the 30 to 40 years in which the regime developed and operated. And the novel technical and political problems that have recently provoked a reassertion of high state politics over the permissive framework of the leading players also suggests the need for new regime players and mechanisms that state-based authorities cannot provide. So far, it appears that the powerful states understand this but have been unable to take decisive steps down the road to a new series of regimes. Instead they rely increasingly on their own inadequate resources.

The realization that something new is likely to be required is, however, a sign of some evolution that may at least ameliorate the effects of the current gridlock and suggest some plausible ways out of it in the longer term. In particular, there may be some hope for the international community to move through the gridlock phenomenon via a shift in the interests of the major powers, at least in some of the more pressing recent problems thrown up by WMD technologies, coupled with the potential role that specialist groups could play in a neo-functionalist fashion, and particularly if they can link with more adaptive intergovernmental institutions. Incremental change, and some amelioration of gridlock symptoms, might be anticipated in this way. A move beyond gridlock, however, is more difficult to discern. There are attempts to move beyond gridlock and escape from the phenomenon in a wide coalition of reformist states and elements of civil society, but there is little evidence of political traction for this coalition over the short to medium term. On the other hand, there is scope for strong and internationalist leadership, even in the short term, to build on a shared understanding of the new dangers inherent in WMD technologies to build on what incremental progression might be evolving to reassert the value of a regime-based approach to WMD and move it beyond the current gridlock. Whether such potential will be realized, however, must remain an open question.

The WMD Control Regime

What can be loosely described as the current global regime to combat the use and proliferation of weapons of mass destruction is based around a multi-level series of agreements spanning more than 50 years, beginning with the Partial Nuclear Test Ban Treaty of 1963. As the destructive pinnacle of WMD technologies, nuclear weapons have dominated the political agenda of the regime for most of these years. The bilateral nuclear relationship between the United States and the Soviet Union represented the realpolitik essence of the regime; what was possible between them became possible for the wider international community, and vice versa. Despite massive changes since the end of the Cold War, the current bilateral relationship between the US and Russia still plays a highly pivotal role in setting the political limits and opportunities not just for the nuclear arms control regime but also for the wider WMD regime that draws moral and political authority from it.

At the most formal level, the regime can draw from a treaty and international law-based foundation. There are some "core treaties," as they are frequently called, dependent as they are on the high politics among the major states who agree them (Knopf 2016: 1). The "core treaty" basis was built around the US–Soviet bilateral deals enshrined in the nuclear arms control agreements that benefited from the atmosphere around the Partial Nuclear Test Ban Treaty. The Strategic Arms Limitations Treaty (SALT I) was concluded in 1972 and followed in 1979 by a SALT II Treaty. This was refined in a Strategic Arms Reduction Treaty (START I) in 1991, which entered into force in 1994. A successor START II treaty was negotiated but never ratified and the negotiations for a START III were abandoned without agreement.

The specific legal basis of the regime was constructed on the political foundations that these bilateral treaties helped to provide. The Treaty on the Non-Proliferation of Nuclear Weapons, or Non-Proliferation Treaty (NPT), was concluded in 1968 and entered into force in 1970 as another "core treaty." The NPT is a multilateral treaty, backed by the authority of the UN, which commits the nuclear weapons states to refrain from enlarging their own nuclear weapons stocks and from transferring any nuclear technologies to non-nuclear weapons states, and to pursue nuclear disarmament in good faith. In return, the non-nuclear weapons states are assisted in their pursuit of civil nuclear technologies, under supervision to ensure they are not being diverted to weapons programmes. The treaty proved powerful in refocusing the International Atomic Energy Agency (IAEA) – already in existence – and enhancing it as an enforcement mechanism to monitor compliance, to report to its superior, the UN Security Council, and to maintain its own scientific expertise as nuclear technologies progress.

The SALT/START treaties, the NPT and the enhanced role of the IAEA were all agreed, ratified and entered into force. On the back of these solid foundations other treaties were negotiated. The Comprehensive Nuclear-Test-Ban Treaty (CTBT) was signed in 1996 and awaits the full ratification process to enter into force. Preliminary negotiations have taken place to try to conclude a Fissile Material Cut-Off Treaty to prohibit the production of weapons-grade nuclear material. Such initiatives are promoted in the UN Conference on Disarmament in Geneva which serves as the standing 65-member multinational negotiating forum and which works by consensus.

Beneath this formal level of treaty-based agreement the regime has been bolstered by a range of informal initiatives, some more politically potent than others. The most prominent informal mechanisms have been the Six-Party Talks to address North Korea's nuclear proliferation; the P5+1 grouping to deal with Iran's evident progress towards crossing the nuclear threshold; the Nuclear Suppliers Group of 46 advanced states working to prevent any nuclear technologies reaching states either outside the NPT or non-compliant with IAEA commitments; and the Missile Technology Control Regime, which attempts to keep missile technologies away from those states with illegal nuclear or other WMD capabilities. Another tranche of informal mechanisms has also been created to address the challenges of "loose nukes" over the last decade and a half. At the end of the Cold War there was great concern that nuclear weapons and related materials might be insecure in the hiatus created by the collapse of the Soviet Union and its replacement by 15 separate states. That concern subsequently extended beyond the former Soviet Union. The US led and largely funded the Cooperative Threat Reduction Programme, the Global Threat Reduction Initiative and the Global Initiative to Combat Nuclear Terrorism. Other states have taken up this lead in initiating the G8 Global Partnership against the Spread of Nuclear Weapons. The US also launched the Proliferation Security Initiative (PSI) in 2003, in a direct attempt to choke off flows of nuclear expertise and technology to states "of proliferation concern" or to terrorist groups.

Finally, these formal and informal parts of the nuclear non-proliferation regime have been occasionally refocused and energized by particular summits. The NPT is formally reviewed every five years, which serves as an international stock-taking of the regime. Such meetings normally try to push new approaches as far as the prevailing political framework will allow. In the same vein, President Obama convened a biannual Nuclear Security Summit, beginning in 2010 and dealing in particular with the threats of terrorist access to nuclear devices and materials. Though increasingly divisive by the time of the fourth Nuclear Security Summit in 2016, the forum nevertheless brought together over 50 states to address proliferation issues.

Those parts of the overall WMD regime dealing with chemical and biological weapons tend to parallel the multiple structures evident in the more complex non-nuclear regime. The most important part of the anti-chemical proliferation regime is undoubtedly the Chemical

Weapons Convention (CWC), signed in 1993 and entering into force in 1997. The CWC is notable for banning the possession, transfer or use of a complete class of WMD agent, and requires the destruction of any chemical weapons stocks still in existence. It is backed up by the Organisation for the Prohibition of Chemical Weapons (OPCW), though this has far fewer powers and less influence than its nuclear counterpart, the IAEA. Nevertheless, in the years since 1997 more than 60 per cent of the world's declared chemical weapons stockpiles have been successfully eliminated in five of the seven declared chemical weapons possessor states. Of similar legal status to the CWC, the Biological Weapons Convention (BWC) was concluded in 1972 and entered into force in 1975; also banning a complete class of WMD agent, though without any backing from a multilateral enforcement agency. The BWC is intended to be implemented bilaterally and multilaterally by the states parties to the convention. Finally, these treaty-based elements of the CWC and BWC parts of the regime are also backed by less formal mechanisms that arise in response to particular challenges. The Australia Group is the most prominent among these. Formed in 1985, the Australia Group includes 40 states, plus the European Commission, which attempt to restrict the transfer of any technologies or equipment related to chemical and biological agents, including dual-use technologies, to possible state or non-state proliferators.

As international regimes go, the WMD non-proliferation regime is impressive and, by some estimates, has been one of the most effective and cohesive international regimes since 1945 (van der Meer 2011: 37). Until 1991 only Israel, India and Pakistan developed nuclear weapons programmes outside the Cold War non-proliferation structure that the NPT institutionalized. Nuclear proliferation was not nearly as extensive as had been feared in the 1960s, and on the dissolution of the Soviet Union in 1991 all but Russia among the 15 successor states acceded to the NPT, including three that had inherited Soviet nuclear systems – Kazakhstan, Belarus and Ukraine (Cirincione 2007: 61). In addition, Iraq was formally disarmed of its nuclear capacity in the 1990s; South Africa voluntarily dismantled its existing six nuclear weapons in 1990 and became a non-nuclear weapon state; Brazil and Argentina likewise abandoned their independent nuclear weapons programmes in 1991, as did Libya in the aftermath of the 2003 Iraq War. Then, too, the CWC has been generally effective, though in an area where most of the member states have not chosen to push against the norms of non-use and the traditional taboos surrounding chemical release (Fidler 2007; Thakur and Haru 2006).

Regime Gridlock

Despite all this, the WMD non-proliferation regime has been in some trouble in recent years, as key UN officials have acknowledged (Dhanapala 2000; Annan 2005). The most prominent cause of existing institutional gridlock is not hard to discern. The "high politics" that naturally characterize nuclear weapons proliferation has had a fundamental effect on the whole regime since 1991. The treaty-based regimes and the international institutions that for the last half century have structured the international regime against WMD proliferation, and which have shaped and been shaped by the political relationships between the major powers standing behind them, funding them, staffing them, using them when it suited, are now struggling for effectiveness against their great power political constraints.

The underlying limitations of such progress as described above have become increasingly significant. The successes in unilateral and multilateral nuclear disarmament in the traditional regime were all driven by governmental or state-to-state action, rather than by any momentum from the international organizational elements of the regime – though such elements were undoubtedly important in backing up the realpolitik between the states themselves. Most significantly, however, a number of the key initiatives that created and sought to develop the core treaties of the regime did not prove to be self-sustaining. The dynamics of the SALT/START process had run their course by the early 1990s when a dominant US faced an enfeebled Russia. Nuclear capabilities were one of the few superpower attributes the Kremlin had left and there was a renewed Russian emphasis on their relevance as it confronted its other weaknesses. In 2009 the START treaties finally expired and were replaced in 2011 only with a "New START Treaty" for ten years that simply recognizes existing US and Russian nuclear force levels. The CTBT has failed to come into force for lack of sufficient ratifications. Some 166 states have ratified the treaty and 17 others, including the US, Israel and Iran, have signed but not ratified. The CTBT cannot, in any case, come into force until all 44 of its "Annex 2 states," which include India, Pakistan and North Korea, have signed and ratified the treaty. This became a distant prospect after the nuclear tests in India and Pakistan in 1998 and then successive North Korean tests since 2006. This reflects the fact that the near universality of the NPT regime has failed to grip, except tangentially, the nuclear proliferation of Israel, India, Pakistan and North Korea (North Korea left the NPT in 2003). The NPT was extended indefinitely at its review point in 1995, its twenty-fifth year, but has not made any meaningful progress since. The UN Conference on Disarmament in Geneva has been deadlocked for 20 years in its attempt to make a Fissile Material Cut-Off Treaty effective. Meanwhile, the IAEA continues its detailed work but still lacks the capacity or authority that would allow it to create a genuine step change in the international control of nuclear proliferation, or to get to grips with the diversification and minia-turization of nuclear technologies and their potential availability to non-state groups.

Gridlock, as described in the original volume on this subject (Hale, Held and Young 2013) outlines four characteristic dynamics of the process, all of which are discernible in the case of WMD non-proliferation. The "problems" are certainly "harder" to resolve as the technologies behind WMD are increasingly civilianized and more available to both states and non-state groups. For the same general reason there is a high degree of "fragmentation" across the various treaties and regimes grappling with WMD. Dealing with new technologies crosses many institutional boundaries and there is a dearth of sufficiently *qualified and independent* expertise to help the institutions rise to their new conceptual challenges. But the other two dynamics of gridlock feature most in this picture in a mutually reinforcing way. "Institutional inertia" has emerged very strongly, where decision-making authority has been locked into a static concep-tion of an institution's rationale and purposes, particularly in multi-functional organizations that should be good at adaptation, such as the European Union (Zwolski 2011). The focal points for success and development in institutions – the cognitive grip of an organization on its mission – have not altered as quickly as the external land-scape of the organization has changed. At the root of such inertia lie the overtly political pressures created by the fourth dynamic, that of "growing multipolarity." Such multipolarity is expressed not only in the great power political sphere but also in the macro-economic, cyber and technological spheres of world politics (Miller 1994; Stein 2002; World Bank 2011a). Even in these spheres there has been an apparent retreat from the expectation of ever greater global cooperation in the last decade – partly as a result of successive security and economic crises, and partly as a populist response to the limitations on national action that rapid globalization has created.

Global security politics have changed immeasurably since their institutional foundations were laid down in the post-1945 era. Since the collapse of the Soviet Union a postmodern era has taken shape where the forces of globalization have had major political and social impacts on all societies. Great power dynamics have seldom shifted so quickly as in the last 30 years and the transfer of economic weight in global GDP from North America to Asia is acknowledged as the most rapid in international economic history. Whatever short-term tactics may indicate, Russia is structurally weak, China is structurally strong, new regional powers are asserting themselves and traditional authority structures throughout the Western world are vigorously challenged. The trends of "growing multipolarity" that Hale, Held and Young have noted are therefore particularly relevant in the high politics of WMD proliferation in the way they have affected exactly those powers whose agreement is most essential to create and maintain the "core treaties" that underpin the whole regime: Russia, China, India, and in particular the US in its reactions not only to these powers but also to nuclear developments in Iran and North Korea. The power politics between all these states is presently in flux, which has reduced their incentive to maintain or develop regime structures that they fear would reduce their future security options. It would be surprising if the institutional basis for dealing with WMD proliferation had evolved as quickly as these great power developments, and the reassertion of state policy and sovereign rights over such evident symbols of national power is not unexpected.

There was an evolving shift from the late 1990s, and particularly in the US after 2001, from a "non-proliferation" approach to a "counter-proliferation" perspective that relies far more on the individual, largely technological and military, ability of states to counter the proliferation challenges they see directly in front of them (Litwak 2015). These are exercises in essential national interest rather than contributions to international order or the "global commons." As a former MI6 chief expressed it, "War between the great powers is once again a possibility. For better or worse, we are returning to a world of great power balance" (Sawers 2016). Leaders have put more faith in their own coercive abilities to deal with proliferation challenges as their faith in the erstwhile WMD regime dwindles.

In 2009 President Obama tried to break out of the gridlock in an act of overt international leadership. It was almost entirely unsuccessful. His 2009 Prague Declaration assumed a "moral responsibility" to promote a "world free of nuclear weapons." But this was overwhelmed by the renewed Russian determination under President Putin to modernize and emphasize the relevance of Russia as a strategic nuclear power, alongside Obama's own agreement to a US$1 trillion, 30-year upgrade programme for US nuclear forces, effectively embedding a new nuclear arms race between Washington and Moscow.

This particular antagonism played out in other areas of WMD control. In 2013 Obama declared a "red line" against the use of chemical weapons by government forces in the ongoing civil war in Syria. But the President could not carry his own country in enforcing this declaration. The red line was gradually, then repeatedly, crossed by Syrian forces using chemical agents. In 2015 Russia intervened militarily in the conflict to ensure the survival of the Assad government, regardless of its persistent use of chemical weapons. There were many subsequent, reliable reports of the use of chemical devices by Islamic State groups and other rebel factions fighting in the war. The Chemical Weapons Convention has been flagrantly ignored. The Syrian government acceded to the treaty in 2013 and had its declared stocks removed and destroyed in 2014, yet it continued to use other chemical agents against the civilian population of Syria. The CWC had no competence to deal with non-state groups using chemical devices and the adversarial relationship between the US and Russia meant that one great power condemned the use of chemical warfare but could not enforce its will, while the other was complicit in President Assad's use of chemical weapons and was prepared to ignore it. The effect was not just that "red lines" had been crossed with impunity but that within two years the general taboo on the use of chemical agents was visibly breaking down in substate warfare.

The Obama Administration could point to its 2015 nuclear deal with Iran as a significant legal contribution to non-proliferation. Its conclusion was a key US objective; a device to shape new strategic relations across the Middle East and a deal to which Russia acquiesced, which also involved the P5 plus Germany and the European Union. This might be presented as a good example of modern global governance. But the incoming US Administration had pledged to kill the deal and there were also powerful constituencies against it in Tehran, Riyadh and Tel Aviv. As a new beginning in non-proliferation the deal simply lacked the breadth of political consensus that had attended earlier regime building blocks.

In relation to North Korean nuclear proliferation the Six-Power Talks have been moribund since North Korea walked out of them in 2009. There is no other treaty or international organizational framework presently competent to monitor, let alone restrain, North Korea's nuclear programme since it withdrew from the NPT in 2003 following a series of nuclear tests. The international response to the most unpredictable nuclear proliferator is an ad hoc sanctions policy subject to all the cross-cutting pressures between the great powers which must enforce them as each North Korean crisis arises.

Not least, the US has been unable to enter into any meaningful nuclear arms control dialogue with China as Beijing sought to create its own countervailing deterrent to overwhelming US nuclear superiority, and the George W. Bush Administration became frankly disinterested in regime approaches to nuclear arms control and disarmament. As an influential group of four US writers observed a decade ago, a progressive, global nuclear disarmament process would have to evolve from the Permanent Five in the United Nations, starting with the US and Russia, and then extending the initiative to China, before working to draw in the other most relevant nuclear actors (Shultz et al. 2007; 2008). If China was seen to be part of a second step in this general process, a decade later the reality is that even the first step on the road has become all but impossible to envisage.

Pathways through and beyond Gridlock

All this is bad news for the supporters of a cooperative approach to the problems of WMD and they acknowledge that there have been significant shifts in the assumptions and expectations of the great powers as they confront them. Counter-proliferation is far more prevalent in great power thinking than non-proliferation; national actions are more favoured than regime approaches; and expectations for the future are not generally regime-centric. "Multipolarity" – both cause and effect of "institutional inertia" – has stymied the progress of the regime more than the other dynamics of gridlock.

Nevertheless, in the globalization challenges and great power shifts that have gridlocked the regime it is also possible to discern the emergence of some plausible ways through it, and out of it. Inventive officials in the policy process and committed outsiders are constantly looking for ways to ameliorate the effects of gridlock or even escape from the effects of it, and while there are no guarantees of success, some hybrid paths to progress are possible. These do not escape from the dynamics of multipolarity determining regime progress, but they do tend to get the attention of political leaders at key moments, which has always been the necessary, if not sufficient, condition for regime building and sustainment.

Cyber dimensions of WMD

Cyber threats are increasing in all domains of global politics and those emerging in relation to WMD are particularly challenging, not least in their potential consequences. There are possibilities of a pathway through, though not beyond, gridlock in the way technical expertise may emerge, in a neo-functionalist fashion, to address these problems. The idea that cyber attacks on the critical national infrastructure of major states could somehow have the same effect as the use of WMD has been encapsulated in speculation about a full-blown "cyber war" between major states. This is generally regarded as an overstated scenario that would lack the true destructive power and the psychological impact of nuclear, chemical or biological weapons employed in a general war between highly developed countries (Rid 2013; Singer and Freedman 2014: 155).

Nevertheless, the cyber domain impinges on more traditional WMD scenarios to create new dangers and opportunities for potential protagonists. The nuclear powers increasingly worry about the integrity of their nuclear command and control procedures. Any compromise of such procedures might prevent a nuclear power from launching its weapons in a war; interfere with their flight or functioning once launched; create an unauthorized launch; disguise an incoming attack until it was too late to respond; create fear and uncertainty by simulating aspects of an attack or an accidental launch; or be used to steal nuclear technologies or even weapons themselves. Not least, cyber attacks might also be directed against the secondary infrastructures that support command and control systems or those that support the manufacture of the system components or even of the weapons themselves. The scope for cyber spying and sabotage in the nuclear field is, in principle, immense and of very high value to the perpetrator. The perceived stability of mutually assured destruction – the assumed basis of deterrence – between those nuclear powers capable of threatening each other could be completely undermined by a cyber attack on many aspects of nuclear forces but more particularly on their associated infrastructure (Futter 2016).

The response to such challenges has mirrored the informal initiatives that characterized the traditional WMD regime, driven by some evident shift in the way major powers perceive their core interests, though without the treaty or international law foundations on which that regime has been based. A UN Group of Governmental Experts (UNGGE) have been considering the problem of cyber security since 2010, but have not been able to have a significant policy impact (Grigsby 2015). There has also been much discussion in the last decade of promoting "cyber arms control" initiatives (Litwak and King 2015). But the difficulties of modelling cyber arms control on the formal treaties of the nuclear age display some potentially fatal flaws. Those treaties of a previous era were based on the assumption that controls could be exercised over large and observable weapons stocks. Cyber attacks, however, might involve nothing but a few lines of code and be so deeply embedded in the civil sphere as to be hidden in plain sight. One of the greatest problems in applying nuclear deterrent (and hence arms control) logic to cyber attack is that of timely identification of the perpetrators. Any retaliation against the perpetrators has a much different character if it is months in coming and even more if it turns out to be against the wrong target.

On the other hand, examples of the informal initiatives of that arms control era have been thought to have some utility, if only as confidence-building measures. The UNGGE recommended some voluntary limitations that states could agree in peacetime, such as not targeting those aspects of any country's critical national infrastructure that have particular relevance to civilian welfare, and this was subsequently endorsed by the G20 nations. A number of confidence-building measures have also been proposed to reduce the impact of a cyber event on nuclear strategic stability. Non-governmental experts in NATO have suggested draft rules of international cyber engagement in the case of war. In September 2015 the US and Chinese presidents agreed some mutually convenient norms on the use of cyber instruments between them, in a dialogue that was intended to deepen between the two countries. Devoid of any treaty foundations, this nevertheless represents awareness at the level of core national interests that a new challenge to strategic stability should be addressed. As such it represents a potential "pathway out of gridlock" though it cannot be said so far to represent a clearly defined pathway.

Another effect of cyber insecurity has been to emphasize the difference between the three biggest nuclear weapons states – the US, Russia and China – which are in a position to erect effective cyber defences for their strategic nuclear forces, as opposed to all the others. In effect, recent cyber insecurities have raised the price of *effective* entry to the nuclear club by an amount that cannot so far be determined but which may be very considerable. The United Kingdom and France have spent significant sums to secure the cyber security of their nuclear weapons systems but doubts remain about the reliability of their command and control systems over the long term. In the near term, it is generally acknowledged that other nuclear powers such as India, Pakistan, even Israel and North Korea, are open to professional cyber penetration; and in the case of Pakistan, in particular, to private or terrorist-led expertise (Sukumar and Sharma 2016). The "Stuxnet" computer virus that was first reported in 2010 as penetrating the most sensitive parts of the highly secretive Iranian uranium enrichment process indicates what is possible with only moderately sophisticated state-sponsored malware. And in November 2012, the group Anonymous claimed to have hacked the IAEA and threatened to release "highly sensitive data" on the Israeli nuclear programme that they had allegedly seized (Kelley 2012). Whether true or not, the ability of a private group such as Anonymous to do this is not doubted.

The cyber specialists who can protect the command and control systems of the existing nuclear powers do not exist in sufficient numbers, even in the major nuclear powers – though the degree of reassurance for these states can be somewhat higher (US Department of Defense 2013). But the long-term cyber vulnerability of the United Kingdom's nuclear weapons, for example, is now commonly cited as a major risk of embarking on the "successor programme" to replace the independent nuclear deterrent in the late 2020s (Browne 2015). Why invest over £100 billion, the argument runs, in a programme running into the 2050s if it could be rendered deeply vulnerable well within that time? In other respects and for other countries the challenges are more immediate. The IAEA provides assistance and training in cyber security to member states running military and civil nuclear programmes but lacks the necessary resources to address an ever growing demand.

Nuclear establishments in all the nuclear weapon states have increasingly to draw on expertise from the civil sector if they are to remain secure – not just in the "crown jewels" of their early warning and launch procedures, but in the deeper engineering, scientific and military infrastructures that support their whole programmes. As a potential path through gridlock this may represent a form of legitimizing technical expertise; something more akin to the neo-functionalism of international technical elites. Gaining legitimacy from the UN (as in the UNGGE process), or through IAEA outsourcing – of which there is already a fair amount – it may become possible to discern the corpus of a cyber security establishment operating around the nexus of major international cyber companies. The cyber challenge extends deep into the underlying infrastructures of nuclear weapon systems and the reliance on civilian cyber security specialists is likely both to expand and deepen. As the "Internet of Things" becomes a reality the expectation is that this reliance will increase exponentially.

Such reliance will have different effects within the diverse range of polities that span the current nuclear weapons states. The non-P5 nuclear powers are especially vulnerable to fragmentation and external influences, both governmental and non-governmental. There is growing international concern, and for different reasons in each country, about the security of nuclear weapons and related materials in India and Pakistan (Sukumar and Sharma 2016), for example. It is probably premature to herald the existence of a neo-functionalist cyber security elite in the world, still less one that would embody a baseline minimal commitment to securing all nuclear forces against malicious cyber activity. But the conditions exist for such an elite to arise and the necessity for the work it would do has been recognized as a matter of urgency in the last decade among both state and non-state actors. The way the current nuclear weapons states handle the growing gaps in their cyber security expertise will have big effects on the credibility and security of their respective nuclear deterrents.

Institutional adaptation to the terrorist WMD threat

The possibility of international terrorists using elements of WMD in their attacks was only regarded as a serious proposition after Al Qaeda's attacks on the United States in 2001. Chemical and radiological agents, in particular, have formed the most likely parts of a new threat scenario that the security agencies, no less than the nonproliferation community, have tried to tackle. Terrorist groups are judged to have little effective capacity to employ biological warfare agents; and building, stealing – or even being gifted – a viable nuclear device is regarded as improbable and unlikely to work even if it were possessed. Chemical and radiological scenarios, however, are all too easy to credit (Hafemeister 2016: 353).

The institutional response has been interestingly different in the case of chemical, as opposed to radiological threats. As it happens, the 1993 Chemical Weapons Convention somewhat fortuitously includes several provisions that could help its signatories to prevent chemical terrorism or manage the consequences of an attack. Certainly, the CWC has made progress in eliminating chemical stocks (Walker 2010).[1] Nevertheless, 30,000 metric tons still await destruction, and several suspected possessor states remain outside the CWC regime. The CWC has not shown institutional adaptation in rising to its more immediate challenges. The provisions in the convention that could address terrorist use of chemical agents are not effectively used to increase international collaboration and the OPCW has found its role in preventing and responding to incidents of chemical terrorism highly constrained by political differences among its leading members (Tucker 2012).

The European Union, encompassing 28 of the 30 to 40 states most threatened by chemical terrorism, and embodying the security services to monitor illicit chemical transits around Europe, has been very slow to respond. After the 9/11 attacks the EU took on the responsibility of dealing more coherently with the threat of terrorism in all its forms, but only in 2009 did it really include potential WMD elements in the mix (Cebeci 2013). Little has been achieved at an institutional level. It is evident that the EU encompasses too many different security agencies in the counter-terrorism sphere, from individual national police forces and judicial authorities to the EU's law enforcement agency, Europol; the judicial cooperation agency, Eurojust; the EU's Intelligence Analysis Centre, INCENT; and the border management agency, Frontex. They represent a classic case of the "institutional fragmentation" identified by Hale, Held and Young (2013) as a symptom of gridlock. These agencies are either underfunded or constructed in a way that does not facilitate much genuine collaboration between them, while national police forces are frequently in competition with their own security agencies (Dempsey 2016). Belgian authorities admitted as much after the 2016 terror attacks in Brussels. The current crisis across the Middle East and the spate of terror attacks in France and Belgium in 2015–16 led to more concern about the potential for chemical terrorism across EU member states, but the response has remained overwhelmingly within different national policy frameworks (Lloyd's 2016: 7).

NATO has been somewhat more adaptive in this respect since it has taken practical measures against chemical terrorism for the last 15 years and alliance membership includes countries that have traditionally developed military-based skills in countering chemical warfare. Mature skills and facilities exist in the Czech Republic and Turkey, where NATO's Combined Joint CBRN [Chemical, Biological, Radiological and Nuclear] Defence Task Force has created centres of expertise, training and (most crucially) operational capacity that could be drawn on at short notice in a chemical terror event. There is a degree of operational practicality in the response of NATO, though as a collective defence alliance, this is more about consequence management than arms control at the higher political level. Neither NATO nor the EU have emerged as adaptive organizations in the face of new challenges in chemical terrorism and have not made any discernible impression on the CWC, or at the UN level, in shifting the international anti-chemical warfare regime into new conceptual territory.

The situation is different, however, over the potential for radiological terrorism, another example of the way in which nuclear symbols and technologies command more political attention than other parts of the WMD spectrum. In the case of radiological terrorism there are some understandable reasons for this. The examples of radiological contamination provided by the disasters at the Chernobyl nuclear power plant in 1986 and at Fukushima in Japan in 2011 have provided practical yardsticks of the threat that radiological terrorism might pose. Despite the experience of Iraqi chemical attacks on Halabja in 1988 and attacks in Syria since 2013, such radiological disasters stick more in the political imagination; no matter that such a concentration of radiological elements would be far more challenging for any terrorist group than a comparable and deliberately destructive event using chemical agents. The most likely scenario is the detonation of a "dirty bomb" where a conventional explosion is encased in mixed radiological materials that might be stolen, or supplied by a rogue state, derived from a wide range of civilian sources, from a nuclear power industry, or even from military nuclear stocks.

In this realm it is possible to discern a potential pathway out of gridlock since there has been a clear shift in the perception of core interests among the most relevant state leaderships in the world. The 9/11 attacks on the US in 2001 emphasized not just the nihilistic ambitions of the new terrorists but also their willingness to use novel modes of attack that might also involve radiological or other WMD elements. As the then UK Prime Minister Tony Blair subsequently expressed it, "If they [jihadi terrorists] got hold of them, there could be little doubt on the evidence of September 11 that they would use them." And how much worse might the 9/11 experience have been, leaders reasoned, if elements of WMD had been involved as well? "It was obvious to me," said Blair, "that our attitude towards the trade, transfer and development of such weapons had to be of a wholly different kind" (2011: 357). Clearly, internationally coordinated action was necessary and justified by such new challenges.

Representing the same sentiments and a clear shift in the perception of core interests, the United States embarked on a carefully targeted campaign nationally, and also through the United Nations, to launch the Proliferation Security Initiative in 2003 (Dunne 2013; Belcher 2016). It was a new orientation in non-proliferation, being directed specifically at the dangers that non-state groups might pose, and some 105 nations have endorsed the initiative, intended, in the words of the US State Department, "to make PSI a flexible, voluntary initiative geared toward enhancing individual and collective partner nations' capabilities to take appropriate and timely actions to meet the fast-moving situations involving proliferation threats"

(US Department of State 2016). The PSI does not create any new legal authority, although its terms are already included in the UN Security Council's key anti-terrorism resolutions 1373 and 1540, and other arms control treaty obligations.[2]

The PSI, however, began to run out of political steam. It was independently judged after 2014 to have exhibited no improvement in measures, including on-site physical protection, security during transport or the ability to recover lost radioactive materials. As the Nuclear Threat Initiative put it, "The nuclear security summits have had a positive effect, but the strategic goal of developing an effective global nuclear security system remains unachieved" (Spetalnick and Brunnstrom 2016) Finally, it succumbed to the political fall-out of the deteriorating relations between Washington and Moscow when Russia ostentatiously refused to attend the final PSI summit in 2016. It was the victim of a crisis in bilateral relations largely over the Ukraine/Crimea and then Syria – two regions that are prime candidates for the illicit supply or transit of radiological materials in terrorist hands.

Other voluntary and ad hoc initiatives have also emerged, one of which, the 2006 Global Initiative to Combat Nuclear Terrorism (GICNT) is a voluntary international partnership of 86 nations and five international organizations committed to strengthening global capacity to prevent and respond to nuclear terrorism (Alcaro 2009). It was established with the US and Russia as co-chairs, and the Netherlands leading the Implementation and Assessment Group under the guidance of the co-chairs. This arrangement has endured and the GICNT has an active agenda through to the 2020s and has generated a great number of international meetings to share best practice and evaluate capacities. Nevertheless, the GICNT places few demands on its members and the control of fissile materials in the most vulnerable regions and countries is still hampered by a chronic lack of financial provision (Cameron 2016).

Such flexible and voluntary arrangements are backed up by the more structured support offered by the IAEA and NATO, both of which have been more active on nuclear terrorist challenges than has been generally acknowledged. In particular, their role and the synergy they can offer with arrangements such as the PSI or the GICNT has been galvanized to a significant extent by the Fukushima disaster (Pandza 2011).

The net conclusion must be that though there are mechanisms in the existing regime structure that could have been used to address both of these new challenges, and though there have been some evident shifts in the perception of core interests, the major players have not put their faith in regime approaches and have instead sought national or bilateral action, or else purely voluntary arrangements at the international level.

Pathways beyond Gridlock?

The WMD arena demonstrates many of the old frustrations as well as some of the new hopes of navigating out of institutional gridlock in the present international environment. One of the recognized pathways out of any gridlock – a coalition between reformist states and the wider international civil community – has been increasingly frustrated since 1991. The traditionalists within the arms control community, both governments and individuals, have shown a natural tendency to try to build coalitions at the global level. As a pathway out of gridlock and in a debate so charged with moral condemnation, there has been a major attempt to try to create momentum behind a moral climate that puts civilized thinking ahead of barbarism (Risse-Kappen 1995). But this has become more a substitute for genuine policy action – at best a contribution to the milieu around the central issues – rather than a new impetus for WMD regimes.

A long-standing attempt through the UN is underway to create an international effort to declare a ban on nuclear weapons – a straightforward "nuclear weapons treaty." More than 100 members of the UN have made common cause with a large coalition of non-governmental organizations over recent years to propose, for 2017, the opening of negotiations for a treaty that would ban nuclear weapons; to close the "legal gap" in the existing regime governing nuclear weapons, as recognized by the UN's "humanitarian pledge." It is an anomaly, it is argued, that these are the only weapons of mass destruction not yet prohibited under international law in a comprehensive and universal manner, since chemical and biological weapons, anti-personnel landmines and cluster munitions are all expressly prohibited through international conventions. The practical utility of declaring an outright "ban" has been hotly disputed by those organizations and states which argue that a "convention," designed around a "prohibition," would be more realistic, since the objective is to follow the examples set by the conventions on anti-personnel landmines and on cluster munitions, and to create a growing momentum that would delegitimize and stigmatize the possession of nuclear weapons in the eyes of world opinion (Pearce 2016). The fact remains, however, that none of the nuclear weapons states, and none of the so-called "umbrella states" which believe they are the recipients of deterrence extended from a nuclear weapons state, have supported the initiative. At best, the signing of such a convention would restate and perhaps reinforce the existing obligations undertaken in the current NPT and within existing declared Nuclear Weapons Free Zones. It is understood that any attempt to delegitimize nuclear weapons, albeit through a large and loose coalition of prominent individuals, non-state groups and sympathetic governments, must be regarded chiefly as an aspirational goal to bring pressure on future generations of policymakers in the nuclear states (Ritchie 2014: 622–3). Contributing to a global intellectual milieu is not without value in helping light a path that may in the future lead out of gridlock, but it has made no policy progress to date and is arguably less influential than it might have been even during the Cold War era, let alone in the lost decade of arms control after 1991.

At the other end of the spectrum, a pathway out of gridlock based on political leadership among the key state players might have been seen as more promising. In the event, one US President tried to offer inspirational national leadership in 2009 at the beginning of his term of office. But President Obama's attitude towards an explicit regime approach to WMD proliferation – deeply held and explicitly foreshadowed (Obama 2007: ch. 8) – was out of kilter with the previous US Administration of 2001–9, the incoming Administration of 2017, and the approaches of the other most important nuclear players in Russia, China and India whose policy trajectories pointed in the opposite direction. In the current era not even a deeply committed US President could engineer a shift in the perceptions of core interests either among his international interlocutors or his own congressional and defence establishments. This is in sharp historical contrast to the case of President Ronald Reagan who, as a right-wing Republican leader, was able to seize the moment in 1987 to agree the Intermediate-Range Nuclear Forces Treaty with his Soviet counterpart that saw the abolition of a complete class of nuclear weapons – over 2,500 of them – within four years and create a shared aspiration to highly ambitious nuclear disarmament goals (Kissinger 2014: 312–14). In that era, and within a brief political window, the moment was right. The WMD regime seemed set to make substantial, and unexpected, progress for which an unlikely presidential champion takes the historical credit. It was, said observers, "a Republican-built regime" (Cirincione 2000: 6–8). Thirty years later, however, Barack Obama was the Democratic President who, against his instincts, was forced to accept the logic of a modernization arms race in the nuclear forces of the major powers and, the Iran nuclear deal aside, saw all his attempts at global leadership in this realm come to nothing (Luce 2016). No other significant world leaders currently in a position to affect ongoing policy on WMD have stepped forward as Obama tried to do.

Nor has there been any such leadership on the more immediate breaking of taboos on the use of chemical agents in conflict; quite the reverse. The current zone of warfare extends in an arc from Nigeria in West Africa to Pakistan in South Asia, covering around 1 billion of the world's 6.2 billion inhabitants (Pinker and Santos 2016). Within that arc, conflicts of fragmentation are overwhelmingly predominant and such taboos as had existed on the use of chemical agents in conflict have been significantly eroded.

Despite these setbacks, other identified pathways out of gridlock may show some signs of vitality, particularly in relation to new and conceptually challenging scenarios posed by cyber threats to nuclear stability and terrorist access to WMD. In both these areas it is possible to discern some shifts in the core interests of the major players. In the case of "chemical terrorism" it is difficult to discern what is genuinely different, other than greater awareness and expressions of concern. The possibilities of "nuclear terrorism," however, have created some impetus to institutional evolution – reorientating the work of some traditional institutions such as the IAEA and NATO, and attempting to create more voluntary structures to complement them through initiatives such as the PSI or the GICNT. Such international institutionalization is also dependent for its success on the capabilities of national security and law enforcement agencies in the most significant states. Though all this exists through the agencies of sovereign states and at the impetus of high politics, there is a necessary pyramid of mutual dependence that runs from the UN Security Council down to domestic law enforcement at the local level. This is replete with vulnerabilities, of course, but also with different potential drivers of political impetus, albeit within the frameworks of sovereign authority.

Perhaps most interestingly, the challenges posed to strategic nuclear stability by the potential for cyber interventions or attacks are only now being grasped by policymakers within the WMD regimes. Unlike with most forms of criminality, the state's security and enforcement apparatus is inadequate to deal with cyber challenges on its own. It must have the cooperation of the private sector. Nuclear forces, of course, are encased in the best security arrangements a state can provide. But the evidence is growing that this may not extend to all the cyber vulnerabilities that are now possible, and in particular, not to those arising from the deep physical and social infrastructures upon which nuclear forces depend. If policymakers in the nuclear states want to address this problem, top-level agreements, as between the US and China in 2015, will not suffice, however binding they may appear. They will need to cooperate, to co-opt from the private sector, and to mutually enforce across cyberspace a determination to maintain the operational integrity of their nuclear forces. The alternative for policymakers would be to accept cyber competition between them as intrinsic to their deterrent relationship, with all the unknown vulnerabilities and uncertainty that would bring.

It would be a great irony if a new impetus in great power nuclear non-proliferation was sparked by a recognition that the major powers needed to cooperate to enforce their collective will on cyberspace – one of the great engines of globalization – in order to maintain their conception of mutually assured destruction. It would be a latter-day return to the notion of nuclear arms control, protecting stability rather than trying to reduce weapons themselves or the number of states possessing them. But the original WMD regimes, the core treaties that underpinned them, began in a similar way in the 1960s. The big difference in this case would be that any arrangements could not remain at the high political level but would have to embrace large swathes of the internet industries and extend deep into the activities of civil society. As one route out of current institutional gridlock, that would be unprecedented but not impossible given the stakes for which the great powers would be playing. A combination of renewed political leadership, based on a perception of core interests, but linked explicitly to the vigour of economic elites and civil society is still a realistic aspiration for future global governance (Mazower 2012: 426).

This suggests that new regime-based approaches to modern proliferation challenges would have to approach the central concerns indirectly, building on shared core interests to prevent anarchy being brought to the strategic relationships that underpin WMD possession through cyber attacks or widespread possession or use by terrorists of significant WMD elements. None of this would address directly the return of the great powers to nuclear arms racing or the trends towards more regional WMD proliferation in the Middle East or Asia. But it may represent the most plausible way forward, as long as the limited and pragmatic measures which political leaders are beginning to see as desirable are also interpreted to include large parts of the civil and technological sectors whose involvement is critical to their implementation. The challenge of moving a reformed WMD regime from one largely dominated by the high politics of national security towards one that recognizes the limitations of the key states to protect themselves from these new challenges and requires such a degree of neo-functional cooperation below the political level may become an impetus to make it more of a reality. One hopes this might be the case before some catastrophic use or accident in WMD technology makes it seem an imperative. A precautionary reform of the currently failing regime would be greatly preferable to a retrospective one.

13

Conclusion

Breaking the Cycle of Gridlock

Thomas Hale and David Held

In *Gridlock*, we set out to explain why multilateral cooperation is stalling across many areas of world politics. We argued that trends towards multipolarity, harder problems, institutional inertia, and fragmentation, all rooted in the previous successes of global governance, now make cooperation more difficult. Because the argument emphasized long-term, structural, partially endogenous trends, it could say little about how to resist or escape gridlock. The implication was that global governance had become systematically stuck and would likely remain so until things deteriorated into a major crisis, after which it would be possible, perhaps, to rebuild. This "punctuated equilibrium" model of history is as intuitively compelling as it is grim.

Beyond Gridlock has attempted to challenge this conclusion. Recognizing the range of exceptions and anomalies to the gridlock logic, it has tried to identify systematic pathways through and beyond. It has explored these pathways empirically across a wide range of issues in the hope of informing efforts to undo gridlock.

Has it succeeded? In part. As we review below, the previous chapters have described critical areas where global governance remains robust and resilient despite gridlock, showing the endurance of some institutions even in the face of significant political changes. The chapters also show how global governance can be surprisingly adaptive and responsive, changing institutional form or modus operandi to achieve its goals via alternative means when gridlock arises. Much of this resilience and innovation springs not from the kind of long-term structural trends emphasized in *Gridlock*, but from the agency, strategic responses, and leadership of key actors in world politics.

But readers hoping for a panacea will be disappointed. The chapters in this book show the resilience of some existing patterns of cooperation and instances of incremental progress, but they offer fewer examples of transformative change. In other words, the preponderance of the book's findings address pathways through gridlock, not pathways truly beyond it. Indeed, in some areas, gridlock is worsening. This decay stems in part, as we explain below, from an anti-global backlash for which unmanaged globalization is partially responsible.

Will these negative trends erode remaining areas of resilience and undo the incremental progress made thus far, returning us to the grim implications of the gridlock argument? Not necessarily, we conclude. The existence of pathways through gridlock means that a positive difference can be made by bolstering resilient areas of global governance and by creatively seeking incremental progress. The previous chapters offer concrete examples that can be built on and applied to other domains. But the book's findings also strongly imply that the kinds of successes described here will ultimately be insufficient. Moving truly beyond gridlock will require more far-reaching and radical political changes than have been possible to date. Building the political conditions to manage globalization effectively must therefore be seen as a long-term political project, akin to the struggle to institutionalize national self-determination or liberal democracy. The challenge will be to do this while also resisting the further deepening of gridlock and its effects. In sum, in the twenty-first century our global political institutions are caught between interlocking forces of progress and decay. Our essential task is to tilt the balance toward the former.

Self-Reinforcing Gridlock and the Rise of Nationalism

While this book has explored exceptions to gridlock, in some ways it has found the phenomenon to be even more entrenched than first described. One of the central concepts developed in *Gridlock* was "self-reinforcing interdependence" (Hale, Held and Young 2013), the mutually enabling relationship between globalization and the institutionalization of world politics that profoundly deepened interdependence over the postwar period. The idea is that international cooperation is not just a response states use to manage existing interdependence; over time, cooperation also increases the links between economic and social systems across borders, deepening interdependence further. For example, trade agreements create incentives for companies to develop global supply chains and invest in technologies that facilitate cross-border production, changing their business models and building new constituencies for trade. The resulting increase in interdependence creates additional political incentives for countries to cooperate further, beginning the cycle again. We argued in *Gridlock* that this historical process of partially endogenous interdependence deepened to such a degree over the postwar period that a number of "second order" cooperation problems arose, causing gridlock.

It now seems clear that gridlock itself also has a self-reinforcing element. The global rise of nationalism and populism has multiple and complex origins. But this trend can be seen as part of a downward spiral in which gridlock leads to unmanaged globalization or unmet global challenges, which in turn help to provoke anti-global backlashes that further undermine the operative capacity of global governance institutions (figure 13.1).

Consider each dynamic in turn. First, as per the gridlock argument, we face a multilateral system that is less and less able to manage global challenges, even as growing interdependence increases our need for such management. Nearly every chapter in this volume has found evidence of gridlock, defined as multilateral dysfunction stemming from the four gridlock mechanisms, and all chapters have identified urgent global issues that are inadequately managed. These results reaffirm our 2013 argument that the condition is pervasive across contemporary world politics, even if specific pathways through and beyond it can also be identified.

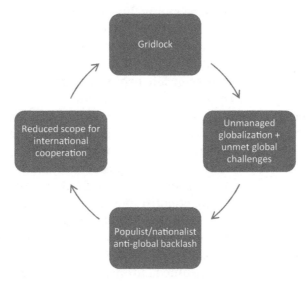

Figure 13.1 Self-reinforcing gridlock

Second, in many areas this inability to manage globalization or to meet global challenges has led to real, and in many cases severe, harm to many sectors of the global population, often creating complex and disruptive knock-on effects. Perhaps the most spectacular recent example of harm caused by mismanaged interdependence was the 2008–9 financial crisis. A product of inadequate regulation in major economies and at the global level, the crisis wrought havoc on the world economy. We should not be surprised that such significant impacts have led to further destabilization.

Third, what has become clear only several years after the crisis is the scale of the political destruction to which the crisis contributed. Rising economic inequality, a long-term trend in many economies, has been made more salient by the crisis. It reinforced a stark political cleavage between those who have benefited from the globalization, digitization, and automation of the economy, and those who feel left behind in the wake of these powerful disruptions. The global financial crisis is not the only cause of many of the political disruptions that have come to characterize and realign politics in major countries in the last few years, but it has been a critical contributing factor in several of them. Perhaps most importantly, the financial crisis sharpened the divide between working-class voters in industrialized countries, who were hit hard by the events, and other segments of the population. This division is particularly acute in spatial terms: the cleavage between global cities and their hinterlands. Global cities like London, Paris, Shanghai, New York, and San Francisco have become nodes of power and influence in the global economy, linked to each other through a variety of social and economic networks. Their citizens have benefited directly as opportunities have sharply risen. By contrast, those in the hinterlands, typically rural areas and deindustrialized cities, but not exclusively so, have often been left behind in absolute and relative terms, building up frustrations and resentments.

The effect on politics has been profound, with a number of nationalist and populist movements emerging and, in some cases, winning elections (or otherwise seizing power) in many countries. Again, we should not be surprised that people exposed to the negative effects of globalization will turn against it. Research shows that over the course of history, right-wing populist movements and financial crises are strongly correlated (see Funke, Schularick and Trebesch 2016). Relatedly, the 2008 crisis exacerbated many of the woes that have beset the eurozone since 2010, such as the repeated bailouts of Greece and other countries that consumed European politics and drove voters on both the creditor and debtor side of the political chasm towards

Euro-scepticism. And more broadly, the impact on the centre-left parties that have traditionally supported global and regional cooperation has also been severe, with the differential affects of globalization straining the traditional coalition of between metropolitan progressives and the working class.

But the financial crisis is only one area where gridlock has undercut the management of global challenges and therefore undermined political support for global cooperation. Consider the global response to terrorism. International cooperation, though effective in many areas, has failed to prevent extremists from attacking civilians around the world. While relatively cohesive and centralized networks like Al Qaeda have been largely taken apart through a combination of aggressive policing, surveillance, drone attacks, and other techniques, more inchoate movements like the Islamic State are much harder to root out. The attacks by these groups, for example in Paris in 2015, have been all too effective in creating a public discourse in many countries that sees perpetual war between Islamists and the West. This sentiment, in turn, creates political pressure for militarized responses from the West that can create as many terrorists as they eliminate.

These negative effects also spill across issue areas. The failure to manage terrorism and the wars in the Middle East have had a particularly destructive impact on the global governance of migration. With millions of refugees fleeing their countries in search of safety and a better life for their families, many of them heading for Europe, the global forced migration regime has been overwhelmed. Many recipient countries have seen a potent political backlash from right-wing national groups and disgruntled populations, which further reduces the ability of countries to generate effective solutions at the global level.

This undermining of global cooperation, whether for migration, terrorism, financial regulation, climate change, or other areas, is the fourth and final element of self-reinforcing gridlock. As the global trend to nationalism and populism cuts the effectiveness of global institutions even further, the whole cycle begins anew. We see such trends across many different kinds of countries, from Trump's United States to Duterte's Philippines, from Putin's Russia to Brexit Britain, from Modi's India to Erdoğan's Turkey. The anti-global backlash is heterogeneous. It encompasses terrorism in the name of Islam and Islamophobic discrimination against Muslims. It includes leftist rejection of trade agreements and right-wing rejection of environmental agreements. The powerful tie that unites these disparate movements is a rejection of interdependence and collective efforts to govern it. Global institutions and (perceived) cosmopolitan elites have always

been a potent and politically expedient whipping boy for national-
ists and populists, even when those institutions, or some other form
of international cooperation, are needed to tame the socio-economic
forces that inflamed populist movements to begin with.

In short, the destructive power of unmanaged interdependence has
been unleashed by, in no small part, deepening gridlock in critical
areas of global governance. It is important to note that such dynamics have long been familiar to many countries in the global South,
which have always felt the sharpest edges of globalization and interdependence in the form of IMF structural adjustments, military interventions, and other intrusive forms of global governance. For many
years, the developed countries' wealth and political power insulated
them from the worst elements of globalization, while their welfare
states softened global capitalism enough to make it politically palat-
able for comfortable majorities of the population. This compromise
of "embedded liberalism" (Ruggie 1982) – in which social democracy
gave populations the control and protection they needed to liberalize their economies – a cornerstone of the postwar order, now seems
increasingly inadequate and threadbare.

This system has eroded in part because gridlock has reduced our
ability to manage globalization effectively. But we should also recognize that the embedded liberalism of the middle of the twentieth
century existed only for a small set of industrialized democracies. As
the world economy began to change, and new entrants emerged in the
1980s (Japan, South Korea, Taiwan) and the late 1990s (China, India,
Brazil, among others), the position of the developed countries began
to alter. The world's centre of economic gravity progressively shifted
south and east (Quah 2011). Some countries in the developing world
have been able to socially embed the global economy as they have
developed, but most have not. Meanwhile, power has shifted. This
process was given an enormous impetus by the financial crisis of 2008,
which for several years saw a collapse and subsequent stagnation of
growth in much of the West, while the Asian economies continued
to grow at a rapid pace (Wolf 2013). While in the 1990s emerging
countries' combined GDP (at market exchange rates) amounted to less
than a third of the G7 countries' combined GDP, today this gap has
practically closed (Quah and Mahbubani 2016). Reflecting a decline
in international income inequality, the world order, shaped by the
West for so many centuries, has begun to undergo seemingly irre-
versible change. The West can no longer rule the roost as it once
did and with this change comes not just increasing competition for
employment, production and innovation, but also a growing sense
of unease and powerlessness in the "left behind" segments of many

Western populations, which reinforces anti-global, pro-national political forces. And while global markets have created many new beneficiaries in the developing world, they have also brought significant
social and political disruption, without, in most cases, forging the
kind of embedded liberalism that has traditionally made integration
sustainable. In sum, gridlock not only emerges from self-reinforcing
global trends, but is also compounded through its pernicious effects
on national politics. However, as this book has argued, it can also lead
to and enable opposite reactions. We turn to these now.

Pathways through and beyond Gridlock

With powerful, mutually reinforcing trends working to undermine
effective global governance, the recognition, strengthening, and reinforcement of causal pathways through and beyond gridlock become
all the more important. This book has traced seven such pathways
across eleven areas of world politics. Gridlock may be self-reinforcing,
but it is not inevitable. While the issues focused on in the previous chapters are not necessarily representative of all areas of world
politics, they do cover a sufficiently broad range of topics to support
some more general claims. Below we offer some reflections on each
of the pathways, and some issues that cut across them. What emerges
is a comparative analysis of many core sectors in global politics that
allows us to understand the conditions and mechanisms for significant policy innovation in diverse areas.

Shifts in major powers' core interests

Unsurprisingly, the shifting interests of major nation-states provide
one of the most important pathways through and even beyond gridlock. As observed in the previous chapters, from health, to climate
and energy, to investment, to human rights, shifts in the policy goals
of big countries have helped unblock multilateral institutions in
important ways. In investment, these shifts have the potential to
truly remake the regime in a fundamentally different way, creating a
pathway beyond gridlock. It remains to be seen, however, if the major
powers' interests do indeed align to make this happen. In climate and
health, by contrast, action by major powers has provided an important
pathway through previous gridlock, but does not yet qualify as transformational. In health, there has been a vast increase in funding for
critical diseases, but not yet a full-fledged effort to build robust health

systems around the world to make diverse populations more resilient. In climate, shifting interests in the United States and China allowed the regime to evolve with the adoption of the Paris Agreement. But such shifts cannot be taken for granted. For climate, the election of Donald Trump in the United States provides a vivid example of how major powers' priorities can suddenly shift against more effective cooperation (a possibility also for China and other major powers). This reversibility highlights a key limitation of this pathway. There is no guarantee that major powers' interests will shift in a way that counterbalances gridlock. Indeed, given global trends towards nationalism, the opposite may be more likely in the foreseeable future. So while shifts in major powers may lead to occasional breakthroughs in specific areas – the previous chapters posit that nuclear security and cyber security may at some point benefit from such a shift – the mechanism in general is unlikely on its own to provide a long-term pathway beyond gridlock.

Autonomous and adaptive international institutions

Several areas of contemporary world politics are, largely to their benefit, populated by relatively strong, independent international institutions. These institutions are somewhat insulated from the political whims of their member states (at least in certain areas), and possess sufficient authority and resources to at least partially adapt to the expanding governance needs generated by deepening interdependence. Trade, finance, investment, monetary cooperation, nuclear proliferation, and human rights stand out in this regard. Note that institutions in these realms include both those that deal with "high politics" questions (like human rights, state-to-state trade disputes, or nuclear security) and more technocratic issues. Even in areas with sharp distributional implications or high sovereignty costs, some institutions have proven sufficiently autonomous and adaptive to chart a course through gridlock. The WTO's dispute settlement mechanism is a case par excellence, a quasi-legal body that has managed to retain its authority even as the issues before it expanded far beyond those originally envisioned by members of the WTO. The power of law and formal legal rules is important to note in this regard. In a different realm, the IAEA has been able to conduct inspections of nuclear sites even in challenging countries.

One of the interesting features of this pathway is the ability of such institutions to reassert their centrality in an increasingly plural institutional landscape. This book has argued that a reinvigorated WTO may be able to strengthen its coordination of the welter of preferential trade agreements that have proliferated in recent years and therefore bring greater coherence to global trade rules. It has also found evidence of the IMF taking steps in this direction to coordinate the increasingly important arrangements between national central banks and the credit swaps set up between them. In the climate realm, we have seen how the UNFCCC has consciously embraced the proliferation of transnational and sub- and non-state governance initiatives. These interactions suggest that the relatively strong international institutions that exist today can become focal points around which more comprehensive and effective global governance arrangements may accrete, merging with the pathway explored below. Still, this potential remains largely prospective in the cases considered in this book. Instead, the chief contribution autonomous and adaptive international institutions have made so far is to maintain existing patterns of cooperation even under difficult conditions.

Multiple, diverse organizations and institutions coalesce around common goals/norms

In several issue areas, authors saw progress being made when a proliferation of institutions and actors cohered around a common purpose. Such a structure is vigorously in evidence in the realms of health and climate and energy, for example, where private actors, multi-stakeholder initiatives, and networks of cities, businesses, NGOs, and other sub/non-state actors have completely reshaped the governance landscape. In climate, for example, it is estimated that the actions of cities, businesses, and other sub/non-state actors will reduce as much carbon from the atmosphere as the pledges of nation-states (UNEP 2016). Similarly, in global health, private funds and funding channelled through hybrid vehicles now constitute the majority of money going towards the management and mitigation of critical diseases in the developing world. In other words, for both these issues, nation-states and formal intergovernmental processes have been joined by a wide array of complementary actors and institutions, which have made a qualitative improvement in the global governance of these areas.

A critical characteristic of these domains is that the proliferation of institutions and actors work towards a common goal. In climate, the common objective of limiting temperature change to 2°C or 1.5°C this century, established by the UNFCCC, has been directly translated into the objectives of many cities, businesses, regions, and other actors. In global health, the International Health Regulations and numerous WHO guidelines (e.g. regarding what drugs to use) give coherence to the wider range of efforts now being undertaken. In addition, in the domain of human rights, national and transnational networks of non-state actors have used the international human rights regime developed in the 1960s and 1970s as a lever to insert the human rights agenda into numerous national polities. This is not to say that such polycentric systems do not suffer from relatively high transaction costs for coordination and some degree of redundancy. But the existence of common norms and objectives makes plurality a virtue in these contexts.

A proliferation of actors and institutions around a common goal or norm was also observed with more limited success in humanitarianism, and envisioned as a potential way forward in the realm of investment. In the former, the existence of a coordinating committee with an established division of labour for humanitarian actors provides an important degree of coherence, though practice in the field has lagged behind the decisions taken by the global bodies headquartered in Geneva. For investment, the norms dominating the field are now in a state of flux, so it is unclear if one will emerge to provide a focal point for different dispute resolution institutions to cohere around.

Of all the pathways, this merger of plurality and coherence seems to have the most transformative potential. In climate, health, and human rights, for example, the regimes have made enormous progress by tapping this broader array of actors. That said, the pathway also faces a critical scope condition: it only appears in areas where a wide range of actors possess the ability to make a positive contribution to the governance challenge in question. Because any number of actors and entities can affect climate, health or human rights, those issues are more amenable to a pluralistic strategy. This would not be the case for, say, nuclear security or tariff barriers, where the actors with the capacity to affect the problem are almost entirely nation-states.

Mobilization of domestic constituencies

Relatively few issues areas provided evidence for this pathway. In the human rights realm, international courts, tribunals, and other institutions have served to strengthen the hand of pro-compliance groups in domestic societies, notably in Latin America, in a way that strengthens the global governance of human rights. Though not emphasized in this book, the trade regime has also been reinforced by giving exporters access, through their governments, to legal redress. This arrangement entrenches support for the WTO in domestic interests. In the climate realm, the Paris Agreement is envisioned to bolster domestic constituencies for progressively more stringent climate action through the review and ratchet process, but whether it does or not remains to be seen. In other areas, the book did not find systematic efforts to build domestic constituencies that would help move us through or beyond gridlock.

Could such mechanisms be imagined in the future? One of the weaknesses of contemporary global governance is that it is often remote from daily concerns, or seen to be remote. In other words, it has not been adequately embedded socially. Even though global governance affects almost every aspect of society and the economy, it has few constituents. A more robust form of global governance may need to connect more directly to individuals and interest groups in order to retain their support as a bulwark against gridlock. We return to this idea below.

Technical groups with effective and legitimate processes

In almost every area considered in this book, technical cooperation was seen as a critical and successful element of global governance arrangements, even in the face of gridlock. Effective technical processes are often, unsurprisingly, "under the radar," but this does not diminish their importance. For example, while state-to-state treaty negotiations over reducing trade barriers get the most attention in the trade realm, standard setting, commercial dispute resolution, and export finance cooperation are also critically important to the global economy. Global governance in these areas, dominated by technocratic groups, many of them mixing state and non-state actors, seems to be working quite well. Similar effectiveness can be observed in scientific cooperation around climate change, or in the realm of nuclear safety. The importance of this pathway suggests that, in many ways, we take significant areas of global governance for granted, even in the academic literature. The gridlock narrative is thus missing out on important swathes of cooperation that are reassuringly robust even in the face of challenging structural trends.

But by the same logic, this pathway is better at preserving cooperation and finding incremental gains than in fundamentally transforming our capacity to manage interdependence. In none of the chapters did we find evidence that technical groups following a strong process could, through their own actions, overturn the fundamental barriers to effective global governance. This is to be expected. Significant change requires, virtually by definition, political mobilization, coalition building, and contestation.

Civil society coalitions with reformist states

In contrast to the incremental benefits of technocratic processes, civil society coalitions with reformist states have at least the potential to move us fundamentally beyond gridlock. In the 1990s civil society organizations and social movements played a key role, often in alliance with states, in pushing many core issues onto the global agenda, from issues around AIDS/HIV and reproductive rights to broader issues of nuclear disarmament, war crimes and climate change. Yet, in the proceeding chapters, such potential was identified only in two realms: investment and humanitarianism. In the former, some developing countries have been seeking to leave the investor–state dispute settlement system, while the EU has sought to create a public alternative to private arbitration. In both cases, governments have been pushed by, and worked in tandem with, civil society activists. While it remains unclear whether the regime will fully shift as a result of these efforts, the potential to do so seems strong.

In contrast, in three other areas, nuclear proliferation, human rights, and financial regulation, we found little evidence that civil society movements could fundamentally alter global gridlock. This finding is striking and discouraging because these areas have traditionally been targets for widespread activism, such as the peace and disarmament movements of the 1960s and 1970s, the struggle for human rights, most marked in the 1970s and 1980s, and the Occupy Wall Street movement that emerged after the 2008 crisis. We are thus left with the somewhat bleak conclusion that one of the most reliable traditional pathways to effective political change, and one of the pathways with the greatest transformative potential, seems to have a fairly narrow window for application at the present time. This may, of course, change in due course as politics in many countries becomes more contentious and new generations redevelop social movements. But to the extent this possibility exists, it remains in the future.

Innovative leadership as a reaction to gridlock

More encouragingly, in several areas authors found states and other actors responding positively and strategically to gridlock by exercising leadership of various kinds. In climate, for example, the way top UN officials and national diplomats shifted the regime from a "regulatory" to a "catalytic" model, by articulating a new vision of what multilateral institutions should do, helped unlock new political possibilities. In health, the steep increase in funding for critical diseases by G7 countries and private entities like the Gates Foundation has made a crucial difference to the global disease burden. These kinds of constructive actions result from farsighted and public-spirited decisions taken by key individuals, some of them motivated by failures of global governance they could no longer abide. In this sense they represent "leadership" of the highest order.

Gridlock is a theory of long-term structural trends, and so it puts relatively little weight on the individual agency of key actors. But at least a few chapters in this book suggest that the exceptions to the gridlock logic can be very significant indeed. Recognizing this is important, because it means that effective global governance is not necessarily doomed, even if numerous factors push against it. Beyond climate and health, it is encouraging that the chapters on nuclear and cyber security posit effective leadership as at least a potential path beyond gridlock. How can we stimulate more of it? And would good leadership be sufficient to overcome gridlock trends? We now turn in closing to these urgent questions.

Breaking the Hold of Gridlock and the Anti-global Backlash?

What does *Beyond Gridlock* tell us? In the first instance, globalization creates huge opportunities but also dislocations and risks. Opportunities because individuals, nations and countries have the capacity to communicate and engage across the world, often yielding spectacular benefits, for example, substantial increases in trade, growth in employment and productivity, and enhanced prosperity over many years. But these benefits are not distributed equally. Trade may make the world richer on average, but it does so by taking from some to give to others. Similarly, increased cultural exchange may liberate some members of a society but challenge the sacred beliefs of others. Moreover, globalization also creates huge risks if the economic and social interconnections and networks within and between countries are not subject to rules, standards, and coordination. Without this, globalization easily becomes subject to the law of winner takes all, and thus unsustainable. Ungoverned, globalization sows the seeds of its own destruction. This combination of opportunity and risk is highlighted by the fact that the world economy has grown annually since 1950 (Wolf 2017), while income inequality, as measured by the gap between the richest 10 per cent and the poorest in a country, has substantially increased in many parts of the world, even as the gap between countries has shrunk (see Held and Kaya 2006; OECD 2011; Piketty 2014; Milanovic 2016). Unregulated globalization can create havoc in the lives of individuals and nations across the world, as both are subject to the intensive competition of global markets. The latter can lead to large-scale shifts in patterns of industrialization and employment, meaning a reduction in real wages for many and, for the more educated and mobile, holders of capital, and the rising middle classes in emerging countries, spectacular gains.

Embedded liberalism and multilateralism have been and remain our core institutional response to the opportunities, dislocations, and risks of globalization. If the hugely unequal effects of globalization – including income inequality, exchange rate instability, financial turbulence, uneven patterns of job loss and creation, and environmental damage – are to be not just contained but governed in ways that are acceptable to domestic populations, then embedding markets in structures of fair rules, policies and institutions remains of the utmost importance. The radically uneven distributional consequences of globalization need to be addressed within and across countries if the frustration and anger of those left behind are not to focus simply on the reassertion of nationalism and the anti-global. Yet, the havoc that ungoverned globalization can create affects not just the routine and daily issues that influence the quality of everyday life, but also poses many dangerous existential risks, from the spread of WMD, to deadly pathogens, to climate change. These cannot be addressed other than through global cooperation and collaboration focused on mitigation and amelioration, on the one side, and creating the conditions of pacific and sustainable life across the world, on the other.

How do we manage globalization? One of the key lessons of this book is that one size does not fit all. That is to say, there are several pathways to significant policy change and it is necessary to understand what works and why in different sectors. Understanding how different issues and sectors are amenable to different pathways of change creates a capacity for practical strategies for working through and beyond gridlock. While well-managed institutions, the rule of law, redistributional policies, and progressive political coalitions can advance good governance, the seven pathways make it clear that being sensitive to different policy contexts is necessary if change is to be effective and durable.

Although it has been shown that most change is incremental, transformative change beyond gridlock does happen. Major leaps forward in the institutional structures of nations and the world order often follow major wars and calamities. But political wisdom requires that we learn to make significant and strategic changes before tragedies unfold, and not just with hindsight. And our ability to harm ourselves has increased; when weapons of mass destruction, global pandemics, and environmental collapse loom, reform-through-crisis becomes a very unattractive option. Looking back at the institutional world order set down after 1945, and the reasons for its successes and failures, it is clear that we have to understand and grasp these if we are to avoid the cycle of calamitous tragedies and institutional change. *Beyond Gridlock* reveals that the conditions of change can be understood and analysed both in relation to routine circumstances in the governance of trade, finance, and human rights, and also in relation to the global challenges like climate change and the control of WMDs. How we shift from the postwar institutional order to a new structure of "sustainable interdependence" is a major long-term question, but what *Beyond Gridlock* shows is that productive steps are available, here and now. Building and strengthening institutions, shifting preferences in major states, new transnational coalitions of civil society working in partnership with states, and other shifts are an important part of this story. And innovative leadership is a significant channel to build these pathways through and ultimately beyond gridlock.

The theory of gridlock helps us understand why the remarkable period of global cooperation that began with the foundation of the UN, and ushered in a new era of governed globalization, has now run into deep difficulties. The vicious circle of self-reinforcing gridlock compounds the problems and adds to the conditions that have spurred the rise of nationalism and the anti-global backlash. Donald Trump, Tayyip Erdoğan, Vladimir Putin, Narendra Modi, and Nigel Farage are, among others, all riding this wave of nationalism and reasserting the interests of particular peoples and places. They all promise that by putting their nation first, bringing to an end intrusive regional and international agreements, weakening or dismantling the hold of supranational institutions, and rolling back the tide of various global linkages – free trade, migration, international rules and norms – they can establish a new era of national greatness. By reasserting sovereignty, reasserting control over national assets, and reasserting essentialist national identities, they claim they can make their countries pre-eminent again.

This urge to retreat makes sense at a time when globalization affects us all and gridlock prevents effective management of globalization. But in a globalized world, the reassertion of national autonomy does not increase control, it weakens it. Simply tearing down global institutions would only exacerbate the very problems that gave rise to discontent in the first place. In other words, the nationalist dream is an illusion. Any short-term advances will be undercut by long-term damage to the prospects of managing the global challenges of our time. There is at present no viable alternative to the complex structures of international and transnational cooperation and collaboration we have built since 1945, even if their political sustainability is increasingly weakened. Since World War II we have learned that the challenges of war and conflict, trade and prosperity, financial instability, sustainable growth and the well-being of peoples – from their health to their environment – can only be protected through national, regional and global cooperation and collaboration. It is in the institutions that are built, the networks that are created, and the delicate pathways of change that are established that we have learned to manage global risks and solve problems. If we dismantle these achievements, humankind will be left to the raw risks of mismanagement and existential threats.

We must not underestimate the potential consequences. Global challenges threaten to overwhelm human life in the twenty-first century. Acting alone or asserting national interests is precisely what led to the calamitous world wars and the Great Depression that shaped the first half of the twentieth century. Acting alone now, in a more densely interconnected and fragile world order, risks repetition of these disasters, but on an even more frightening scale. The pathways through and beyond gridlock set out in this book show the complex processes required to reach effective governance; to ignore these is to ignore the ways we have learnt to manage our collective problems in a period of dense interdependence. Such misjudgement will lead to a period of institutional destruction and with it the concomitant risks of profound damage to the fabric of human life.

How do we avoid this fate? How do we construct the effective and legitimate – and therefore sustainable – global governance we require? Understanding and deploying the pathways through gridlock, the areas of resilience and innovation explored in this book, can help us manage globalization and take some of the oxygen out of the anti-global backlash. This means, for example, identifying and bolstering the relatively obscure technical institutions on which we rely. It means finding new ways to bring broad transnational networks of actors around common norms. It means working to alter the interests of major countries by building domestic constituencies for cooperation over time. It means creative and bold leadership. As the chapters show, such work has not been and will not be easy. To create sustainable global cooperative institutions and networks takes a great deal of time and effort. Success will often be defined as avoiding harm – toiling in relative obscurity to prevent a financial crisis, a terrorist attack, or a pandemic – as opposed to making a significant step forward. When progress does come, it will typically be incremental, with few silver bullets.

But at the same time we must reach beyond our current efforts. While this book has found concrete ways forward, nothing in our analysis suggests these incremental steps through gridlock will necessarily lead into trajectories beyond it. In some cases, they may be too little too late. In other cases, the book has identified at least the potential for transformation. For example, in areas like climate and health the diverse array of actors coordinating around common norms may yet grow into a decisive transformation. While reformist civil society coalitions have not proven themselves during the current period to be a pathway beyond gridlock, some chapters suggest they may become one in the future. The point is that, contra the gridlock logic, the pathways through and beyond gridlock demonstrate the possibility, if not the inevitability, of building the global governance we so badly need, and chart some specific ways to advance it.

Because we have found the current pathways to be largely incremental, this project must be a long-term one. It must address both the global organizations, networks, and institutions described in this book and the national political contexts in which they are embedded. Moving beyond gridlock – that is, constructing legitimate and effective global governance – should therefore be seen as a generational political effort, not something to be achieved in a few bullet points of policy recommendations. But therein lies one of the great difficulties of our era. To mitigate existential threats is an essential and immediate task; building institutions and pathways of change takes a much greater period of time. We must try to do both simultaneously. We can hope that by understanding what has worked in the past, and why, and what might work again in the future, and why, we will be able to act in an appropriate way and in time. It is only by understanding these pathways through and beyond gridlock, and their complex possibilities, that we can initiate progressive change.

Notes

1 Introduction: Pathways beyond Gridlock

1 As we have noted elsewhere, the growth of transnational governance institutions, not captured in the formal international organization statistics, may partially account for this seeming paradox. Global governance functions are increasingly being performed by a wide range of actors and institutions beyond states and intergovernmental organizations (Hale and Held 2011), which may account for some of the drop-off we observe. At the same time, however, we have also argued that such institutional innovations represent, at best, only a partial solution to the issue of gridlock, above all because of the problem of reaching a sufficient scale in activity to make a difference in a specific policy domain (Hale and Held 2012).

2 Camila Duran, Ann Florini, Lucas Kello, Andreas Klasen, Kyle McNally, Eva Marie-Nag, James Orbinski, Thomas Pegram, Robert Wade, Taylor St John, Oliver Stuenkel, Vanda Felbab-Brown, Seyom Brown, Michael Clarke, and Kevin Young joined David Held and Thomas Hale.

2 Finance: Risk and Progress

1 Abbott, Green and Keohane (2016) note that private transnational regulatory organizations have lower entry costs than intergovernmental organizations, and that they are more flexibly able to find "niches" in which they can thrive. While some of the parameters and specificities of their argument don't capture what is going on in global financial governance, this is a useful characterization when thinking about gridlock in particular.

2 Many grateful thanks to Stefano Pagliari for compiling and sharing these data.

3 These data were also used in Young 2014a.

3 Monetary Policy: Making Fragmentation Work

1 The G20 comprises the following countries and institutions: Argentina, Australia, Brazil, Canada, China, France, Germany, India, Indonesia, Italy,

Japan, South Korea, Mexico, Russia, Saudi Arabia, South Africa, Turkey, United Kingdom, United States and European Union, represented by the European Commission and the European Central Bank.

2   In a currency swap agreement, a central bank swaps its own currency for another (usually, a stronger currency) and assumes the obligation of repurchasing its currency on a later date at a predetermined rate.

3   The SDR is an international asset allocated by the IMF. It was created in 1969 to serve as a source of unconditional liquidity to the Fund's members.

4   Source: IMF statistics; COFER database.

5   On the basis of purchasing power parity. Source: IMF statistics.

6   Source: IMF statistics.

7   "Our collective response to the crisis has highlighted both the benefits of international cooperation and the need for a *more legitimate and effective IMF*" (emphasis added), G20 Leaders' Statement, Pittsburgh Summit, 24–25 September 2009.

8   It had also intervention objectives to influence the value of the emerging countries' currencies and incentivize exports.

9   These emerging powers were Brazil, Mexico, South Korea and Singapore.

10   This regional monetary arrangement is formed by the ten members of the Association of Southeast Asian Nations (ASEAN) and Japan, China and South Korea (the "plus 3" countries).

11   Originally, the ASEAN+3 Macroeconomic Research Office was created as a company limited by guarantee, according to the laws of Singapore. Since February 2016, it has been an international organization.

12   Brazil, Russia, India, China and South Africa.

13   However, in the framework of the North American Free Trade Agreement (NAFTA), Mexico and the US have a currency swap facility of US$6 billion, with the Federal Reserve and the US Treasury each participating up to US$3 billion (Henning 2002: 51).

14   The Local Currency Payment System (SML) is a clearing house to settle commercial transactions using Brazilian real and Argentinean peso as well as Uruguayan peso. The SML is a *continuum* of the Agreement on Reciprocal Payments and Credits, created in 1982 by the ALADI (Latin American Integration Association) and formalized by the central banks of Argentina, Bolivia, Brazil, Chile, Colombia, Ecuador, Mexico, Paraguay, Peru, the Dominican Republic, Uruguay and Venezuela.

15   The Federal Open Market Committee (FOMC) of the Fed stated in 1998 that "in light of 15 years of disuse, the bilateral swap arrangements of the Federal Reserve...were jointly deemed no longer to be necessary in view of the well established present-day arrangements for international monetary cooperation" (US Fed, FOMC minutes, 17 November 1998, http://www.federalreserve.gov/fomc/minutes/19981117.htm).

16   See the account of these swaps at the Fed's website (Federal Reserve 2017).

17   Item 2 of the Joint Statement of the 19th ASEAN+3 Finance Ministers' and Central Bank Governors' Meeting, 3 May 2016. At http://asean.org/joint-statement-19th-asean3-finance-ministers-central-bank-governors-meeting-3-may-2016-frankfurt-germany/.

18   IMF-related assets (SDR holdings and reserve tranche) accounted for 3.4 per cent of total international reserves at the end of 2013 (IMF at https://www.imf.org/external/pubs/ft/ar/2014/eng/pdf/a1.pdf).

19 In 2015, China declared its intention of keeping capital account controls by: (1) macroprudential management of the private sector's external debt; (2) management of short-term speculative capital flows; (3) adoption of temporary capital controls in case of "abnormal" fluctuations in international markets, or balance of payments problems; and (4) monitoring of cross-border financial transactions, which involve money laundering and financing of terrorism, as well as the exploitation of tax havens (Xiaochuan 2015: 6).

5   Investment: Contestation and Transformation

1 Although outright expropriation is easy to identify, there are deep-seated historical disagreements about the appropriate standard of compensation for expropriation. The Hull Rule is identified with the US and capital-exporting states, while the Calvo Clause is identified with capital-importing states; Newcombe and Paradell 2009: 11–18.
2 The EU has also secured agreement on the investment court system from two TPP signatories: Vietnam and Canada. The Canadian government renegotiated an agreement that had already been signed to replace investor–state arbitration with an investment court system. At the time of writing, the US government has not publicly responded to the EU's proposal.

6   Energy: A Fundamental Transformation?

1 See https://en.wikipedia.org/wiki/Joule.
2 All of these units and the many others in which energy and power are measured can be converted into one another. The American Physical Society has a good concise explanation of the bewildering variety of energy units and the formulas to compare them, at https://www.aps.org/policy/reports/popa-reports/energy/units.cfm.
3 This chapter does not address one potentially significant contributor to the electricity generation component of energy supply: nuclear power. The nuclear regime, with the Non-Proliferation Treaty and the International Atomic Energy Agency at its core, was designed to encourage peaceful uses of nuclear technology while reducing the associated risks of the proliferation of nuclear weapons. Whether or not nuclear power is or should be a major part of the energy transition, however, the global governance of nuclear energy is quite distinct from the rules, systems, and organizations of fossil fuels and renewable energy, and thus does not figure in this assessment of the governance of the energy transition.
4 See https://www.ief.org/about-ief/organisation/member-countries.aspx.
5 Thanks to Roland Kupers for detailed comments on this section.
6 See http://www.cleanenergyministerial.org/Our-Work/Ministerial-Meetings.
7 See http://www.se4all.org/flagship-programmes.
8 See http://www.g20australia.org/sites/default/files/g20_resources/library/g20_principles_energy_collaboration.pdf.

8   Human Rights: Leveraging Compliance

1 For extremely useful comments, I thank Par Engstrom, Thomas Hale and David Held and the participants at the two project workshops held at Durham University and the University of Oxford.

2   The US supported the referral by the UN Security Council of Saif Gaddafi to the jurisdiction of the ICC in 2011 regarding possible crimes committed in Libya. To date, Gaddafi has not been rendered to the court.

11   Cyber Security: Gridlock and Innovation

1   This work was written under the auspices of the Cyber Studies Programme at the University of Oxford.
2   In this paper, therefore, the term "cyberwar" excludes espionage activity and attacks that fall below the recognizable threshold of an act of war.
3   Although in the public perception the terms cyberspace and the internet are sometimes used coterminously, they in fact have different meanings. Cyberspace denotes all computers and networks in existence – including the "cyber archipelago," which consists of machines that for security reasons are not joined to the internet, such as industrial controllers at nuclear facilities (Kello 2013).

12   Weapons of Mass Destruction: Incremental Steps

1   The OPCW has overseen the safe and verified demilitarization of more than 43,000 metric tons of deadly chemical agents in almost 4 million weapons and containers since the convention's entry into force in April 1997.
2   The two most relevant are the Convention for the Suppression of Acts of Nuclear Terrorism, and the Convention on the Physical Protection of Nuclear Material.

References

Abbott, K., Genschel, P., Snidal, D. and Zangl, B. 2015. "Orchestration: Global Governance through Intermediaries." In K. Abbott, P. Genschel, D. Snidal and B. Zangl (eds), *International Organizations as Orchestrators*. Cambridge: Cambridge University Press.

Abbott, K., Green, J. and Keohane, R. 2016. "Organizational Ecology and Institutional Change in Global Governance." *International Organization* 70(2): 247–77. doi:10.1017/S0020818315000338.

Abbott, K. and Snidal, D. 2013. "Taking Responsive Regulation Transnational: Strategies for International Organizations." *Regulation and Governance* 7(1): 95–113.

Acharya, A. 2013. "The R2P and Norm Diffusion: Towards a Framework of Norm Circulation." *Global Responsibility to Protect* 5(4): 466–79.

Aggarwal, V. K. and Lee, S. 2011. "The Domestic Political Economy of Preferential Trade Agreements in the Asia-Pacific." In V. K. Aggarwal and S. Lee (eds), *Trade Policy in the Asia-Pacific*. New York: Springer.

Aizenman, J. and Pasricha, G. K. 2010. "Selective Swap Arrangements and the Global Financial Crisis: Analysis and Interpretation." *International Review of Economics and Finance* 19(3): 353–65.

Albin, C. 2008. "Using the Negotiation to Promote Legitimacy: An Assessment of Proposals for Reforming the WTO." *International Affairs* 84(4): 757–75.

Alcaro, R. 2009. "The Global Initiative to Combat Nuclear Terrorism: Big Potential, Limited Impact?" *International Spectator* 44(1): 99–112.

Allen, W. and Moessner, R. 2010. "Central Bank Co-operation and International Liquidity in the Financial Crisis of 2008–9." LSE Financial Markets Group Paper 187. London School of Economics.

Alschner, W. and Skougarevskiy, D. 2016. "Mapping the Universe of International Investment Agreements." *Journal of International Economic Law* 19(3): 561–88.

Alston P. 2011. "Hobbling the Monitors: Should UN Human Rights Monitors Be Accountable?" *Harvard International Law Journal* 52(2): 561–649.

Amemiya, T. 2007. *Economy and Economics of Ancient Greece*. New York: Routledge.

Annan, K. A. 2005. "Break the Nuclear Deadlock." *New York Times*, 30 May.

Arquilla, J. and Ronfeldt, D. 1993. *Cyberwar is Coming!* Santa Monica: RAND.

Bäckstrand, K. and Lövbrand, E. 2016. "The Road to Paris: Contending Climate Governance Discourses in the Post-Copenhagen Era." *Journal of Environmental Policy and Planning*: 1–19.

Bagshaw, S. 2005. *Developing a Normative Framework for the Protection of Internally Displaced Persons*. Ardsley: Transnational.

Baker, A. 2010. "Restraining Regulatory Capture? Anglo-America, Crisis Politics and Trajectories of Change in Global Financial Governance," *International Affairs* 86(3): 647–63.

Baker, A. 2013. "The Gradual Transformation? The Incremental Dynamics of Macroprudential Regulation." *Regulation and Governance* 7(4): 417–34.

Ban, C. and Gallagher, K. 2015. "Recalibrating Policy Orthodoxy: The IMF since the Great Recession." *Governance* 28(2): 131–46.

Barnes, A. and Brown, G. W. 2011. "The Idea of Partnership in the Millennium Development Goals: Context, Instrumentality and the Normative Demands of Partnership." *Third World Quarterly* 32(1): 165–80.

Barnes, A., Brown, G. W. and Harman, S. 2015. *The Global Politics of Health Reform in Africa: Performance, Participation and Policy*. London: Palgrave.

Barnett, M. 2011. *Empire of Humanity: A History of Humanitarianism*. New York: Cornell University Press.

Barnett, M. 2014. "Refugees and Humanitarianism." In E. Fiddian-Qasmiyeh et al. (eds), *The Oxford Handbook of Refugee and Forced Migration Studies*. Oxford: Oxford University Press.

Barnett, M. and Finnemore, M. 2005. *Rules for the World*. Ithaca: Cornell University Press.

Barroso, J., Fallin, M. and Foxx, V. 2016. *The 2016 Republican Party Platform*. Washington, DC: Republican National Committee.

Bax, T. 2014. "Poll: Will the BRICS Bank Shift the Balance of Power?" *Guardian*, 25 July. At http://www.theguardian.com/global-development-professionals-network/poll/2014/jul/25/brics-bank-world-bank-power.

BCBS (Basel Committee on Banking Supervision). 2012. "Report to the G20 Ministers and Central Bank Governors on Basel III Implementation." October. Basel: Bank for International Settlements.

BCBS (Basel Committee on Banking Supervision). 2014. "Regulatory Consistency Assessment Programme (RCAP) Assessment of Basel III Regulation: European Union." December. Basel: Bank for International Settlements.

Belcher, E. 2016. "The Proliferation Security Initiative: The Achievements and Limits of an Informal Approach to Cooperation." In J. W. Knopf (ed.), *International Cooperation on WMD Nonproliferation*. Athens: University of Georgia Press.

Bennett, C. 2015. "Kremlin's Ties to Russian Cyber Gangs Sow US Concerns." *The Hill*, 11 October.

Bentham, J. 2014. "The Scenario Approach to Possible Futures for Oil and Gas." *Energy Policy* 64: 87–92.

Berman, F. 2009. "Evolution or Revolution?" In C. Brown and K. Miles (eds), *Evolution in Investment Treaty Law and Arbitration*, pp. 658–672. Cambridge: Cambridge University Press.

Berners-Lee, T. and Cailliau, R. 1990. "WorldWideWeb: Proposal for a HyperText Project." 12 November. At https://www.w3.org/Proposal.html.

Betts, A. 2010. "The Refugee Regime Complex." *Refugee Studies Quarterly* 29(1): 12–37.

Beyani, C. 2012. "Meeting Summary: The Mandate of the Special Rapporteur on the Human Rights of Internally Displaced Persons." 22 February. At https://www.chathamhouse.org/sites/files/chathamhouse/public/Research/International%20Law/220212summary.pdf.

Biersteker, T. J. and Eckert, S. E. (eds). 2007. *Countering the Financing of Terrorism.* London: Routledge.

Biofuels International. 2016. "Poet-DSM Ramps up Production at Iowa-Based Cellulosic Ethanol Plant." 29 April. At http://biofuels-news.com/display_news/10458/poetdsm_ramps_up_production_at_iowabased_cellulosic_ethanol_plant/.

Blair, T. 2011. *A Journey.* London: Arrow.

Blitz, J. 2013. "UK Becomes First State to Admit to Offensive Cyber Attack Capability." *Financial Times,* 29 September.

Bloomberg New Energy Finance. 2016. "Executive Summary." *New Energy Outlook 2016.*

Bond, P. and Garcia, A. (eds). 2015. *BRICS: An Anti-Capitalist Critique.* London: Pluto Press.

Bosco, D. 2014. *Rough Justice.* New York: Oxford University Press.

Botzem, S. 2012. *The Politics of Accounting Regulation: Organizing Transnational Standard Setting in Financial Reporting.* Cheltenham: Edward Elgar.

Boughton, J. M. 2001. *Silent Revolution: The International Monetary Fund, 1979–1989.* Washington, DC: International Monetary Fund.

Bowcott, O. 2015. "UK and Saudi Arabia 'in Secret Deal' over Human Rights Council Place." *Guardian,* 29 September.

Braun, C. 2014. "Responsibility for the Rose: Environmental Policy and the WTO." *UMKC Law Review* 82(2): 537–59.

Brenner, J. 2011. *America the Vulnerable: Inside the New Threat Matrix of Digital Espionage, Crime, and Warfare.* New York: Penguin Press.

Broad, W. J. and Sanger, D. E. 2016. "As U.S. Modernizes Nuclear Weapons, 'Smaller' Leaves Some Uneasy." *New York Times,* 11 January.

Broome, A., Clegg, L. and Rethel, L. 2015. *Global Governance Crisis.* London: Routledge.

Brown, G. W. 2015a. "Knowledge, Politics and Power in Global Health." *International Journal of Health Policy and Management* 4: 111–13.

Brown, G. W. 2015b. "The 2015 G7 Summit: A Missed Opportunity for Global Health Leadership." *Global Policy,* June. At http://www.globalpolicyjournal.com/sites/default/files/inline/files/Brown%20-%20The%202015%20G7%20summit,%20A%20missed%20opportunity%20for%20global%20health%20leadership.pdf.

Brown, G. W. and Stoeva, P. 2014. "Reevaluating Health Security from a Cosmopolitan Perspective." In S. Rushton and J. Youde (eds), *The Routledge Handbook of Health Security.* London: Routledge.

Brown, O. 2008 "Climate Change and Displacement: The Numbers Game." *Forced Migration Review* 31. At http://www.fmreview.org/FMRpdfs/FMR31/08-09.pdf.

Browne, D. 2015. "Trident 'Could be Rendered Obsolete by Hackers.'" *BBC News,* 24 November. At http://www.bbc.co.uk/news/uk-politics-34903327.

Broz, J. L. 2015. "The Politics of Rescuing the World's Financial System: The Federal Reserve as a Global Lender of Last Resort." *Korean Journal of International Studies* 13(2): 323–51.

Bruen, C. and Brugha, R. 2014. "A Ghost in the Machine? Politics in Global Health Policy." *International Journal of Health Policy and Management* 3: 1–4.

Brunsden, J. 2012. "EU Criticized with US for Bank Rules Weaker Than Basel III." *Bloomberg*, 11 June.

Brysk, A. 2013. *Speaking Rights to Power: Constructing Political Will*. Oxford: Oxford University Press.

Bulkeley, H. et al. 2014. *Transnational Climate Change Governance*. Cambridge, Cambridge University Press.

Bull, H. 2003. *The Anarchical Society: A Study of Order in World Politics*, 3rd edn. London: Palgrave.

Burkeman, O. 2002. "America Forced Me Out, Says Robinson." *Guardian*, 31 July.

Busch, M., Reinhardt, E. and Shaffer, G. 2009. "Does Legal Capacity Matter? A Survey of WTO Members." *World Trade Review* 8(4): 559–77.

Büthe, T. and Mattli, W. 2011. *The New Global Rulers: The Privatization of Regulation in the World Economy*. Princeton: Princeton University Press.

Cabral, L., Russo, G. and Weinstock, J. 2014. "Brazil and the Shifting Consensus on Development Co-operation: Salutary Diversions from the 'Aid-effectiveness' Trail?" *Development Policy Review* 32(2): 179–202.

Cameron, G. 2016. "Formal and Informal Mechanisms for Countering Nuclear Terrorism: The ICSANT and the GICNT." In J. W. Knopf (ed.), *International Cooperation on WMD Nonproliferation*. Athens: University of Georgia Press.

Capling, A. and Higgott, R. 2009. "Introduction: The Future of the Multilateral Trade System – What Role for the World Trade Organization?" *Global Governance* 15: 313–25.

Carpenter, C. 2007. "Setting the Advocacy Agenda: Theorizing Issue Emergence and Nonemergence in Transnational Advocacy Networks." *International Studies Quarterly* 51: 99–120.

Carroll, T. J. and Sovacool, B. 2010. "Pipelines, Crisis and Capital: Understanding the Contested Regionalism of Southeast Asia." *Pacific Review* 23(5): 625–47.

Carver, R. 2010. "A New Answer to an Old Question: National Human Rights Institutions and the Domestication of International Law." *Human Rights Law Review* 10(1): 1–32.

Carver, R. 2013. "Does Torture Prevention Work?" Report on Research Project Commissioned by the Association for the Prevention of Torture.

Cebeci, M. 2013. "The European Union and Weapons of Mass Destruction Terrorism." *Defence against Terrorism Review* 5(1): 77–98.

Cerf, V. G. and Kahn, R. E. 1974. "A Protocol for Packet Network Interconnection." *IEEE Transactions on Communications*, Com-22 (5): 637–48.

Chan, M. 2011. "WHO Director-General Addresses First Meeting of BRICS Health Ministers." Remarks delivered at the first meeting of BRICS health ministers, Beijing, 11 July. At http://www.who.int/dg/speeches/2011/BRICS_20110711/en/.

Chan, S. et al. 2015. "Reinvigorating International Climate Policy: A Comprehensive Framework for Effective Nonstate Action." *Global Policy* 6(4): 466–73.

Chang, Y. and Li, Y. 2013. "Renewable Energy and Policy Options in an Integrated ASEAN Electricity Market: Quantitative Assessments and Policy Implications." In F. Kimura, H. Phoumin and B. Jacobs (eds), *Energy Market Integration in East Asia: Renewable Energy and Its Deployment into the Power System*. ERIA Research Project Report 2012-26. Jakarta: Economic Research Institute for ASEAN and East Asia.

Chayes, A. and Chayes, A. 1993. "On compliance." *International Organization* 47(2): 175–205.

Chen, Y., Ebenstein, A., Greenstone, M. and Li, H. 2013. "Evidence on the Impact of Sustained Exposure to Air Pollution on Life Expectancy from China's Huai River Policy." *Proceedings of the National Academy of Sciences of the USA* 110(32): 12936–41. At www.pnas.org/cgi/doi/10.1073/pnas.1300018110.

Chey, H-k. 2006. "Explaining Cosmetic Compliance with International Regulatory Regimes: The Implementation of the Basle Accord in Japan, 1998–2003." *New Political Economy* 11(2): 271–89.

Chey, H-k. 2012. "Why Did the US Federal Reserve Unprecedentedly Offer Swap Lines to Emerging Market Economies during the Global Financial Crisis? Can We Expect Them Again in the Future?" GRIPS Discussion Paper 11-18. National Graduate Institute for Policy Studies, Tokyo.

Chonghaile, C. N. 2015. "Ebola Spending: Will Lack of a Positive Legacy Turn Dollars into Dolour? *Guardian*, 13 February. At http://www.theguardian.com/global-development/2015/feb/13/ebola-spending-positive-healthcare-legacy-west-africa.

Chorev, N. 2005. "The Institutional Project of Neo-liberal Globalism: The Case of the WTO." *Theory and Society* 34(3): 317–55.

Choucri, N. 2013. *Cyberpolitics in International Relations*. Cambridge, MA: MIT Press.

Chwieroth, J. 2014. "Controlling Capital: The International Monetary Fund and Transformative Incremental Change from within International Organizations." *New Political Economy* 19(3): 445–69.

Cirincione, J. (ed.). 2000. *Repairing the Regime: Preventing the Spread of Weapons of Mass Destruction*. London: Routledge.

Cirincione, J. 2007. *Bomb Scare: The History and Future of Nuclear Weapons*. New York: Columbia University Press.

Clapper, J. R. 2013. "Worldwide Threat Assessment of the US Intelligence Community." US Senate Select Committee on Intelligence, March. Washington, DC: US Government Printing Office.

Clark, D. D. 1988. "The Design Philosophy of the DARPA Internet Protocols." Proceedings of the SIGCOMM '88. *Computer Communication Review* 18(4): 106–14.

Clark, D. D. 2016. "Designs for an Internet." Draft version 2.0 ed. MS.

Clark, P. 2015. "Carbon Capture: Miracle Machine or White Elephant?" *Financial Times*, 9 September. At https://www.ft.com/content/88c187b4-5619-11e5-a28b-50226830d644.

Clarke, R. A. and Knake, R. 2010. *Cyber War: The Next Threat to National Security*. New York: HarperCollins.

Clinton, H. R. 2010. "Clinton's Speech on Internet Freedom, January 2010." Council on Foreign Relations. At http://www.cfr.org/internet-policy/clintons-speech-internet-freedom-january-2010/p21253.

Cohen, B. J. and Benney, T. M. 2014. "What Does the International Currency System Really Look Like?" *Review of International Political Economy* 21(5): 1017–41.

Cohen, R. and Deng, F. M. 1998a. *The Forsaken People: Case Studies of the Internally Displaced*. Washington, DC: Brookings Institution.

Cohen, R. and Deng, F. M. 1998b. *Masses in Flight: The Global Crisis of Internal Displacement*. Washington, DC: Brookings Institution.

Colgan, J. D., Keohane, R. O. and Van de Graaf, T. 2012. "Punctuated Equilibrium in the Energy Regime Complex." *Review of International Organizations* 7: 117–43.

Collier, P. 2013. *Exodus: How Migration Is Changing Our World*. Oxford: Oxford University Press.

Cook, T. 2016. "A Message to Our Customers." Apple.com, 16 February. At http://www.apple.com/customer-letter/.

Coombs, C. A. 1976. *The Arena of International Finance*. New York: John Wiley & Sons.

Cosbey, A. and Mavroidis, P. C. 2014. "Heavy Fuel: Trade and Environment in the GATT/WTO Case Law." *Review of European, Comparative and International Environmental Law* 23(3): 288–301.

Council on Foreign Relations. 2013. "The Global Human Rights Regime." At http://www.cfr.org/human-rights/global-human-rights-regime/p27450.

Coyne, C. J. and Williams, C. R. 2014. "Can International Aid Improve Health?" In G. W. Brown, G. Yamey and S. Wamala (eds), *Global Health Policy*, pp. 375–92. Oxford: Wiley-Blackwell.

Cronin, B. (ed.). 2003. *Institutions for the Common Good: International Protection Regimes in International Society*. Cambridge: Cambridge University Press.

Cyber Consequences Unit. 2009. "Overview by the US-CCU of the Cyber Campaign against Georgia in August of 2008." Special Report, US Cyber Consequences Unit.

Czuczka, T. 2016. "Germany Tightens Asylum Rules as Merkel Stems Refugee Flow." *Bloomberg*, 25 February. At https://www.bloomberg.com/news/articles/2016-02-25/germany-tightens-asylum-rules-as-merkel-seeks-to-stem-refugees.

Dai, X. 2013. "The 'Compliance Gap' and the Efficacy of International Human Rights Institutions." In T. Risse, S. C. Ropp and K. Sikkink (eds), *The Persistent Power of Human Rights*, pp. 85–102. Cambridge: Cambridge University Press.

Davenport, C. 1999. "Human Rights and the Democratic Proposition." *Journal of Conflict Resolution* 43(1): 92–116.

Davies, H. 2014. "The Spider of Finance." *Project Syndicate*, 16 October.

Davies, S. E. and Glanville, L. 2010. *Protecting the Displaced: Deepening the Responsibility to Protect*. Leiden: Martinus Nijhoff.

Davis, Z. S. 1993. "The Realist Nuclear Regime." *Security Studies* 2 (3–4): 77–99.

de Búrca, G. 2015. "Experimentalism and the Limits of Uploading: The EU and the UN Disability Convention." In Jonathan Zeitlin (ed.), *Extending Experimentalist Governance? The European Union and Transnational Regulation*, pp. 295–323. Oxford: Oxford University Press.

Delimatsis, P. 2014. "Transparency in the WTO's Decision-Making." *Leiden Journal of International Law* 27: 701–26.

Dempsey, J. 2016. "Time for an EU Counter-Terrorism Agency." Judy Dempsey's Strategic Europe, Carnegie Europe, 21 April.

DeNardis, L. 2009. *Protocol Politics: The Globalization of Internet Governance*. Cambridge, MA: MIT Press.

DeNardis, L. and Raymond, M. 2013. "Thinking Clearly about Multistakeholder Internet Governance." Eighth Annual GigaNet Symposium.

Destradi, S. and Jakobeit, C. 2015. "Global Governance Debates and Dilemmas: Emerging Powers' Perspectives and Roles in Global Trade and Climate Governance." *Strategic Analysis* 39(1): 60–72.

Development Initiatives. 2017. "Dataset 1: International Humanitarian Response." Global Humanitarian Assistance. At http://www.globalhumanitarianassistance.org/data-guides/datastore.

DFID (Department for International Development). 2013. *Multilateral Aid Review Update*. London: DFID.

Dhanapala, J. 2000. "The State of the Regime." In J. Cirincione (ed.), *Repairing the Regime: Preventing the Spread of Weapons of Mass Destruction*. London: Routledge.

Dolzer, R. 2002. "Indirect Expropriations: New Developments?" Colloquium on Regulatory Expropriation. *New York University Environmental Law Journal* 11(1): 64.

Dolzer, R. and Schreuer, C. 2012. *Principles of International Investment Law*, 2nd edn. Oxford: Oxford University Press,

Donnelly, J. 2007. *International Human Rights*, 3rd edn. Boulder: Westview Press.

Douglas, Z. 2006. "Nothing If Not Critical for Investment Treaty Arbitration: Occidental, Eureka, and Methanex." *Arbitration International* 22(1): 27–51.

Downs, A. 1967. *Inside Bureaucracy*. Boston: Little Brown.

Downs, G. W., Rocke, D. M. and Barsoom, P. N. 1996. "Is the Good News about Compliance Good News about Cooperation?" *International Organization* 50(3): 379–406.

Drezner, D. 2012. "The Irony of Global Governance: The System Worked." Working Paper, Council on Foreign Relations.

Drezner, D. 2014. *The System Worked: How the World Stopped Another Great Depression*. Oxford: Oxford University Press.

Drissel, D. 2007. "Internet Governance in a Multipolar World: Challenging American Hegemony." *Cambridge Review of International Affairs* 19(1): 105–20.

Drysdale, D. 2015. "Why the OECD Arrangement Works (Even Though It Is Only Soft Law)." In A. Klasen and F. Bannert (eds), *The Future of Foreign Trade Support*. Durham: Global Policy.

Dunne, A. 2013. "The Proliferation Security Initiative: Legal Considerations and Operational Realities." SIPRI Policy Paper 36, May. Stockholm International Peace Research Institute.

Dunning, J. 2000. "The Eclectic Paradigm as an Envelope for Economic and Business Theories of MNE Activity." *International Business Review* 9(2): 163–90.

Duran, C. V. 2015a. "Avoiding the Next Liquidity Crunch: How the G20 Must Support Monetary Cooperation to Increase Resilience to Crisis." GEG/BSG Policy Brief, October. Global Economic Governance Programme, University of Oxford.

Duran, C. V. 2015b. "The International Lender of Last Resort for Emerging Countries: A Bilateral Currency Swap?" GEG Working Paper 108. Global Economic Governance Programme, University of Oxford.

The Economist. 2001. "When Is a Refugee Not a Refugee?" 1 March. At http://www.economist.com/node/518172.

The Economist. 2013. "The Digital Arms Trade." 30 March. At http://www.economist.com/news/business/21574478-market-software-helps-hackers-penetrate-computer-systems-digital-arms-trade.

The Economist. 2015. "Europe's Boat People: The EU's Policy on Maritime Refugees Has Gone Disastrously Wrong." Editorial, 25 April. At http://www.economist.com/news/leaders/21649465-eus-policy-maritime-refugees-has-gone-disastrously-wrong-europes-boat-people.

Eichengreen, B. 2011. *Exorbitant Privilege: The Rise and the Fall of the Dollar and the Future of the International Monetary System*. Oxford: Oxford University Press.

Elsig, M. 2016. *The Functioning of the WTO: Options for Reform and Enhanced Performance*. Geneva: International Centre for Trade and Sustainable Development and World Economic Forum.

Engle-Merry, S. 2006. *Human Rights and Gender Violence*. Chicago: University of Chicago Press.

Engstrom, P. 2015. "The Inter-American Human Rights System: Notable Achievements and Enduring Challenges." In C. Lennox (ed.), *Contemporary*

Challenges in Securing Human Rights, pp. 141–6. London: Institute of Commonwealth Studies.

Erkkilä, T. and Piironen, O. 2014. "(De)politicizing Good Governance: The World Bank Institute, the OECD and the Politics of Governance Indicators." *Innovation* 27(4): 344–60.

European Commission. 2015. "Refugee Crisis: European Commission Takes Decisive Action." Press Release IP/15/5596, 9 September. At http://www.europeansources. info/showDoc?ID=1206552.

Evangelista, M. 1999. *Unarmed Forces: The Transnational Movement to End the Cold War*. Ithaca: Cornell University Press.

Falkner, R. 2016. "The Paris Agreement and the New Logic of International Climate Politics." *International Affairs* 92(5): 1107–25.

Falkner, R., Stephan, H. and Vogler, J. 2010. "International Climate Policy after Copenhagen: Towards a 'Building Blocks' Approach." *Global Policy* 1(3): 252–62.

Falliere, N., Murchu, L. O. and Chien, E. 2011. "W32.Stuxnet Dossier (Version 1.4)." Symantec Security Response. Cupertino: Symantec.

Federal Reserve. 2017. "Credit and Liquidity Programs and the Balance Sheet: Central Bank Liquidity Swaps." Board of Governors of the Federal Reserve System. At https://www.federalreserve.gov/monetarypolicy/bst_liquidityswaps.htm.

Fidler, D. P. 2007. "The Chemical Weapons Convention after Ten Years: Successes and Future Challenges." *ASIL Insights* 11(12), 27 April.

Finnemore, M. and Toope, S. J. 2001. "Alternatives to 'Legalization': Richer Views of Law and Politics." *International Organization* 55(3): 743–58.

Fischer, S. 1999. "On the Need for an International Lender of Last Resort." *Journal of Economic Perspectives* 13(4): 85–104.

Florini, A. 2011. "The International Energy Agency in Global Energy Governance." *Global Policy* 2(s1): 40–50.

Florini, A. and Saleem, S. 2011. "Information Disclosure in Global Energy Governance." *Global Policy* 2(s1): 144–54.

Foley, S. 2013. "NY Fed Warns on 'Go It Alone' Regulations." *Financial Times*, 22 April.

Frenk, J. and Moon, S. 2013. "Governance Challenges in Global Health." *New England Journal of Medicine* 368: 936–42.

Frontex. 2014. "Annual Risk Analysis 2014." Warsaw: Frontex, European Border and Coast Guard Agency.

Frontex. 2015. "Annual Risk Analysis 2015." Warsaw: Frontex, European Border and Coast Guard Agency.

Funke, M., Schularick, M. and Trebesch, C. 2016. "Going to Extremes: Politics after Financial Crises, 1870–2014." *European Economic Review* 88: 227–60.

Futter, A. 2016. *Cyber Threats and Nuclear Weapons: New Questions for Command and Control, Security and Strategy*. London: Royal United Services Institute.

G7. 2016. "G7 Ise-Shima Leaders' Summit Declaration." G7 Ise-Shima Summit, Japan, 26–27 May. At http://www.mofa.go.jp/files/000160266.pdf.

G20 Research Group. 2016. "G20 Leaders' Communiqué: Hangzhou Summit." University of Toronto. At http://www.g20.utoronto.ca/2016/160905-communique.html.

Galvanizing the Groundswell of Climate Actions. 2015. "Lima-Paris Action Agenda (LPAA) Independent Assessment Report." 7 December. At http:// www.climategroundswell.org/blog-test/lpaa/report.

Garcia, F. J., Ciko, L., Gaurav, A. and Hough, K. 2015. "Reforming the International Investment Regime: Lessons from International Trade Law." *Journal of International Economic Law* 18: 861–92.

Gautier, L., Harmer, A., Tediosi, F. and Missoni, E. 2014. "Reforming the World Health Organization: What Influence Do the BRICS Wield?" *Contemporary Politics* 20(2): 163–81.

Geers, K. 2009. "The Cyber Threat to National Critical Infrastructures: Beyond Theory." *Information Security Journal: A Global Perspective* 18(1): 1–7.

Germain, R. 2001. "Global Financial Governance and the Problem of Inclusion." *Global Governance* 7: 411–26.

GFATM (Global Fund to Fight AIDS, Tuberculosis and Malaria). 2016. *Impact and Results Report 2016*. Geneva: Global Fund. At http://www.theglobalfund.org/en/impact/.

Ghosh, A. and Chawla, K. 2016. "Can the International Solar Alliance Change the Game?" *The Hindu*, 26 August.

Gill, S. 2015. *Critical Perspectives on the Crisis of Global Governance*. London: Palgrave.

Gilpin, R. 1981. *War and Change in World Politics*. Cambridge: Cambridge University Press.

Ginsburg, T. and Shaffer, G. 2012. "The Empirical Turn in International Legal Scholarship." *American Journal of International Law* 106(1): 1–46.

Goldin, I. 2013. *Divided Nations: Why Global Governance Is Failing, and What We Can Do about It*. Oxford: Oxford University Press.

Goldsmith, J. 2011. "Cybersecurity Treaties: A Skeptical View." Stanford: Hoover Institution Task Force on National Security and Law.

Goldthau, A. and Sitter, N. 2015. *A Liberal Actor in a Realist World: The European Union Regulatory State and the Global Political Economy of Energy*. Oxford: Oxford University Press.

Goldthau, A. and Witte, J. M. 2011. "Assessing OPEC's Performance in Global Energy." *Global Policy* 2(s1): 31–9.

Goodman, R. and Jinks, D. 2013. *Socializing States*. New York: Oxford University Press.

Goodman, R. and Pegram, T. 2012. *Human Rights, State Compliance and Social Change*. New York: Cambridge University Press.

Grigsby, A. 2015. "The UN GGE on Cybersecurity: What Is the UN's role?" Net Politics, Council on Foreign Relations, New York.

Grimes, W. W. 2011. "The Asian Monetary Fund Reborn? Implications of Chiang Mai Initiative Multilateralization." *Asia Policy* 11: 79–104.

Grossman, L. K. 1995. *The Electronic Republic: Reshaping Democracy in the Information Age*. New York: Viking Penguin.

Grossman, L. 2015. "Inside the Quest for Nuclear Fusion: Clean Energy's Holy Grail." *Time*, 22 October.

Guzman, A. 2008. *How International Law Works*. Oxford: Oxford University Press.

Haas, P. M. 1992. "Introduction: Epistemic Communities and International Policy Coordination." *International Organization* 46(1): 1–35.

Hafemeister, D. 2016. *Nuclear Proliferation and Terrorism in the Post-9/11 World*. New York: Springer.

Hafner-Burton, E. and Ron, J. 2009. "Seeing Double: Human Rights Impact through Qualitative and Quantitative Eyes." *World Politics* 61(2): 360–401.

Hale, T. 2011. "A Climate Coalition of the Willing." *Washington Quarterly* (Winter).

Hale, T. 2014. "What Is the Effect of Transnational Commercial Arbitration on Trade?" In W. Mattli and T. Dietz (eds), *International Arbitration and Global Governance*. Oxford: Oxford University Press.

Hale, T. 2015. *Between Interests and Law*. Cambridge: Cambridge University Press.

Hale, T. 2016. "'All Hands on Deck': The Paris Agreement and Nonstate Climate Action." *Global Environmental Politics* 16(3): 12–22.

Hale, T. and Held, D. 2011. *Handbook of Transnational Governance: Institutions and Innovations*. Cambridge: Polity Press.

Hale, T. and Held, D. 2012. "Gridlock and Innovation in Global Governance: The Partial Solution." *Global Policy* 3(2): 169–81.

Hale, T., Held, D. and Young, K. 2013. *Gridlock: Why Global Cooperation Is Failing When We Need It Most*. Cambridge: Polity Press.

Hale, T., Held, D. and Young, K. 2016. "Response to Critics." *Philosophy and Public Issues* 6(3): 55–76.

Hale, T. and Urpelainen, J. 2015. "When and How Can Unilateral Policies Promote the International Diffusion of Environmental Policies and Clean Technology?" *Journal of Theoretical Politics* 27(2): 177–205.

Hameiri, S. and Wilson, J. D. 2015. "The Contested Rescaling of Economic Governance in East Asia: A Special Issue." *Australian Journal of International Affairs* 69(2).

Hanley, S. 2016. "China, Japan, Russia, and South Korea Plan Renewable Energy Super Grid." CleanTechnica, 21 September. At https://cleantechnica.com/2016/09/21/china-japan-russia-south-korea-plan-renewable-energy-super-grid/.

Hansen J. et al. 2013. "Assessing 'Dangerous Climate Change': Required Reduction of Carbon Emissions to Protect Young People, Future Generations and Nature." *PLoS ONE* 8(12): e81648.

Harmer, A. and Buse, K. 2014. "The BRICS: A Paradigm Shift in Global Health?" *Contemporary Politics* 20(2): 127–45.

Harrigan, J., Wang, C. and El-Said, H. 2006. "The Economic and Political Determinants of IMF and World Bank Lending in the Middle East and North Africa." *World Development* 34(2): 247–70.

Harris, S. 2014. "Black Market for Malware and Cyber Weapons Is Thriving." *Foreign Policy*, 25 March.

Hassner, P. 1998. "Refugee: A Special Case for Cosmopolitan Citizenship?" In D. Archibugi, D. Held and Köhler, M. (eds), *Re-Imagining Political Community*. Stanford: Stanford University Press.

Hathaway, O. 2002. "Do Human Rights Treaties Make a Difference?" *Yale Law Journal* 111: 1935–2042.

Hawkins, D. 2004. "Explaining Costly International Institutions: Persuasion and Enforceable Human Rights Norms." *International Studies Quarterly* 48(4): 779–804.

He, B. 2014. "Global Social Justice at the WTO? The Role of NGOs in Constructing Global Social Contracts." In J. Linarelli (ed.), *Research Handbook on Global Justice and International Economic Law*. Cheltenham: Edward Elgar.

Held, D. 2004. *Global Covenant: The Social Democratic Alternative to the Washington Consensus*. Cambridge: Polity Press.

Held, D. and Kaya, A. (eds). 2006. *Global Inequality*. Cambridge: Polity Press.

Held, D. and McGrew, A. G. 1999. *Global Transformations: Politics, Economics, and Culture*. Cambridge: Polity Press.

Held, D. and Roger, C. (eds). 2013. *Global Governance at Risk*. Cambridge: Polity Press.

Held, D. and Young, K. 2013. "From the Financial Crisis to the Crisis of Global Governance." In D. Held and C. Roger (eds), *Global Governance at Risk: New Powers and the Restructuring of World Order*, pp. 170–201. Cambridge: Polity Press.

Helleiner, E. 2010. "What Role for the New Financial Stability Board? The Politics of International Standards After the Crisis." *Global Policy* 1(3): 282–90.

Helleiner, E. 2012. "The Limits of Incrementalism: The G20, FSB and the International Regulatory Agenda." *Journal of Globalization and Development* 2(2): 1–19.

Helleiner, E. 2014. *The Status Quo Crisis: Global Financial Governance after the 2008 Meltdown*. Oxford: University Press.

Helleiner, E. and Pagliari, S. 2010. "Crisis and the Reform of International Financial Regulation." In E. Helleiner, S. Pagliari and H. Zimmerman (eds), *Global Finance in Crisis: The Politics of International Regulatory Change*, pp. 1–18. London: Routledge.

Helleiner, E. and Pagliari, S. 2011. "The End of an Era in International Financial Regulation? A Post-Crisis Research Agenda." *International Organization* 65(1): 169–200.

Helleiner, E. and Porter, T. 2010. "Making Transnational Networks More Accountable." *Economics, Management and Financial Markets* 5(2): 158–73.

Henderson, D. 1999. *The MAI Affair: A Story and Its Lessons*. London: Royal Institute of International Affairs.

Henning, C. R. 2002. *East Asian Financial Cooperation*. Washington, DC: Peterson Institute for International Economics.

HM Government. 2010. *A Strong Britain in an Age of Uncertainty: The UK National Security Strategy*. Cm 7953. London: Cabinet Office.

Ho, D. 2002. "Compliance and International Soft Law: Why Do Countries Implement the Basel Accord?" *Journal of International Economic Law* 5: 647–8.

Hoekman, B. M. and Mavroidis, P. C. 2007. *The World Trade Organization*. London: Routledge.

Hoffmann, M. 2011. *Climate Governance at the Crossroads: Experimenting with a Global Response after Kyoto*. Oxford: Oxford University Press.

Hopgood, S. 2014. *The Endtimes of Human Rights*. Ithaca: Cornell University Press.

Hummels, D. 2007. "Transportation Costs and International Trade in the Second Era of Globalization." *Journal of Economic Perspectives* 21(3): 131–54.

Hyndman, J. 2000. *Managing Displacement: Refugees and the Politics of Humanitarianism*. Minneapolis: University of Minnesota Press.

ICC (International Criminal Court). 2002. "Rome Statute of the International Criminal Court." A/CONF.183/9. At https://www.icc-cpi.int/nr/rdonlyres/ea9aeff 7-5752-4f84-be94-0a655eb30e16/0/rome_statute_english.pdf.

ICRC (International Committee of the Red Cross). 2015. "International Humanitarian Law and the Challenges of Contemporary Armed Conflicts." Doc. 32IC/15/11, October. Report for 32nd International Conference of the Red Cross and Red Crescent, Geneva, 8–10 December.

ICSID (International Centre for Settlement of Investment Disputes). 2007. "Award." *Sempra Energy International v The Argentine Republic* (ICSID ARB/02/16). At http:// www.italaw.com/sites/default/files/case-documents/ita0770.pdf.

IDMC (Internal Displacement Monitoring Center). 2015. "Global Figures." At http:// www.internal-displacement.org/global-figures.

IEA (International Energy Agency). 2013. *Technology Roadmap: Carbon Capture and Storage*. At http://www.iea.org/publications/freepublications/publication/ technologyroadmapcarboncaptureandstorage.pdf.

IEA (International Energy Agency). 2016. *Key World Energy Statistics 2016*. At https://
www.iea.org/publications/freepublications/publication/key-world-energy-
statistics.html.

IEA (International Energy Agency) and World Bank. 2015. *Progress toward
Sustainable Energy 2015: Global Tracking Framework Report*. Washington, DC: World
Bank. At http://www.se4all.org/sites/default/files/l/2013/09/GTF-2105-Full-Report.
pdf.

IEO IMF (Independent Evaluation Office of the International Monetary Fund).
2014."IMF Response to the Financial and Economic Crisis: Evaluation Report."
Washington, DC: International Monetary Fund.

Ignatieff, M. 1997. *The Warrior's Honor: Ethnic War and the Modern Conscience*. New
York: Metropolitan.

IHME (Institute for Health Metrics and Evaluation). 2015. "Transition in an Age
of Austerity." Seattle, WA: IHME. At http://www.healthdata.org/policy-report/
financing-global-health-2013-transition-age-austerity.

Ikenberry, G. J. 2001. *After Victory: Institutions, Strategic Restraint, and the Rebuilding
of Order after Major Wars*. Princeton: Princeton University Press.

IMF (International Monetary Fund). 2010a. "The Fund's Mandate – The Future
Financing Role: Reform Proposals." Finance, Legal, and Strategy, Policy and
Review Departments. Washington, DC: IMF.

IMF (International Monetary Fund). 2010b. "Public Information Notice: The
Fund's Mandate – Future Financing Role." PIN 10/124, 3 September. At https://
www.imf.org/en/News/Articles/2015/09/28/04/53/pn10124.

IMF (International Monetary Fund). 2012. *Global Financial Stability Report*.
Washington, DC: IMF.

IMF (International Monetary Fund). 2013. *Global Financial Stability Report*.
Washington, DC: IMF.

IMF (International Monetary Fund). 2014. "Review of Flexible Credit Line, the
Precautionary and Liquidity Line, and the Rapid Financing Instrument." IMF
Policy Paper, 27 January. Washington, DC: IMF.

IMF (International Monetary Fund). 2015. "Review of the Method of Valuation
of the SDR – Initial Considerations." IMF Policy Paper, 3 August. Washington,
DC: IMF.

IMF (International Monetary Fund). 2016. "Adequacy of the Global Financial Safety
Net." IMF Policy Paper, 10 March. Washington, DC: IMF.

IMF News. 2016. "IMF Adds Chinese Renminbi to the SDR basket."
International Monetary Fund, 30 September. At http://www.imf.org/en/News/
Articles/2016/09/29/AM16-NA093016IMF-Adds-Chinese-Renminbi-to-Specia
l-Drawing-Rights-Basket.

IPCC (Intergovernmental Panel on Climate Change). 2014. *Climate Change 2014:
Synthesis Report*. IPCC Fifth Assessment Report: Summary for Policymakers. At
http://www.ipcc.ch/pdf/assessment-report/ar5/syr/AR5_SYR_FINAL_SPM.pdf.

IRENA (International Renewable Energy Agency). 2015. *Battery Storage for Renewables:
Market Status and Technology Outlook*. Abu Dhabi: IRENA.

IRENA (International Renewable Energy Agency). 2016. "What We Do." At http://
www.irena.org/Menu/index.aspx?PriMenuID=53&mnu=Pri.

James, H. 1996. *International Monetary Cooperation since Bretton Woods*. Oxford:
Oxford University Press.

James, S. 2009. "Incentives and Investments: Evidence and Policy Implications."
Investment Climate Department, World Bank Group, Washington, DC. At

http://documents.worldbank.org/curated/en/945061468326374478/Incentive
s-and-investments-evidence-and-policy-implications.

Janis, M., Kay, R. and Bradley, A. 1995. *European Human Rights Law: Text and Materials*, rev. edn. New York: Oxford University Press.

Johnson, K. 2016. "Envisioning the Hack that Could Take Down New York City." *New York Magazine*, 13 June.

Johnson, L. and Bernasconi-Osterwalder, N. 2013. "New UNCITRAL Arbitration Rules on Transparency: Application, Content and Next Steps." Columbia Center on Sustainable Investment. At http://ccsi.columbia.edu/files/2014/04/UNCITRAL_Rules_on_Transparency_commentary_FINAL.pdf.

Jones, E. and Macartney, H. 2016. "TTIP and the 'Finance Exception': Venue-Shopping and the Breakdown of Financial Regulatory Cooperation." *Journal of Banking Regulation* 17: 4–20.

Kahler, M. 2013. "Economic Crisis and Global Governance: The Stability of a Globalized World." In M. Kahler and D. Lake (eds), *Politics in the New Hard Times*, pp. 27–51. Ithaca: Cornell University Press.

Kahler, M. and Lake, D. 2013. "Introduction." In M. Kahler and D. Lake (eds), *Politics in the New Hard Times*, pp. 1–26. Ithaca: Cornell University Press.

Kaldor, M. 2012. *New and Old Wars: Organized Violence in a Global Era*. Cambridge: Polity Press.

Kastner, L. 2014. "Much Ado about Nothing? Transnational Civil Society, Consumer Protection and Financial Regulatory Reform." *Review of International Political Economy* 21(6): 1313–45.

Keck, M. and Sikkink, K. 1998. *Activists beyond Borders: Advocacy Networks in International Politics*. Ithaca: Cornell University Press.

Kelley, J. and Simmons, B. 2016. "The Power of Ranking? The Ease of Doing Business as Soft Power." Draft presented at the International Studies Association conference, 18–21 March.

Kelley, M. 2012. "Anonymous Hacks Top Nuclear Watchdog Again to Force Investigation of Israel." *Business Insider*, 3 December.

Kello, L. 2013. "The Meaning of the Cyber Revolution: Perils to Theory and Statecraft." *International Security* 38(2): 7–40.

Kello, L. 2014–15. "The Virtual Weapon: Dilemmas and Future Scenarios." *Politique étrangère* 79(4) (Winter): 139–50.

Kello, L. 2017. *The Virtual Weapon and International Order*. New Haven: Yale University Press.

Keohane, R. O. 2001. "Governance in a Partially Globalized World." *American Political Science Review* 95(1): 1–13.

Keohane, R. O. 2002. *Power and Governance in a Partly Globalized World*. London: Routledge.

Keohane, R. O. and Martin, L. 1995. "The Promise of Institutionalist Theory." *International Security* 20(1): 39–51.

Keohane, R. O. and Nye, J. S. 1974. "Transgovernmental Relations and International Organizations." *World Politics* 27(1): 39–72.

Keohane, R. O. and Nye, J. S., Jr. 1999. "Power and Interdependence in the Information Age." *Foreign Affairs* 77(5): 81–94.

Keohane, R. O. and Ooms, V. D. 1975. "The Multinational Firm and International Regulation." *International Organization* 29(1): 169–209.

Keohane, R. O. and Oppenheimer, M. 2016. "Paris: Beyond the Climate Dead End through Pledge and Review?" Discussion Paper 2016-85. Harvard Project on Climate Agreements, Belfer Center for Science and International Affairs, Harvard Kennedy School.

Keohane, R. O. and Victor, D. 2011. "The Regime Complex for Climate Change." *Perspectives on Politics* 9(1): 7–23.

Kerner, A. 2014. "What We Talk about When We Talk about Foreign Direct Investment." *International Studies Quarterly* 58(4): 804–15.

Kickbusch, I., Lister, G., Told, M. and Drager, N. (eds). 2013. *Global Health Diplomacy: Concepts, Issues, Actors, Instruments, Fora and Cases*. New York: Springer.

Kickbusch, I. and Reddy, K. 2015. "Global Health Governance: The Next Political Revolution." *Public Health* 129(7): 838–42.

Kindleberger, C. 1973. *The World in Depression: 1929–1939*. Berkeley: University of California Press.

Kindleberger, C. and Aliber, Z. R. 2011. *Manias, Panics, and Crashes: A History of Financial Crises*, 6th edn. New York: Palgrave Macmillan.

King, G., Pan, J. and Roberts, M. 2013. "How Censorship in China Allows Government Criticism but Silences Collective Expression." *American Political Science Review* 107(2): 1–18.

King, I., 2004. "Internationalising Internet Governance: Does ICANN Have a Role to Play?" *Information and Communications Technology Law* 13(3): 243–58.

Kissinger, H. 2014. *World Order: Reflections on the Character of Nations and the Course of History*. London: Allen Lane.

Klasen, A. 2011. "The Role of Export Credit Agencies in Global Trade," *Global Policy* 2(2): 220–2.

Klasen, A. and Bannert, F. 2015. "Introduction: The Future of Foreign Trade Support." In A. Klasen and F. Bannert (eds), *The Future of Foreign Trade Support*. Durham: Global Policy.

Klein, H. 2002. "ICANN and Internet Governance: Leveraging Technical Coordination to Realize Global Public Policy." *Information Society* 18(3): 193–207.

Knaack, P. 2015. "Innovation and Deadlock in Global Financial Governance: Transatlantic Coordination Failure in OTC Derivatives Regulation." *Review of International Political Economy* 22(6): 1217–48.

Knopf, J. W. (ed.). 2016. *International Cooperation on WMD Nonproliferation*. Athens: University of Georgia Press.

Kobrin, S. 1984. "Expropriation as an Attempt to Control Foreign Firms in LDCs: Trends from 1960 to 1979." *International Studies Quarterly* 28(3): 329–48.

Kobrin, S. 2005. "The Determinants of Liberalization of FDI Policy in Developing Countries: A Cross-Sectional Analysis, 1992–2001." *Transnational Corporations* 14(1): 67–104.

Krasner, S. 1976. "State Power and the Structure of International Trade." *World Politics* 28(3): 317–47.

Krasner, S. 1999. "Globalization and Sovereignty." In: D. A. Smith, D. J. Solinger and S. C. Topik (eds), *States and Sovereignty in the Global Economy*. London: Routledge.

Kriebaum, U. 2007. "Regulatory Takings: Balancing the Interests of the Investor and the State." *Journal of World Investment and Trade* 8(2): 717–44.

Labonte, R., Schrecker, T., Packer, C. and Runnels, V. (eds). 2009. *Globalization and Health: Pathways, Evidence and Policy*. London: Routledge.

Lake, D. A. and Morgan, P. M. 2010. *Regional Orders: Building Security in a New World*. University Park: Penn State University Press.

Lamy, P. 2014. "The Global Governance Deficit." Interview with the Oxford Martin School, July. At http://www.oxfordmartin.ox.ac.uk/publications/view/1697.

Lamy, P. and Goldin, I. 2014. "Addressing the Global Governance Deficit." *Huffington Post*, March. At http://www.huffingtonpost.com/pascal-lamy/addressing-the-global-gov_b_4646573.html.

Lastra, R. M. 2015. *International and Financial Law*. Oxford: Oxford University Press.

Laville, S. 2016. "Child Sex Abuse Whistleblower Resigns from UN." *Guardian*, 7 June.

Lavopa, F., Barreiros, L. and Bruno, V. 2013. "How to Kill a BIT and Not Die Trying: Legal and Political Challenges of Denouncing or Renegotiating Bilateral Investment Treaties." *Journal of International Economic Law* 16(4): 869–91. doi:10.1093/jiel/jgt025.

Lee, D. 2012. "Global Trade Governance and the Challenges of African Activism in the Doha Development Agenda Negotiations." *Global Society* 26(1): 83–101.

Levit, J. K. 2008. "Bottom-up Lawmaking: The Private Origins of Transnational Law." *Indiana Journal of Global Legal Studies* 15(1): 49–73.

Levy, D. and Prakash, A. 2003. "Bargains Old and New: Multinational Corporations in Global Governance." *Business and Politics* 5(2): 131–50.

Lewis, J. A. 2010. "A Note on the Laws of War in Cyberspace." April. Washington, DC: Center for Strategic and International Studies.

Lewis, J. I. 2014. "The Rise of Renewable Energy Protectionism: Emerging Trade Conflicts and Implications for Low Carbon Development." *Global Environmental Politics* 14(4): 10–35.

Libicki, M. 2009. *Cyberdeterrence and Cyberwar*. Santa Monica: RAND.

Libicki, M. 2015. *Iran: A Rising Cyber Power?* Santa Monica: RAND.

Liff, A. P. 2012. "Cyberwar: A New 'Absolute Weapon'? The Proliferation of Cyberwarfare Capabilities and Interstate War." *Journal of Strategic Studies* 35(3): 401–28.

Lindo, D. and Fares, A. 2016. *Representation of the Public Interest in Banking*. Brussels: Finance Watch.

Lindsay, J. R. and Kello, L. 2014. "Correspondence: A Cyber Disagreement." *International Security* 39(2): 181–92.

Litwak, R. S. 2015. "Counterproliferation and the Use of Force." In J. F. Pilat and N. E. Busch (eds), *Routledge Handbook of Nuclear Proliferation and Policy*. Abingdon: Routledge.

Litwak, R. S. and King, M. 2015. *Arms Control in Cyberspace?* Washington, DC: Wilson Center.

Lloyd's. 2016. *Use of Chemical, Biological, Radiological and Nuclear Weapons by Non-State Actors: Emerging trends and Risk Factors*. London: Lloyd's/Chatham House.

Lowe, V. 2002. "Regulation or Expropriation?" *Current Legal Problems* 55(1): 447–66.

Luce, E. 2016. "Obama's Disappointing Nuclear Legacy Looms over Hiroshima Visit." *Financial Times*, 24 May.

Lupovici, A. 2011. "Cyber Warfare and Deterrence: Trends and Challenges in Research." *Military and Strategic Affairs* 3(3): 49–62.

Lynch, J. 2016. "Interview with John Lynch." Steptoe Cyberlaw Podcast by S. Baker, 21 January. At http://www.steptoecyberblog.com/2016/01/21/steptoe-cyberlaw-podcast-interview-with-john-lynch-2/.

Lynn, W. J., III. 2010. "Defending a New Domain." *Foreign Affairs* 89(5): 97–108.

MacFarlane, S. N. and Weiss, T. G. 1992. "Regional Organizations and Regional Security." *Security Studies* 2(1): 6–37.

Majumdar, D. 2015. "America's F-35 Stealth Fighter vs. China's New J-31: Who Wins?" *National Interest*, 25 September.

Mallet, V. and Crabtree, J. 2015. "India's Raghuram Rajan Urges IMF and World Bank Reforms." *Financial Times*, 7 October. At https://www.ft.com/content/0e299960-6ca8-11e5-8171-ba1968cf791a.

Malmström, C. 2015. "Proposing an Investment Court System." Blog Post of the European Commission, Commissioner Cecilia Malmström, 16 September. At https://ec.europa.eu/commission/2014-2019/malmstrom/blog/proposing-investment-court-system_en.

Manger, M. 2005. "Competition and Bilateralism in Trade Policy: The Case of Japan's Free Trade Agreements." *Review of International Political Economy* 12(5): 804–28.

Marcussen, M. 2009. "'Scientization' of Central Banking: The Politics of A-politicization." In K. Dyson and M. Marcussen (eds), *Central Banks in the Age of the Euro: Europeanization, Convergence and Power*. Oxford: Oxford University Press.

Markoff, M. 2015. "Advancing Norms of Responsible State Behavior in Cyberspace." Dipnote: US Department of State Blog, 9 July.

Martens, K. 2004. "Bypassing Obstacles to Access: How NGOs Are Taken Piggy-Back to the UN." *Human Rights Review* 5(3): 80–91.

Matsushita, M., Schoenbaum, T. J. and Mavroidis, P. C. 2015. *The World Trade Organization*. Oxford: Oxford University Press.

Maurer, T. 2011. "Cyber Norm Emergence at the United Nations – an Analysis of the UN's Activities Regarding Cyber-security." Belfer Center Discussion Paper 2011-11. Cambridge, MA: Harvard Kennedy School.

Mazower, M. 2012. *Governing the World: The History of an Idea*. London: Allen Lane.

McAfee, J. and Loggia, R. 2015. "We Have Created a Cyberwar Doomsday Machine that Isis Can Turn against Us." *International Business Times*, 15 December.

McCarty, N., Poole, K. T. and Rosenthal, H. 2006. *Polarized America: The Dance of Ideology and Unequal Riches*. Cambridge, MA: MIT Press.

McDowell, D. 2012. "The US as 'Sovereign International Last-Resort Lender': The Fed's Currency Swap Programme during the Great Panic of 2007–2009." *New Political Economy* 17(2): 157–78.

McKinnon, R. 1993. "The Rules of the Game: International Money in Historical Perspective." *Journal of Economic Literature* 31(1): 1–44.

Medlock, K. B., Jaffe, A. M. and O'Sullivan, M. 2014. "The Global Gas Market, LNG Exports and the Shifting US Geopolitical Presence." *Energy Strategy Reviews* 5: 14–25.

Mehrling, P. 2015. "Elasticity and Discipline in the Global Swap Network." Working paper for "China and the Global Financial System" conference, Institute for New Economic Thinking and Shanghai Development Research Foundation, 6–7 August.

Menon, N., George-Cosh, D. and Douglas, J. 2013. "BOC's Carney: Ring-Fencing Foreign Ban Units Reduces Efficiency." *Wall Street Journal*, 25 February.

Meyer, G. 2016. "Us Shale Hotspot Defies Doldrums with Near Record Output." *Financial Times*, 25 August. At https://www.ft.com/content/fbf0f91a-6a3e-11e6-a0b1-d87a9fea034f.

Meyer, H. and Klasen, A. 2013. "What Governments Can Do to Support their Economies: The Case for a Strategic Econsystem." *Global Policy* 4(s1): 1–9.

Micha, R. et al. 2012. "Estimating the Global and Regional Burden of Suboptimal Nutrition on Chronic Disease: Methods and Inputs to the Analysis." *European Journal of Clinical Nutrition* 66(1): 119–29.

Michaelidis, P., Kardasi, O. and Milios, J. 2011. "Democritus's Economic Ideas in the Context of Classical Political Economy." *European Journal of the History of Economic Thought* 18(1): 1–18.

Milanovic, B. 2016. *Global Inequality. A New Approach for the Age of Globalization.* Cambridge, MA: Harvard University Press.

Miller, B. 1994. "Polarity, Nuclear Weapons and Major War." *Security Studies* 3(4): 598–649.

Miller, G. 2005. "The Political Evolution of Principal–Agent Models." *Annual Review of Political Science* 8(1): 203–25.

Millimet, D. L. and Roy, J. 2015. "Multilateral Environmental Agreements and the WTO." *Economic Letters* 134: 20–3.

Milner, H. 1988. *Resisting Protectionism: Global Industries and the Politics of International Trade.* Princeton: Princeton University Press.

Mims, C. 2016. "Why Electric Cars Will Be Here Sooner Than You Think," *Wall Street Journal*, 28 August. At http://www.wsj.com/articles/why-electric-cars-will-be-here-sooner-than-you-think-1472402674.

Minor, M. 1994. "The Demise of Expropriation as an Instrument of LDC Policy, 1980–1992." *Journal of International Business Studies* 25(1): 177–88.

Moessner, R. and Allen, W. 2010. "Banking Crises and the International Monetary System in the Great Depression and Now." BIS Working Paper 333. Bank for International Settlements.

Mohan, R. and Kapur, M. 2015. "Emerging Powers and Global Governance: Whither the IMF?" IMF Working Paper 15/2019. Washington, DC: International Monetary Fund.

Monaco, L. O. 2016. "Administration Efforts on Cybersecurity: The Year in Review and Looking Forward to 2016." Blog, 2 February. Washington, DC: The White House.

Montagu, D. and Yamey, G. 2011. "Pay-for-Performance and the Millennium Development Goals." *Lancet* 377 (9775): 1383–5.

Mooney, E. 2005. "The Concept of Internal Displacement and the Case for Internally Displaced Persons as a Category of Concern." *Refugee Survey Quarterly* 24(3): 9–26.

Moravcsik, A. M. 1989. "Disciplining Trade Finance: The OECD Export Credit Arrangement." *International Organization* 43(1): 173–205.

Morgan, P. M. 2010. "Applicability of Traditional Deterrence Concepts and Theory to the Cyber Realm." In *Proceedings of a Workshop on Deterring Cyberattacks: Informing Strategies and Developing Options for U.S. Policy.* Washington, DC: National Academies Press.

Morse, J. C. and Keohane, R. O. 2014. "Contested Multilateralism." *Review of International Organizations* 9(4): 385–412.

Moschella, M. and Tsingou, E. (eds). 2013. *Great Expectations, Slow Transformations: Incremental Change in Post-Crisis Regulation.* Colchester: ECPR Press.

Moyn, S. 2012. *The Last Utopia: Human Rights in History.* Cambridge, MA: Harvard University Press.

Mueller, J. 1990. "The Obsolescence of Major War." *Security Dialogue* 21(3): 321–8.

Mueller, M. L. 2002. *Ruling the Root: Internet Governance and the Taming of Cyberspace.* Cambridge, MA: MIT Press.

Mueller, M. L. 2010. *Networks and States: The Global Politics of Internet Governance.* Cambridge, MA: MIT Press.

Mueller, M. L., Mathiason, J. and Klein, H. 2007. "The Internet and Global Governance: Principles and Norms for a New Regime." *Global Governance: A Review of Multilateralism and International Organizations* 13(2): 237–54.

Mügge, D. 2013. "Resilient Neo-liberalism in European Financial Regulation." In V. Schmidt and M. Thatcher (eds), *Resilient Liberalism in Europe's Political Economy*, pp. 201–25. Cambridge: Cambridge University Press.

Muzaka, V. 2011. *The Politics of Intellectual Property Rights and Access to Medicines.* Basingstoke: Palgrave.

Narlikar, A. 2010a. *Deadlocks in Multilateral Negotiations: Causes and Solutions.* Cambridge: Cambridge University Press.

Narlikar, A. 2010b. "New Powers in the Club: The Challenges of Global Trade Governance." *International Affairs* 86(3): 717–28.

Naughton, J. 1999. *A Brief History of the Future: Origins of the Internet.* London: Weidenfeld & Nicolson.

Neal, C. 2012. "A Sustainable Development Goal on Energy Would Help Replicate Germany's Solar Example." World Bank blog, 17 July. At http://blogs.worldbank.org/energy/a-sustainable-development-goal-on-energy-would-help-replicate-germany-s-solar-example.

Neumayer, E. 2004. "The WTO and the Environment: Its Past Record Is Better Than Critics Believe, but the Future Outlook Is Bleak." *Global Environmental Politics* 4(3): 1–8.

Newcombe, A. 2005. "The Boundaries of Regulatory Expropriation in International Law." *ICSID Review* 20(1): 1–57.

Newcombe, A. and Paradell, L. 2009. *Law and Practice of Investment Treaties: Standards of Treatment.* The Hague: Kluwer Law International.

Nölke, A. 2010. "The Politics of Accounting Regulation: Responses to the Subprime Crisis." In E. Helleiner, S. Pagliari and H. Zimmerman (eds), *Global Finance in Crisis: The Politics of International Regulatory Change*, pp. 37–55. London: Routledge.

Nölke, A. 2015. "Second Image Revisited: The Domestic Sources of China's Foreign Economic Policies." *International Politics* 52(6): 657–65.

Nölke, A. and Perry, J. 2006. "The Political Economy of International Accounting Standards." *Review of International Political Economy* 13(4): 559–86.

Nye, J. S., Jr. 2011. *The Future of Power.* New York: PublicAffairs.

Nye, J. S., Jr. 2014. "The Regime Complex for Managing Global Cyber Activities." Issue Paper 1, May. Global Commission on Internet Governance.

Nye, J. S., Jr. 2017. "Deterrence and Dissuasion in Cyberspace." *International Security* 41(3): 44–71.

O'Connell, P. 2007. "On Reconciling Irreconcilables: Neo-liberal Globalisation and Human Rights." *Human Rights Law Review* 7(3): 483–509.

O'Neal, J. and Russett, B. 1997. "The Classical Liberals Were Right: Democracy, Interdependence and Conflict, 1950–1985." *International Studies Quarterly* 41(2): 267–94.

Oatley, T. 2001. "The Dilemmas of International Financial Regulation." *Regulation* 23(4): 36–9.

Obama, B. 2007. *The Audacity of Hope: Thoughts on Reclaiming the American Dream.* Edinburgh: Canongate.

Obama, B. H. 2009. "Remarks by the President on Securing Our Nation's Cyber Infrastructure." Washington, DC: White House Press Office.

Obstfeld, M. 2011. "The SDR as an International Reserve Asset: What Future?" Working Paper, International Growth Centre, 27 March.

OCHA (Office for the Coordination of Humanitarian Affairs). 2004. *Guiding Principles on Internal Displacement*, 2nd edn. Geneva: United Nations. At https:// docs.unocha.org/sites/dms/Documents/GuidingPrinciplesDispl.pdf.

OCHA (Office for the Coordination of Humanitarian Affairs). 2015. *Global Humanitarian Overview for 2016*. At http://www.unocha.org/node/207851.

OCHA (Office for the Coordination of Humanitarian Affairs). 2016. *World Humanitarian Data and Trends 2016*. At http://www.unocha.org/datatrends2016/ WHDT2016.pdf.

OCHA (Office for the Coordination of Humanitarian Affairs). 2017. "Cluster Coordination." At http://www.unocha.org/what-we-do/coordination-tools/cluster-coordination.

OECD (Organisation for Economic Co-operation and Development). 2004. "'Indirect Expropriation' and the 'Right to Regulate' in International Investment Law." OECD Working Papers on International Investment 2004/04. At http:// dx.doi.org/10.1787/780155872321.

OECD (Organisation for Economic Co-operation and Development). 2011. "An Overview of Growing Income Inequalities in OECD Countries: Main Findings." In *Divided We Stand: Why Inequality Keeps Rising*. Paris: OECD.

Ooms, G. 2014. "From International Health to Global Health: How to Foster a Better Dialogue between Empirical and Normative Disciplines." *BMC International Health and Human Rights* 14(36): 1–10.

Orbinski, J. 2008. *An Imperfect Offering: Humanitarian Action for the Twenty-First Century*. New York: Walker.

Orchard, P. 2010. "Protection of Internally Displaced Persons: Soft Law as a Norm-Generating Mechanism." *Review of International Studies* 36(2): 281–303.

Osborne, G. 2015. "Chancellor's Speech to GCHQ on Cyber Security." 17 November. At https://www.gov.uk/government/speeches/chancellors-speech-to-gchq-on-cyber-security.

OSCE (Organization for Security and Co-operation in Europe). 2013. "Initial Set of OSCE Confidence-Building Measures to Reduce the Risks of Conflict Stemming from the Use of Information and Communications Technologies." Decision No. 1106. OSCE Permanent Council.

Oxford Geoengineering Programme. 2017. "What Is Geoengineering?" Oxford Martin School, University of Oxford. At http://www.geoengineering.ox.ac.uk/ what-is-geoengineering/what-is-geoengineering/.

Pagliari, S. 2012a. "A Wall around Europe? The European Regulatory Response to the Global Financial Crisis and the Turn in Transatlantic Relations." *Journal of European Integration* 35(4): 391–408.

Pagliari, S. 2012b. "Who Governs Finance? The Shifting Public–Private Divide in the Regulation of Derivatives, Rating Agencies and Hedge Funds." *European Law Journal* 18: 44–61.

Pagliari, S. and Young, K. 2016. "The Interest Ecology of Financial Regulation: An Empirical Analysis." *Socio-Economic Review* 14(2): 309–37.

Pagliery, J. 2015. "ISIS Is Attacking the U.S. Energy Grid (and Failing)." CNN Money, 15 October. At http://money.cnn.com/2015/10/15/technology/isis-energy-grid/.

Pair, L. M. and Frankenstein, P. 2011. "The New ICC Rule on Consolidation: Progress or Change?" *Emory International Law Review* 25(3): 1061–85.

Pandza, J. 2011. "Managing the Consequences of Nuclear Terrorism." *Survival* 53(5): 129–42.

Park, I. 2009. "Regional Trade Agreements in East Asia: Will They Be Sustainable?" *Asian Economic Journal* 23(2): 169–94.

Pauwelyn, J. 2014. "At the Edge of Chaos? Foreign Investment Law as a Complex Adaptive System, How It Emerged and How It Can Be Reformed." *ICSID Review* 29(2): 372–418.

Pearce, B. 2016. "The Beginning of the End of Nuclear Weapons?" Royal United Services Institute. *RUSI Newsbrief* 36(5): 22–4.

Pegram, T. 2015. "Global Human Rights Governance and Orchestration: National Human Rights Institutions as Intermediaries," *European Journal of International Relations* 21(3): 1–26.

Pegram, T. 2017. "Stewardship and Intermediation: Comparative Lessons from Human Rights Governance." *Annals of the American Academy of Political and Social Science* 670 (March).

Phuong, C. 2005. *The International Protection of Internally Displaced Persons*. Cambridge: Cambridge University Press.

Piketty, T. 2014. *Capital in the Twenty-First Century*. Cambridge, MA: Harvard University Press.

Pinker, S. and Santos, J. M. 2016. "Colombia's Milestone in World Peace," *New York Times*, 26 August.

Plender, J. 2013. "Global Banking Retreat Risks Cutting Financial Capacity." *Financial Times*, 24 April.

Posner, E. 2014. *The Twilight of Human Rights Law*. Oxford: Oxford University Press.

Poulsen, L. S. 2014. "Bounded Rationality and the Diffusion of Modern Investment Treaties." *International Studies Quarterly* 58(1): 1–14.

Power, J. 2001. *Like Water on Stone: The Story of Amnesty International*. Harmondsworth: Penguin.

Président de la République. 2013. *Le Livre blanc. Défense et sécurité nationale*. Paris: La Documentation Française.

Price, R. and Tannenwald, N. 1996. "Norms and Deterrence: The Nuclear and Chemical Weapons Taboos." In P. J. Katzenstein (ed.), *The Culture of National Security: Norms and Identity in World Politics*. New York: Columbia University Press.

Psaki, J. 2013. "Statement on Consensus Achieved by the UN Group of Governmental Experts on Cyber Issues." Washington, DC : US Department of State.

Quah, D. 2011. "The Global Economy's Shifting Centre of Gravity." *Global Policy* 2(1): 3–9.

Quah, D. and Mahbubani, K. 2016. "The Geopolitics of Populism." *Project Syndicate*, 9 December. At http://prosyn.org/2FraZs7.

Rayner, S. and Caine, M. 2015. *The Hartwell Approach to Climate Policy*. London: Routledge.

Reinhart, C. and Trebesch, C. 2016. "The International Monetary Fund: 70 Years of Reinvention." *Journal of Economic Perspectives* 30(1): 3–28.

Rengger, N. 2011. "The World Turned Upside Down? Human Rights and International Relations." *International Affairs* 87(5): 1159–78.

Reus-Smit, C. 2011. "Human Rights in a Global Ecumene." *International Affairs* 87(5): 1205–18.

Reuter, O. J. and Szakonyi, D. 2015. "Online Social Media and Political Awareness in Authoritarian Regimes". *British Journal of Political Science* 45(1): 29–51.

Reuters News. 2014. "UN to Give Evidence in Australian Asylum Seeker Test Case." 13 October.

Reyes, J., Wooster, R. and Shirrell, S. 2014. "Regional Trade Agreements and the Pattern of Trade: A Network Approach." *World Economy* 37(8): 1128–51.

Rid, T. 2013. *Cyber War Will Not Take Place*. London: Hurst.

Risse, T., Ropp, S. C. and Sikkink, K. (eds). 2013. *The Persistent Power of Human Rights: International Norms and Domestic Change*. Cambridge: Cambridge University Press.

Risse-Kappen, T. (ed.). 1995. *Bringing Transnational Relations Back In: Non-State Actors, Domestic Structures and International Institutions*. Cambridge: Cambridge University Press.

Ritchie, N. 2014. "Waiting for Kant: Devaluing and Delegitimizing Nuclear Weapons." *International Affairs* 90(3): 601–23.

Rogin, J. 2012. "NSA Chief: Cybercrime Constitutes the 'Greatest Transfer of Wealth in History.'" *Foreign Policy*, 9 July.

Rolland, S. E. 2007. "Developing Country Coalitions at the WTO: In Search of Legal Support." *Harvard International Law Journal* 48: 483–551.

Romm, T. 2016. "WikiLeaks Supporters Claim Credit for Massive U.S. Cyberattack, but Researchers Skeptical." *Politico*, 21 October.

Rosecrance, R. N. 2013. *The Resurgence of the West: How a Transatlantic Union Can Prevent War and Restore the United States and Europe*. New Haven: Yale University Press.

Ruffing, K. G. 2010. "The Role of the Organization for Economic Cooperation and Development in Environmental Policy Making." *Review of Environmental Economics and Policy* 4(2): 199–220.

Ruggie, J. G. 1982. "International Regimes, Transactions, and Change: Embedded Liberalism in the Postwar Economic Order." *International Organization* 36(2): 379–415.

Ruggie, J. G. 2001. "Global_Governance.net: The Global Compact as Learning Network." *Global Governance* 7: 371–8.

Ruggie, J. G. 2006. "Interim Report of the Special Representative of the Secretary-General on the Issue of Human Rights and Transnational Corporations and Other Business Enterprises." UN Doc E/CN.4/2006/97. United Nations.

Rushton, S. 2011. "Global Health Security: Security for Whom? Security for What?" *Political Studies* 59(4): 779–96.

Rushton, S. and Youde, J. (eds). 2014. *Global Health Security*. Abingdon: Routledge.

Salacuse, J. 2010. *The Law of Investment Treaties*. Oxford: Oxford University Press.

San Juan, E. 2011. "Contemporary Global Capitalism and the Challenge of the Filipino Diaspora." *Global Society* 25(1): 7–27.

Sánchez-Garzoli, G. 2004. "Collection of Global Course Syllabi Relating to Internally Displaced Persons." The Brookings–SAIS Project on Internal Displacement. At http://www.brookings.edu/~/media/Projects/idp/Collection-of-Course-Syllabi-on-IDPs-(2004).pdf?la=en.

Sandalow, D. 2015. "Mission Innovation: Interview with Secretary Moniz." Center on Global Energy Policy, Columbia University, 11 December. At http://energypolicy.columbia.edu/on-the-record/mission-innovation-interview-secretary-moniz.

Sandalow, D. 2016. "The History and Future of the Clean Energy Ministerial." Center on Global Energy Policy, Columbia University, 31 May. At http://energypolicy.columbia.edu/publications/commentary/history-and-future-clean-energy-ministerial.

Sanger, D. E. 2012. *Confront and Conceal: Obama's Secret Wars and Surprising Use of American Power*. New York: Broadway Books.

Sawers, J. 2016. "We Are Returning to a World of Great Power Rivalry." *Financial Times*, 20 October.

Schill, S. 2009. *The Multilateralization of International Investment Law*. Cambridge: Cambridge University Press.

Schmitt, E. and Shanker, T. 2011. "U.S. Debated Cyberwarfare in Attack Plan on Libya." *New York Times*, 17 October.

Schmitt, M. N. (ed.). 2013. *Tallinn Manual on the International Law Applicable to Cyber Warfare*. Cambridge: Cambridge University Press.

Scholte, J. A. 2010. "Governing a More Global World." *Corporate Governance* 10(4): 459–74.

Schrijver, N. and Prislan, V. 2013. "The Netherlands." In C. Brown (ed.), *Commentaries on Selected Model Investment Treaties*. Oxford: Oxford University Press.

Seabrooke, L. and Wigan, D. 2015. "Powering Ideas through Expertise: Professionals in Global Tax Battles." *Journal of European Public Policy* 23(3): 1–18.

SEATINI (Southern and Eastern Africa Trade Information and Negotiations Institute), TARSC (Training and Research Support Centre) with Limpopo, U. 2016. "Implementing the International Health Regulations in East and Southern Africa: Progress, Opportunities and Challenges." EQUINET Policy Brief 40, EQUINET Harare.

Senthilingam, M. 2015. "Are We Ready for the Next Global Epidemic?" CNN, 13 February. At http://edition.cnn.com/2015/02/13/health/are-we-ready-for-global-outbreak/index.html.

Sheppard, D. and Raval, A. 2015. "LNG Trade Prepares to Come out of Oil's Shadow: With US Supplies Coming On Line, Liquefied Natural Gas Is Set for a Transformation." *Financial Times*, 28 May. At https://www.ft.com/content/2ab4c50e-0539-11e5-8612-00144feabdc0.

Sherwood, H. 2015. "Human Rights Groups Face Global Crackdown 'Not Seen in a Generation.'" *Guardian*, 26 August.

Shiffman, J. 2014. "Knowledge, Moral Claims and the Exercise of Power in Global Health." *International Journal of Health Policy and Management* 3(6): 297–9.

Shultz, G. P., Perry, W. J., Kissinger, H. A. and Nunn, S. 2007. "A World Free of Nuclear Weapons." *Wall Street Journal*, 4 January.

Shultz, G. P., Perry, W. J., Kissinger, H. A. and Nunn, S. 2008. "Towards a Nuclear-Free World." *Wall Street Journal*, 15 January.

Siegfried, K. 2016. "Migration: What if Trump Does Win." *IRIN News*, 7 November. At https://www.irinnews.org/analysis/2016/11/07/migration-what-if-trump-does-win.

Simmons, B. 2009. *Mobilizing Human Rights: International Law in Domestic Politics*. Cambridge: Cambridge University Press.

Singer, P. W. and Freedman, A. 2014. *Cybersecurity and Cyberwar: What Everyone Needs to Know*. Oxford: Oxford University Press.

Skultety, S. 2006. "Currency, Trade and Commerce in Plato's Laws." *History of Political Thought* 27(2): 189–205.

Slaughter, A.-M. 2004. "Disaggregated Sovereignty: Towards the Public Accountability of Global Government Networks." *Government and Opposition* 39(2): 159–90.

Slaughter, A.-M. 2017. *The Chessboard and the Web: Strategies of Connection in a Networked World*. New Haven: Yale University Press.

Smith, C. R. 2003. "Cyber War against Iraq." NewsMax.com, 12 March. At http://www.newsmax.com/Pre-2008/Cyber-War-Against-Iraq/2003/03/12/id/674588/.

Soldatov, A. and Borogan, I. 2016. *The Red Web: The Struggle between Russia's Digital Dictators and the New Online Revolutionaries*. New York: PublicAffairs.

Solis, G. D. 2016. *The Law of Armed Conflict: International Humanitarian Law in War*. Cambridge: Cambridge University Press.

Sovacool, B. K., Walter, G., van de Graaf, T. and Andrews, N. 2016. "Energy Governance, Transnational Rules, and the Resource Curse: Exploring the Effectiveness of the Extractive Industries Transparency Initiative (EITI)." *World Development* 83: 179–92.

Spetalnick, M. and Brunnstrom, D. 2016. "Nuclear Terrorism Fears Loom over Obama's Final Atomic Summit." Reuters, 31 March.

Sridhar, D. and Gostin, L. 2011. "Reforming the World Health Organization." *JAMA: The Journal of the American Medical Association* 305(15): 1585–6.

Steckel, J. C., Edenhofer, O. and Jakob, M. 2015. "Drivers for the Renaissance of Coal." *Proceedings of the National Academy of Sciences* 112(29): E3775–81. At http://www.pnas.org/content/112/29/E3775.full.pdf.

Steger, D. P. 2009. "The Future of the WTO: The Case for Institutional Reform." *Journal of International Economic Law* 12(4): 803–33.

Stein, J. A. 2002. "Globalisation, Science, Technology and Policy." *Science and Public Policy* 29(6): 402–8.

Stern, J. 2016. "The New Japanese LNG Strategy: A Major Step towards Hub-Based Gas Pricing in Asia," Oxford Institute of Energy Studies, June.

Stiglitz, J. E. and members of a UN Commission of Financial Experts. 2010. *The Stiglitz Report: Reforming the International Monetary and Financial Systems in the Wake of the Global Crisis*. New York, New Press.

Stoddard, A. et al. 2015. *The State of the Humanitarian System 2015*. Active Learning Network for Accountability and Performance in Humanitarian Action (ALNAP). At http://sohs.alnap.org/.

Stoll, C. 1989. *The Cuckoo's Egg: Tracking a Spy through the Maze of Computer Espionage*. New York: Doubleday.

Streltsov, A. A. 2007. "International Information Security: Description and Legal Aspects." UNIDIR Disarmament Forum. Geneva: United Nations Institute for Disarmament Research.

Sukumar, A. M. and Sharma, R. K. 2016. *The Cyber Command: Upgrading India's Nuclear Security Architecture*. New Delhi: Observer Research Foundation.

Swanson, R. C. et al. 2015 "Strengthening Health Systems in Low-Income Countries by Enhancing Organizational Capacities and Improving Institutions." *Globalization and Health* 11(5): 1–8.

Szulecki, K., Pattberg, P. and Biermann, F. 2011. "Explaining Variation in the Effectiveness of Transnational Energy Partnerships." *Governance* 24(4): 713–36.

Tannenwald, N. 1999. "The Nuclear Taboo: The United States and the Normative Basis of Nuclear Non-Use." *International Organization* 53(3): 433–68.

Tannenwald, N. 2005. "Stigmatizing the Bomb: Origins of the Nuclear Taboo." *International Security* 30(1): 5–49.

Terry, F. 2002. *Condemned to Repeat? The Paradox of Humanitarian Action*. Ithaca: Cornell University Press.

Thakur, R. and Haru, E. 2006. *The Chemical Weapons Convention: Implementation, Challenges and Opportunities*. Tokyo: United Nations University Press.

Thiemann, M. 2014. "In the Shadow of Basel: How Competitive Politics Bred the Crisis." *Review of International Political Economy* 21(6): 1203–39.

Thomas, K. 2007. "Growing Use, Uncertain Benefits, Uneven Controls: An Exploration of Government Measures to Attract Investment." Geneva: International Institute for Sustainable Development.

Timberg, C., Nakashima, E. and Douglas-Gabriel, D. 2014. "Cyberattacks Trigger Talk of 'Hacking Back.'" *Washington Post*, 9 October.

Toohey, L. 2014. "Reinvigorating the WTO from the Inside Out – Revisiting the Role of the Secretariat." *Asian Journal of WTO and International Health Law and Policy* 9(2): 385–405.

Trakman, L. 2012. "The ICSID under Siege." *Cornell International Law Journal* 45: 603–65.

Tsao, J., Lewis, N. and Crabtree, G. 2006. "Solar FAQs." At http://www.sandia.gov/~jytsao/Solar%20FAQs.pdf.

Tsingou, E. 2010. "Regulatory Reactions to the Global Credit Crisis: Analyzing a Policy Community under Stress." In E. Helleiner, S. Pagliari and H. Zimmerman (eds), *Global Finance in Crisis: The Politics of International Regulatory Change*, pp. 21–36. London: Routledge.

Tsingou, E. 2015. "Club Governance and the Making of Global Financial Rules." *Review of International Political Economy* 22(2): 225–56.

Tucker, J. B. 2012. "The Role of the Chemical Weapons Convention in Countering Chemical Terrorism." *Terrorism and Political Violence* 24(1): 105–19.

Turing, A. M. 1937. "On Computable Numbers, with an Application to the Entscheidungsproblem." *Proceedings of the London Mathematical Society* 2(42): 230–65.

Tyler, A. 2011. "Enforcing Enforcement: Is the OECD Anti-bribery Convention's Peer Review Effective?" *George Washington International Law Review* 43(1): 137–73.

Underhill, G. R. D. and Zhang, X. 2008. "Setting the Rules: Private Power, Political Underpinnings, and Legitimacy in Global Monetary and Financial Governance." *International Affairs* 84(3): 535–54.

UNEP (United Nations Environment Programme). 2016. *The Emissions Gap Report 2016: A UNEP Synthesis Report*. Nairobi: UNEP.

UNEP Inquiry. 2015. *The Financial System We Need: Aligning the Financial System with Sustainable Development*. Geneva: Inquiry into the Design of a Sustainable Financial System, United Nations Environment Programme.

UNEP Inquiry. 2016a. "Government Subsidies to the Global Financial System: A Preliminary Exploration." Inquiry Working Paper 16/11, July. Geneva: Inquiry into the Design of a Sustainable Financial System, United Nations Environment Programme.

UNEP Inquiry. 2016b. *Green Finance for Developing Countries: Needs, Concerns, and Innovations*. Geneva: Inquiry into the Design of a Sustainable Financial System, United Nations Environment Programme.

UNFCCC (United Nations Framework Convention on Climate Change). 2017. "NAZCA: Tracking Climate Action." At http://climateaction.unfccc.int/.

UN General Assembly. 2003. "Creation of a Global Culture of Cybersecurity." Resolution 57/239. New York: United Nations.

UN General Assembly. 2015. "Report of the Group of Governmental Experts on Developments in the Field of Information and Telecommunications in the Context of International Security." A/70/174. New York: United Nations.

UNHCR (UN Refugee Agency). 2010. "Convention and Protocol Relating to the Status of Refugees." 1951 Refugee Convention and 1967 Protocol. At http://www.unhcr.org/pages/3b66c2aa10.html.

UNHCR (UN Refugee Agency). 2016. *Global Trends: Forced Displacement in 2015*. At https://s3.amazonaws.com/unhcrsharedmedia/2016/2016-06-20-global-trends/2016-06-14-Global-Trends-2015.pdf.

UNHCR (UN Refugee Agency). 2017. "History of UNHCR." At http://www.unhcr.org/uk/history-of-unhcr.html.

UNHCR Canberra. 2016. "Detaining Asylum Seekers and Refugees in Offshore Detention Centres Subject to International Obligations, Despite High Court Decision." 5 February. UNHCR Regional Representation in Canberra.

UN IGME (UN Inter-agency Group for Child Mortality Estimation). 2013. *Levels and Trends in Child Mortality: Report 2013*. New York: UNICEF.

Union of International Associations. 2014. *Yearbook of International Organizations: Statistics, Visualizations and Patterns*. Berlin: De Gruyter.

Union of International Associations. 2016. *Yearbook of International Organizations 2016–2017: Statistics, Visualizations and Patterns*. Berlin: De Gruyter.

United Nations. 2008. "First Annual Report of the Subcommittee on Prevention of Torture and Other Cruel, Inhuman or Degrading Treatment or Punishment." UN Doc. CAT/C/40/2. At http://www2.ohchr.org/english/bodies/cat/opcat/docs/CAT.C.40.2.pdf.

United Nations. 2011. "Guiding Principles on Business and Human Rights." At http://www.ohchr.org/Documents/Publications/GuidingPrinciplesBusinessHR_EN.pdf.

United Nations. 2012. "Report of the Secretary-General's Internal Review Panel on United Nations Action in Sri Lanka." November. At http://www.un.org/News/dh/infocus/Sri_Lanka/The_Internal_Review_Panel_report_on_Sri_Lanka.pdf.

US Department of Defense. 2013. *Task Force Report: Resilient Military Systems and the Advanced Cyber Threat*. Defense Science Board, January. At http://www.acq.osd.mil/dsb/reports/ResilientMilitarySystems.CyberThreat.pdf.

US Department of State. 2016. "Proliferation Security Initiative." At http://www.state.gov/t/isn/c10390.htm.

US Intelligence Board. 1966. "Impact of a Threshold Test Ban Treaty on Soviet Military Programs." National Intelligence Estimate Number 11-11-66. Washington, DC: United States Intelligence Board.

US Senate Armed Services Committee. 2010. "Hearings before the Committee on Armed Services United States Senate One Hundred Eleventh Congress Second Session on Nominations of Elizabeth A. McGrath [...] Ltg Keith B. Alexander, USA [...]." Washington, DC: US Government Printing Office.

US Trade Representative. 2016. "Strategic Importance of TPP." At https://ustr.gov/sites/default/files/TPP-Strategic-Importance-of-TPP-Fact-Sheet.pdf.

van Asselt, H. et al. 2016. "Maximizing the Potential of the Paris Agreement: Effective Review of Action and Support in a Bottom-up Regime." At http://ssrn.com/abstract=2781270.

van Boven, T. 2000 "The Role of the United Nations Secretariat [1992]." In F. Coomans et al. (eds), *Human Rights from Exclusion to Inclusion: An Anthology from the Work of Theo C. van Boven*, pp. 145–76. The Hague: Kluwer Law International.

Van de Graaf, T. 2015. "The IEA, the New Energy Order and the Future of Global Energy Governance." In D. Lesage and T. van de Graaf (eds), *Rising Powers and Multilateral Institutions*, pp. 79–95. London: Palgrave Macmillan.

Van de Graaf, T. and Colgan, J. 2016. "Global Energy Governance: A Review and Research Agenda." *Palgrave Communications* 2 (26 January).

Van de Velde, J. R. 2016. "War in Peace." *American Interest*, 6 September.

van der Meer, S. 2011. "Not That Bad: Looking Back at 65 Years of Nuclear Non-proliferation." *Security and Human Rights* 22(1): 37–47.

van Os, R. and Knottnerus, R. 2011. "Dutch Bilateral Investment Treaties: A Gateway to 'Treaty Shopping' for Investment Protection by Multinational Companies." 1 October. At http://somo.nl/publications-en/Publication_3708.

Verma, S. 2012. "Carney Aims to Make FSB More Than Just a Talking Shop." *Euromoney*, October.

Vestergaard, J. and Wade, R. H. 2013. "Protecting Power: How Western States Retain the Dominant Voice in the World Bank's Governance." *World Development* 46: 153–64.

Victor, D. G. 2011a. *Global Warming Gridlock: Creating More Effective Strategies for Protecting the Planet*. Cambridge, Cambridge University Press.

Victor, D. G. 2011b. "Why the UN Can Never Stop Climate Change." *The Guardian*, April 4.

Vincent, J. 1986. *Human Rights and International Relations*. Cambridge: Cambridge University Press.

Wade, R. H. 2011. "Emerging World Order? From Multipolarity to Multilateralism in the G20, the World Bank, and the IMF." *Politics and Society* 39(3): 347–78.

Waibel, M. 2007. "Two Worlds of Necessity in ICSID Arbitration: CMS and LG&E." *Leiden Journal of International Law* 20(3): 637–48.

Walker, P. F. 2010. "Abolishing Chemical Weapons: Progress, Challenges and Opportunities." *Arms Control Today* 40 (November).

Walter, A. 2001. "NGOs, Business, and International Investment: The Multilateral Agreement on Investment, Seattle, and Beyond." *Global Governance* 7(1): 51–73.

Walter, A. 2008. *Governing Finance: East Asia's Adoption of International Standards*. Ithaca: Cornell University Press.

Waltz, K. 2010. *Theory of International Politics*. Long Grove, IL: Waveland Press.

Walzer, M. 2015. *Just and Unjust Wars: A Moral Argument with Historical Illustrations*, 5th edn. New York: Basic Books.

Weaver, C. 2008. *Hypocrisy Trap: The World Bank and the Poverty of Reform*. Princeton: Princeton University Press.

Welsh, J. M. 2009. "Implementing the 'Responsibility to Protect.'" Policy Brief No 1/2009. Oxford: Oxford Institute for Ethics, Law, and Armed Conflict.

WHO (World Health Organization). 2015a. "Implementation of the International Health Regulations (2005): Responding to Public Health Emergencies." Report by the Director-General, A68/22, 15 May.

WHO (World Health Organization). 2015b. "Universal Health Coverage." Fact Sheet. At http://www.who.int/mediacentre/factsheets/fs395/en/.

WHO Africa (2015) *Integrated Disease Surveillance Quarterly Bulletin*, 31 May. Brazzaville: World Health Organization Regional Office for Africa.

Wilkinson, R., Hannah, E. and Scott, J. 2014. "The WTO in Bali: What MC9 Means for the Doha Development Agenda and Why It Matters." *Third World Quarterly* 35(6): 1032–50.

Witton, B. 2016. "How Immigration Is Fuelling Sweden's Economic Boom." *Independent*, 5 October. At http://www.independent.co.uk/news/world/europe/sweden-immigration-economic-boom-theresa-may-refugee-crisis-tory-conference-a7347136.html.

Wolf, M. 2013. "The Shift and the Shock: Prospects for the World Economy." In D. Held and C. Roger (eds), *Global Governance at Risk*. Cambridge: Polity Press.

Wolf, M. 2017. "The Risks That Threaten Global Growth." *Financial Times*, 3 January. At https://www.ft.com/content/00b89fbe-ce8c-11e6-b8ce-b9c03770f8b1.

World Bank. 2011a. *Multipolarity: The New Global Economy*. Washington, DC: World Bank.

World Bank. 2011b. *World Development Report 2011: Conflict, Security and Development*. At https://openknowledge.worldbank.org/handle/10986/4389.

World Bank. 2016. "Pandemic Emergency Facility: Frequently Asked Questions." At www.worldbank.org/en/topic/pandemics/brief/pandemic-emergency-facility-frequently-asked-questions.

World Energy Council. 2015. "Foreword." *2015 World Energy Issues Monitor*. At https://www.worldenergy.org/wp-content/uploads/2015/01/2015-World-Energy-Issues-Monitor.pdf.

WTO (World Trade Organization). 2015a. *International Trade Statistics 2015*. Geneva: WTO.

WTO (World Trade Organization). 2015b. *WTO Dispute Settlement*. Geneva: WTO.

Xiaochuan, Z. 2015. "IMFC Statement by Zhou Xiaochuan, Governor, People's Bank of China." Statement to the 31st Meeting of the International Monetary and Finance Committee, International Monetary Fund, 18 April.

Yagci, A. H. 2016. "The Great Recession, Inequality and Occupy Protests around the World." *Government and Opposition*, online 23 March. doi:10.1017/gov.2016.3.

Yamin, A. and Parra-Vera, O. 2009. "How Do Courts Set Health Policy? The Case of the Colombian Constitutional Court." *PLoS Med* 6(2): 1–4.

Youde, J. 2014. "Global Health Partnerships: The Emerging Agenda." In G. W. Brown, G. Yamey and S. Wamala (eds), *Global Health Policy*, pp. 505–18. Oxford: Wiley-Blackwell.

Young, K. 2012. "Transnational Regulatory Capture? An Empirical Examination of Transnational Lobbying over the Basel Committee on Banking Supervision." *Review of International Political Economy* 19(4): 663–88.

Young, K. 2014a. "The Complex and Covert Web of Financial Protectionism." *Business and Politics* 15(4): 579–613.

Young, K. 2014b. "The Politics of Global Financial Regulation." In T. Oatley and W. Winecoff (eds), *Handbook of the International Political Economy of International Monetary Relations*. Cheltenham: Edward Elgar.

Young, K. and Pagliari, S. 2017. "Capital United? Business Unity in Regulatory Politics and the Special Place of Finance." *Regulation and Governance*, online. doi:10.1111/rego.12098.

Young, K. and Park, S. H. 2013. "Regulatory Opportunism: Cross-National Patterns in National Banking Regulatory Responses Following the Global Financial Crisis." *Public Administration* 91(3): 561–81.

Yu, P. K. 2008. "Access to Medicines, BRICS Alliances, and Collective Action." *American Journal of Law and Medicine* 34(2–3): 345–94.

Zwolski, K. 2011. "The External Dimension of the EU's Non-proliferation Policy: Overcoming Inter-institutional Competition." *European Foreign Affairs Review* 16(3): 325–40.

Index